I0032110

Iraq

Oil and Gas Industry

In the Twentieth Century

Ghanim Anaz

Nottingham
University Press

First published by Nottingham University Press

This reissued original edition published 2023 by 5m Books Ltd www.5mbooks.com

Copyright © Nottingham University Press 2023

All rights reserved. No part of this publication
may be reproduced in any material form
(including photocopying or storing in any
medium by electronic means and whether or not
transiently or incidentally to some other use of
this publication) without the written permission
of the copyright holder except in accordance with
the provisions of the Copyright, Designs and
Patents Act 1988. Applications for the copyright
holder's written permission to reproduce any part
of this publication should be addressed to the publishers.

British Library Cataloguing in Publication Data
Iraq Oil and Gas Industry in the 20th Century

ISBN 9781789182873

Disclaimer

Every reasonable effort has been made to ensure that the material in this book is true, correct, complete and appropriate at the time of writing. Nevertheless the publishers and the author do not accept responsibility for any omission or error, or for any injury, damage, loss or financial consequences arising from the use of the book. Views expressed in the articles are those of the author and not of the Editor or Publisher.

Typeset by Nottingham University Press, Nottingham

EU GPSR Authorised Representative
LOGOS EUROPE, 9 rue Nicolas Poussin, 17000, LA ROCHELLE, France
E-mail: Contact@logoseurope.eu

CONTENTS

Dedication

I am greatly honoured and humbled

To be able to dedicate this book to my beloved

Country Iraq, as a sign of gratitude and appreciation

For affording me that rare and precious opportunity

To have been sent at that very tender age on a

Scholarship to study in the United Kingdom,

Which has enabled me today, with the

Help of God, to write this book.

May God bless and protect

Iraq and all its people.

Ghanim Anaz

Background and Acknowledgements

Throughout my 47 years of work in the oil and gas industry in Iraq, the United Kingdom and the United Arab Emirates, I have had the good fortune of working with some of the industry's most capable men. I spent most of the 1960s and early 1970s in the Development Engineering Department of the Iraq Petroleum Company (IPC) in Kirkuk which dealt with the preparation of the design, drawings and contract documents for the company's small and medium size locally generated projects since the major projects were generated in the IPC's head office in London. Nonetheless the drawings and a lot of the details of such major projects were sent to the Development Engineering Department in Kirkuk for information and records. This put me in close contact with some of the highly experienced Iraqi and expatriate staff working in this field both in Kirkuk and the IPC's London Office. As a result I was able to acquire an in depth knowledge of the extent of the Company's vast operations both in Iraq and other parts of the Middle East and a good understanding of the oil and gas industry. This led to my rapid promotion in 1969 to become the superintendent of the Development Engineering Department at the age of 32.

This experience was soon to be made use of and greatly enhanced after the nationalisation of the IPC in June 1972 by being appointed as Head of a newly established Projects Department which expanded the Northern Iraqi oilfields production and export facilities from one million barrels per day to 1.2 and then to 1.4 million barrels of crude oil per day. The projects were vast involving all aspects of the planning, design, construction and operations of the production, processing and pipeline facilities. The cost of the projects was in excess of one billion US dollars equivalent to several billion dollars in today's terms.

This background enabled me after leaving Iraq to join the newly established Sharjah Liquid Petroleum Gas (LPG) Company, (Shalco) in January 1986. This new company was a joint venture between the Government of Sharjah, UAE, the American Oil Company (AMOCO) and two Japanese companies Itochu and Tokyo Boeki. As the company's Technical Manager, I was involved in the management of latter stages of the construction of the company's LPG plant and terminal. Once the project was completed and the plant and terminal were commissioned, I went to manage the operations and export activities of the company. This was followed in 1994 by the expansion of the LPG plant by 70% from its original capacity of 440 to 750 million cubic feet per day.

In the meantime and during my entire service of over 21 years, I was also the secretary to the Board of Directors of Shalco which got me involved in the company's overall policy, long term planning, budget, management and other top decision making.

All this experience had put me in close contact with a large number of highly professional people working in the oil and gas industry including most of the senior Iraqi oilmen throughout the country, those of the IPC, the American Oil Company (AMOCO), the British Petroleum Company (BP), Crescent Petroleum Company, Dana Gas Company, the French contractors Entropose, the German contractors Mannesmann, Japan Gas Company (JGC) and many other international and local companies.

It must be emphasised that many of my very capable Iraqi friends and colleagues had similar experiences as mine, acquiring a vast expertise in their own fields of work which had helped us all in building Iraq's vast and successful oil and gas industry during the 1970s and 1980s.

The irony of all this is that, though the oil and gas industry had been and continues to be the life blood of Iraq, those who had participated so successfully in building and running it had been marginalised and overshadowed by other historical events, political upheavals and intrigues which were hatched by the power hungry politicians. These included the never ending political and social unrests, the numerous coups and counter coups, the futile revolutions, the destructive and tragic wars, the inhumane United Nations sanctions, and finally the vengeful invasion of Iraq in 2003 which sent the county back to the (Stone Age) almost exactly as threatened by James Baker the former US Secretary of States in 1990 after the invasion of Kuwait.

It is with sadness that one can look back now to see how such a heaven sent blessing of abundant revenues from the export of crude oil, which could have been spent wisely on the development of the country and the welfare of its people, could have been so grossly wasted on the very destruction of the country and the killing and impoverishment of its people.

It is such tragic and disastrous events that prompted me to reflect back and sum it all up in the following short poem.

Iraq

A country floating on oil

Some oil was set on fire
to get the whole oil boil

To brew a fatal stew
of war, blood and toil

Courtesy of Chefs greed,
Ignorance and broil

It is unbelievable if not maddening to see that nothing has changed and no lessons seem to have been learnt since, even today in 2011, these very ugly master chefs and many others like them are still hard at work preparing their new and more sophisticated recipes for even deadlier stews. As a result and since the invasion of Iraq in 2003, hundreds of thousands more people have been killed, tens of thousands have been left homeless, hundreds of thousands more people have fled the country to bring the total to some three to four million. Poverty and disease are more widespread than before, law and order have broken down completely with people disappearing, being murdered in daylight, or bombed in the streets or in their own homes. Basic services such medical care, clean water, electricity, drainage and more amazingly, in the country floating on oil, it is becoming difficult to secure ones need of the essential products of that oil. This is despite the fact that nearly two and a half million barrels of that oil is still flowing every day as it has been doing so for decades.

In the meantime the huge revenues which are being generated by the export of the oil are still going to waste down the drain through the funnels of mismanagement, greed and corruption.

Will we ever learn, will we ever stop and think rationally, will sanity ever prevail, will Iraq return to normality and when? The answer must be yes since this great county had experienced similar if not much worse tragedies throughout its history and came out triumphant. We must remember that this is the same country that is known as the cradle of civilisation, the land of Babylon and its hanging gardens. It is the same country of the golden civilisation of Haroun Al-Rasheed and his fabulous capital Baghdad and its legendry tales of the one thousand and one nights. It is the home of a great nation, it will, it must stand back on its feet with its head high amongst the nations of the world and very soon at that.

Back to our book and away from the distressing state of current affairs, it is worth highlighting that though many books and hundreds of papers and articles had been published dealing with certain aspects, branches, political or historical events relating to Iraq's oil industry, to my knowledge, no single comprehensive book had been written covering all of these aspects over a long period of time.

Therefore I was convinced that it was about time that a book was written about the industry and its professionals and technocrats that would give them back their long overdue recognition and appreciation which had been denied them by the mainly amateur politicians who had ruined and finally brought the country to its knees through their unbelievable short-sightedness and utter mismanagement.

However, while we still wait for such serious recognitions to appear in the Iraqi media, we find the media in the Western World had been much quicker in doing so. Many articles and papers have been published in the newspapers and on the internet on the subject and finally, we find Greg Muttitt in his recent book in 2011, " Fuel on the Fire/Oil and Politics in Occupied Iraq" writes in page xxvii the following :

"Most Iraqis say they want oil production to stay in the public sector. This attitude has been dismissed by occupation officials and Western commentators as old-fashioned, ideological or even Ba'athist. Yet when one looks at the Iraqi oil industry, one finds a proud engineering culture. It achieved great successes immediately after nationalisation in the 1970s and maintained Iraq's facilities and operations through the hardships of three wars and 13 years of sanctions. In place of financial capital, they relied on human endeavour. In place of modern technology, they improvised with what they had.

For many Iraqi oil technocrats, their industry-taking into account its environmental, economic and political circumstances-can be run most efficiently in the public sector."

He then writes on page 18 the following:

"During the 1970's the Iraqi engineers deployed the skills they had leaned working for the British-run IPC before nationalisation to build an industry that was the envy of oil producers around the world. Between 1972 and 1979 the Iraq National Oil Company (INOC) increased production from 1.5 to 3.5 million barrels per day. From 1972 to 1977 Iraqi exploration teams discovered new oil at a rate of 6 billion barrels of oil a year, matching the best years for the whole of the rest of world put together. They found some of Iraq's largest fields: West Qurna,East Baghdad, Majnoon and Nahr Bin Omar."

Hence, following my retirement in 2007, several of my Iraqi friends and colleagues in the industry who were aware of the extent of my broad and diverse experience approached me suggesting that I write a book about Iraq's oil and gas industry. Many were enthusiastic and encouraging by offering to contribute relevant information from their own vast and varied experiences in the industry and its history.

It seems that the writing and the publication of my Arabic poems over the years, which had been well circulated and received, had brought my name to the forefront to fulfil this uneasy task of writing such a book which I proudly agreed to undertake and have done my best to be as accurate, factual and fair as possible in writing it.

Meanwhile it is important to highlight that the archive of the Iraq Petroleum Company Limited is held within the archive of the British Petroleum Company at the University of Warwick, Coventry, United Kingdom.

It is however unfortunate that this archive, which contains all the IPC's main records including the Concessions' Agreements and the Minutes of the Board of Directors, could not be made available to me since it is closed for thirty years. Hence there is no doubt that new information and additional important facts will be revealed when this archive is finally opened which would, no doubt throw new lights that would enhance what has been recorded in this book.

Faced with the non-availability of the IPC's archive, which would have afforded me the most reliable and accurate source of information for the period stretching between the First World War and the nationalisation of the IPC in 1972, I started to look for other reliable sources of information for the various chapters of the book such as:

1.   The Development of the Oil and Gas Fields and the Export Pipelines.

   Not to my surprise, such sources of accurate information on the Historical and Technical aspects of the Development of the Oil and Gas Fields as well as the Export and other Pipelines were very limited and when found they usually had the relevant information incoherent and scattered here and there within such sources. However after some further intensive research I was fortunate enough to find, at least, some of what I wanted from the following sources:

a.   Some of the IPC's publications

A few such publications came to hand mainly through helpful IPC colleagues that included:

- The Iraq Petroleum Company and Its Associated Companies' Handbook, first Edition 1948.

- What Do You Know About The Water Injection Scheme In Kirkuk, 1964.

- Iraq, Basrah And Mosul Petroleum Companies, Revue For 1965.

- Guide To Iraq Petroleum Company, Kirkuk, 1966.

- Kirkuk Field – 500 Million Tons, December 1966. This is the total cumulative crude oil produced from this field since its discovery in 1927 to December 1966.

Though the information in these documents were limited compared to the vast scope of the subject, nonetheless they were very reliable in helping the completion of the book as well as decorating it with some rare photographs.

b.   The IPC Society Newsletters

The IPC society was established in the early 1970s when it started to publish its quarterly Newsletter and continues to do so until now with over 150 such issues having been published to date. These Newsletters not only contained personal news of the members but also various articles about the authors recollections of their work experiences, stories, adventures etc during their services whether in London Office, Iraq or the rest of the Middle East.

The relevant Technical and Historical articles contained a wealth of information about the development of Iraq's oil and gas fields and export pipelines as well as some unique old photographs, all of which proved to be of great assistance in writing this book. It goes without saying that the information in these articles were firsthand experiences of those who wrote them and no doubt rank as some of the most authentic and trustworthy sources of information that could be found.

c.   My Own First Hand Personal Experience And Those Of Other Iraqi Oilmen.

In the 1952 Concession Agreement, the IPC Group had agreed to send 50 Iraqi students on scholarship to the United Kingdom at its own expense every year to study engineering, technology, science and other related subjects to the oil and gas industry, with the total number of students not exceeding 250 s at any one time.

After their graduation, these students returned to Iraq from the late 1950s onwards to join the Iraq, Basra and Mosul Petroleum Companies as well as the other government oil and gas departments. They then began to acquire a vast expertise in their own fields of work and finally took over the running of Iraq's vast and successful oil and gas industry. Many of these colleagues contributed generously and freely to the completion of this book by supplying vital information based on their first hand experiences which again rank as some of the most accurate and trustworthy sources that could be found.

d.   Iraq-International Relations and National Development, by Edith and E.F Penrose, , first published in 1978.

Though this book dealt with all aspects of the National Development of modern Iraq up to the mid 1970s, it contained some of the most interesting historical and technical information about the oil and gas industry that I have read in one single book. Hence it was of great value in assisting to compare and cross-check various data in order to arrive at the most accurate information that has been included in this book.

e.   The History of the British Petroleum Company, Volume 1, by R.W. Ferrier, The Development Years 1901-1932, published in 1982.

This book covers the history of the D'Arcy concession in Persia in 1901 and it final discovery of oil in May 1908 in Masjidi Sullaiman, an area about 130 miles upstream of the river Karun. The D'Arcy interest then joined forces with the interest of another concern, the Burma Oil Company, to form the famous Anglo-Persian Oil Company (APOC), our present time British Petroleum Company (BP).

The Turkish Petroleum Company (TPC) was then established in 1912, in which APOC ultimately became a major shareholder, and obtained its first oil concession in Iraq and went to find oil on Kirkuk in 1927. The name of the TPC was finally changed to the Iraq Petroleum Company IPC in 1928

The book contains detailed information about the history of oil in Persia and Iraq in these early days of the twentieth century and afforded a good source of reliable information which helped in the completion of this book.

2. The Concessions' Negotiations and the Relationship Between the Iraqi Governments and the IPC Group During the Period 1921-1952.

As for the various concessions' negotiations and the relationship between the Iraqi Governments and the IPC Group, I was very lucky to come across the following book:

- The Political History of the Oil Concessions in Iraq, Between 1925-1952, by Nori Abdul Hamid Khalil, first published in Arabic in 1980.

I was very fortunate indeed to have been able to obtain a copy of this University of Baghdad Ph.D. thesis which had a limited number of copies and hence was very rare and difficult to find. The thesis is a very lengthy, elaborate and detailed document of more than 400 pages. It is also very well documented and referenced. A lot of its information is based on the relevant documents of the British Colonial Office, Foreign Office, Air Ministry and the India Office. Other accurate information are mainly based on the minutes of meeting of the Iraqi Cabinets as well as other relevant official documents from the archives of the Iraqi Ministry of Economy, Ministry of Oil, Foreign Ministry and Ministry of Communications and Works.

The thesis also included some other important but less substantiated information from various Iraqi newspapers of that period. As a whole the thesis proved to be of great assistance in arriving at the most authentic and reliable information that could be included in this book.

Again, Edith and E.F Penrose's book, Iraq-International Relations and National Development, contained some good information on this subject and helped to compare and verify information from the other sources.

3. The Relationship and Negotiations between the Iraqi Governments and the IPC Group during the 1950s and the 1960s.

Once more I was more than fortunate to find a lot of what I was looking for in the following important book:

- Iraqi Oil Negotiations, 1952 – 1968, by Abdullah Ismail, first published in Arabic 1989.

This is one of the most detailed and comprehensive books that I have come across on the controversial subject of the various disputes and negotiations between the Iraqi Governments and the IPC Group during the turmoil periods of the 1950s and 1960s. It's importance, in my view, stems from the fact that the author was one of the most senior and long serving officials in the Ministry of Economy and later on in the Ministry of Oil during these critical times. Furthermore he was the secretary to the Committee which conducted the difficult and at times very strained and bitter negotiations during the period 1958-1961 which were conducted during their later stages by General Qassim himself and which ultimately failed and resulted in the legislation of the famous Law 80 which expropriated 99.5% of the IPC Group's concession areas.

Abdullah was also a member of the committee which conducted the similarly very important and controversial negations between the Ministry of Oil and the IPC Group during the period 1964-1965, which were headed by Abdul Aziz Al-Wattari the then Minister of Oil. These negotiations were more balanced and businesslike and almost succeeded in the creation of the much talked about ill-fated Baghdad Oil Company (BOCO).

Though these negotiations have also been mentioned in other books including Edith and E.F Penrose's Iraq-International Relations and National Development, various memoirs and numerous articles, none of these rank as complete, accurate and reliable as Ismail's book, though they were very useful for comparison and cross-checking purposes. Hence without this book the information included in this book would have been grossly inadequate.

It is of interest to record that the mention of Abdullah Ismail has always brought back to me some of the most cherished memories from my younger days. That is when I was interviewed with many other students in the summer of 1954 by a committee from the Ministry of Economy and the IPC, which included Abdullah, for the selection of the successful students who would be sent on the renowned Ministry of Economy (later on Ministry of Oil) Scholarship Scheme to study in the United Kingdom.

4.   Iraq's Oil And Gas Fields

Most of the oil and gas fields which were discovered in the twentieth century have been fairly well documented though scattered in different books, papers and articles. Based on these diffident sources, a complete up to date list and description of these fields are included in this book together with the unique additional first hand information of Nathim Al-Qazzar who is considered to be one of the small number of people who have such an in depth knowledge about them.

It is, however, also fair to highlight that much more comprehensive, detailed and thorough reports about Iraq's oil and gas fields as well as scores of promising structures could be found advertised on the internet and in journals. However these include elaborate detailed geological information, petroleum and reservoir engineering data as well as detailed maps that are mainly of interest to the specialists and the prospective oil companies. However each of these reports could cost anything from a few thousands to tens of thousands of dollars, depending on the information they contain.

Furthermore, it is to be highlighted that though this book deals with oil and gas related events that took place during the twentieth century, certain important and controversial other events have taken place during the first decade of the twenty first century. These include the signing of several Production Service Contracts by the Ministry of Oil of the Central Government in Baghdad with a number of the international oil companies.

Furthermore a large number of Exploration and Production Sharing Agreements were awarded by the Kurdistan Regional Government for a much larger number of promising oil and gas structures though these Agreements are considered illegal by the Central Government in Baghdad and have been the subject of bitter disputes between the Central Government and the Kurdistan Regional Government. Nonetheless the exploration and drilling work went ahead and several oil and gas fields have since been discovered, developed and went on production.

Hence, due to the importance and the controversial aspect of this subject it was considered appropriate to include these fields in the book. It is however important to highlight that though no detailed information has been made available about such fields except through the companies' press releases and statements, every effort has been made to include the most up to date reliable information and data about them. These will no doubt be updated during their ongoing evaluation in the coming months and years.

5.   Oil Refineries, Gas Industry and Other topics

The technical aspects of refineries and gas processing plants are well documented in hundred of books, journals and articles as well as the various engineering data books such as The Engineering Data Book, tenth edition 1987, by the Gas Processors Suppliers Association, Tulsa, Oklahoma 74145, USA, and hence there was no shortage of reference books to rely upon.

Unfortunately there was precious little written references about the relevant history or detailed technical information about Iraq's refineries and gas processing plants. Again I was fortunate to discover that there were no shortage of colleagues who volunteered to supply the required information based on their first hand experience in the industry.

I am therefore greatly indebted to the large number of friends and colleagues whose names could not all be recorded. However those who were instrumental in supplying information, guidance and encouragement included the following friends:-

- Dr. Nadhim Al-Qazzaz was the contributor of most of the vital chapter eight on Iraq's oil and gas fields. Nadhim had spent most of his working life, of almost fifty years, in Iraq's oil and gas industry which made him one of the authorities on the subject.

  He Joined the Mosul Petroleum Company in 1959 as a production engineer before being transferred soon after to the Iraq Petroleum Company in Kirkuk as Area Production Engineer till 1967. He spent the next five years in higher education at the University of Victoria, Victoria, B.C., Canada, obtaining his MSc. in 1969 and his PhD in 1972.

  Nadhim returned to Kirkuk after the nationalisation of the IPC to join the newly formed Iraqi Company for Oil Operations (present day North Oil Company) in 1973. He held the post of Area Production Engineer before becoming Senior Reservoir Engineer in 1975, Chief Reservoir and Fields Development Engineer in 1979 and finally the Head of Petroleum Engineering Department in 1984. He continued to hold this post until his retirement in 1990. As a result, Nadhim has had a firsthand in depth knowledge of all the oil and gas fields in northern Iraq as well as the additional knowledge of all the other fields throughout the country which made him one of the small number of people who had such wealth of knowledge about Iraq's oil and gas fields.

  Nadhim was also generous in his assistance on other subjects such as drilling, production and other operational matters. Hence without Nadhim's contribution this book could not have been presented in its current form and therefore I am truly grateful and indebted to this dear lifetime friend of almost sixty years .

Nadhim moved to the UK in 1990 to work as consultant mainly in the field of oil and gas for the following 18 years until his second and final retirement in 2009.

- Faik Mohammed Abdul Aziz who was the head of the Electrical Engineering Department during the latter years of the IPC and the subsequent years after its nationalisation. He continued in the same role until he left the company in 1984 to work as a consultant in Iraq, the UAE and the UK till his retirement in 2008. Faik had a wealth of both technical and historical knowledge which proved to be vital for the completion of the book. He was also generous in reading the lengthy draft, contributing additional information and proposing amendments to many paragraphs. Again without Faik's help this book would have been grossly incomplete and I am again truly indebted to this dear lifetime friend of over fifty years.

- Mishal Hammodat was one of the truly early pioneers of the oil and gas industry in Iraq with an experience stretching from the early 1950s when the industry was almost entirely in the hands of the expatriates. He is considered as the father of the crude oil refining industry in the country. He was also instrumental in the successful establishment of the petroleum products and liquid petroleum gas (LPG) production and distribution. Mishal served in the Ministry of Oil for many years and was involved in the country's top oil decision making and policy setting and had published two books about the subject. The wealth of knowledge he contributed about the refineries and the LPG industry was vital for the completion of this book. Above all Mishal's overwhelming generosity, guidance and encouragements were paramount in the completion of this book and I am very grateful to him.

- Dr Tariq Irhayim, who is a very dear old friend of mine and who had spent most of his working life in the Petroleum Engineering Department in Kirkuk, played a pivotal role in supplying information about the old sulphur plant and the LPG underground salt cavern storage facilities. He also became my central contact with some of our colleagues in the industry in Kirkuk. For all his help and countless emails I am very grateful.

- Abdul Karim Mohammad whose name had become synonymous with the Process Plants for decades was a true friend and colleague who was the generous provider of most of the information about the Process Plants, which were and still are the central and vital installations in the crude oil production facilities at Kirkuk. Though he is nearly ninety years old, I find his mind still as sharp as ever not to mention his down-to-earth attitude and lovely sense of humour. Again I am greatly indebted and thankful to him.

- Abdul Razzak Al-Battawi who had spent practically all his working life in the operations of the main IPC Mediterranean export pipelines, was one of the main contributors of information about the pump stations and their various facilities. He was instrumental in supplying some of the historical as well as most of the technical details of the numerous oil and gas equipment at these vital stations. I am therefore grateful to Abdul Razzak for all his help in making the writing this book possible.

- Issam al-Chalabi, the deputy and later on the Minister of Oil during the 1980s was truly generous in his encouragement and in providing the vital information and block diagrams about the huge South Gas Project. Issam who is still publishing his important articles about Iraq's past and current oil and gas affairs has become an authority in this field and I am grateful for all his help and contribution.

- My cousin Anwar Abdul Rahman Dawood and Husam Majeed Al-Shamma' were extremely generous in contributing most of vital information about the twin Iraq/Turkey export pipelines to the port of Ceyhan on the Mediterranean and the Iraq/Saudi export pipeline to the port of Yanbu on the Red Sea and I am extremely grateful and indebted to both of them.

- My profound thanks and appreciation must also go to the authors of numerous articles published in the IPC Society Newsletters, a few of whom are known to me and the vast majority I have never met, who have afforded me some of the vital information and unique photographs that have been included in this book.

- I also would like to say thank you to my other friends who either supplied information or gave encouragement. They are so many that I beg to be forgiven for mentioning only a few of them such as Tariq Shafiq, Dr. Fadhil al-Kazily, Abdul Jabber Neseyif, Hosam Raof, Saleh Ali and Fakhri Sharief.

It goes without saying that the completion of this book could not have been possible without the patience and continuous encouragement of my wife who had also helped throughout the months in reading, checking, editing and finally proof reading the final draft, to whom I am extremely grateful.

In the meantime, I am reproducing two of my poems, the first in Arabic, "The Cradle Of Civilisation", which is published on the "almosul.org" website together with the whole of my collection of 38 poems. The poem talks about that glorious old civilisation and compares it with the present miserable , chaotic and shameful state of affairs and ends with expressing hope and optimism for a bright and honourable future for this great country.

The second poem in English "The Talking Oaks Of Cassiobury Park" is a more light hearted poem which was published by the IPC Society in its newsletter, issue 145 of January 2010.

Ghanim Anaz
August 2011
Watford,
United Kingdom

مَهدُ الحضارةِ

غانم عنّاز

جلستُ أرنو إلى ما حَلَّ في بـلدي   ذاكَ العراقُ الذي ما غابَ عن خَلَدي

ذاك الحبيبُ الذي قد ذابَ في المُهَجِ   وأصبح راسخًا في العقلِ والجسدِ

عَرفتُهُ رافعًا رأسًا بلا خطَلٍ   ومُسعِفًا شعبًا إنْ ضيمَ من أحدِ

مهدُ الحضارةِ يا مَنْ علّمَ الأممَا   كتابةَ الحرفِ واستنساخهِ بيدِ

سَنَنْتَ أوّلَ قانونٍ بلا جَدلٍ   لِتنشُرَ العَدلَ بينَ الناسِ للأبدِ

عَجائبُ الدنيا منها جَنائنُكَ   مُعَلَّقاتٍ في يُسرٍ وفي رَغدِ

وعدتُ أصغي لعلّي أسمعُ فرَحًا   فلمْ أجدْ غيرَ ما يُدمي من الكمدِ

مَضَتْ ثلاثون عامًا أنت في صَخبٍ   تُصارعُ الشرَّ يأتيكَ بلا رصدِ

فلم أرَ غيرَ حربٍ لم تكنْ هَمَدتْ   حتى تلاها غَزوٌ طالَ في الأمدِ

وبينَ هذا وذاكَ حِصارٌ قـذِرٌ   لِيُهلكَ النسلَ عنْ قصدٍ وعنْ حَسَدِ

خيراتُكَ أصبحتْ نهبًا بلا رصدِ   وأرضُكَ مُنحتْ حقلاً لِمنْ يَفدِ

وأهلكَ هُجِروا قسْرًا بلا سَببٍ   وشعبُكَ أصبحَ صَيدًا لِمنْ يصِدِ

آثارُكَ سُرقتْ منَ الغُزاةِ ضُحى   لتُصبحَ سِلعةً في أيدي مَنْ يَـزِدِ

فارقتُكَ مُرغمًا لا طالبًا طمَعا   كي أرجعَ بعدَ أنْ تَـشفى منَ الأوَدِ

طالَ انتظاري وما خفتْ مَصائبُكَ   ها أنتَ ذا سِلعةً للساسةِ الجددِ

وعُدتُ أزجرُ نفسي صائحًا عَجبٌ   كنتِ التي تَنصحينَ الناسَ بالجَلدِ

تفاءَلي وانشُري ما بيننـا أمَلاً   أنتِ التي دائمًا تدعينَ للرَشدِ

واتفورد – ضواحي لندن

تشرين الثاني 2011

THE TALKING OAKS OF CASSIOBURY PARK

This is the story of a few ancient oak trees standing close to both the river Gade and the Grand Union Canal in Cassiobury Park in Watford, Herts., United Kingdom.

It was written for the author's grand children, two of them twin girls age six and lived overseas. The poem was read to the twins and fired their imaginations. They couldn't wait for their summer holiday to come to visit the trees. When they arrived in Watford, their Gran took them to the park and were excited to see the trees and suddenly started talking to them. When they heard no answer they asked their Gran why weren't they answering them back? Their Gran was quick to explain that they are magic trees and would only talk to their grandfather!

While I stood admiring the ancient oak
I hopefully asked, tell me, can you talk?
Though you don't seem to move at all
Yet you have grown so thick and tall

The answer came in a nice whispering tone
As you know, my origin was a humble corn
In this park, I was planted a long time ago
Perhaps five or six hundred years or so

Though my trunk has grown so very thick
I my youth, I was such a skinny stick
And though my life is full of nice memories
Yet, I have also had my share of agonies

The memories that I remember and cherish best
Are of courting couples having me as a love nest
Names have been lovingly carved in my trunk
Beautiful hearts and arrows also deeply sunk

My trunk has been home to so many squirrels
Amusing me with their love N rowdy quarrels
On my branches, birds have peacefully rested
Sang their hearts out, courted and finally nested

People love to rest in my inviting shade
After their walks in the nearby glade
Sometimes, I just love to stand still and dream
While my feet get washed by the gentle stream

Other times, I prefer relaxing in the breeze
Letting my leaves dance with perfect ease
And so my friend as you can see
A busy life can also be led by an oak tree

Watford, Herts
Sept 1994

1

IRAQ OIL AND GAS INDUSTRY IN THE TWENTIETH CENTURY

Introduction

This book is about the history of the discovery of Crude Oil and Gas Fields and the subsequent development of the oil and gas industry in Iraq. It is the history of some of the unique oil and gas organisations, which stretched over most of the 20th century and which are still going very strong in the twenty first century.

It is the story of the Iraqi Ministry of Oil, the Iraq Petroleum Company (IPC) and its successors, after nationalisation, the Iraqi Company for Oil Operations (ICOO) which was renamed North Petroleum Organisation, (NPO) to become at the present North Oil Company (NOC). It is that of the Mosul Petroleum Company (MPC), the Basra Petroleum Company (BPC) and its successor after nationalisation, the South Petroleum Organisation (SPO) which became at the present South Oil Company (SOC). It is also the story of the Iraq National Oil Company (INOC) and other organisations such as the Iraqi Refineries, the Natural Gas and Liquid Petroleum Gas (LPG), and the distribution of Petroleum Products and LPG.

It is also a tribute to the tens of thousands of people who planned, managed, built and operated the vast facilities of these organisations.

The spheres of activities of these organisations covered the whole of Iraq and beyond with their crude oil pipelines terminating at the Mediterranean coast at Haifa in Palestine, Tripoli in Lebanon, Banias in Syria, and Ceyhan in Turkey. Other pipelines terminated at the Red Sea coast at Yanbu in Saudi Arabia and in the Gulf at the Iraqi deep water oil terminals of Khor al-Amayah and Mina al-Bakr.

They finished the twentieth century as truly giant oil and gas organisations with the following impressive and envious achievements:

- The discovery of more than 70 oil and gas fields some of which are real giants and amongst the largest in the world with a proven recoverable crude oil reserves of 143 billion barrels.

- An impressive expansion of the country's production and export facilities from the initial modest capacity of 80,000 barrels per day to 3.8 million barrels of oil per day.

- Drilling and completion of thousands of oil, gas, observation, water injection and potable water wells.

- Construction of scores of degassing stations of various capacities to suit the different oil fields.

- Construction of two oil processing plants each having a capacity of one million barrels of oil per day.

- Construction of a water injection plant with a capacity of up to one and quarter million barrels per day of highly purified water for injection in the Kirkuk oil reservoir to maintain its pressure.

- Laying of tens of thousands of kilometres of crude oil, gas and petroleum products pipelines of numerous sizes of up to 56 inch in diameter all over Iraq and across many countries traversing over mountains, deserts and crossing major rivers.

- Building of tens of oil pumping stations, some of them in the middle of nowhere, with oil pumping capacities of up to 1.6 million barrels per day, each complete with all the necessary supporting industrial facilities in addition to the residential and recreational amenities.

- Construction of many refineries all over Iraq with a total capacity of some 700,000 barrels per day.

- Installation of many natural gas and Liquid Petroleum Gas plants

- Installation of many petroleum products and Liquid Petroleum Gas depots, underground storage facilities and LPG bottling plants.

- Building of thousands of kilometres of service roads all over Iraq and across Jordan, Palestine, Syria and Lebanon.

- Building of thousands of houses, offices, workshops, schools, clubs, cinemas, golf courses and many other industrial, community and recreation facilities.

- Establishment of a home ownership scheme for the Iraqi staff and employees mainly in the cities of Kirkuk, Basra and Mosul, which helped them to own their own homes, as well as participating in the development of these cities by creating the much needed additional employment opportunities for the local communities.

- Construction of a main power station and several power-generating plants together with the relevant sub-stations, and laying the necessary high and low voltage cable networks to supply all the industrial and domestic needs with electric power.

- Installation of several water supply systems to satisfy the industrial and domestic requirements.

- Sending thousands of their staff and technicians abroad on scholarships to universities and colleges and many more for training at the factories and workshops of their equipment suppliers.

- Establishment of Training Centres that provided the much needed technicians and artisans for the county's oil and gas industry

All this required the dedicated effort of men and women of different professions and skills, the number of which reached over seventy thousands by the end of the century.

A Brief History of Crude Oil

We are all familiar with the products of Crude Oil in one form or another. The most commonly used products are petrol, diesel oil and kerosene sold at our local petrol stations to fill up our cars, run our machines and heat our homes, offices factories and shops. Other products exist in one form or another in the manufacturing of thousands of our daily use commodities.

Crude oil is found in abundance all over the world. It has been known and utilised for thousands of years. Tar has been seeping to the surface of the ground in Iraq, Azerbaijan, and Persia and other part of the world.

It is thought that the Sumerians, in the south of Iraq, seem to have utilised tar to waterproof some of their boats which were made of entwined local reeds some five thousand years ago. It is also thought that the reed circular boat the "Quffa" which is still being used today on the river Tigris has its origin in Sumer.

Asphalt was also employed as a water proofing material by the Babylonian in the construction of their Ziggurats and the walls of their fabulous city of Babylon with its hanging gardens over three thousand years ago.

A fishing Quffa on the River Tigris - Mid 20th Century

Ancient Arabic poetry and history books dating back to the early centuries of the first millennium AD are full of references about their beloved camels, which were their main vehicle of transport across the desert as well as a source for their milk and ultimately meat. These books also often refer to the successful use of tar for treating Mange, the skin disease that affected these much valued ships of the desert.

A passenger Quffa on the River Tigris-Baghdad - Early 20ᵗʰ Century

Tar, was also known to have been used by the Arabs for paving some of the main roads during the construction of their new and fabulous city of Baghdad in 762AD.

Petroleum was distilled in the ninth century AD by the well-known Persian chemist and physician Mohammad Al Razi to produce kerosene in the Alembic (Arabic al-Imbiq), which was used in kerosene lamps. Arab and Persian chemists are also known to have distilled crude oil to produce flammable products for use in their mangonels. It was through the Arabic and Islamic golden civilisation in Spain that the distillation of petroleum became available to Western Europe in the twelfth century AD.

Naphtha is known to have been extracted from the oil fields in the areas around Baku, Azerbaijan, as early as the ninth century AD. The well-known Arab explorer and geographer Ali Al Masoudi referred to the white oil in that area in his famous book " Morouj Al Dhahab and Maadin Al Jowhar" after he visited the area in the tenth century AD during his elaborate journey though Egypt, Syria, Palestine, the Caucasus, Persia, India, Ceylon, and parts of China well before Marco Polo.

When Marco Polo visited the city of Baku in Azerbaijan in 1264, he saw oil being collected from oil pits. He also mentioned that he saw a fountain from which oil springs in great abundance. Hand-dug holes of up to 35 metres deep were in use in Baku in 1594. By 1830 more than 100 such oil wells were in production in the vicinity of Baku

Native Americans are known to have been digging small pits in the oil seepage area for medicinal usage in the early years of the fifteenth century. European settlers in America had for years been skimming the oil from the oil seeps and using petroleum product from it in their oil lamps.

During the later years of the first half of the nineteenth century, oil was already being refined and one of its products, Kerosene, was being commercially marketed.

THE OIL RUSH

The most important oil well ever drilled was in the middle of a quiet farm country in north-western Pennsylvania in1859. For, this was one of the first successful oil wells that were drilled for the purpose of finding oil. Known as the Drake well, after (Colonel) Edwin Drake, the man responsible for the well, it started an international search for petroleum, and in many ways eventually changed the way we live. The well was drilled by a simple rig to a depth of about 21 metres and left over night. It was not until the next morning when the driller noticed oil was floating in the hole which he had left empty the night before. By today's standards, it was a pretty unremarkable hole, probably producing 20 barrels or less of oil per day, where as some of the later wells can gush over 100,000 barrels per day. Almost overnight the quiet farming region changed in much the same manner as the gold rush of the Wild West. Suddenly this once quiet area became louder than anyone could have imagined, with steam engines and other types of machinery necessary to run the hundreds of wells that sprang up in the area in the first couple of years. This sudden discovery was very significant and marked the early establishment of the modern oil industry.

THE DAWN OF THE MOTOR CAR

Up to 1886, the market for crude oil products was confined to kerosene for lighting and lubricants, mainly for the steam engines. In 1885 the German Karl Benz designed and built his four-stroke internal combustion engine that was used in his automobile. He then went to patent his automobile in 1886, which became the first automobile in production in the world. He was soon to be followed by others the like of the Germans Rudolf Diesel and Gottlieb Daimler and the American Henry Ford.

By the end of the nineteenth century and the beginning of the twentieth century the use of the motorcar was beginning to increase steadily and with it came the increasing demand for gasoline and crude oil.

By the end of the First World War the use of the internal combustion engine spread quickly, to power all sorts of vehicles trucks, buses, passenger and cargo ships, military tanks, armoured vehicles, civil and military aeroplanes, agricultural and industrial machinery and many others.

This was followed by the development of the enormous petrochemical industry and its countless domestic, industrial and pharmaceutical products, which together with the internal combustion engine resulted in an explosive demand for crude oil and its products, which led to the modern ever expanding crude oil industry.

THE WORLD'S FIRST OIL GUSHER

There had long been suspicions that oil might be under (Spindletop Hill) in Beaumont, Texas. As a result drilling was started there and on 10th January 1901, at a depth of 347 metres oil was struck and started to blow over 46 metres in the air at a rate of some 100,000 barrel per day. It took nine days before the well was brought under control. The Spindletop well was the largest gusher the world had seen at that time and represented a turning point for Texas and the United States, which soon after became the leading oil producer in the world.

The Race for the Middle East Oil

In view of the increasing demand for the petroleum products in the western world during the later years of the nineteenth century and the early years of the twentieth century, it became a matter of national priority for two of the world major powers of that time, Britain and Germany, to ensure the continuity of their reliable supplies of crude oil.

Since it had been known that there were plenty of signs for the existence of oil in the Middle East, it prompted these two powers together with others to support the establishment of their own national oil companies. Such indications also encouraged them to despatch their exploration parties to the Middle East to locate the possible oil rich regions and to send their trade missions to Istanbul and Teheran to obtain oil concessions. As a result, the geologists from many European countries were roaming all over the region exploring and trying to identify the most likely locations of such lucrative oil fields.

Iraq had been singled out as a very promising country for the existence of oil deposits based not only on the geological assessments but also on the abundant oil tell tale signs, such as the asphalt and crude oil seepages at Qayarah, Kirkuk, Pulkanah and Heet as well as the escaping natural gas of the legendary Eternal Fires in the Baba Gurgur area near Kirkuk.

Crude oil had been collected for a long time from these seepages by the local people and filled in goat skins to be transported on horses and donkeys. From about the seventeenth century such seepages were leased to traders such as the Naftchi (crude oil trader) family of Kirkuk who had obtained their lease by a Farman (Decree) from the Ottoman Sultan. Their lease covers the crude oil seepages in the Kirkuk region which included the famous seepage of Wadi al-Naft (Oil Wadi) which runs behind the present Process Plant and the Baba degassing station. The collection of crude oil from this seepage continued until the middle of the twentieth century. By then the oil was filled in special ten containers and transported to be used mainly as fuel for the various public Turkish baths in Kirkuk and the nearby towns.

An attempt was made by Madhat Basha (1869-1872), the progressive Ottoman Wali (governor) in Baghdad to develop the oil in the Mandili region with the assistance of the Germans. Another attempt was made by the French towards the end of the nineteenth century to utilise the crude oil in the Kirkuk and Pulkanah regions. Finally in 1905 the Ottoman authorities started to import equipment for the production of the crude oil in Iraq but these efforts were hindered by the political events of the following years and to be finally over taken by the start of the First World War.

It was not until May 1901, that William Knox D'Arcy, a British adventurer, was granted a concession by the Shah of Persia to search for crude oil in the region of Khuzistan. After a long period of exploration and drilling and just before abandoning the whole adventure, due to shortage of capital, he struck oil in May1908 at Masjidi Sullaiman area about 130 miles upstream of the river Karun. The D'Arcy interest then joined forces with the interest of another concern, the Burma Oil Company, to form the famous Anglo-Persian Oil Company (APOC), which became our present time British Petroleum Company (BP). APOC then proceeded to exploit this Persian oil find and went from there to explore for other fields in the region. This was the first commercially significant crude oil find in the Middle East, which whetted the appetites of many other companies to obtain similar concessions for the exploration of the lucrative crude oil.

Iraq was, in these days, part of the Ottoman Empire, which was very weak and dubbed at that time as the "Sick Man of Europe". The world's super powers of that time had the necessary leverage on the "Sick Man" to secure the much sought after rights for the exploration of the oil deposits in Iraq. This led the oil companies of these powers to hold a series of separate and sometimes overlapping negotiations with the Ottoman authorities with the view of securing concessions for such mineral deposits.

The Anatolian Railway Company, which was owned by the German Deutsche Bank, had already obtained a concession to build a railway in Turkey. It proceeded later on to secure a permission to extend its railway to the Gulf and at the same time it obtained a promise of special preferential treatment for mineral exploration rights. Finally the famous Baghdad Convention, which was signed in 1903, gave the Anatolian Railway Company these promised preferential rights to explore for oil on each side of the proposed route of the Railway which was planned to run from Konia in Turkey to Baghdad and ends in Basra. This was to form the basis of the much talked about "Berlin to Baghdad" railway which was to become a famous slogan later on. The company obtained in 1904 a one year option to explore the area and report. However the company did not meet some of the conditions and as a result the concession was considered in July 1907 to have lapsed.

In the meantime, following their success in discovering oil in Persia, the D'Arcy group began to show interest in securing a further oil concession in Iraq. As a result the D'rcy group approached the Ottoman authorities in 1906 with the support of the British embassy in Istanbul for the purpose of obtaining a concession for the exploration of oil in Iraq. These negotiations dragged on for many years without any agreement.

Meanwhile the American and the Italian governments were also in contact with the Ottoman authorities for securing a concession for their companies.

As a result of the different interests of these countries, a diplomatic race was started by their diplomatic missions in Istanbul to secure the necessary concessions from the Ottoman Empire for exploration, finding and producing such oil.

Successive rival negotiators, mainly German and British, dealt first with the Sultan's Privy Purse, to which all oil-bearing properties were transferred in late eighteen eighties, which after 1909, came under the control of the reformed Turkish Government.

THE BRITISH NAVY AND THE ANGLO-PERSIAN OIL COMPANY

Meanwhile the British Foreign Office as well as other government departments especially the Admiralty had become convinced that Britain should not only control the oil fields from which she expect to secure her future oil supplies, but that the companies that hold the concessions to such oil fields should also be British. The Persian oil was already in the hands of the British through the Anglo-Persian Oil Company, APOC, and the British government was determined to ensure that any Iraqi oil should similarly stay in the hands of a British company.

The British navy under Churchill (1912-1915) after a lengthy debate had finally decided to convert the navy fuel from coal to oil. On 17 July 1913 he spoke in the debate on the navy and envisaged that quote,

> "The Admiralty should become the independent owner and producer of its own supplies of liquid fuel; firstly by building up an oil reserve in the country sufficient to make us safe in war and be able to override price fluctuations in peace; secondly by acquiring the power to deal in crude oils as they come cheaply into the market." Churchill finished his speech by proclaiming "on no one quality, on no one process, on no one country, on no one route and on no one field must we be dependent. Safety and certainty in oil lie in variety and variety alone"

In the meantime the Anglo-Persian Oil Company was facing financial difficulties and after some lengthy and elaborate discussions between the British government and APOC, an agreement was finally concluded between them by which the government acquired a 51% controlling interest in APOC for £2.2 million. The agreement was approved by the Cabinet on 13 May 1914 and by Parliament on 17 June.

It is of interest to record that the Government sold its shares, except the golden share, during the privatisation policy of the 1980s.

THE TURKISH PETROLEUM COMPANY

Meanwhile, in 1912, a group consisting of the National Bank of Turkey (a British concern), and another British concern associated with it, the Asiatic Petroleum Company which was a subsidiary of the Royal Shell Group, together with the Deutsche Bank had joined forces to form the Turkish Petroleum Company, TPC, which began seeking to obtain an oil concession in Iraq. Fifty percent of the shares were held by the National Bank of Turkey and the other two companies had 25% of the shares each. This powerful group representing the British, German and Dutch interests became a new real competitor to be taken in consideration.

The royal Dutch Shell which had 60% Dutch interest and 40% British interest had been the main competitor of the APOC and since it was believed by the British that the Dutch at that time were under the influence of the Germans, Shell was considered non-British and hence was regarded with some doubt. As a result of the pressures exerted by the Germans for promoting the TPC cause and those exerted by the British for promoting the D'Arcy cause, none of the two companies could obtain a concession from the Turkish government.

In an effort to reconcile the German, British and other conflicting interests, different negotiations were carried out between the D'Arcy group, the Turkish Petroleum Company with contributions from the British Foreign Office, the Turkish government and the German government representatives. The result of these lengthy negotiations was an agreement entitled, "Arrangements for Fusion of the Interests in the Turkish Petroleum Concessions of the D'Arcy Group and the Turkish Petroleum Company" which became to be known as "The foreign Office Agreement". This agreement was signed on 19 March 1914 by representatives of the German government, the British government, the National Bank of Turkey, the Anglo-Saxon Petroleum Company (the Royal Dutch Shell subsidiary), the Deutsche Bank and the D'Arcy Group.

This was a compromise designed to prevent rivalry between the British and the Germans and at the same time to fend any effort by others from obtaining an exploration concession.

The Original shares of the Turkish Petroleum Company, TPC were divided between the main three shareholders, as follow:

- The National Bank of Turkey, 50.00%

- The Anglo- Saxon Petroleum Company (a subsidiary of Royal Dutch Shell), 25.00%

- The Deutsche Bank (as assignee of the German Baghdad Railway Company), 25.00%.

However as a result of "The foreign Office Agreement", the shareholding in the TPC was reallocated as follows:-

- The 50.00% interest of the National Bank of Turkey in TPC was divided by mutual agreement between the Deutsche Bank and the Royal Dutch Shell giving each one of them 50.00% of the shares.

New shares equal in number to the existing shares were created and allocated to the D'Arcy group. The new shareholdings thus became:

- 50.00% for D'Arcy group (Anglo- Persian Oil Company, APOC)

- 25.00% for the Deutsche Bank.

- 25.00% for the Royal Dutch Shell.

Then 2.50% each were taken from the D'Arcy group and Royal Dutch Shell and the resulting 5.00% was given to Gulbenkian.

As a result of this redistribution the final shareholdings in the TPC were as follows:

- 47.5% for D'Arcy group (Anglo- Persian Oil Company, APOC).

- 25.0% for the Deutsche Bank.

- 22.5% for the Royal Dutch Shell.

- 5.0% for Calouste Gulbenkian (Mr 5%) who had the necessary influence and the proper channels of contact with the hierarchy of the Ottoman

Empire and who had also owned 15% interest in the National Bank of Turkey.

It is worth highlighting that this "Foreign Office Agreement" contained a "Self-Denying" clause which prevented the shareholders from having any interest in the production or manufacture of oil in the Ottoman Empire except through the TPC.

A PRIZE LETTER

The disappearance of rivalry between the British and the Germans and their coordinated efforts to secure a concession for their joint Turkish Petroleum Company was soon to give a fruitful result. Both the British and the German ambassadors in Istanbul had sent in June 1914 a similar letter to the Grand Vizier of the Ottoman Empire requesting the award of an oil concession in the Vilayets of Baghdad and Mosul to the Turkish Petroleum Company.

The answer came in the form of an amazing letter dated 28th June 1914, written by the Grand Vizier to the British Ambassador in Istanbul, stating that the Minister of Finance has agreed to lease to the TPC the Petroleum Deposits already discovered or to be discovered in the Vilayets of Mosul and Baghdad and reserves the right to participate in it and agreeing its general terms and conditions.

The terms and conditions of such an extremely important, well sought after and lucrative Lease were not stated in that letter but left open for future settlement.

This letter looked very much like the behind the scene work of Mr Gulbenkian, which earned him his fabulous 5%, cut of the shares of the Company and made him later on one of the richest people in the world. It is also suspected that he must have satisfied the thirst for wealth of the hierarchy of the Ottoman Empire, with the most generous rewards.

Soon after, on 22 July 1914, the Ottoman government informed its representative in London to advise the TPC to send its representative to Istanbul to agree on the terms and conditions of the Lease which would take place in the presence of representatives from the British and the German embassies in Istanbul. However the deterioration in relations between the Ottoman Empire and Britain and the declaration of war between them on 5 November 1914 prevented any further discussion of the Lease.

It is to be noted that this very important letter was to become just as important and valuable, after the First World War, when it was cleverly and cunningly used by the Company to constitute the claim and the basis of the TPC application for securing the final Oil Concession from the newly formed Iraq Government for the areas named.

THE FIRST WORLD WAR

During the First World War, the Ottoman Empire had entered the War with Germany against Britain and France and all contacts regarding the subject of the TPC Concession had been lost. Both Germany and the Ottoman Empire came out of the War defeated and had no longer any say in dictating any terms on the fate of the Middle East territories and its destiny, wealth, mineral deposits or any other important issues. All such issues were basically left in the hands of Britain and France to deal with in accordance with their own mutual, and at times, conflicting national wishes and interests.

The French government had originally anticipated as early as 1916, that, after the War, the Vilayet of Mosul to fall under its mandated share of the Middle East, but as soon as it became apparent that Mosul may fall under the British mandate it started to make claims to participate in any future Iraq oil concession. As a result the shareholding in the TPC became a major issue at the San Remo conference in 1920 where the future of the non-Turkish territories of the Ottoman Empire was finally decided.

THE SAN REMO CONFERENCE

The San Remo Conference was held for the purpose of ratifying the decisions made at the Paris peace conference of May 1919. Representatives of Great Britain, France, Italy, Japan, Greece, and Belgium met at San Remo, Italy in April 1920; to discuss problems arising from the First World War. Though, members of the supreme council of the Allies took leading parts, the United States did not attend the Conference.

At the conference, Britain was awarded mandates over Iraq and Palestine, while France was awarded mandates over Syria and Lebanon. Technically a mandate held the territories in trusteeship for the League of Nations until the political systems of these territories were developed enough to warrant independence and admission to the League of Nations.

The mandated territories were divided into three classes, according to their economic and political development. Class (A) consisted of Iraq and Palestine (British), Syria and Lebanon (French). At the same time the Mandates gave the Mandatory Powers the right to practically run these countries including the powers to legislate and to enforce the laws.

The text of the San Remo Resolution dated April 25, 1920 is as follows:

"It is agreed

(a) To accept the terms of the Mandates Articles as given below with reference to Palestine, on the understanding that there was inserted in the process, verbal undertaking by the Mandatory Power that this would not involve the surrender of the rights hitherto enjoyed by the non-Jewish communities in Palestine; this undertaking not to refer to the question of the religious protectorate of France, which had been settled earlier in the previous afternoon by the undertaking given by the French Government that they recognised this protectorate as being at an end.

(b) That the terms of the Mandates Articles should be as follows:

The High Contracting Parties agree that Syria and Mesopotamia shall, in accordance with the fourth paragraph of Article 22, Part I (Covenant League of Nations), be provisionally recognised as independent States, subject to the rendering of administrative advice and assistance by the mandatory until such time as they are able to stand alone. The boundaries of the said States will be determined, and the selection of the Mandatory made by the Principle Allied Power.

The High Contacting Parties agree to entrust, by application of the provision of Article 22, the administration of Palestine, within such boundaries as may be determined by the Principle Allied Powers, to a Mandatory, to be selected by the said Powers. The Mandatory will be responsible for putting into effect the declaration originally made on November 8, 1917, by the British Government, and adopted by the other Allied Powers, in favour of the establishment in Palestine of a national home for the Jewish people, it being clearly understood that nothing shall be done which may prejudice the civil and religious rights of existing non-Jewish communities in Palestine, or the rights and political status enjoyed by the Jews in any other county."

The San Remo Resolution had a special oil agreement attached to it revising the old TPC share holding by giving the German share to the French as mentioned before. It also stipulated that Iraq be allowed 20% of the TPC shares if it elected to do so by investing in it. Iraq was denied this right of participation by the TPC and the issue remained a source of mistrust and irritation over the following decades between Iraq and the IPC.

IRAQ'S PROVISIONAL INDEPENDENCE

In accordance with the San Remo Resolution, Iraq became, in 1921, provisionally independent and soon after a National Government was formed, though under the protection and advice of the British Government and its administrative organisation in Iraq. Faisal the First became the first King by popular vote and the blessing of the British Government.

However, in practical terms, Iraq was completely administered by the British Advisers, albeit under the banner of the Iraq National Government. That included the Internal Administration and Foreign Policy, as well as the Economic affairs, including the granting of any important minerals and crude oil concessions

POST WAR RIVALRY

(a) Britain and France

The secret Sykes-Picot negotiations which took place between the British and the French governments during the First World War, had envisaged that Syria, Lebanon as well as Mosul, which was considered to be rich in oil, were included in the French sphere of interest.

This understanding, however, became later on unacceptable to the British government which decided to retain Mosul under her sphere of interest and as a result France found herself deprived of any oil rich region and began to make claims for participation in any post war arrangement affecting the oil and mineral resources of the conquered territories of the Ottoman Empire.

As a result France claimed the pre-war German share in the Turkish Petroleum Company, which had been taken by the British Custodian of enemy property in 1915, and early in 1919 an agreement was made between Walter Long, First Lord of the Admiralty, and Senator Berenger, the French Commissioner – General of Petroleum Products. This agreement provided for a French interest of 20% in the TPC, with 70% for British interest and 10% for native government. In return the French government was to facilitate the construction of pipelines for the transport of Iraq and Persian oil across Syria to the Mediterranean.

Although the Long-Berenger agreement was ratified by the British Foreign Office, it was not accepted by the British Prime Minister Lloyd George.

The main principles of this agreement were nevertheless embodied after the war in the San Remo Oil Agreement of 24 April 1920 which maintained the old TPC arrangement of 1914 by substituting France for Germany. As a result the French government established the Compangnie Francaise des Petroles, CFP which was authorised to hold its 25% shareholding in the TPC.

(b) Britain and the United States

No sooner had the differences between the British and the French government settled by offering the German share in the TPC to France than a new bitter dispute erupted this time between the British and the American governments. The Americans attacked the San Remo agreement protesting to the British Foreign Office that the Agreement had established an Anglo-French monopoly in the areas mandated to them. They insisted on the "open door policy" of equal opportunity for nationals of countries in the mandated territories with no concession to be granted so large as to be exclusive

The San Remo Resolution had deliberately excluded the United States from participating in the Turkish Petroleum Company on the grounds that it had not declared war on Turkey and was therefore not concerned with the Peace Treaty as evident from its absence from the San Remo Conference.

The Americans were furious when the agreement came to light. They delivered a strong note to the British government implying that they were trying to establish an Anglo-French monopoly in the areas mandated to them reminding them that the United States of America had helped them to win the war. The British countered that America had a dominant position in world oil as evident of the fact that while Britain merely had 4.5% of the world's oil America controlled 82%.

This was followed by high-level negotiations, with the American pressing their claim on the basis of the "Open Door Policy". That policy was initiated by John Hay the United States Secretary of State in 1899 after several Western Powers in addition to Japan had established a large sphere of interests in China with each power trying to get all the trading rights for its self. As a result Hay sent notes to the competing powers asking them to maintain complete equality for all nations that wished to trade with China. After some hesitation, these powers accepted Hay's proposal agreeing to observe the" Open Door Policy".

The Americans maintained their relentless pressure to join the TPC in accordance with the Open Door Policy reminding the British that they, amongst the other nations, had accepted it. They also challenged the validity of the letter of June 1914 from the Grand Vizier for the Petroleum deposits concession to the TPC on the ground that the right to grant any such concession could not now be derived from the Ottoman government's letter but rested with the people of the new country and proposed going to arbitration on the issue of its validity.

The British government was faced with the difficult choice of either to continue its dispute with the American government and face the threat of arbitration or to somehow come to an agreement with it. This subject was discussed during a meeting held on 16 January 1922, chaired by John Shuckburgh from the Colonial Office and representatives from the Foreign Office and the Petroleum Department at the end of which it was recommended to avoid the confrontation with the Americans by offering them a share in the TPC. This recommendation met with the approval of the Secretary of the Colonial Office and the authorisation of the TPC to establish contacts with the American companies to resolve the dispute. Subsequent negotiations took place between the TPC and the American oil companies which resulted in defusing the tension between the British and American governments.

Understanding was soon to be established between the shareholders of the TPC, represented by APOC, CFP, Royal Dutch Shell and Gulbankian and the seven American companies represented by Standard oil of New Jersey (SONJ) in which they agreed on the principle of the participation of American companies in the TPC.

THE TURKISH PETROLEUM COMPANY'S WORKING AGREEMENT

The partners began their internal negotiations to find a Working Agreement which would govern the relations among themselves as well as those between them and the government of Iraq. These negotiations were conducted over some six years. The negotiations between the TPC and the government lasted over a period of some three year between 1922 and March 1925 when the Concession agreement was signed. These negotiation will be dealt with separately.

However the internal negotiations between the partners stretched over a much longer period between 1922 and 1928. In the meantime these negotiations did not affect the exploration and drilling works which went ahead and finally resulted in the discovery of the Kirkuk oilfield in 1927.

During these lengthy internal negotiations, the following principles were agreed upon between the partners:-

1. The Open Door Policy and the Plot System

    Standard Oil of New Jersey representing the American companies proposed maintaining the Open Door Policy to satisfy the American government by adopting the "Plot System". It proposed that the TPC would select within two years not more than 12 blocks of 16 square miles each for its own exploration out of the entire concession area and make the rest of the area of some 159,000 square miles available for leasing to any other company, including the partners in the TPC.

    Gulbankian reacted sharply to this proposal since it would enable the partners of the TPC to ensure that his five per cent interest in the company would relate only to oil found in these proposed 12 blocks of 192 square miles whereas he believed that he had rights to the exploitation of all the oil of the vilayets of Mosul and Baghdad. He found support from the French who were also determined, that any arrangement between the British and the Americans should not reduce their share in all Iraqi oil.

    In the meantime the old proposal of 12 plots of 16 square miles each was replaced at a later date by a new system based on 24 plots of 8 square miles each

    Though the Plot System was incorporated in the 1925 Concession Agreement, it was abolished in the 1931 Concession Agreement and replaced by a new huge single concession area of 32,000 square miles east of the river Tigris.

    It is of interest to record that the Open Door Policy which the Americans had insisted on was basically to get them through the Door of the club of oil producers in Iraq. Once they were admitted that door was soon to be slammed close behind them in the face of anyone else by adopting the Self Denying Policy which resulted in the exclusive club of the Red Line Agreement.

2. Iraq's Participation in the TPC

    Though the San Remo Resolution had a special oil agreement attached to it stipulating that Iraq be allowed 20% of the TPC shares if it elected to do so by investing in it, the TPC partners had decided to deny Iraq that right. They had no intention of permitting the government to examine the company's accounts or interfere in its financial affairs or have a say in the oilfields development plans or any other major management decisions.

3.   Royalties

There were no internationally recognised prices for the crude oil in those days. As a result the TPC had decided that the Iraq Concession be based on a royalty of four Shillings per ton, bearing in mind that the Pound sterling at that time was equal to twenty Shillings. This, they argued was fair and comparable to the rate offered in the United States where royalties were a percentage of the wellhead value of the oil. They were also ready to argue that the fixed royalty which would provide revenues to the government without any risk to itself and without committing any resources of her own, that it didn't have much of at that time, is the more suitable option.

4.   The TPC, Non-Profit Company

The American companies had raised the question of double taxation which would affect them if the profit of the TPC, which is a British registered company, would be distributed. In such case they would be taxed by both the British and the American governments which was not acceptable to them. To overcome this problem the partners decided that the TPC role would be restricted for the sole purpose of holding a concession and producing oil for its parents companies, which will result in no profit accruing to the TPC itself. This was to be achieved by allocating the available oil to each partner in the proportion of their shareholding at cost of operation and transportation plus a nominal fee.

5.   TPC Board of Directors

That the proposed TPC Board of Directors which manages the company's business should be free from any interference from the Iraqi government and, as a result, Iraq should be discouraged from participating in the Board of Directors.

6.   The Term of the Concession

That, the duration of the crude oil concession should be in the region of ninety nine years. This, as we shall see, was reduced during the negotiation between the TPC and the Government to 75 years.

7. Exemption from Iraqi Taxes

   The TPC had also decided to avoid being subjected to Iraqi taxes which may be imposed by the government. Such taxes over which the TPC would have no control could become unreasonable and exacting in the future. This subject was discussed during the Concession negotiation and a compromise was finally reach whereby the TPC accepted the right of the government to impose the same taxes on it, its property and employees as those imposed on other industrial undertaking in Iraq.

8. The Final Distribution of Shareholdings

   The discovery of the Kirkuk oilfield in October 1927 brought the question of the shareholding in the TPC as well as finalisation of a formal agreement between the partners to the forefront._

   The distribution of the shareholdings was to become highly contentious. As we have seen the original shareholdings of the TPC were as follows:

   - 47.50% for D'Arcy group (Anglo- Persian Oil Company, APOC).
   - 25.00% for the French company CFP through replacing the Deutsche Bank interest.
   - 22.50% for the Royal Dutch Shell.
   - 5.00% for Calouste Gulbenkian.

   It became obvious that the largest contribution towards the American companies' shareholdings would have to come from the APOC which was reluctant to do so. However the other partners did not want a distribution which would allow any two shareholders exercise majority shareholding and a controlling vote. Hence it was finally agreed make the 5.00% Gulbenkian shareholding as non-voting shares and to distribute the remaining shares equally between the four other partners. Thus the final shareholding became as follows:

   - 23.75% for APOC.
   - 23.75% for CFP.
   - 23.75% for Royal Dutch Shell.
   - 23.75% American group.
   - 5.00% for Gulbenkian.

To compensate APOC for giving up half of its shares, APOC was given an overriding royalty of 10% of all the oil produced from the group concession area.

It is to be highlighted that by early 1928 the original seven American companies had been reduced to five only. These five companies then went to organised the Near East Development Corporation to hold their interest in the TPC. These five companies were reduced later on to two only being Standard Oil of New Jersey (now Exxon) and Standard Oil of New York (now Mobil)

9.   The Self Denying Clause and the Red Line Agreement

After the TPC had secured the 1925 Concession, discovered the Kirkuk oilfield and settled most of the major internal issues between the partners, the question of the "Self Denying" clause which formed part of the "foreign Office Agreement" of 19 March 1914 was still outstanding. The American companies had consistently refused to accept the restrictions imposed on all shareholders of the TPC by this Agreement. On the other hand, both the French and Gulbenkian were consistently insisting on maintaining the Agreement. They were afraid that the other much bigger shareholders of the TPC, if permitted to obtain oil elsewhere in the area other than through the TPC, they would prefer to develop such areas rather than develop the production from the TPC area. The French wanted oil since they had none and felt that they would be at a disadvantage in relation to other shareholders when it came to bidding for oil concessions. They knew that their interest would be best protected by ensuring that all the partners had to work through the TPC itself.

A compromise was eventually reached under which the American companies agreed to accept the principle of the "Self Denying" clause within the area of the former Ottoman Empire. With this important agreement, the opportunity was taken in 1928 to formulate the Group Agreement between its various members of the major oil concerns of the four powerful nations, as to their relations and mutual obligations within a defined area. This area being that of the Asiatic Ottoman Empire of 1914 marked on a map in red. This was to be known as the famous Red Line Agreement, which was signed on July 31, 1928, in Ostend, Belgium.

The agreement included the "Self Denial" clause and marked the creation of an oil monopolistic cartel of immense power and influence, spanning a vast territory of the Middle East. This in effect was contrary to the spirit of the Open Door Agreement that the major powers had preached before but the Self-Denial clause suited their interests at this time and as a result no real objection was raised.

In the meantime and after some confusion between the partners as what exactly the ex Ottoman Empire territory included, it was said that Calouste Gulbenkian took out a large map, laid it on the table and drew with a thick red pencil an outline demarcating the boundaries of the Self Denial clause would be in effect. He apparently said that this is the boundary of the Ottoman Empire, as he knew in 1914. He should know, he added, since he was born in it and lived in it. The other representatives of the mighty major oil companies of the time looked on attentively like school children and did not object since they had more or less anticipated such a boundary and were awaiting someone to tell them.

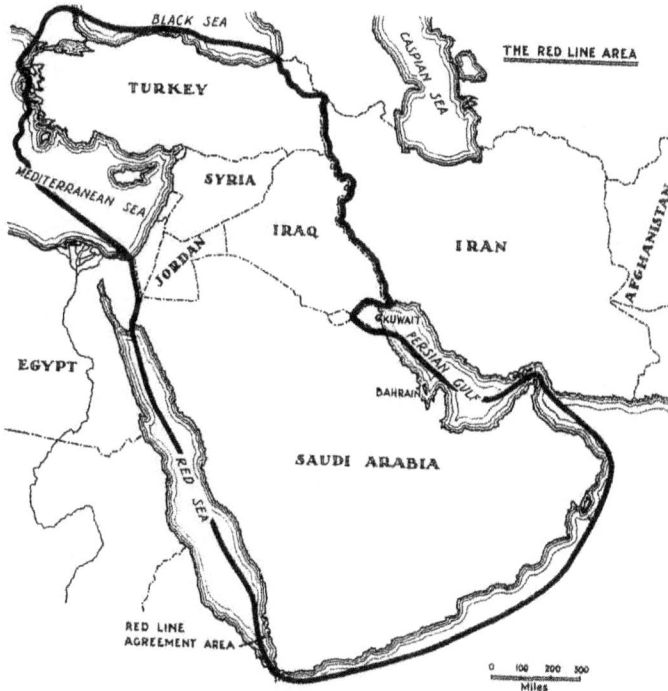

The Red Line Map

The Red Line around the territories which circumscribed the entire ex-Ottoman territory in the Middle East included Iraq, Syria, Lebanon,

Palestine, Jordan, the Arabian Peninsula as well as Cyprus and Turkey with the exception of Kuwait.

It was said that Gulbenkian commented later that there never was an "Open Door" so hermetically sealed.

10.   The Chairman of TPC

The shareholders agreed that the TPC should always have a British chairman.

THE IRAQ PETROLEUM COMPANY - IPC

In the meantime the name the "Turkish Petroleum Company" had become obsolete, after the establishment of the national Iraqi Government and the discovery of oil, and was finally changed in October 1928 to the "Iraq Petroleum Company" and thus came to be commonly known as the famous IPC.

2

IRAQ'S OIL CONCESSIONS

The Turkish Petroleum Company Concession

The First World War had demonstrated, beyond any doubt, to the British government the dependence of its war machine on oil, especially the navy, which had converted from coal to oil just before the war.

Hence when Mr C. Greenway, the chairman of the TPC, put forward a formal application to the Foreign Office for obtaining an oil concession in Iraq it was vigorously supported by admiral Sir E. Slade who had written in 1918 that, quote,

> "We must therefore at all costs retain our hold on the Persian and Mesopotamian oilfields, and any other fields which may exist in the British Empire, and we must not allow the intrusion in any form of any foreign interests, however much disguised they may be."

This was to become Britain's strategic policy for securing crude oil at source. As a result the British Government, which had participated in the formation of the TPC and held 51% interest in it, had no hesitation in blessing the application.

We have seen that the TPC had discussed some of the principles of its "Working Agreement" and agreed on the terms of the draft concession to be presented to the Iraqi government.

In the meantime Sir Percy Cox, the British High Commissioner in Baghdad had presented as early as 1922 a letter to King Faisal recommending that Iraq offers an oil concession to the TPC based on the Ottoman government letter of 28th June 1914, agreeing to lease to the TPC the Petroleum Deposits already discovered or to be discovered in the Vilayets of Mosul and Baghdad.

From there on the question of the terms on which the oil resources were to be exploited occupied much of the time of the King, the Iraqi governments, the local press and public opinion.

The general prevailing views of the Iraqis on the subject of oil concession could be summarised as follows:

- That the Iraqi government must not be seen as following the advice of the British Government and its administration in Iraq blindly during its negotiations of the oil concession.

- Though still under mandate, Iraq must assert its sovereignty especially with regards to the sensitive issue of the terms of the oil concession, which would demonstrate its independence as far as the commercial business is concerned.

- The Iraqi governments were conscious of the mistrust of the Iraqi population of the British Administration in the country and the 1920 revolt against the British was still fresh in the mind of the nation. Hence the governments were under pressure to safeguard Iraq's rights and secure a fair concession agreement.

- The Iraqis were aware that the fate of the vilayet of Mosul was still not settled and aware as well of the British Administration's disguised and sometimes open threats that such fate may depend on the offering of a favourable oil concession to the Turkish Petroleum Company.

- That Iraq was in need of revenues for the development of the impoverished country as soon as possible and hence should try to conclude a concession as soon as possible.

- The Iraqis were aware at the same time that the TPC was just as anxious to secure the oil concession as soon as possible.

- Though the Iraqis were unaware at that early time of the San Remo's side letter, which gave Iraq the right to 20% ownership in the concession, they wanted to participate in the company's shareholdings.

- The duration of the concession should not be too long, preferably in the region of some thirty to fifty years.

- They also wanted to have an oil refinery of their own.

Based on the blessing of the British government, the Turkish Petroleum Company applied for the oil concession on 30 August 1923 by presenting its proposed Concession Agreement to the newly formed Iraq Government basing its case on the Ottoman Vizirial Promise, which it had previously obtained in 1914.

In the meantime, the British Administration had advised the Iraqi government, which had very limited funds available and in need of developing the young country quickly, not to venture into the ownership of the risky business of oil exploration, a business which requires huge capital and in which it had no previous experience. Hence it advised that it would be much more advantageous for Iraq to base the oil concession on Royalties, which would result in regular revenues with no risk to itself.

As a result the Iraqi government of Abdul Muhsin al-Sadoon appointed on 5 September 1923 a committee for the negotiation with the TPC. The Committee was composed of Yasin al-Hashimi, Minister of Communications and Works, Naji Al- Suwaydi, Minister of Justice, Colonel S. Slater, a British adviser in the Ministry of Finance and E. Drower a British adviser in the Ministry of Justice.

The Committee met then to study and discuss the proposed Concession and made the following recommendations:-

- That the concession should not include the Basra region and the transferred territories.
- That the period of the concession should be no more than 60 years.
- That the government should obtain 20% free participation in the shareholding of the company.

These recommendations were approved by the cabinet which advised the High Commissioner on 8 September of its dissatisfaction with the terms of the proposed concession.

The TPC had appointed E.H Keeling as its negotiator with the Iraqi government. Keeling was reporting to H.E Nichols, the TPC Managing Director in London who in turn reports to the Board of Directors and who at the same time kept the British Government fully informed of the proceedings.

Keeling arrived in Baghdad on 20 October 1923 and subsequent to his arrival, the TPC presented on 2 November a revised Concession Agreement to the Government.

As a result a new committee was appointed composed of Yasin al-Hashimi, Minister of Communications and Works, Chairman, Naji al- Suwaydi, Minister of Justice and Sasoon Hesgail, Minister of Finance.

The first session of negotiations was held in Baghdad on 2 November and continued into December 1923. Though the negotiations dragged over many meetings during this period, differences remained regarding many issues such as, the duration of the concessionary period, the commitment for a drilling programme, the royalty payments, the right of Iraq to share in participation, the right of the Iraqi government to impose taxes and the place of the company registration amongst other issues.

It must be noted that the Iraqi negotiators were not aware at this stage of the attachment to the San Remo agreement, which gave Iraq the right to participate in the ownership of the TPC by up to 20% if it elected to do so by investing in it.

Meanwhile the Iraqi Cabinet resigned and a new cabinet was formed with Jaafar al-Askari as prime minister. As a result a new oil negotiating committee was appointed composed of Ali Jawdat al- Ayubi, Minister of Interior, chairman, Abdul Muhsin Shlash, Minister of Finance and Sabih Nashaat, Minister of Communications and Works.

Several sessions of negotiations took place during December 1923 and January 1924 during which Keeling pressed the TPC terms forcefully, which were met by the refusal of the committee which insisted on the right of participation of the government in the company and the registration of the company in Iraq.

In the meantime the subject of the concession was being debated between the Foreign Office, the Colonial Office, the High Commissioner and the TPC. The opinions regarding the signing of the concession were divided. Whereas the latter three wanted the finalisation and the signing of the concession to go ahead as soon as possible, the Foreign Office was adamant that this should be delayed until after resolving the status of Mosul, since Turkey was still at that time claiming Mosul and that an agreement between the partners in the TPC especially the Americans was still not finalised.

As a result of this and the presence of an opportunity for the ratification of the Anglo-Iraqi Treaty in an amicable atmosphere it was decided by the High Commissioner to postpone the concession negotiation and as a result Keeling left Baghdad in mid May 1924.

In the meantime the duration of that government did not last long after being criticised for its ratification of the Anglo-Iraqi Treaty and its resignation was announced on 2 August 1924.

A new government was subsequently formed with Yasin al-Hashimi as a Prime Minister.

This was followed by the appointment of a new negotiating committee composed of Yasin al-Hashimi himself, Muzahim al-Pachachi, Minister of Communications and Works, Hesgail Sasoon, Minister of Finance and Rasheed Ali al-Qailani, Minister of justice.

It was not until September 1924 when the TPC negotiators returned to Baghdad that the negotiations started again. It seems that by this time the Iraqi Government had become aware of the attachment to the San Remo Agreement, which gave Iraq the right to participate in the ownership of the TPC.

The negotiations dragged on with some serious objections being raised by the Iraqi negotiators, who showed considerable skill, with regards to the following issues: -

- The replacement of the fixed four shillings per ton royalty, which had been proposed by the TPC, by the more favourable variable scale arrangement.

- The insistence that the royalty payments should be based on the Pound Sterling Gold Standard since the Pound may get devalued in the future as had happened during the First World War.

- The participation of the Iraq Government in the ownership of the Company as required by the attachment letter to the San Remo Agreement.

- The duration of the concession, which the Iraqi side preferring it to be limited to no more than 60 years instead of the 99 years as proposed by the TPC.

- The appointment of an Iraqi director to the TPC board of directors.

- A commitment to an elaborate and firm drilling programme.

- A commitment for an export pipeline to the Mediterranean.

- The requirement for a minimum production levels.

- The objection to the 24 plots arrangement with sub leasing, which the Iraqi team thought it to infringe on Iraq's sovereignty.

- The preference of having a large area single concession instead of the complicated small plots arrangement.

- An Iraqi right to veto any sub-leasing.

- The reversion to the Iraq Government of the TPC property outside Iraq after the expiry of the concession period.

- That the TPC should be liable for custom duties.

- That the Iraqi government should have the right to impose taxes.

- That the TPC should be registered as an Iraq based company.

Opinions within the British Government were divided on the subject of participation of the Iraq government in the shareholding of the TPC. While the Foreign Office was sympathetic to the exclusion of Iraq from shareholding, it could not support it on the basis of the attachment letter to the San Remo Agreement. However the Colonial Office was more inclined to support the TPC's desire to the exclusion of the Iraq participation.

Also while the Foreign Office had wanted the negotiations between the Iraq government and the TPC to drag on until after the status of Mosul had been settled, the Colonial Office had contested that view in order to maintain pressure on the Iraqi government.

Furthermore Sir Henry Dobbs, the High Commissioner in Iraq had supported the Colonial Office views and urged the British government to intervene on behave of the TPC. In the meantime he made every effort to persuade the Iraqi government to accept the company proposal and not to insist on the participation issue, he even allowed them to believe that the political future of Mosul and Britain's willingness to support the new state might depend on the signature of the concession agreement.

Nevertheless, both the company and the British government consistently recognised that the Iraqi demand for an ownership share was legitimate.

In the meantime the League of Nations had dispatched a Commission of Inquiry to Iraq to examine the dispute between Iraq and Turkey regarding the territories of Mosul. The Commission arrived in Baghdad on 16 January 1925. It stayed in Baghdad for a few days before travelling to Mosul. It seems that the impression gained from the Commission's members was in favour of awarding Mosul to Iraq as had been expected by the British government. This was confirmed by the Commission's report of 25 December 1925, in which they considered that the sentiments of the majority of the people of the region supported the union with Iraq and which was accepted by the League's Council.

This seems to have satisfied the Foreign Office condition about the fate of Mosul and as a result, the concession negotiations continued to make progress and by the end of February 1925, agreement had been reached on most of the disputed issues with the exception of the sticky issue of the Iraqi participation.

However, as a result of the relentless insistence of the Iraqi team on participation, the British government had advised the TPC in early March 1924 to agree to a compromise under which Iraq would receive free of charge special non-voting shares equal to 20 per cent of the total shares. These shares would be entitled to dividends, but would confer no right to interfere in the commercial policy or general management of the company, and royalties would be reduced by the amount of dividends paid. The company agreed since it had already told the Iraqis that if they insisted on participation, the royalties would be reduced, since the high royalty rate that they had offered was based on the assumption that the ownership rights would be relinquished. However the TPC negotiators delayed presenting this proposed compromise officially to the Iraqi government.

Meanwhile, Sir Henry Dobbs the High Commissioner in Iraq was giving contrary advice to King Faisal, who was unaware of the TPC's readiness to accept the principle of participation, urging him to accept the principle of non-participation. In the meantime King Faisal was under opposing pressures, those from the British Administration regarding the possible loss of Mosul and those from the widespread unrest and resentment of the Mandate and the unpopular British dominance in the running of the country. He was also aware that time was passing by quickly and the election of the proposed parliament may result in further complications to the delicate ongoing negotiations.

The King was also aware of the dire financial situation of the country and the urgent need for substantial revenues for early development. He was also coming under increasing pressure from the British government and its administration in Iraq to bring in early revenues to the Iraqi treasury, which would help to lessen the British burden of financial liabilities in the country.

As a result of all this, the King and the Cabinet finally accepted, in good faith, the High Commissioner's advice and authorised Muzahim al-Pachachi, the Minister of Communications and Works on 14 March 1925 to sign the concession agreement without the right to participation but subject to some minor points. One of these point is a modified clause on participation which read :

"Whenever an issue of shares is offered by the Company to the general public, subscription lists shall be opened in Iraq simultaneously with lists opened elsewhere, and Iraqis in Iraq shall be given preference to the extent of at least twenty per cent of such issue."

King Faisal I

This was a goodwill political gesture to the Iraqi government by the TPC, which was of no real commercial value since the TPC knew well that it had no intention whatsoever of issuing shares to the general public.

Thus this ratification of the concession, which deprived Iraq from its legal right to participate in the ownership of the TPC, prompted the resignation of two Iraqi cabinet ministers as a sign of protest. They were the Minister of Justice the famous Rasheed Ali al-Gailami, and the Minister of Education, Mohammad Ridha al-Shibibi. It is to be recorded that Muzahim al-Pachachi himself had also tendered his resignation at an earlier date but withdrew it later on.

The ratification also resulted in a public outcry and a widespread unrest and resentment at the time as well as continuing to be a cause of deep bitterness with the Iraqi public and several subsequent governments for many decades to come.

It must also be highlighted that the principle of not allowing the producing countries to participate in their concessions was never forgotten despite the continual refusal of the oil companies. Hence it was not until early 1972 when the Saudi Aramco after bitter negotiations agreed to allow the Saudi Arabian Government a 20% ownership in their lucrative concession. Furthermore Aramco agreed reluctantly and under protest that the compensation for the 20% part ownership should be based on book value of the company's assets. This historic principle of participation, which was denied Iraq almost fifty years earlier, was quickly to spread to other producing countries and soon after that, the governments of the United Arab Emirates, Qatar and Kuwait were able to obtain similar 20% participations in their concessions.

However the government of Iraq by that time had, more or less, made up its mind to nationalise the IPC, as it finally did on the first of June 1972, and hence did not bother to press for a similar participation.

THE MAIN TERMS OF THE 1925 OIL CONCESSION

The Main terms of the Concession were as follows: -

- The standard rate of Royalty was fixed at 4 Shillings (gold) per ton, with possible adjustment after 20 years, (bearing in mind that the Pound Sterling at that time was equivalent to 20 Shillings).

- The linking of royalties to profits made from Iraqi oil, with a minimum royalty of two and a maximum of six Shillings (gold), with this clause not to come into force before twenty years.

- The right of the Iraqi public to subscribe up to 20% in the TPC ownership as and when such subscription is offered to the general public.

- The duration of the concession was for 75 years.

- The government has the right to impose taxes on the TPC similar to those imposed on other industrial establishments in Iraq.

- The Company has the right to select, within 32 months, for testing and exploration, twenty four plots each having an area of eight square miles, with the obligation to intensively drill there.

- The Government itself was, within 4 years, to select another 24 similar plots to offer them on lease by auction to all interested parties.

- The TPC to build a pipeline for export as soon as possible but in any case within four years after its plots were fully tested.

- The Company to have five drilling rigs working simultaneously within three years from the date of the concession agreement.

- The Company was to: -

  - Make all its geological information available,

  - To act as Government Agent in all its future leases.

- Other Lessees were to undertake obligations similar to the Company's, and to enjoy a certain percentage use of the Company's pipeline.

- Full facilities were to be given or permitted by the Government to the Company and to the other Lessees to enjoy for their operations.

A few other less important clauses have not been included above.

THE BLACK GOLD WAS FOUND

The months before and after the granting of the TPC 1925 concession were occupied by intensive geological exploration activities including the organising of human resources and the establishment of a management and operations base at Sulaiman Beg near Tuz Khurmato not too far from the city of Kirkuk. This was followed by the shipment of the necessary drilling rigs, and other necessary supporting equipment, plants, materials and camp requirements as well as the establishment of the various necessary organisations in preparation for the actual exploration drilling work.

Actual drilling was finally started in earnest; the first well to be spudded was PulkanahNo.1 which took place on 5 April 1927 in the presence of His Majesty King Faisal the first.

This was followed by other wells such as Pulkanah No.2, Khash al-Ahmar No.1, Injanah No.1, and Qaiyarah No.1.

Seepage of Crude Oil at Pulkanah - Early 20ᵗʰ Century

Courtesy of IPC

The sixth well was Baba Gurgur No.1 (renamed Kirkuk No. 1) was spudded on 30 June 1927. Drilling in this well went on over the summer months and well into autumn and when a depth of 1521 feet was reached, a 10.75 inch diameter casing was cemented in place.

Inauguration of drilling - Kirkuk No. 1

Courtesy of IPC Society Newsletters

At midnight of 13/14 October a new drilling crew went on shift. They bailed out most of the mud left in the casing after cementing, keeping 500 feet of fluid at the bottom as a precaution against a blowout and the drilling tools were then run in. As soon as the bit cracked through the cement at the casing shoe, oil started to flow into the well. Within a few moments the oil was blowing over the crown of the derrick to a height of about 140 feet.

The following quotation from an account by the resident geologist T. F. Williamson throws some light on what happened next:

> "The driller ran to the boilers and extinguished the flames and when daylight came the scene of the oil discovery was marked by a black pall of gas and oil vapours and the oil was flowing like a river down Wadi Naft. At two o'clock in the afternoon the heavy drilling string was blown up into the derrick with a mighty roar.

> Three days passed before the control valve could be closed. Soon the ground all around the well was saturated with oil to a depth of several inches and the slight breeze which rose daily was blowing some of it long distances. Men arriving from southern areas reported that it began to fog their windscreens as far as 10 miles from the well. With all this inflammable liquid lying in pools everywhere, one carelessly struck light might have caused a most disastrous fire. The famous Burning Fiery Furnace of Shadrack, Meshak and Abednego,

Baba Gurgur, Kirkuk - Well K-1- 14 October 1927

Courtesy of IPC Society Newsletters

Well K-1 - "Oil flowing like a river down Wadi al-Naft"

Courtesy of IPC Society Newsletters

half a mile away, was hurriedly smothered with earth and a constant watch had to be kept to ensure that it was not relit nor any other fire stated. Had there been one heavy rain storm all the hastily thrown up dams in the wadi would have burst and the thousands of tons of oil which they were holding up would have run downstream to the River Tigris with consequences that would have been catastrophic. Yes we were very lucky indeed with that well"

The sight of the oil gushing violently out of the ground caused considerable anxiety in Kirkuk town. The residents were at first afraid and one said:

"Though oil was not new to us, since our people had been collecting it for centuries from seepages, the violent way it burst through, with the poisonous gases , led many of us to believe that Allah was punishing them for their wrongdoing."

It was not until 17 October when the gate valve was closed and the well was finally brought under control. The well was then tested with the flow estimated at 90,000 barrel per day. With that, the well was then closed in on 23 October.

This was then a sure sign of the discovery of a huge structure, which would reveal itself as one of the most remarkable in the world at that time.

It is to be noted, with great interest, that the location of this famous well, Kirkuk No. 1, was no more than a few hundred metres away from the legendary Eternal Fires which have attracted the attention of the ordinary people as well as the geologists over the centuries.

The Eternal Fires - Baba Gurgur, Kirkuk

Courtesy of IPC

Thereafter, up to nine rigs were working for the next three years with the result that operations in unpromising areas could be suspended or abandoned and most of the Company's attention devoted to the development of the Kirkuk structure in preparation for full exploitation. The necessary organisation and installations, roads, water supply, power plant, offices and dwellings, stores and workshops were put in hand and provisionally completed while the drilling of wells proceeded both for future production and for observation.

GREAT OIL DISCOVERY

The news of the discovery of oil in Kirkuk was reported in many newspapers around the world such as the following article that appeared in the British Daily Telegraph:-

From the Daily Telegraph - 18th October, 1927

Great "Gusher" in Irak Oil Field.

5,000 tons in 24 hours

A sudden outburst

Baghdad, Monday.

The Turkish Petroleum Company, a powerful international syndicate, in which the Anglo-Persian Oil Company has a large interest, has struck oil at one of its drilling installations near Kirkuk. At three o'clock in the morning, without warning, oil began to flow, a few minutes later shooting into the air, it is stated, at the rate of 5,000 tons every 24 hours. This oil is now being burnt pending arrangements for closing the well until commercial production is required-Reutter.

Predictions verified. **The pipeline project**-from a Correspondent.

Although quite recently it stated in the House of Commons that there was no justification for assuming that oil would be found in Iraq in quantities that would be commercially profitable, not only experts, but others who knew Irak at first hand, were confident that it was only a matter of time before a "gusher" would be discovered, exactly as "gushers" were found in south Persia, in the fields of the ANGLO-PERSIAN OIL COMPANY. There, as in Kirkuk, the discovery was often so sudden that drillers could not at once control the flow, and has no option but to burn the oil. In past days "crude" was invariably burnt, and many thousands tons went up in flames on the hills of Persia and elsewhere. That was before the "crude" was recognised, and it is not likely that much of Irak's production will so vanish in thin air.

There always has been evidence of oil in Irak, and the task of the geologists sent out by the Turkish Petroleum Company was to find out whether there was enough to justify the establishment of large refineries, and possibly a pipe-line to the Mediterranean. The later project will now become something worthy of almost immediate achievement. In Northern Irak there are many parts of the desert which are black with oil, and the Arabs themselves, in a small and primitive way, had been disposing of it for scores of years. The district around Kirkuk is much of this description, there have been shallow wells, formerly worked by the Irakis, in the neighbourhood.

The Turkish Petroleum Company, on whose field the "gusher" has been discovered, was founded in 1912. After many vicissitudes its position, so far as the present concession is concerned, was made definitive in 1925. The concession covers the whole territory of the Kingdom of Irak, except the Liwa of Basrah and the territories transferred to Turkey from Persia in 1913, where the oil rights had already been exclusively acquired by the ANGLO-PERSIAN OIL COMPANY. In the convention conferring the concession it was stipulated that the company should always have a British chairman.

Towards the end of last year drillers and machinery were sent out to Iraq on a scale that suggested the company was certain of result. The port of Basrah had not for years been so busy, while in Baghdad there was difficulty in finding accommodation for the company's staff. This activity gave rise to many rumours of discovery of "gushers", but one after another were contradicted. It is only now, after many months of patient work, that a well "fit to tell the world about" has been met.

A "gusher", of course, is merely a well from which oil flows without pumping. It is often come across in the Middle East belt and few, perhaps, of the best well have not been "gushers".

The discovery is of tremendous importance to Irak commercially, and gives promise of great prosperity. Not only will the country benefit from royalties, but it will also benefit indirectly. The concession directs that an overwhelming percentage of Irakis must be employed by the company, and therefore unemployment is likely to become greatly diminished in the country. We are likely to find repeated the success in this direction that has attended the Anglo-Persian Oil Company, who have developed what may be termed a "self contained" colony of workers, more intent on the prosperity of the company than on political matters.

Hitherto dates have been the principle export of Irak, but this old industry, though certain to remain flourishing, must now take second place.

Kirkuk is a town of some importance about 120 miles SE of Mosul and a rather greater distance to the north- east of Baghdad.

AN IMPORTANT EVENT - Financial Aspect –From Our City Editor.

The above announcement is important, particularly for the Anglo-Persian Oil Co. and the Royal Dutch-Shell undertakings, because the former holds a 47.5 per cent, interest in the Turkish Petroleum Company and the latter 22.5 per cent , the balance being owned as to 25 per cent by a French group and as to 5 per cent by Mr. C.S. Gulbenkian. The issued capital of the Turkish Petroleum Company , which has a concession for seventy-five years, originally granted by the Turkish Government to work the oil deposits over 90,000 square miles in the Mosul and Baghdad vilayats in Irak now amounted to £1,000,000 to which it was raised in 1925, when a convention was signed by the Irak Government. The shares, which are of the denomination of £1, are not quoted. With the present world over production, fresh oil supplies obviously are not required for the time being, and, in accordance with the usual practice, the well will be closed, but the new discovery will materially strengthen the position of the Anglo-Persian and Shell groups in the future."

The Iraq Petroleum Company Concession

THE EXPIRY OF THE 1925 CONCESSION

The period of 32 months specified in the 1925 Concession Agreement within which the TPC was to have chosen its 24 plots was due to expire during November 1927. By the first half of 1927, the TPC was not ready to meet the target date and as a result requested a one-year extension to complete its exploration work. As a result a one year extension was granted by the government of Iraq which would expire in November 1928.

However the real reasons for the failure on the part of the TPC to name its plots and abide by the terms of the concession were as follows: -

• The TPC had wanted to make sure that the Vilayet of Mosul was allocated to Iraq. This as we have seen had dragged on through the League of Nations and as a result the northern frontier of Iraq with Turkey was not settled until July 1926. This had delayed any serious expenditure on exploration and drilling and subsequently delayed the discovery of the Kirkuk oilfield until October 1927. The extent and magnitude of the field need to be evaluated which could take some time.

- It became clear to the TPC, after the discovery of the Kirkuk oilfield, that the field covers a much larger area than the eight square miles specified in the Concession's Plot System. Furthermore that the possibility of the discovery of similar large oilfields had made the total concession area of 194 square miles (24 plots of eight square miles each), completely inadequate and hence wanted a much larger area for its exclusive exploration that would put such fields out of reach of possible competitors.

- The Company's Group Agreement between the partners had dragged on well beyond the target date and was not finalised and signed until 31 July 1928.

NEW CONCESSION NEGOTIATIONS

By mid 1928 the TPC had still not decided to choose its plots and requested a further five years extension on the ground that it needed the extra time to be able to evaluate geological structures and other exploration data.

Meanwhile during this period of time, a company by the name of British Oil Development (BOD), which included British, Italian and German shareholding had been formed in 1928.

BOD had approached the Iraqi government to select its plots in accordance with the 1925 concession agreement so that it could present its proposal for a concession of such plots. Furthermore the BOD had offered to build a railway to the Mediterranean as part of its proposal, a project desired by the government but refused by the TPC, and introduced the new principle of Dead Rent. This offer appeared much more favourable than that of the TPC concession and gave the government a good bargaining power with the TPC which resulted in the ultimate refusal of the TPC's request for the five years extension.

The refusal of the extension of time resulted in the opening of fresh negotiations between the government and the TPC and subsequently with Iraq Petroleum Company, IPC (the new name adopted on 8 June 1929 instead of the TPC).

The government primary objectives of these negotiations were: -

- To obtain a commitment for minimum revenues regardless of the quantities of the actual crude oil exported.

- The introduction of the principle of Dead Rent similar to that proposed by the BOD.

- A firm commitment for constructing the Mediterranean Pipeline and the beginning of export of crude oil by a specified date.

- To maintain the right to impose taxes on the Company as specified in article 27 of the 1925 concession agreement.

- The construction of an oil refinery or the provision of petroleum products at low prices for the internal Iraqi market.

The IPC primary aims were: -

- The elimination of the plots system after securing the American shareholders agreement for the Red Line Agreement and to obtain instead as large area as possible for its new concession.

- The elimination of the Tax provision.

- The sowing of doubts regarding the financial and technical capabilities of the B.O.D. to discourage the government from accepting a concession bid from it.

The negotiations between the government and the IPC were complicated and prolonged and centred on two main points the first was the route of the pipeline to the Mediterranean which was not only a point of dispute between the partners themselves but also between the TPC and the government and second the tax regime as specified under article 127 of the 1925 concession agreement.

Both the Iraqi and the British governments preferred the pipeline to terminate at Haifa in Palestine. From the British government point of view it was important that the pipeline remains under its control by passing through the territories under its mandate. Iraq on the other hand did not want the pipeline to pass through Syria and become under the control of the French government that had removed King Faisal from the throne of Syria in 1920. On the other hand the French did not trust the British and wanted the pipeline under their control and both the Americans and Gulbankian sided with the French since that was the shortest and hence the cheapest route. This dispute continued for a long time until it was finally resolved by a compromise to build two pipelines one through the three countries under the British mandate namely Iraq, Jordan and

Palestine terminating at Haifa and the second passing through Syria terminating at Tripoli in Lebanon which were both under the mandate of France. The completion of these two pipelines was also a point of dispute since each side wanted its pipeline to be completed first. This was resolved by an agreement which stipulated that the two pipelines should be constructed simultaneously and completed at the same time.

On the taxes issue, the IPC had a rethink about article 127 of the 1925 concession agreement which had given the government the right to impose taxes on the company similar to those imposed on other industrial establishments in Iraq. It felt that the absence of any restriction on the rate at which such taxes could be imposed by future governments would leave the company unacceptably vulnerable to unreasonable taxes that may result in substantial sums of money.

On the other hand the Iraqi government felt that any restriction on its ability to impose ordinary taxation on the company was an unacceptable interference with its national sovereignty and would subject the government to severe criticism by the parliament, the opposition parties, the press and the general public.

The negotiations continued for three years during the governments of Tawfeeq al-Sowaidi who resigned in August 1929, Abdul Muhsin al-Saadoon who commited suicide on 13 October 1929 and finally Nuri al-Said who became prime minister in March 1930. The IPC negotiators were headed by its chairman John Cadman.

The negotiations continued without real progress and at times it seemed as if they were near breakdown on the issue of taxation.

In an effort to resolve this sticky issue the cabinet on 7 June 1930 authorised the Prime Minister Nuri al-Said, who was due to visit London on other outstanding issues between the British and Iraqi governments, to discuss the subject of the Concession.

Negotiations which were held in London between the Prime Minister and Cadman resulted in the following understanding:-

• That the IPC would construct a pipeline to the port on the Mediterranean acceptable to Iraq.

• That the new concession area would cover that east of the river Tigris in the Liwas of Mosul and Baghdad.

- The IPC would pay Iraq £300,000 annually as Dead Rent and a loan until the start of the export of oil.

- The provision of cheap oil to Iraq by up to £100,000 annually.

- That Iraq would forfeit her right to impose taxes on the IPC as required by article 127 of the 1925 concession agreement.

Cadman was unable to present these terms to the Board of Directors and Nuri al-Said advised Cadman in September 1930 that he is finding difficulties in persuading his cabinet accepting the allocation of the area east of the river Tigris and compensation for forfeiting the Taxes.

In a final effort to resolve the outstanding issues, it was decided to send Cadman to Baghdad. The negotiations started soon after his arrival in Baghdad in early January 1931. The Iraqi team was headed by Nuri al-Said the Prime Minister, Muzahim al-Pachachi the Minister of Communications and Economy, Rustem Haidar the Minister of Finance and Jamal Baban the Minister of Justice. Both King Faisal and Humphrys the High Commissioner attended part of the negotiations.

The main issues remained with both side insisting on their point of views. The only possible compromise that remained was the payment of an annual lump sum by the IPC instead of the Taxes. As a result the government proposed that the sum should be £500,000 per year.

On 8 March 1931, the IPC presented a counter proposal offering £60,000 for the first 4 million tons oil then a £20,000 for every additional one million tons.

Further negotiation resulted in the agreement that the IPC would pay Iraq £9,000 (gold) annually for the taxes with effect from 1932 until the beginning of the export of oil and from that time on to pay £60,000 (gold) for the first 4 million tons of oil then a £20,000 (gold) for every additional one million tons.

The new agreement was met with suspicion and some fierce opposition from Hisb al-Ikha al-Watani (National Brotherhood party) led by Yasi al-Hashimi and Hisb al-Watani al-Iraqi (Iraqi National party) led by Jaafar Abu al-Timman.

It also came under the relentless criticism of Rashid Ali Al-Gailani and other members of parliament such as Ali Jawdat al-Ayubi who both together with Yasin al-Hashimi resigned their seats in the Chamber of Deputies on 8 March.

Amongst those opposed to the agreement from within the cabinet was Muzahim al-Pachachi the Minister of Communications and Economy who as a sign of protest also tendered his resignation from the cabinet.

The agreement was subsequently presented to the parliament on 17 March for approval and though it was criticised by many it was finally approved. It was then presented to the Upper House and met with similar criticism but received the necessary approval.

The agreement was then met with the Cabinet approval and was signed on 24 March 1931.

THE IPC CONCESSION AGREEMENT OF 24 MARCH 1931

The main terms of the revised concession agreement that included some fundamental and important modifications were as follows:

- The abolition of the plots system.
- A new Concession area of 32,000 square miles east of the river Tigris was secured against the relinquishment of the previous small area west of the Tigris.
- The royalty of four shilling (gold) per ton remained unchanged.
- An annual fixed tax of £9,000 (gold) was agreed for up to the commencement of commercial export of oil, and thereafter £60,000 (Gold) on the first four million tons produced and £20,000 (Gold) on each additional million ton. (These payment are made in compensation for the exemption of the IPC from taxes)
- The introduction of a new fixed payment of £400,000 (gold) payable annually until the beginning of export of crude oil by pipeline. Half of such payments would be Dead Rent (non-recoverable) with the other half to be recoverable from future years Royalties in excess of £400,000.
- A minimum annual payment of £400,000 for the first twenty years beginning with the first export was guaranteed regardless of the level of oil export.
- A pipeline of three million tons annual crude oil capacity became a definite obligation to be completed by the end of 1934.
- The duration of the concession was reduced from 75 to 70 years

- The Royalty rate, however, remained unchanged at 4 Shillings (gold) per ton.

- The supply of petroleum products for internal consumption, were to be secured by the IPC and sold at specified prices.

- That twenty years after the beginning of exports, the rate of royalty was to be increased or decreased in proportion to the extent to which the profit or loss of the company was greater or less than during the immediately preceding five years than it had been during the first fifteen years of the twenty year period. Profit and loss were defined to include the cost of refining and distributing the products made from Iraqi crude oil. A minimum of two Shillings and a maximum of six shillings per ton was stipulated.

- The right of the Iraqi public to subscribe up to 20% in the IPC ownership as and when such subscription is offered to the general public.

It could be said that the government of Iraq had achieved four of its five objectives in full i.e. to obtain a commitment for minimum revenue regardless of the quantities of oil exported, the introduction of the principle of Dead Rent, the firm commitment for building the Mediterranean Pipeline and in securing the country's internal petroleum products requirement at reasonable prices.

However it only succeeded partially in achieving its fifth objective of the right to impose taxes on the Company. This was one of the most difficult issues, which faced the negotiating teams. From the Iraqi point of view any restriction on the government's rights to impose ordinary taxation on a commercial concern was considered as an unacceptable infringement on Iraq's National Sovereignty. This was reinforced by the bitter opposition from many of the prominent politicians, the national press and the public at large who were not only resentful of the British domination of the country's affairs but also of the IPC's apparent intransigence and unfair attitude. On the other hand, the IPC felt that the absence of any restriction on the rate at which taxes could be imposed on it would leave it at the mercy of the future governments that may demand unreasonable if not extortionate rates. At the end and after some bitter and prolonged exchanges, the two parties agreed on the fixed lump sum payments arrangement as detailed in the final concession agreement above.

It could also be said that the IPC achieved two of its objectives in full i.e. securing a much larger area for its concession and the elimination of the old plots system. Though it failed to avoid the payment of taxes, it did however succeed in restricting their limits. It also succeeded in keeping the British Oil Development at bay for the time being.

The Kaniqin Oil Company Concession

THE TRANSFERRED TERRITORIES

No real borders problem existed between Iraq and Iran until the rise of the Ottoman Empire. Some serious military conflicts, across these borders, developed in 1514, during the reign of the Ottoman Sultan, Selim the First. Further clashes followed between the Ottoman Empire and the Persian Safawi Dynasty which wanted control over the Holy Cities of Karbala and Najaf..

As a result of these frequent conflicts, both sides signed the Treaty of Zuhab in 1639, which did little to prevent further conflicts.

By the nineteenth century some of these disputes began to affect the shipping routes in the Shatt-Al Arab River and the upper Arabian Gulf region, which was vital to British shipping.

Russia by then was thinking of building a road from its southern borders to Iraq to have access to the Arabian Gulf, became also interested in settling the Iraq-Iran borders issue. Pressure was exerted by these two powers on both sides, which resulted in the acceptance of the Second Treaty of Erzurum of 1848. This again did not settle the dispute completely especially in the Shatt-Al Arab and upper Gulf region.

However oil was discovered in Persia in 1908 in the Masjidi Sullaiman Field and a safe access to it through the upper reaches of the Gulf to the Karun River became a matter of urgency for the British Empire. Intense pressure was mounted again on both sides and as a result serious negotiations between the Ottaman Empire, Persia, Britain and Russia continued over a three-year period ending in the signature of the Constantinople Protocol on 17 November 1913, when the delination was clarified in considerable detail. The final boundary was, then demarcated by pillars in 1914.

It is worth recording that at the time of the discovery of oil in Persia, a large region of Arabstan, on the eastern side of the Shatt Al Arab River including the island of Abadan near the mouth of the River Karun, was under the rule of

Sheikh Khazaal of Mohammara. Following this discovery, it was decided to lay a pipeline from the Masjidi Sulaiman Field to the island of Abadan where a refinery would be constructed. Some serious negotiations between the Anglo-Persian Oil Company and Sheikh Khazaal regarding the purchase or rental of

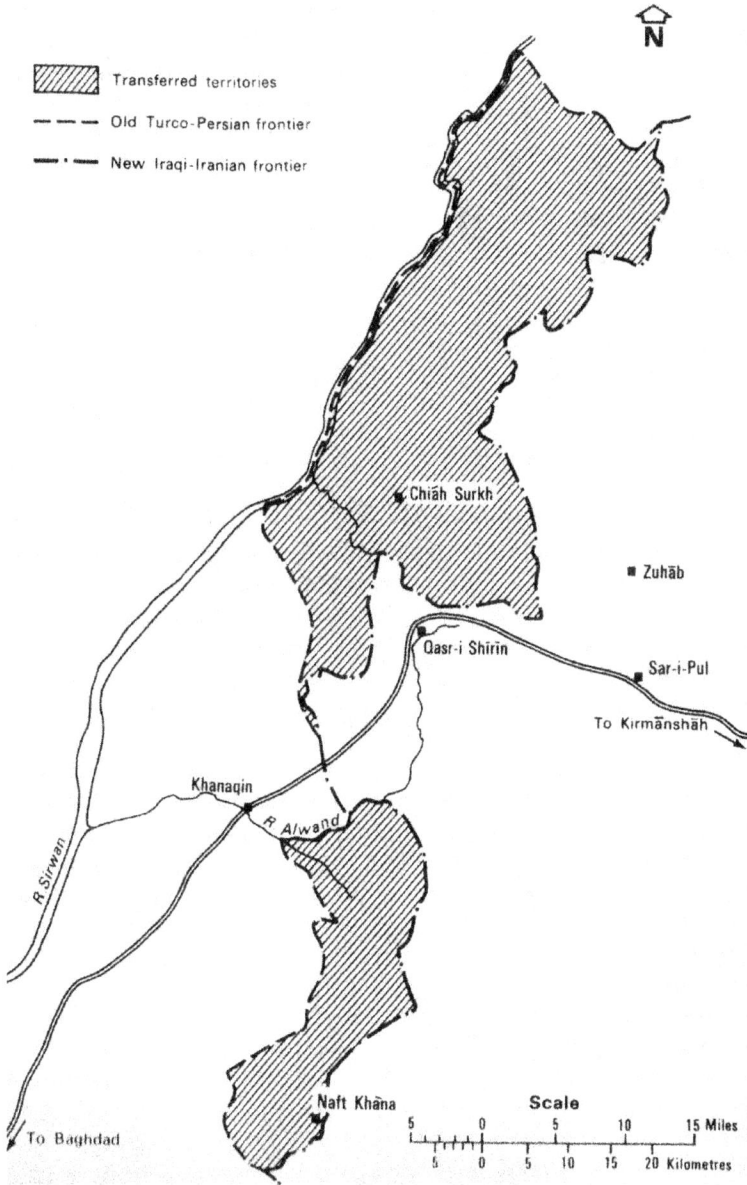

Transferred territories

the site of the refinery at Abadan were conducted in early 1909. Agreement was finally reached on the financial terms with the exception of the Sheikh's demand that the agreement should include a clause reverting the rights of the agreement to his sons and lineal decedents. This was not acceptable from the point of view of the British Government since it represents a political commitment, which may be seen as interference in the local politics by the Persian Government. Further delays could not be tolerated by the British Government and it was finally, under the direct undisguised threat of the British Resident Sir Percy Cox, that the Sheikh agreed to sign the agreement.

Meanwhile the Constantinople Protocol of 1913 and the 1914 boundary demarcation resulted in the transfer of some 800 square miles of territories near the town of Khaniqin from Persia to Iraq, which came to be known as the Transferred Territories. It was recognised by the terms of this Protocol that these territories would continue to form part of the D'Arcy Persian oil concession and that the Ottoman government recognises the validity of this concession.

NAFTKHANAH OILFIELD

After the war, in 1922 the Anglo-Persian Oil Company, APOC, presented to the Iraqi government a copy of its Persian oil concession and of the 1913 Constantinople Protocol claiming its oil exploration rights in the Transferred Territories which was recognised in principle by the Iraqi government.

A committee was formed on 13 May 1922, consisting of the Minister of Finance, Sasoon Hesqail, Minister of Justice, Abdul Muhsin al-Saadoon, Minister of Communications and Works, Sabih Nashaat, and Jaafar Abu al-Timman, Minister of Commerce to study the subject and prepare a report about it. The committee contacted APOC which proposed giving the government 20% share for 39 years. This was too brief and ambiguous, which prompted the committee to prepare a somewhat elaborate proposal which included in its terms 20% of the profit, the provision of cheap oil for Iraq, the establishment of a new company and the participation in its management. This proposal met with the approval of the cabinet on 19 June 1922 and was then sent to the High Commissioner.

This was studied by the Colonial Office and the Petroleum Department that suggested a new proposal which came to be known as the Colonial Office Agreement of May 1923, which revised the concession period to 47 years instead of 39 and replaced the profit article by a royalty of three Rupees per ton and set the price of oil for the local market at cost plus 10%.

Meanwhile the Anglo-Persian Oil Company, which was drilling in that region, struck oil in May 1923 and the well caught fire and burnt for a week before being brought under control. The oilfield was named Naftkhanah and though it proved to be rather small, it extended inside Persian where it came to be called Nafti-Shah field.

It was decided later to hold direct negotiation between the government and the company and a committee was formed in early September 1923 consisting of Yasin al-Hashimi, Minister of Communications and Works and Slater, acting Minister of Finance. Subsequent negotiations between the committee and the company ended without reaching an agreement.

By 1924 the company has studied the production capability of the Naftkhanah field and decided that it would not be economical to construct a pipeline to the sea and proposed instead the construction of a local refinery to utilise the modest production of oil from the field.

Nonetheless the negotiations between the government, the High Commissioner and the company continued over many months until after the signature of the Turkish Petroleum Company, TPC Concession Agreement of 14 March 1925.

As a result a new committee was formed in August 1925 from Naji al-Suwadi, the Minister of Justice and Sabih Nashaat the acting Minister of Communications and Works to study the subject again. The committee did not take long in presenting its finding on 20 August, recommending basing the new agreement on the terms of the 1925 TPC Concession Agreement. It recommended the establishment of a new company, a four Shillings (Gold) per ton of oil, the provision of cheap petroleum products and the validity of the concession to 1996. This was approved by the cabinet and a concession agreement was subsequently signed on 30 August by Sabih Nashaat the acting Minister of Communications and Works and Greenwood on behalf of the new company by the name the Khaniqin Oil Company, KOC, a subsidiary of the Anglo-Persian Oil Company, subject to its ratification by the parliament.

Further negotiations followed and it was not until March 1926 that the company offered new prices for its petroleum products based on a reduction of 25% as compared to those in Swansea and the government wanted 35%. Further negotiations resulted in an agreement by which the KOC accepted not to sell its oil in Iraq at higher prices than those of the Turkish Petroleum Company and would not export its crude oil until it satisfies the Iraqi market. The cabinet approved this and authorised the Minister of Communications and Works Mohammad Ameen Zaki to sign the agreement which was signed also by Jacks on behalf of the KOC on 24 May 1926.

The agreement was debated and approved by the parliament on 13 June and by the Upper House on 14 June 1926.

KOC completed the construction of its Al-Wand refinery which came on stream in February 1927, taking its crude oil feed from the NaftKhanah field and from there on established itself as the major supplier of petroleum products in the northern provinces of Iraq.

The KOC then went to establish a subsidiary company by the name of the Rafidain Oil Company which became the main distributor of petroleum products in the northern provinces of the country.

It is to be recorded that prior to the commissioning of the Persian Abadan refinery in 1912 the main supplier and distributor of petroleum products in Iraq and the rest of the Middle East, which was mainly kerosene, was the American Standard Oil Company.

However by the time the Abadan refinery was successfully commissioned, it was decided to force Standard Oil out of the Middle East Markets. Instructions were issued to the Refinery agents in all the regions to undercut the prices of Standard Oil at any cost in order to force it out of the region and thereby monopolise the markets. With Standard Oil at a disadvantage due to its higher freight cost it was easily forced out of Iraq, Persia and the rest of the Gulf region. Kerosene and benzene were packed and marketed in standard two-gallon tins and the prices were subsequently raised after the departure of Standard Oil, a typical monopoly strategy, similar to that practiced by standard Oil itself.

The British Oil Development Company Concession
The Mosul Petroleum Company

As we have already seen, a company by the name of British Oil Development (BOD) had been formed and was looking for an oil concession in Iraq.

The company was formed on 1 March 1928 with a capital of £82,000 by Lord Wemyss and several influential British entrepreneurs. The original main aim of the company was to obtain an oil concession in Iraq for the Plots that the Iraqi government would select in accordance with the TPC concession agreement. This was expected to take place after 6 March 1929 the deadline by which the TPC had to select its 24 plots after which Iraq can then select her plots. By this the BOD did not want to infringe on the TPC rights and thus maintain good relationship with it. The company was also planning the construction of a railway line between Iraq and the Mediterranean.

Wemyss arrived in Baghdad on 17 May 1928 and met with King Faisal to put his proposal which included:

- That the BOD majority shareholding will be maintained in the hands of the British and the Iraqi nationals though it may include others such as Americans, French Italians and others in accordance with the Open Door policy.

- That the BOD was ready to develop the discovered oil and to construct the railway to the Mediterranean as soon as possible.

- The BOD was ready to cooperate with the TPC and other companies.

- The Company was ready to deposit an amount of money in an Iraqi bank as a goodwill gesture.

On 12 December 1928 a new proposal was submitted by which the BOD would select 24 plots which would be presented to the government. Tenders will then be invited for these plots after 6 March 1929 and if the BOD tender was accepted it proposed the following:

- The BOD will lend the government £2,100,000 for 30 years with an annual interest rate of 5.5% for the construction of a bridge in Baghdad and a railway line between Kirkuk and Mosul.

- 25% of the share of the company will be offered to Iraq.

The proposal was considered by the cabinet and was subsequently rejected since it was dependant on the outcome of the tender.

The news of the BOD proposals became known to the parliament and the press and became the subject of a national debate over the next few months.

Meanwhile the Italians, who were hoping to get a share in the TPC, felt that they were sidestepped and began demanding a share in Iraq's oil and as a result the establishment of the BOD presented them with a new opportunity to obtain such a share.

In the meantime the entire BOD shareholders have so far been British and it was decided to give the Italians a share in accordance with the Open Door policy.

Negotiations were subsequently conducted between the Italian government and the BOD after which an agreement was reached on 22 August 1929 by which the Italian government owned company Azienda Generale Italiana Petroli (AGIP) obtained a 40% shareholding in the BOD.

It was felt wise to give the Germans also some shareholding and after negotiatons with a group of German interests it was agreed on 12 April 1930 to redistribute the shareholding again with 51% for the British, 34% for the Italians and 15% for the Germans.

In the meantime the French felt that they were left out and in June 1930 they were admitted through the Open Door and the new shareholdings became 51% British, 25% Italian, 12% German and 12% French/Swiss.

After the conclusion of the TPC concession agreement on 24 March 1931 which gave the region east of the river Tigris to the TPC, the region west of the Tigris became available for concessions and as a result a new proposal was submitted by the BOD to the Iraqi government on 27 May 1931 for that region on the following terms:

- A concession for the area west of the river Tigris north of latitude 33 for a period of 75 years.

- A Royalty rate of four shillings per ton of oil.

- The Government has a right take 20% of the shares or 20% of the oil produced.

- The company would construct a pipeline within seven years unless other means became available.

- An annual Dead-Rent of £50,000 will be paid in January 1933 rising to £100,000 in January 1934 and the years after until the completion of the Pipeline.

- A similar tax arrangement to that of the TPC will be made.

- Three Iraqis will be sent on scholarship to Europe to study oil related subjects.

In the meantime the Americans felt that they have been left out and asked in accordance with the Open Door policy to be included in any future bidding for concessions.

Based on this, the Iraqi ministry of Economy and Communications on 26 May 1931 advised the companies that had submitted requests for oil concession to submit their new proposals and advertised in the local and foreign press inviting other companies that want to bid.

Four bids were received from the following companies:

- The British Oil Development Company, BOD.
- The British company S.Pearson & Sons.
- The American Company G. F. Getty.
- The French Company Etudes Financieres d'Entreprises.

The bids were studied by a committee headed by Mohammad Ameen Zaki, the Minister of Economy and Communications, the Head of the Oil Affairs and other advisers.

The committee submitted its report on 3 November 1931 and recommended that the area west of the river Tigris be divided into two, the first, north of Qaiyarah and the second between Qaiyarah and Baghdad, be offered to the BOD and Pearson and Sons. However, if both of these companies declined to accept the concession for the less promising area between Qaiyarah and Baghdad, then the whole region should be given as one concession.

The cabinet considered the recommendation during its meeting on 9 November and decided to exclude both the American and the French companies and to invite the BOD to start the negotiations and to advise Pearson & Sons to be ready if called for negotiations.

Both Lord Wemyss and Sir Mountain the representatives of the BOD arrived in Baghdad for the negotiations while the cabinet on 27 November authorised Rustam Haidar, the Minister of Finance and Mohammad Ameen Zaki to conduct the negotiations. The negotiations did not progress much and as a result both Wemess and Mountain left Iraq.

The negotiation were resumed on 9 April 1931 and this time made good progress which resulted in an agreement based on the following main terms:

- A concession for the area of some 46,000 square miles west of the river Tigris north of latitude 33 for a period of 75 years.

- A Royalty rate of four shillings (Gold) per ton of oil provided that the annual government revenue would not be less than £200,000 for the twenty years following the first export of oil.

- The oil export shall not be less than one million tons per year after seven and a half years from the date of the concession.

- The Government has a right, at wellhead, to 20% of all oil won in kind or in equivalent cash, but such oil will not be for export purposes.

- An annual Dead-Rent of £100,000 (Gold) will be paid in January 1933 rising by £25,000 annually up to a maximum of £200,000 in 1937 and the years after.

- A similar tax arrangement to that of the TPC will be made.

- A heavy drilling obligation was stipulated.

- Three Iraqis will be sent on scholarship to Europe to study oil related subjects.

The cabinet approved the agreement on 20 April 1931 and authorised Mohammad Ameen Zaki, the Minister of Economy and Communications to sign it.

The agreement was then debated by the parliament on 14 May and was approved. It was subsequently debated by the Upper House on 19 May and was also approved.

It is to be noted that the terms of this Concession were a big improvement on those of the Iraq Petroleum Company by the introduction of a new clause, being that of the right to wellhead oil.

It is also worth highlighting too that Iraq though still under a substantial influence of the British administration, its Government had gained some further experience in the art of negotiation and some political confidence and as a result was able to dictate the improved terms and conditions.

Meanwhile the Iraq Petroleum Company had watched the success of the BOD with some alarm. This unwelcomed and unexpected intruder that had managed in such a short time to get the huge area of 46,000 square miles which is larger than its own and as a result established itself as a serious competitor in Iraq. It had also seen how the BOD's offers, had undermined its negotiating position and strengthened that of the Iraqi government during their negotiations that had forced the IPC to improve the terms of its 1925 concession agreement. Hence this unwelcome intruder was not to be left in peace by the powerful and resentful IPC, which would patiently and cunningly awaits its chance to bring its downfall and final takeover as we shall see.

In the meantime, soon after securing its concession, the BOD started its exploration and drilling works but within a short time found itself short of financial resources. As a result another private company by the name of, Mosul Oilfields Limited, was formed in November 1932 mainly to finance the BOD, and again had some substantial Italian, German, British, French, Dutch, Iraqi, and Swiss participation. In the meantime in early August 1934, both the French and the Swiss sold their 12% shareholdings in the BOD to the Italian AGIP. A further 10% was secured by AGIP from the British shareholders. Thus the shareholding of the BOD became 47% Italian, 41% British and 12% German.

King Ghazi I

With time the BOD found itself in need of additional capital to settle an outstanding Dead Rent payment of over quarter of a million Stirling becoming due at the end of March 1936. The suggestion that if the Company was to become unable to settle this payment on time, the concession might be taken over by the Italian State Company (AGIP), was rejected by the Iraqi government.

As a result discussions were held between the BOD and the IPC on possible ways of arriving at some sort of agreement to solve this problem.

This led to the Iraq Petroleum Company Group itself forming in 1936, a new company by the name of Mosul Holdings Limited. The main purpose of this company was to provide the desperately required additional capital by the BOD against acquiring some shares and direction in the Mosul Oilfields which it managed to achieve without much difficulties. Soon afterwards, however the name of the Mosul Holdings Limited was to be changed to Mosul Petroleum Company, the M.P.C.

Then, between 1936 and 1940, the IPC Group progressively managed to assume further control of the BOD interests and ultimately full control of its operations.

The BOD itself then in 1941 assigned its entire Iraq Concession to the Mosul Petroleum Company.

The position of these different companies was finally simplified in 1943 by the liquidation and hence the disappearance of both B.O.D. and Mosul Oilfields Limited and the original BOD Concession and Operations came under the sole control of the Mosul Petroleum Company one of the successful Daughters of the IPC.

Thus within less than ten years, the IPC had managed to liquidate its unwelcome competitor in Iraq and to bring some 78,000 square miles under its control, virtually the whole region of northern Iraq.

The MPC then went on to discover and develop two separate and adjacent oilfields namely those of Ain Zalah and Batmah and by 1952 the MPC was able to export its first quantity of crude oil. These two fields proved to be rather small, nonetheless they managed to continue to produce the Concession minimum requirement, of 1,000,000 tons of oil per year, albeit with some difficulty at times, up to the time of the abandonment of the MPC concession after the nationalisation of the IPC in 1972.

It is to be highlighted that though the MPC remained an independent company from legal and financial points of view its management and operations came under the direct control of the IPC and as a result it looked to the outsider as if it was an integral part of the IPC.

The Basra Petroleum Company Concession

The existence of oil in southern Iraq was not well known as it had been in the north since no telltale signs of oil seepage had been seen and the geology of the surface of the land is flat and featureless. However, the telltale signs of oil in southern Iran and the successful discovery of oil in Masjidi Sulaiman in 1908 as well as the subsequent discovery of oil in Bahrain in 1932 highlighted the possibility of similar oil deposits in southern Iraq and the Arabian peninsula. As a result the IPC Group as well as other companies began to approach the Iraqi government expressing their interest in obtaining a concession.

Several such companies submitted their requests for concessions including:

- Burma Oil Company in 1936, a British company which became associated with the Anglo-Persian Oil Company, APOC.

- Dawood al-Haidari in1936, an Iraqi national who had a small shareholding in the British Oil Development in north Iraq.

- Najm al-Saadoon 1937, an Iraqi national.

- Iraq Petroleum Company IPC in 1937, the company that holds the oil concession in northern Iraq.

- Seaboard Oil Company in 1937, an American company which had connections with Standard Oil of California and, represented by C. Hart, an ex ambassador to Iran.

- B. L. Hunting Company in 1937, a British company with tankers interests.

A committee was formed in July 1937 by Hikmat Sulaiman the Iraqi Prime Minister, consisting from Mohammad Ali Mahmoud, Minister of Finance, Ali Mahmoud al-Shaikh Ali, Minister of Justice and Abbas Mahdi Minister of Economy and Communications to study these applications and submit its findings.

However a new government was formed after a month or so in August 1937 by Jameel al-Madfae, and as a result the committee was unable to continue with its work.

It seems that only two companies were considered as serious contender, the IPC Group and Seaboard Oil.

It was on 22 June 1937 that Seaboard Oil proposed the establishment of a company M. Iraq by offering 25% of it shares to Iraq without mentioning other terms. However in early 1938 Seaboard Oil submitted a new proposal for a concession offering four Shillings per ton royalty and 20% profit.

When this became clear to the IPC Group, it submitted its proposal offering four Shillings per ton royalty and 20% of the wellhead oil.

This presented a new problem for the government since if it were to give such a concession to the IPC Group the whole of the country would come under the sole control of one company. This would no doubt create a real monopoly, prevent competition and come under attack from the different groups of opposition as well as the general public, which have not forgiven the Company for preventing Iraq from participating in the ownership of its previous concession. On the other hand, the bitter experience with the BOD and its financial problems made the government weary of new contenders. Hence, since no such contender has come forward for a similar request, and since the IPC Group has demonstrated their financial ability and technical expertise, the government was willing to consider their request.

A new committee was formed in the Ministry of Finance to study the offers which found the IPC to be in a better position, since it has already demonstrated its financial ability and technical expertise. However the committee recommended that the terms of the new concession to be similar to those of the BOD concession. The recommendation was endorsed by the Ministry of Finance which sent it to the ministry of Economy and Communications for consideration.

Subsequent negotiations took place between the Ministry of Economy and the IPC and agreement was reached on basing the new concession on similar terms of the BOD concession. A recommendation based on these negotiations was sent on 9 July 1938 to the cabinet which met with its approval.

In the meantime the IPC had on 22 July 1938 formed a subsidiary by the name of Basra Petroleum Company and the final agreement was then signed on29 July 1938 by the acting Minister of Economy and Communication on behalf of the government and John Skliros on behalf of the BPC.

This Company was identical in its composition and shareholding with its mother IPC.

The agreement was then debated by the parliament on 12 November and subsequently by the Upper House on 21 November and was approved by both.

The main terms of this Concession are as follows:

- The Concession was for 75 years and covers the southern region of Iraq including Iraq's offshore areas and the Iraq-Saudi neutral zones.

- A Royalty rate of four shillings (Gold) per ton of oil.

- A Dead Rent to be paid at the beginning of 1939 and the years after until the date of the starting of export of oil. The Dead Rent was for £200,000 (gold) in the case of less marketable inferior oil and up to £400,000 (Gold) in the case of the discovery of oil deposits which would prove to be of a standard up to that of Kirkuk oil.

- A heavy drilling obligation was stipulated by which the company will start within three years from the date of the concession agreement.

- An export obligation of one million tons of oil within seven and half years from the date of the discovery of crude oil.

- A free 20% of wellhead oil was also allotted to the Government.

The Company subsequently went to discover the Zubair oilfield in 1948, which was developed quickly to begin export in 1951 after the completion of its pipeline to Fao terminal at the mouth of the Shatt Al-Arab in the Arabian Gulf.

A much larger oilfield was to be discovered soon after also in 1948 being the famous Rumaila oilfield which came on stream in1954. By the time of its nationalisation in 1974, the Basra Petroleum Company had become a major producing company in the Middle East.

BPC Offices-Basra, mid 1950s
Courtesy of IPC Society Newsletters

The IPC Group

The three companies, the Iraq Petroleum Company, IPC, the Mosul Petroleum Company, MPC and the Basra Petroleum Company, BPC that came to control the oil concessions of the whole of Iraq soon began to operate as one organisation controlled by their Board of Directors in London. Hence they will be referred to collectively throughout this book as the "IPC Group", especially when we discuss general matters affecting these three companies. However the term "IPC Group" could also be used in certain cases to include other petroleum companies within the Red-Line Agreement as we shall see soon.

Other IPC Concessions

A MOTHER WITH 12 DAUGHTERS

Based on the monopolistic Red Line Agreement between the shareholders and their Self Denying Clause, the IPC then proceeded to create subsidiary companies (daughters) for obtaining exploration and production rights in numerous territories of the Middle East within the Red Line Area. By 1948 the IPC had 12 such daughters with concessions or exploration licences as follows:

• Mosul Petroleum Co. Ltd.

• Basra Petroleum Co. Ltd.

IPC Group Head Office-1960s, 33 Cavendish Square-London

Courtesy of IPC Society Newsletters

- Petroleum Development (Qatar) Ltd.

- Petroleum Development (Trucial Coast) Ltd

- Petroleum Development (Cyprus) Ltd.

- Lebanon Petroleum Company Ltd.

- Petroleum Development (Palestine)

- Syrian Petroleum Co. Ltd.

- Trans-Jordan Petroleum Co. Ltd.

- Petroleum Development (Oman and Dhofar) Ltd.

- Petroleum Concessions Ltd (for the Aden Protectorates)

- Petroleum Development (Western Arabia) Ltd.

We have already discussed the concessions of two of these successful daughters, the Mosul Petroleum Company, MPC, and the Basra Petroleum Company, BPC that went to discover and export crude oil.

The other two daughters that discovered and exported crude oil successfully were the Petroleum Development (Qatar) Ltd, QPC and Petroleum Development (Trucial Coast) Ltd present day Abu Dhabi Petroleum Company ADPC).

The remaining eight daughters were barren as no crude oil was discovered in their countries by the IPC and as a result their concessions either expired or relinquished. This was due either to the failure of the IPC to explore in the right regions or to its reluctance to act early.

However crude oil was discovered in abundance by other independent companies within some of the Red Line Countries such as Saudi Arabia, Oman, Yemen and Syria.

PETROLEUM DEVELOPMENT (QATAR) LTD., QPC

This is the third daughter of the IPC which obtained a Concession for the oil exploration of the Qatari Peninsula in 1935.

Oil was discovered in 1939 in the Dukhan Field. The development of the Field was delayed during the Second World War but started again after it ended

The first oil shipment was exported through Mesaieed Port in the late1951.

The production rates were gradually increased and reached some 18,000 barrels per day by 1973 and averaged some 62,000 barrels per day in 1977.

Qatar gained its independence in 1977 and in that year it nationalised the Petroleum Development (Qatar) Ltd.

ABU DHABI PETROLEUM COMPANY (ADPC)

(Previously) Petroleum Development (Trucial Coast) Ltd (Pdtc)

This is the fourth daughter of the IPC and the only one that has managed to survive the fate of nationalisation. It is still operating successfully today and it seems certain that it will end its life in the normal peaceful manner after the expiry of its concession in 2014.

This Company started its life early when a company by the name of Petroleum Development (Trucial Coast) Limited, was formed by the same shareholders of the IPC in 1935 for obtaining oil exploration and production rights in all the old Arabian Sheikhdoms of that time currently known as the United Arab Emirates.

The Company was able, in 1939, to obtain a Concession from the Sheikhdom of Abu Dhabi. The Concession was for the normal IPC standard period of 75 years.

The exploration work was delayed by the prolonged Second World War to be started in earnest at last in the late 1940s. At that time, the town of Abu Dhabi itself was no more than a tiny village, and there were no roads in the entire Sheikhdom.

The actual drilling was finally started in 1950, but the search for oil proved to be a prolonged one. In July 1953 a well was drilled in the Bab field, but mechanical difficulties led to it being abandoned despite the evidence of the presence of oil. Further drilling at Bab finally established the potential of the field in 1960. The Bu Hasa field was proved soon after when oil was discovered in commercial quantities, and the first quantity of oil was exported from the Sheikhdom in 1963. In the following year, ADPC relinquished its concession in the other Trucial Sheikhdoms to concentrate its efforts on Abu Dhabi and went to discover other fields such as Asab.

It is worth mentioning that oil was discovered in 1951 offshore on the continental shelf of the Abu Dhabi Sheikhdom but it was ruled that the PDTC concession did not include the continental shelf. Hence the PDTC was deprived of the huge offshore fields, though both British Petroleum and the French Compagnie Française des Pétroles, CFP, (both IPC shareholders) were two of the main shareholders of the lucrative offshore oil and gas fields.

It was, however, not until 1963 when the PDTC decided to change its name to the Abu Dhabi Petroleum Company, ADPC.

A BRIEF HISTORY OF THE IPC SHAREHOLDERS

We have so far seen that the owners of the IPC were five. So why were these owners so powerful to be able to secure the exclusive rights for the exploration of oil in the north of Iraq and subsequently through the 12 subsidiary companies of the IPC in obtaining similar exclusive rights in other countries in the Middle

East and beyond? The answer is obvious when we know that the four big shareholders are either owned or supported by their governments, the victors of the First World War. A brief history of each of these powerful companies is given hereunder as follows:

1. Anglo-Persian Oil Company (Present Day British Petroleum, BP)

In May 1901, William Knox D'Arcy, a British adventurer who had made his fortune during the gold rush in Australia, was granted a concession by the Shah of Persia to search for oil. After a long period of exploration and drilling he finally struck oil in May 1908 at the Masjidi Sullaiman area about 130 miles upstream of the river Karun. This was the first commercially significant find in the Middle East. In 1909, D'Arcy and Burma Oil Company formed the Anglo-Persian Oil Company (APOC) to exploit this Persian find. The company grew slowly until World War I when its strategic importance led the British Government to acquire a controlling interest in the company.

The company went to build the 130 miles pipeline from the oil field to Abadan, the first such crude oil pipeline in the Middle East. The shipment of oil from Abadan was also to mark the first export of crude oil from the Gulf.

Furthermore the company built the famous Abadan refinery, which was the main supplier of petroleum products in the Middle East for a long time.

In 1917, the war allowed it to take the British arm of the German Europaiche Union, which used the trade name British Petroleum. After the war ended, the company, in which the British Government by then had 51% interest, moved to secure outlets in Europe and elsewhere.

However, the APOC main concern was still Persia, following the Anglo-Persian Agreement of 1919 the company continued to trade profitably in that country.

After the First World War the Anglo-Persian Oil Company was awarded the lucrative share of 23 2/3% in the TPC, which became later on the Iraq Petroleum Company (IPC).

In 1931, partly in response to the difficult economic conditions of the times, BP merged their marketing operations in the United Kingdom (only) with those of Shell-Mex to create Shell-Mex and BP Ltd, a company that continued to trade until the Shell and BP brands separated again in 1975.

There was a growing dissent within Persia however at the imperialist and unfair position that APOC occupied. As a result the Shah terminated the APOC concession in 1932. The concession was reinstated within a year, covering a reduced area with an increase in the Persian government's share of profits. Persia was renamed Iran in 1936 and APOC became AIOC, the Anglo-Iranian Oil Company.

Following the turmoil of World War II, the AIOC and the Iranian government resisted nationalist pressures to agree a revised better terms of the concession in 1949. In March 1951, the pro-western Prime Minster Ali Razmara was shot dead on his way to the mosque in April. Soon after Mossadeq was elected as a prime minister and a bill was passed nationalising the oil industry and the Shah was forced to leave the country.

The AIOC took its case against the nationalisation to the International Court of Justice at the Hague, but lost the case. However the British and the United States governments were concerned about the encroachment of the Soviet influence in the area and assisted to hatch a plot against the Iranian administration. They succeeded in their efforts and on august 19th, 1953, the incumbent democratically elected Prime Minster, Mohammed Mossadeq, was forced from office and replaced by the pro western general Fazlollah Zahedi and the Shah was finally able to return to Iran.

The AIOC became the British Petroleum Company in 1954, and briefly resumed operation in Iran with a forty per cent share in a new international consortium. BP continued to operate in Iran until the Islamic Revolution in 1979.

From the late 1960's the Company started to looked beyond the Middle East to the USA and the North Sea.

2. Royal Dutch/Shell

In 1833, a Jewish shopkeeper Marcus Samuel decided to expand his London business. He sold antiques, but now added oriental shells. He aimed to capitalise on a fashion for using them in internal design. His instinct was right; such was the demand that he quickly began importing shells from the Far East laying the foundation for his import/export business.

By 1886 the business had passed to his sons Marcus Samuel junior and his brother Sam. They exported British machinery, textile, and tools to the newly industrialising Japan and the Far East and on return imported rice, silk, china and copperware to the Middle East and Europe. In London, they traded in commodities such as sugar, flour and wheat worldwide.

It was during a trip to Japan that Marcus became interested in the oil exporting business then based in Baku, Russia. The Rothschilds had invested heavily in the 1880s in rail and tunnels to overcome the transport difficulties of getting oil from this landlocked region to the Black Sea and from there to overseas markets. Shipping still posed a problem as the oil was carried in barrels, which could leak and took up much space on the ship's hold.

The Samuels commissioned a fleet of steamers to carry kerosene in bulk, using for the first time the Suez Canal. They also set up bulk oil storage at ports in the Far East and contracted a Russian group of producers controlled by the Rothschilds, for long-term supply of kerosene. Their strategy was high-risk; if the news of their operations got out, they would be squeezed out by Rockfeller's dominant Standard Oil Company. With the maiden voyage of the first bulk carrier, the "Murex", through the Suez Canal in 1892 the Samuels had achieved a revolution in oil transportation. Bulk transport substantially cut the cost of oil by enormously increasing the volume that could be carried. The Samuel brothers initially called their company The Tank Syndicate but in 1897 renamed it The Shell Transport and Trading Company.

Petroleum was also being produced in the Dutch colony of the East Indies and in 1880 a company had been formed to develop an oil field in Sumatra. This is the origin of what was to become the Royal Dutch Petroleum Company. The company then moved to build a pipeline and a refinery in the region. Faced with the competition from the Samuels low bulk transport cost, the Royal Dutch began the construction of tankers and bulk storage installations and set up its own sales organisation.

Samuel Marcus had become a leading businessman in London and was knighted in 1898. However his dependence on the Russian producers left his company vulnerable and he decided to seek other sources of oil.

He signed a contact with the American company Gulf to buy 100,000 tons of crude oil a year at a fixed price for twenty-four years. Soon after, it became apparent that Gulf could not fulfil its contract and Samuel agreed to cancel it.

Following that, the Far East was the obvious place to look and his venture in Borneo brought him up against Royal Dutch, one of the region's biggest oil producers and main marketing competitors. After a while the two companies realised that their main competitor was the mighty Standard Oil of the United States and decided to join forces to protect themselves against it by forming a sale organisation in 1903.

It was not until 1907 that the two companies merged fully to form the Royal Dutch Shell Group, with a share of 60% to Royal Dutch and 40% to Shell.

The Group rapidly expanded across the world with marketing companies formed throughout Europe and many parts of Asia. Its exploration and production went to cover Russia, Romania, the Middle East through its participation in the Iraq Petroleum Company and its daughter subsidiaries, the Basra, Mosul, Qatar and the Abu Dhabi Petroleum Companies as well as Nigeria, Venezuela, Mexico and the United States of America. The company grew to become one of the successful major oil companies in the world.

3. Compagnie Francaise Des Petroles (CFP)

After World War I, the French government had no National Oil Company of its own and as such rejected the idea of forming a partnership with Royal Dutch Shell in favour of creating an entirely French oil company since it was envisaged that Petroleum would be an essential requirement in the case of a new war with Germany. As a result CFP was founded in March 1924.

As we have already seen, the 23.75% share of Deutsche Bank in the Turkish Petroleum Company (TPC), was awarded to France at the San Remo conference as a compensation for the war damages caused by Germany during that war. This share was subsequently awarded to CFP which was converted to a private sector company and was listed on the Paris Stock Exchange for the first time in 1929.

CFP then went to acquire 23.75% of each of the IPC, BPC, MPC, QPC and ADPC as well as other oil interests in the world and to become a world leading oil company.

4. Standard Oil

Standard Oil was established by John Rockefeller in 1870 and became a predominant American integrated oil producing, transporting, refining and marketing company. It grew to become the largest oil refiner in the world. It operated as a major company trust and was one of the world's first and largest multinational corporations, until it was broken up by the United States Supreme Court in 1911.

Its founder, chairman and major shareholder, John Rockefeller, became a billionaire and one of the richest men in the world.

In 1890, Standard Oil controlled 88% of the refined oil flows in the United States. By 1904 Standard controlled 91% of the crude oil production and 85% of final sales of petroleum products in the country. Most of its output was kerosene, of which 55% was exported around the world.

As a result of this dominant control of petroleum products, the Federal Commissioner of Corporations concluded beyond question, that Standard's dominant positioning in the refining industry was due to unfair practices, to abuse of control of pipelines, to railroad discriminations, and to unfair methods of competition.

By 1911, with the public outcry at a climax, the Supreme Court of the United States ruled that Standard Oil must be dissolved and split into 34 companies. Two of these companies were Standard Oil Company of New Jersey, which eventually became Exxon, and Standard Oil Company of New York, which became Mobil. Both these companies as we have seen became shareholders of the Turkish Petroleum Company and subsequently shareholders of the IPC, BPC, MPC, QPC and ADPC with a combined holding of 23.75%.in each of them.

5. Calouste Gulbenkian - Mr. 5%

Calouste Gulbenkian was born in 1869 in Istanbul, the son of an Armenian oil importer/exporter. He was educated at King's College London, where he studied petroleum engineering and gained, after graduation, some experience in the oil industry in Baku. He returned to London and became a naturalised British citizen in 1902 and got involved in arranging the 1907 merger resulting in Royal Dutch/Shell.

His habit of retaining five percent of the shares of the oil companies he developed earned him the nickname "Mr. Five Percent"

In 1912 he was the brain behind the creation of the Turkish Petroleum Company and was instrumental in securing the oil exploration and development rights for the TPC and subsequently the IPC, which earned his usual 5% fee.

It is estimated that by the late 1940s his 5% share in the IPC was yielding him many million US Dollars a year. This was to increase by many folds after the completion of the two 30/32 inch IPC pipelines in the 1950 and 1960s and continued to do so until the nationalisation of the IPC in June 1972.

He amassed a huge fortune and an art collection and later in his life established the Calouste Gulbenkian Foundation for charitable, educational, artistic and scientific purposes, which is still functioning today.

It is regrettable to record that very little of his fortune and his charitable foundation funds was allocated for the social, educational and other humanitarian advancement of Iraq, the county from which he had amassed his fortune in the first place.

This One is mine – Nubar Gulbenkian

It is of interest to quote the following extract from Nubar Gulbenkian's autobiography during his journey along the 12 inch diameter pipeline which was under construction in early 1933. Nubar is the son of Mr. 5%, Calouste.

"My trip along the southern stretch of the pipeline took me through lava country; there was no road and it was the most back-breaking journey I have ever made. To keep out the dust, the windows of the car had to be kept shut and I almost suffocated. I had insisted on inspecting that part of the line because of earlier discussions at headquarters in London. The Iraq Government were very anxious to have a railway and they thought there was no need to pay for one because the IPC would have to build a railway before they could build a pipeline. At the time, the IPC engineers in London said the pipeline could be laid without railway, by using high powered Mack trucks, the last word then in heavy transport. The engineers were right; it could be done and it was done.

And what a job it was. I drove across the desert to watch the work, accompanied by the chief engineer, an American call Stuckey, a most agreeable and capable man. A telegraph line had been laid from Haifa along the proposed pipeline route to Kirkuk and driving was a matter of following the telegraph poles, there was no road and I started counting the poles.

One, two, three, four, five ….nineteen, twenty. That one is mine I said, I was thinking of the Gulbenkian 5 per cent interest in the IPC, notching it up as it were. That was how I first got the name by which my father was afterwards to be known, Mr Five Per Cent. To see a 5 per cent investment in a company like the IPC in terms of telegraph poles, miles of pipeline, coils of wire or

Mack truck is to give a solid reality to the entries on a balance sheet or those in a banks passbook. My father never saw the land from which so much of his wealth came; I am glad I was able to go there.

Pipe carriers, early 1930s

Courtesy of IPC Society Newsletters

Welding -12 inch pipeline

Courtesy of IPC Society Newsletters

One of the most remarkable features of the laying of the pipeline was the energy and keenness of everyone on the job. This first twelve-inch line – the Spaghetti Line as it was called , in comparison with the thirty six inch pipelines of today-was built by the IPC itself ; subsequent increases were built by contract.

Driving across the desert it seemed at first as though there were just the telegraph poles and nothing else; no pipeline and no activity. Then, suddenly, a speck of dust on the horizon became a lorry carrying lengths of pipe and a gang of up to twenty Bedouin under the control of an American foreman; he gave the orders by blowing blasts on a whistle or by making signs with his hands, for he had no common language with workmen. But they certainly jumped to it until the job was finished. As the lorry progressed the men on board heaved the piping on to the ground. As I waited and watched them I became aware of the lengths of the pipe that had been dropped all across the desert and were now snaking across the sand. As we drove on, I saw the way the pipeline was being built. First, there were the gangs welding together the lengths of pipe, each welder working with a sunshade over his head. Then came the trenching machines, gnawing a continuous trench out of the desert, leaving heaps of earth along the sides of the trench. After that came a machine which wrapped the line in what looked like huge rolls of lavatory paper; these rolls were made of bituminous paper and their purpose was to prevent corrosion. Then came another machine to heave the pipeline into the trench, and, finally, one which buried the pipeline by shovelling the earth back into the trench on top of it."

The 12 inch (Spaghetti) Pipeline

Courtesy of IPC Society Newsletters

Summary of Concessions, etc., held in June, 1948, by I.P.C. and Associated Companies

1. In IRAQ

Company	Concession Date	Period in Years	Area Covered	Rights Granted
IRAQ PETROLEUM COMPANY	14/3/25 as modified 29/3/31	75	MOSUL & BAGHDAD VILAYET east of Tigris.	Production, Transport, Refining.
MOSUL PETROLEUM COMPANY (ex BRITISH OIL DEVELOPMENT).	25/5/32	75	IRAQ WEST OF TIGRIS North of lat. 33°.	ditto.
BASRAH PETROLEUM COMPANY.	30/11/38	75	All IRAQ not covered by I.P.C. & M.P.C. (and A.I.O.C.).	ditto.

2. In the LEVANT STATES

Company	Concession Date	Period in Years	Area Covered	Rights Granted
IRAQ PETROLEUM COMPANY.	25/3/31	70	LEBANON	Transit and refining.
ditto.	25/3/31	70	SYRIA	ditto.
ditto.	11/1/31	70	TRANSJORDAN	ditto.
ditto.	11/1/31 supplements 10/7/33 & 29/5/39	70	PALESTINE.	ditto.
SYRIA PETROLEUM COMPANY.	26/3/40	75	All SYRIA north of line E.W. through Damascus.	Production, transport & refining.
TRANSJORDAN PETROLEUM COMPANY.	10/5/47	75	ALL TRANSJORDAN	ditto.

Courtesy of IPC

3. In the GULF

Company	Concession Date	Period in Years	Area Covered	Rights Granted
PETROLEUM DEVELOPMENT (QATAR) LIMITED.	17/5/35	75	QATAR.	Production, transport.
PETROLEUM DEVELOPMENT (TRUCIAL COAST) LTD.	22/5/37	75	DUBAI.	ditto.
	17/9/37	75	SHARJA.	ditto.
	20/12/38	75	KALBAH.	ditto.
	11/1/39	75	ABU DHABI.	ditto.
	21/6/45	75	RAS AL KHAIMA.	ditto.
	20/3/45	75	UMM AL QUWAIN.	ditto.
PETROLEUM DEVELOPMENT (OMAN & DHOFAR) LTD.	24/6/37	75	OMAN & DHOFAR.	ditto.

4. Exploration Licences

Company	Date of Licence	Duration of Licences	Area Covered	
LEBANON PETROLEUM COMPANY.	7/3/38	4 yrs.	500 Km block LEBANON.	Renewed (after war moratorium) 29/4/48. Subject to war moratorium.
PETROLEUM DEVELOPMENT (PALESTINE) LIMITED.	24/2/39 21/7/39	4 yrs. 4 yrs.	11 Licences, total 5,382 sq. km. and 18 Licences, total 8,263 sq. km. in PALESTINE.	
PETROLEUM DEVELOPMENT (CYPRUS) LIMITED	23/4/38	4 yrs.	2,006 sq. m. of CYPRUS.	Renewed annually.
PETROLEUM CONCESSIONS LIMITED.	12/1/38	4 yrs.	ADEN PROTECTORATE	Renewed every 2 yrs.
PETROLEUM DEVELOPMENT (TRUCIAL COAST) LIMITED.	23/3/39	5 yrs.	AJMAN.	Renewed till 1950.

5. Concession Abandoned

Company	Concession Date	Period in Years	Area Covered	Rights Granted
PETROLEUM DEVELOPMENT (WESTERN ARABIA) LTD.	9/7/36	60	100 Km strip of Western SA'UDI ARABIA.	Concession abandoned 1941.

Courtesy of IPC

3

THE RELATIONS BETWEEN THE IRAQI GOVERNMENT AND THE IPC GROUP DURING THE MONARCHY PERIOD

1931-1952

As we have seen the relationship between the Iraqi government and the Iraq Petroleum Company during the difficult negotiations of the concession over the period of several years were far from smooth with the IPC imposing its will on the Iraqi negotiators with the help of the British government and its administration in Iraq. This was demonstrated so clearly by denying Iraq the right for 20 per cent participation in the company despite the fact that this right was given to Iraq by the special side letter attached to the San Remo Agreement of 24 April 1920.

Hence it was not surprising that the disputes between the government and the IPC Group in the interpretation of certain articles of the Concession Agreements began to appear soon after the signature of the first concession agreement beginning with the Gold dispute in early 1932.

The main disputes and disagreements that came to light during the period 1932 and 1951 can be summarised as follows:-

1 - THE GOLD DISPUTE

It is to be noted that the Royalty in the IPC Concession Agreement of 1931 was quoted in Shillings (Gold) bearing in mind that each Pound Sterling was equal to twenty Shillings. The Iraqi negotiators had proposed to link the royalty payment to gold so as to protect the government revenues against any possible financial losses due to any depreciation of the Pound Sterling. They had even gone further to propose the exact equivalent weight and purity of such gold.

77

The Iraqi member of the committee who led the negotiations on this subject was the Finance Minister Sasoon Hesgail. He was a Jewish financier with vast experience, educated in Europe and Istanbul and was elected in 1908 as a member of the Ottoman parliament for Baghdad. He had seen the gold standard for the Pound Sterling suspended during the First World War and though it was reinstated in 1925, he remained sceptical and insisted on including that little magical word.

The IPC did not think that the linking of Sterling to gold was necessary but against the relentless insistence of the Iraqi team it ultimately accepted to insert the word gold after Shilling without a clear specification of such gold. It was however known at that time that the Sterling Gold Standard was equivalent to 7.3 gm of gold.

The Iraqi negotiators were to be proved right soon after the signing of the concession agreement on 24 March 1931 as the Sterling Gold Standard was abandoned a few months later on 21 September 1931 during the Great Depression which resulted in the devaluation of the pound sterling by some 25%.

A payment of £409,000 was due from the IPC to the government in January 1932 and the IPC attempted to refuse to make this payment in accordance with the gold equivalent of the Sterling as required by the clear requirement of the terms of the concession agreement, arguing that there was no clear specification to the word Gold. The IPC as usual sought support from the British and the French governments. They however could not support such a shabby request to avoid such a clear requirement of the concession agreement. The IPC was finally forced to abide by the terms of the Agreement and a payment of £578,000 was made based on the Bank of England's gold price.

It is of interest to highlight that the concession price of a barrel of oil based on four Shillings (gold) per ton was equivalent to US 13 Cents at the end of 1933, however the price of gold was re-valued in February 1934 to $35.00 per ounce and as a result the price of the barrel became equivalent to about US 23 Cents, which represented a jump of some 77% in the government revenues in Dollar terms.

Meanwhile a twist had taken place during the Second World War when the price of gold in the local markets in Iraq and the Middle East in general exceeded the Bank of England price in London and as a result the Iraqi government began to insist on the use of the free market gold price to calculate the royalty payments.

Negotiations between the government and the IPC Group started on 6 January 1949 in Baghdad without reaching agreement. The question of Gold was discussed during several other meetings both in Baghdad and in London with both sides insisting on their points of view until it was finally proposed by the IPC Group that payments should continue to be made in accordance with the Bank of England's price of gold until this issue is finally resolved by an English court. This proposal was accepted by the government on 8 August 1950.

In the meantime it was estimated that the amount in dispute for the period 1940 to 1950 was some 21 million Iraqi Dinars. The government then began to prepare its court case against the IPC and a committee was formed on 9 October 1950 headed by Nadeem al-Pachachi to travel to London to select a legal firm to represent the government in the court. They consulted with legal firms and decided to entrust the case to the lawyer Russell Stoke of Richard Butler and Company. The Company studied the details and after consultation with other well known lawyers they advised that the Bank of England's pricing of gold is based on the British government policy to suit its own requirements and therefore could not be considered applicable in the case of this dispute.

The case was to be heard in the Commercial Court in London and in April 1951 the lawyers of the Iraqi government and the IPC Group met with the Judge who gave the IPC three weeks to present their defence, which they did, denying the Iraqi claims.

The question of gold was kept being discussed during the ongoing negotiation of the other major disputes with the IPC and on 2 July 1951 the Iraqi cabinet wanted to resolve the issue by an amicable settlement and as a result it was finally agreed to postpone the court case indefinitely against the payment of five million Iraqi dinars by the IPC. This settlement was embodied in the 1952 comprehensive agreement between the government and the IPC.

Hence by insisting on inserting the little word "Gold", the shrewd Iraqi negotiators had managed to save Iraq from great financial losses and it remains a story to be told in Iraq until now on how such a small detail can make such a huge difference.

2 - THE MPC OBLIGATION TO PRODUCE OIL WITHIN SEVEN AND A HALF YEARS

The Mosul Petroleum Company concession agreement which was signed on 9 April 1931, had stipulated that the company's oil export shall not be less than one million tons per year after seven and a half years from the date of the concession agreement. This makes the obligation date for the production and export falls at the end of October 1938. The search for oil in the MPC concession area was difficult and prolonged and as a result the IPC Group wanted to concentrate their exploration and drilling efforts on the more promising areas of the IPC .

As a result, in May 1938, the IPC Group requested a ten year extension for the target date for the export of oil from the MPC area against an interest free loan of three million pounds. The government accepted the request but offered an extension of five years only.

In the meantime the IPC concession agreement had stipulated that its crude oil should be exported in equal quantities from Haifa and Tripoli. However due to the Second World War requirements, the IPC wanted to export more from Tripoli and sought the agreement of the Iraqi government for this.

A proposal was presented by the IPC Group to the government to amend the terms of the IPC concession agreement for the unequal oil export from Haifa and Tripoli and the MPC concession agreement for an extension of seven years for its export of oil against an interest free loan of three million pounds.

The government at that time was in a desperate need of money and as a result an agreement based on these terms was signed by Nuri al-Said on behalf of the government and Skliros on behalf of the IPC Group which was ratified by the cabinet on 22 June 1939.

3 - THE REQUEST FOR A MORATORIUM ON MPC AND BPC OBLIGATIONS

The Basra Petroleum Company concession agreement of 21 November 1938, had stipulated that the company will start drilling within three years from the date of the concession agreement. Hence the latest date for the beginning of drilling was 21 November 1941.

However the company was unable to meet the drilling contractual date due to the abnormal conditions of the Second World War which resulted in difficulties in purchasing and transporting the necessary exploration and drilling equipment as well as the shortage of capital.

Meanwhile the seven year extension given to the MPC for the production and export which ends in October 1945 began to look unattainable with the continuation of the War and the MPC wanted a second extension. As a result both the MPC and the BPC submitted their requests on 27 July 1941, for an extension of time to meet their drilling and export obligation until twelve months after the end of the War. The request was initially approved by the cabinet on 16 August 1941 pending the approval of the parliament.

However a new government was formed on 9 October 1941 headed by Nuri al-Said who disagreed with the arrangements made by the previous government since he felt that the agreement would be met with the refusal of parliament and demanded a new interest free loan as a compensation for the loss of early revenues.

The IPC Group then submitted on 29 November 1941 a new proposal for the extensions pleading Force Majeure in accordance with relevant articles in the Concession Agreements. This plea was rejected by the Iraqi government since the postponement of the drilling activities was made at the instruction of the British government and instead proposed going to arbitration to resolve the issue. By then the contractual date for the drilling by the BPC had expired and the Concession Agreement could no longer be considered as valid.

The BPC was not keen on going to arbitration and the negotiations continued to resolve the issue by mutual agreement. The final negotiations took place in Baghdad between Nuri al-Said the Prime Minister and Skliros representing the IPC Group and a draft agreement was initialled by both on 22 March 1943, giving the IPC Group the choice for adopting one of the following three alternatives:-

1. A moratorium on the BPC drilling and crude oil export obligations for a period ending twelve months after the signing of an armistice with the last of the three powers Germany, Italy or Japan, against the payment of an interest free loan of one million pounds on 1 June 1943.

2. A moratorium on both the BPC and the MPC drilling and crude oil export obligations for a period ending twelve months after the signing of an armistice with the last of the three powers Germany, Italy or Japan, against the payment of an interest free loan of one and a half million pounds on 1 June 1943.

3.   The right of the IPC Group to go to arbitration.

The draft agreement was discussed by the Board of Directors of the IPC Group on 25 March which approved the second alternative.

The agreement was then approved by the Iraqi Cabinet and subsequently by the parliament on 10 April 1943.

4 - THE CONSOLIDATION OF THE IPC, MPC AND BPC OBLIGATIONS

As we have seen, the IPC Group was unable to abide by the production and export obligations under the terms of the MPC and BPC Concession Agreements and as a result proposed to consolidate the terms of some of the obligations of the three companies. The aim was to allow the IPC Group to produce its contractual obligations from any of the three concession areas. This would result in the following advantages mainly to itself:-

*   To satisfy its obligation for drilling, production and export under the three concessions through the production and export from the Kirkuk field alone which was well developed and had enough production capacity at that time and expected to have enough export capacity after the completion of the 16 inch diameter pipelines to Haifa and Tripoli. This would have resulted in delaying the development of the MPC and BPC concession areas and consequently result in big savings in exploration, drilling and development costs.

*   Since the production and export costs of the Kirkuk crude were low, this will result in higher profits for the companies.

*   The Kirkuk crude was of high quality and hence has a higher market price which will result again in higher profit for the companies.

*   Both the MPC and BPC concessions allow the Government the right, at wellhead, to 20% of all oil won in kind or in equivalent cash, but such oil will not be for export purposes, while the IPC Concession Agreement did not give the government such a right. As compensation for this, the companies offered 7% of all the oil produced from the three concession areas of the IPC, MPC and BPC.

The government was not interested in such proposals since there was no real benefit for itself and since it wanted to develop the MPC and BPC concession areas as soon as possible and as result the proposal shelved.

5 - THE POLITICAL UNREST DURING THE PREMIERSHIP OF RASHID ALI AL-GAILANI

The relations between the Iraqi and the British governments were strained during the premiership of Rashid Ali al-Gailani, which resulted in a similar relationship between the Iraqi government and the IPC. The disturbances that took place during the first half of 1941, led to some damage to some of the company's property and equipment. This was followed by a serious interruption in the drilling and operation activities. It also resulted in the plugging, of 10 producing wells and 38 observation and other wells by the IPC as a precautionary measure to ensure their denial to the enemy in the event of a German attack. At the same time some 6,000 tons of drilling machinery were removed from Kirkuk oilfield to a safer location in the Basra region.

Nevertheless, sufficient equipment was kept in operation and production to ensure full pipelines throughput and this was maintained throughout this period until early May 1941.

It was on 30 March 1941 that signs of serious trouble began to appear when Iraqi army guards were posted on all oil wells and various plants.

As a result some of the women and children were evacuated to Baghdad and from there to Habbaniya while others were evacuated by the company plane to H-3 pumping station and from there by cars beyond the Iraqi frontiers to Jordan and Palestine.

However it was on 2 May 1941 when a decision was made to shutdown all the wells and the entire production facilities including the process plant. By the evening of that day the 12 inch diameter pipelines to Tripoli and Haifa were also shutdown and the export of oil finally came to a complete halt.

Meanwhile by afternoon of the same day, the IPC Staff were gathered at Arrapha Guest House before being distributed to the 28 bungalows in Arrapha residential area. From there they were then evacuated by the police on 19 May to two schools in the city of Kirkuk.

Events were moving very fast and soon after, Iraq was invaded by the British army and Rashid Ali al-Gailani fled the country and a new government was formed.

As a result it was not until 2 June before the IPC staff and families were allowed back to their homes, with the staff immediately returning to their duties in preparation for the resumption of operation.

All the plants and major equipment were thoroughly checked before returning them to service and by the evening of 2 June 1941 most of the major production facilities were back in service and the oil export was resumed after a stoppage which lasted just over a month.

The British troops then began to make heavy demands for support from the IPC. As a result considerable assistance was afforded by the company to the British Military Forces. This consisted of the supply of large quantities of pipe and other material, the completion of 90 miles of petrol line from Kirkuk to Mosul and the supply of some 15 million gallons of refined petroleum products from the IPC's refinery in Kirkuk.

6 - THE ROYALTY AND THE PROFIT

The Iraq Petroleum Company concession agreement of 1931 stated quote:

> "That twenty years after the beginning of exports, the rate of royalty was to be increased or decreased in proportion to the extent to which the profit or loss of the company was greater or less than during the immediately preceding five years than it had been during the first fifteen years of the twenty year period. Profit and loss were defined to include the cost of refining and distributing the products made from Iraqi crude oil. A minimum of two Shillings and a maximum of six shillings per ton were stipulated" unquote.

The IPC commercial export began in 1934; hence by 1954 the change in royalty payments would be due for consideration. The 15 year period which would set the base for the new calculations would begin in 1939. The Iraqi government kept a close watch on any aspect that may affect the calculation including the price to be charged to the IPC parents for oil.

We have seen that the IPC shareholders had agreed to lift their proportionate shares of crude oil at Cost plus a Fee. So when the IPC started its crude oil production and export from Kirkuk in 1935, it set the Cost plus Fee at the arbitrary Price of 18 Shilling per ton. The Cost elements in this Price included depreciation, amortisation and other items, which can be spread over a longer or shorter period of time resulting in reducing or raising the Cost and subsequently the Price.

So when the government queried the basis of such a price the IPC advised that the price was an arbitrary figure adopted by the companies for their mutual use. The government was not satisfied by such a vague answer and persisted over the years on getting a satisfactory explanation without real success. The IPC explanation was that there was no real clear market price for the Iraqi crude since it was not sold on the open market but lifted by the shareholders in the proportion of their shareholdings at the agreed arbitrary price. Furthermore, the IPC advised that the Iraqi crude was blended with other crudes during transportation, storage and refining and as such there was no way of determining the profit which could be attributed to any particular crude including the Iraqi crude. The issue kept being raised by the government during the 1940s until the IPC suggested the adoption of an agreed price at the Mediterranean but no agreement could be reached on what that price would be. The issue was finally resolved in 1950 when the royalty upper limit of six shillings (gold at the Bank of England's rate) per ton was accepted by the IPC as set by the concession agreement.

As a result of this increase in royalty the government oil revenues more than doubled in 1950 to reach £6.8 million. This late agreement was however swept aside the year after by the introduction of the 50/50 profit sharing agreement which resulted in more than doubling the government revenues again during 1951 to £15.1 million.

7 - THE SUPPLY OF PETROLEUM PRODUCTS FOR IRAQ'S LOCAL MARKET

The Iraq Petroleum Company's concession agreement of 1931 stated that "The supply of petroleum products for internal consumption, were to be secured by the IPC and sold at specified prices."

The IPC did not want to construct a refinery since restriction on prices would make it uneconomical. Furthermore it did not want to engage in the refining and products distribution business which would also result in unnecessary disagreements with the government.

Hence, to fulfil its obligation, the IPC arranged with the Anglo-Persian Oil Company to supply such products from its subsidiary company the Khaniqin Oil Company, the KOC.

The Anglo-Persian Oil Company had in anticipation established the Khaniqin Oil Company in November 1925 to take over the ownership and operation of its Naftkhanah field and Al-Wand refinery. The KOC then established a subsidiary company by the name of the Rafidain Oil Company which became the main distributor of its petroleum products from al-Wand refinery in Northern Iraq. It also became the main importer of the additional petroleum products requirement for distribution in the south of Iraq from Abadan refinery in Iran which is also owned by the Anglo-Persian Oil Company.

Though this arrangement was acceptable to the government during the 1930s and early 1940s, it was not acceptable in later years to have the county's petroleum products market controlled by a foreign company which was charging higher prices than necessary.

As a result an agreement was signed in 1951 between the Iraqi government and the Khaniqin Oil Company by which the government purchased the al-Wand refinery and the Rafidain Oil Company's distribution network. However a ten year service contract was signed with the KOC for the operation of the refinery and the products distribution network. The agreement also extended the Naftkhanah oilfield concession of the KOC on the condition that KOC would raise the crude oil production capacity to two million tons per year within a period of seven years. The KOC was unable to abide by the terms of the new concession agreement and as a result the Naftkhanah and the other potential oil fields in the transferred territories were taken over by the government in December 1958.

In the mean time the embargo on the export of oil from Iran after the nationalisation of its oil industry in 1951, brought to light the danger of relying on imported petroleum products when such products could easily be produced in Iraq. This made the construction of a national oil refinery an urgent matter and as a result it was decided to construct the Daura refinery in Baghdad as detailed separately Chapter 11 of this book.

8 - THE CLOSURE OF THE HAIFA 12 INCH DIAMETER PIPELINE

The Arab Israeli conflict in 1948 resulted in the closure of the 12 inch diameter pipeline to Haifa by the Iraqi government on 17 April of that year. The IPC as expected was unhappy about this closure which deprived it of 50% of its export capacity and began to urge the government to reopen the pipeline. The IPC was supported by both the British and United States governments, and though the pressure was great it was politically impossible for the Iraqi government to reopen the pipeline. However, since most of the Iraqi oil was refined in the local refinery at Haifa, the IPC proposed as a compromise that all the Iraqi crude would be exported from Haifa and hence none of the Iraqi oil would be refined locally. This was again unacceptable to the Iraqi government and despite the continuation of further requests and enticements; the pipeline remained closed and was never used for the export of any Iraqi oil again.

9 - IRAQ'S PARTICIPATION IN THE IPC

The Iraq Petroleum Company concession agreement of 1931as well as those of the MPC and BPC had given the Iraqi public the right to participate in these companies by stating that quote "The right of the Iraqi public to subscribe up to 20% in the IPC ownership as and when such subscription is offered to the general public" unquote.

It was on 14 October 1940 that the BPC decided to issue new shares to its shareholders that prompted the Ministry of Economy to demand that 20% of such shares should be offered to the Iraqi citizens in accordance with the above article. The BPC explained that these shares were offered to the main shareholders only and not to the public and in any case none could be offered to the Iraqi public in case they may be sold by them later on to outsiders.

As a result the government, in an effort to satisfy the BPC objection, issue a law on 20 February 1941 stipulating that no such shares held by the Iraqi public could change hands without the prior approval of the Ministry of Economy. Despite this the BPC continued to refuse the offer of any shares to the public. This should have been realised by the government at the time of signing the concession agreement since it was clear that this article was only meant for cosmetic purposes only.

10 - THE STATUS OF THE IRAQI DIRECTOR

All three concession agreements of the IPC, MPC and BPC had given the Iraqi government the right to appoint an Iraqi director to their boards of directors. However soon differences became clear regarding the role of such a director. While the Iraqi government demanded its director to be involved fully in the companies affairs the companies regarded him as an outside director and hence denied him the participation in the policy making decisions of the companies. As a result he was only invited to attend Board meetings dealing with routine matters and as such was kept in the dark of the serious issues affecting the major decisions. To add to the ineffectiveness of the director the government usually appointed the Ambassador or the first secretary in the Iraqi embassy in London for this post. Since such people had very limited knowledge of the terms and condition of the concessions agreements or of the oil industry and since they were frequently replaced, it was difficult to expect them to be effective in their roles as directors of such huge organisation of very complex oil operations.

Though, as we shall see the IPC Group agreed to the appointment of a second director in the revised agreement of 1952, no real change seems to have affected the stance of the IPC Group regarding the real roles of such directors.

11 - THE TRAINING OF IRAQIS IN THE OIL INDUSTRY

The Iraqi government had complained repeatedly regarding the neglect of proper training for the Iraqis employee of the IPC. It was much easier and cheaper for the IPC to employ Indians for the lower administration posts in the company despite the fact that such jobs could be performed by Iraqis with some basic training. The same thing applies to tradesmen such as mechanics, electricians, carpenters, masons and other artisans. Furthermore no serious effort was made by the company to train Iraqi college graduates to prepare them to fill some of the higher posts in drilling, engineering, operations, administration or finance. This problem was a source of continuous friction and was not addressed properly until its final inclusion in the final 1952 agreement.

12 - THE SLOW EXPANSION OF THE EXPORT OF CRUDE OIL

The export capacity of the IPC had remained stagnant during the 1930s and most of the 1940s, restricted basically by the four million tons per year capacity of the two 12 inch diameter pipelines to Haifa and Tripoli.

The proposed expansion of the pipelines capacity by the construction of the two 16 inch pipelines to Haifa and Tripoli in the late 1940s did little to enhance the export capacity after the closure of the 12 inch diameter and the abandonment of the new 16 inch diameter pipelines to Haifa in 1948. As a result the total crude oil export capacity of Iraq at the end of the 1940s stood at some 6.5 million tons per year which was much lower than the export capacity of some of the late comers such as Saudi Arabia. The reason for this is the cumbersome structure and conflicting interests of the shareholders of the IPC. We have seen that while the British, American and Dutch shareholders had plenty of oil and wanted to hold the Iraqi oil in reserve the French and Gulbenkian did not have such reserves and as a result they pressed for a fast expansion of Iraq's crude export capacity.

This problem was not resolved until after the abandonment of the Red-Line Agreement and its Self Denying Clause in the late 1940s as we shall soon see.

Meanwhile the repeated demands by the Iraqi government for the IPC to expand the export capacity fell on the deaf ears of the company until the late 1940s which resulted in the commissioning of the 16 inch diameter pipeline to Tripoli. This as we have seen did little to satisfy the government demands after the closure of the operating 12 inch pipeline and the abandonment of the new 16 inch diameter pipeline to Haifa.

However as a result of the ceaseless insistence of the government and in order to entice the French and Gulbenkian to abandon the Red-Line Agreement, it was decided to expand the export capacity dramatically through the construction of the 30/32 inch diameter pipeline to Banias in the early 1952 which raised the country's crude oil export capacity from the meagre 6.5 million tons per year to the staggering level of 28 million tons per year.

13 - THE 50/50 PROFIT SHARING

While the Iraqi government and the IPC Group were busy discussing their various differences, the Saudi Government and Aramco were also busy discussing and negotiating royalties and revenues which resulted in their famous agreement of the equal sharing of profits. The agreement was reached in December 1950 but was considered to be valid with effect from January 1950 and provided a profit sharing in the form of a fifty per cent tax. The so called 50/50 agreement was advantageous to both the Saudi government and Aramco, which is an American registered corporation and as such subject to the United States income tax laws. By a special arrangement, the United States Treasury had agreed to permit Aramco to deduct from its United States income tax liability all income taxes paid to the Saudi government. This in effect allowed the company to transfer the income tax that it would have paid to the United States Treasury to the Saudi government at no cost to itself.

In the meantime the agreement became known to the Iraqi government and as a result it demanded from the IPC the application of the 50/50 profit sharing arrangement. However the IPC shareholders were in a very different fiscal position than Aramco and needed a similar tax arrangement from their governments to be able to adopt the 50/50 profit sharing arrangement. Extensive negotiations were conducted between the shareholders themselves and between them and their governments. These negotiations succeeded in persuading the British,French and Dutch governments to accept a similar arrangement of deduction of tax as that of the United States. This finally allowed the IPC to offer Iraq a 50/50 profit sharing arrangement as that of Saudi Arabia.

Since the IPC delivered its crude oil to the shareholders and as a result made no profit itself, it was necessary to create a system by which profits could be attributed to the production of crude oil. Hence it was decided to adopt the "posted prices", a procedure already agreed between the Saudi government and Aramco by which the company published the price at which it would offer specified crude oils for sale from specified export terminals.

In the case of Iraq, the posted prices were the free on board (f.o.b) at terminals to be determined with reference to free market prices for individual commercial sales of full cargos according to a procedure agreed between the government and the company. Since these posted prices are in effect set by the IPC shareholding companies, this resulted in major disputes between the Producing Countries and the oil companies as we shall see later on.

THE DEMISE OF THE RED-LINE AGREEMENT

It is of interest to see that both American partners in the IPC, Standard Oil of New Jersey and Standard Oil of New York that had signed the Red-Line Agreement began to regret that soon after. Oil was discovered in large quantities in Saudi Arabia by other American companies and both these companies wanted to join in the bonanza but were unable to do so by the Self Denying clause of their Agreement.

It is also ironic to notice that the American government, having insistently demanded in the 1920s, the adoption of the Open Door Policy to get the American companies into Iraq, had no intention soon after of opening the Door to Saudi Arabia for the others non American companies including those of their allies the British and the French.

In the meantime the demand of the American partners in the IPC to leave the Red-Line Agreement was met with a strong reaction from the French company CFP and Gulbenkian which escalated as time went on in the initiation of a legal action by Gulbenkian.

This impasse was followed by high level negotiations involving the US State Department, the British government as well as all the IPC shareholders that continued over a period of more than two years from 1946 to 1948.

They all wanted to resolve this embarrassing issue amicably out of courts to avoid parading their monopolistic policy in public. The Americans were worried about the deteriorating diplomatic relations with France, while the British though unhappy about the whole affair did not want to take strong stance since it was thought that they were appeased by the Americans by giving them interest in Kuwait.

A new Group Agreement was finally reached between the shareholders of the IPC in November 1948. The agreement revoked the Red-Line Agreement and Self Denying Clause and removed the restriction preventing the exploration and operation of the individual shareholders inside the Red-Line area, thus both American Companies, the Standard Oil of New Jersey, Exxon, and Standard oil of New York Mobil, became free to enter Aramco and ensure that the Saudi oil remains in the hands of the Americans alone. The British kept their overriding royalty in the IPC; and both the French and Gulbenkian were assured of securing extra oil through the expansion of the IPC output through the construction of the two new 16 inch diameter pipelines to Haifa and Tripoli and the 30/32 inch diameter pipeline to Banias soon after. This expansion of output also had the additional advantage of attempting to satisfy Iraq's continuous demand for higher throughput to match those of other major producing countries even though it did not go far enough to satisfy the Iraqi demands completely.

THE TERMS OF THE 1952 AGREEMENT BETWEEN THE IRAQI GOVERNMENT AND THE IPC GROUP

The negotiations, between the government and the IPC Group that had started soon after the end of the Second World War became more frequent and intensified from the second half of 1948 onwards. Several such high level negotiations took place in Baghdad and in London and all were conducted by Ministerial Committees and led sometimes by the Prime Minister of Iraq at the time. These negotiations covered all the issues listed above and many others of lesser importance. They were heatedly debated at times with the negotiations reaching impasse at other times and near breaking point at others. Meanwhile they continued to receive the attention, guidance and encouragement of the British and to a lesser extent the United States governments. They were also met with suspicion and at times with hostility by the Iraqi opposition parties, the national press and the public at large.

It must be highlighted that during this period another serious dispute and confrontation were taking place between the Iranian government and the oil companies which ended in the nationalisation of the Iranian oil industry on 15 March 1951.As a result, the Iraqi opposition parties and the public opinion were demanding similar steps to those taken by the Iranian government in nationalising the oil industry in Iraq which put both the government and IPC Group on the defensive. As a result of such pressure, the government was forced to adopt a much harder stance in its negotiations with the companies by insisting on the acceptance of its demands which forced the companies at the same time to adopt a more conciliatory stance in the negotiations.

Several proposals and counter proposals had been presented by both sides over the period and it was not until July 1951 that the main terms of a draft agreement had been accepted in principle by both parties. The draft agreement was presented by the IPC Group to the Iraqi government on 20 July 1951 and was approved in principle by the Cabinet on 13 August pending the presentation of the agreement in its final form for a further approval before referring it to the Parliament.

The Agreement in essence is an amendment to the terms of the IPC, MPC and BPC concession agreements and included the following main terms:-

- The agreement covers the concessions of the Iraq Petroleum Company, the Mosul Petroleum Company and the Basra Petroleum Company.

- That the principle of the fifty/fifty profit sharing shall apply to the three companies.

- That part of the fifty per cent profit to be paid by 25% crude oil of the IPC and MPC and 331/3% of the BPC crude oil production.

- The remaining part of the profit to be made as income tax.

- That the combined crude oil production by the IPC and MPC shall be no less than 22 million tons per year by 1954.

- That the crude oil production by the BPC shall be no less than 8 million tons per year by 1955.

- That the combined Iraqi revenue from the three companies shall be no less than 20 million Iraqi Dinars during each of 1953 and 1954, and no less than 25 million Iraqi Dinars during the year of 1955.

- That should any of Iraq's neighbours receives in the future higher revenues per ton of oil produced than Iraq received, then Iraq reserves the right to claim for such higher revenues.

- That the Companies will pay Iraq five million Iraqi Dinars in settlement of all the outstanding disputes between the government and the three companies.

- That the government has the right to appoint a second Iraqi director to join the IPC Group board of directors.

- The IPC Group agrees to send 50 Iraqi students every year on scholarship to the United Kingdom for higher education at its own expense with a total number of students not exceeding 250 at any one time

- That the IPC Group agrees to establish a training centre in Kirkuk and to accelerate the training of their staff and employees.

- That the IPC Group shall not engage any foreign staff for working in the country without informing the Ministry of Economy beforehand.

- That the terms of the agreement are to be implemented with effect from 1 January 1951.

- That the agreement shall be approved by the Iraqi parliament not later than 1 March 1952.

A committee was formed on 1 September 1951 headed by the Prime Minister Nuri al-Said, the Minister of Economy, Abdul Majeed Mahmoud, and Nadim al-Pachachi, the director general of the economic affairs to follow-up the finalisation of the Agreement with the IPC Group in London. The committee engaged the law firm of Richard Butler & Company to help the committee with its task. Though the Prime Minster returned to Iraq at the beginning of October the committee continued its work in finalising the terms of the Agreement which was achieved on 25 October 1951.

A new committee was then formed on the same day from two members of the Iraqi High Court Antowan Shammas and Abdul Jabbar al-Tarkali and the head of the Legislation Department George Georgi to check the final draft of the Agreement.

The final Agreement was then approved towards the end of January by both the Minister of Economy and the IPC Group representative. The Cabinet subsequently approved the Agreement on 31 January 1952 and authorised the Minister of Economy to sign it.

Prince Abdul Ilah & Prime Minister Nuri al-Said

The Agreement was at long last signed on 3 February by the Minister of Economy Abdul Majeed Mahmoud on behalf of the Iraqi government and H. S. Gibson on behalf of the three companies the IPC, the MPC and the BPC.

The Agreement was then sent on 9 February to the parliament for approval. The parliament decided to refer the Agreement to the Economic Affairs Committee to study it and present its report. This was faced with opposition from the members of al-Istiqlal party who proposed referring it to a joint committee from the Ministries of Economy and Finance. This proposal was not adopted and as a result five members of the Istiqlal party submitted their resignation from the parliament on 11 February.

The Agreement was approved by the Economic Affairs Committee, then debated and approved by the parliament on 14 February. It was finally sent to the Upper House when it was debated and approved on 17 February 1952.

The sanction of the Agreement was met with severe criticisms from all the opposition parties, the various trade unions, the university students and the general public which called for a general strike as a sign of protest of what they considered as an unfair agreement. As a result a general strike was observed in Baghdad and most of the large cities on 29 February 1952 which resulted in clashes between the demonstrators and the security forces.

I was a youth at that time and remember taking part in the demonstrations though I was not sure what the whole thing was exactly about except that I knew it would be better for the county to control its own oil resources! However, the question of whether Iraq was able to manage the complex operations of an oil industry which I knew very little about, or not was beside the point to my inexperienced mind at that time and to the vast majority of the other demonstrators for that matter.

New Disputes Between 1953-1958

Different interpretations of the terms of the 1952 concession agreement began to appear soon after its approval as summarised hereunder.

THE 1955 AUDITORS REPORT

The 50/50 profit sharing agreement of 1952 defined the elements of the production costs as follows:-

- Operating and management costs.
- Fixed assets with an annual depreciation rate of 10%.
- Capital expenditures with an annual depreciation rate of 5%.
- A Fixed Production Cost of 23.0 shillings per ton for 1951, 17.6 shillings for 1953 and 13.0 shillings for the following years were agreed for administrative convenience.

It was stipulated that the Actual Costs during any year would apply if they differed from the Fixed Costs by more than 10% during such a year.

As a result, the Fixed Costs of 13.0 shillings per ton was adopted by the IPC for the years 1953, 1954 and 1955, on the basis that the Actual Costs and the Fixed Costs during these three years did not differ by more than the agreed 10%.

However the Government estimated that the Actual Costs per ton during this period must have fallen by more than 10% as a result of the sudden increase of production resulting from the completion of the 30/32 inch diameter pipeline to Banias in 1952.

The government informed the IPC of its doubts regarding this issue as well as many others and as a result appointed the British auditors Hodgson and Harris to examine the IPC's accounts and report their findings. The Auditors presented their report which highlighted the following:-

1. The Recovery of the Dead Rent

    The auditors reported that the Dead Rents had been treated as capital expenditure and as such they have been recovered by the IPC Group at an annual rate of 5%. They advised that this practice is not in accordance with the terms of the 1952 Concession Agreement and recommended the return of the relevant sums to the government. However they did point out that this did not apply to the IPC since no Dead Rent had been recovered after the date of the 1952 concession agreement.

    As for the BPC and MPC, they recommended that the companies should stop this practice and refund the recovered sums to the government.

    The Companies refused to do so and the dispute remained unsolved until the 1958 revolution.

2. The Expensing of the Exploration and Drilling Costs

    Again the Auditors reported that they had found that the IPC Group had been treating the Exploration and drilling costs as production costs and hence in effect recovering these costs during the same year.

    The government objected to this practice and demanded that such costs should be treated as Capital Costs and should be recovered in accordance with the terms of the concession agreement at the annual rate of 5% but the validity of such treatment was disputed by the IPC Group.

    The subject was then referred again to the auditors who advised that there is no single applicable rule for this and suggested the depreciation of the costs of a producing well over the number of years of its production life and the treatment of a dry well as production cost recoverable during that year.

3.   London Office Expenses

The IPC Group had their main offices in London which were shared between the IPC, BPC, MPC, QPC (Qatar Petroleum Company) and ADPC (Abu Dhabi Petroleum Company).

49.4% of the costs of these offices had been charged to the IPC, MPC and BPC and the government had asked the auditors to confirm that this represented a fair share. The auditors examined the accounts and were able to confirm that this indeed represented a fair percentage.

4.   Contributions and Advertisement Costs

The auditors had shown that the IPC had been charging the costs of contribution to different organisations, spending on advertisement, staff recreation etc both inside and outside Iraq and charging these expenses to the production costs. This was objected to by the government despite the fact that these costs were normal and quite small.

5.   Costs of the Students' Scholarships

In the 1952 Concession Agreement, the IPC Group had agreed to send 50 Iraqi students on Scholarship to the United Kingdom at its own expense with a total number of students not exceeding 250 at any one time. It had also agreed to establish a mutual committee to look after the affairs and welfare of these students.

The auditor's report showed that the costs of these scholarships had been included in the IPC Group's production costs.

The government demanded that these costs should be borne by the IPC Group as clearly stated in the Concession Agreement.

6.   Interest on Bank Loans

During the auditing of the IPC Group's accounts in 1957, it was discovered that the Group had been charging the interest on their loans to the production costs with effect from1 January 1955.

This was brought to the attention of the IPC Group and as a result the practice was suspended except in connection with the loans related to the employees Home Ownership Scheme.

OTHER DISPUTES

7.   Posted Prices

The Iraqi government revenue from the sale of its oil was based in the 1931 concession on the fixed royalty of four shillings per ton irrespective of the price at which this oil was sold on the international market and therefore there was no scope of disagreement on the issue of crude oil prices up to the 1952 concession agreement.

However, as a result of the fifty/fifty profit sharing agreements between the producing countries and the major oil companies, the oil producing governments became increasingly interested in the profit calculations and the basis for the pricing of their crude oils.

The 1952 agreement between the Iraqi government and the IPC Group had defined the "prevailing Prices" as the prices free on board (f.o.b.) at terminals to be determined with reference to free market prices for individual commercial sales of full cargos according to a procedure agreed between the company and the government, or by the use of "fair prices" fixed by agreement in the absence of such free market prices, alternatively they should be fixed by arbitration.

There were no independent free market prices at that time and the major oil companies came up in 1952 with the Posted Prices system at which they would offer their specified crude oils for sale at specified terminals and on such prices the calculations for the government's payments are then based. It was agreed that these posted prices for the different world crude oils would be published monthly.

However these posted prices were, in fact artificial since they were being fixed by the major international oil companies themselves and therefore were subject to their own judgement as to what is a fair price as well as to their unilateral decision as to when and by how much such prices to be revised. As a result of this the oil prices were kept deliberately low.

The Iraqi government realised the unfairness of the posted prices system and raised the issue with the IPC Group. The subject was discussed in depth and both sides signed a memorandum as an attachment to the 1952 Concession Agreement dated 24 March 1955 specifying in details the method of arriving at the "Prevailing Prices", "Crude Prices at the Iraqi Borders", "Crude Oil Custody Measurement" and "the conditions and prices for the 12.5% crude oil royalty "

Despite this the IPC Group continued to control the prices unilaterally and as a result decided to reduce the prices of the BPC by five cents per barrel which lasted from 2 February 1956 to 30 November 1956. There was no similar reduction of prices in the other Gulf crudes.

This was met by a strong objection from the government, requiring the BPC to prove that the reduction was made in accordance with the requirement of the terms of the 1952 Concession Agreement and the subsequent memorandum of 24 March 1955..

The BPC could not provide such proof and the government reserved its right to claim the entire outstanding amount. The BPC refused to do so and the issue remained unresolved until the 1958 revolution.

8. The Return of the Unexploited Territories

The subject of the relinquishment of the unexploited territories by the IPC Group, though raised verbally during the 1950s on more than one occasion by the Ministry of Economy, it was not until 21 June 1958 that the new Minister of Economy, Rushdi al-Chalabi, asked the IPC Group in writing to give up some of their territories.

As a result a meeting was held on 6 July 1958 between the government representatives headed by Rushdi al-Chalabi and those of the IPC Group headed by Herridge

The IPC Group informed the government of their willingness to relinquish such territories and their representatives were able to confirm to the government during their meeting on 6 July 1958 of this, pending the finalisation of the details of such territories. The negotiations continued until 13 July 1958 and the news of the negotiations was reported in the newspaper on 14 July, the day of the 1958 revolution.

9. The 2% Discount as Marketing Cost

The Memorandum dated 24 March 1955 had allowed a 2% discount in the exported crude oil prices to the IPC Group as marketing expenses. The purpose of such discount, as claimed by the IPC Group, was to encourage them to keep the Iraqi crude competitive in the international market and increase production and sales. The amount of such discount was to be kept under review from time to time in accordance with the prevailing market conditions.

This was an unnecessary discount since the IPC Group was not involved in the sale of the Iraqi crude oils, but in delivering it to the shareholders in the proportions of their shareholdings. These shareholders in turn would deliver this oil to their refineries and as such there is no marketing of the crude and therefore there should be no marketing expenses.

This discount was applied to the other Middle East oil producing countries and the governments were quick to realise this and wasted no time to try to put a stop to it with a demand for a refund of previous payments. The issue dragged on and was finally taken over by Organisation of the Oil Exporting Countries, OPEC which managed to reduce the discount to 1.0% initially and ultimately to half American Cent per barrel of oil with effect from 1 January 1962.

We have seen that the negotiations during the period 1952 to 1958 covered many disputes that resulted in resolving some of them only. However these negotiations were to become an important background to the subsequent and more intensified negotiations after the 1958 revolution as we shall see soon.

IRAQ'S DEVELOPMENT BOARD

The discovery of crude oil in commercial quantities in the giant Kirkuk field in 1927 and its subsequent development and export of oil in 1934 brought in the much needed revenues to the impoverished Iraqi economy.

The revenues increase modestly in the early 1930s and did not reach one million pounds until after the sustained export of oil in 1935. These revenues increased at modest rates during the next fourteen years before reaching three million pounds in 1949.

However, with the increase of the oil royalty from four to six Shillings per ton, the oil revenues more than doubled to £6.8 million in 1950.

These revenues more than doubled again to £15.1 million in 1951 as a result of the 50/50 profit sharing agreement between the government and the Iraq Petroleum Company. They then surged ahead to £40.8 million in 1952 as a result of the expansion of the crude oil export capacity after the completion of the 30/32 inch diameter pipeline to Banias

The progression continued during the following years due to the gradual expansion of the crude oil export capacity as a result of the subsequent development of the new oilfields such as Ain Zalah, Bai Hassan, and Jambur in northern Iraq and Zubair and Rumaila in the southern region. By 1958 the oil revenues had redoubled again to reach £84.6 million.

In anticipation of the higher oil revenues, the government had commissioned studies on how best to use these revenues in developing the country. One of the early reports is that of the Haigh Commission which had been presented in 1949 on the Control of the Rivers of Iraq and the Utilisation of their Waters. One of the main recommendations of the Haigh Commission Report was the building of the great storage reservoir in the Wadi Tharthar Depression to drain off the water of the Tigris and ensure the protection of Baghdad, since Baghdad and a number of towns and villages had been subjected to periodical devastation by floods over the centuries.

The other important report (The Economic Development of Iraq), of the Mission of the International Bank for Reconstruction and Development which had visited Iraq for nearly four months in 1951. This report confirmed the necessity of flood control, irrigation, and drainage and recommended the allocation of about one third of its proposed development expenditure to these items. It allocated the remaining for the development and reforming of the agricultural system, the improvement of housing and community facilities, health, education, teacher's training and other community related requirements.

The government was aware of the huge task of such a development programme and decided in 1951 to establish the famous independent Development Board.

The idea behind the establishment of such an independent board was to protect it from political pressures and interference and render it independent and immure from the effects of the frequent change of governments.

The Board consisted of eight members, two of whom are the Prime Minister and the Minister of Finance who would maintain liaison with the cabinet and other ministers in general. The other six members, three of whom were to be Experts, were to be appointed for a term of five years.

The Board was charged with preparing and executing a "general economic and financial plan for the development of the resources of Iraq and the raising of the standard of living of her people".

The Board was allocated the total oil revenues as its budget for the year 1951. This was reduced to 70% of the total oil revenues from 1952 onwards, up to 1959 as a result of the dramatic increases in these revenues.

The Board was required to submit its programmes, reports and budgets to the Cabinet and the Parliament for approval otherwise it was independent in implementing these programmes.

The establishment and organisation of the Development Board as a non-political entity was a novelty at that time in Iraq and was widely approved by the public for its expected independence and freedom of action from the interference of the inefficient and red tape infested government establishments.

It was in 1953 that a decision was made to establish the Ministry of Development and make the Minister of Development a member of the Development Board. This was intended to make the Minister answerable to parliament for the Boards decisions and as such insulate the other members of the Board from political pressures. This however imposed some restrictions on the full freedom of the Board's actions.

The impressive sum of 229 million Iraqi Dinars was spent by the Board during the period 1951-1958 on capital investment projects. About one third of this expenditure had gone into the field of agriculture, primarily on dams, barrages and other large flood control and irrigation projects, with the like of Dokan and Darbandikhan dams as fine examples.

Over 50% of that sum was spent on Buildings and Communications. This covered the construction of new housing schemes, major roads, government offices, hospitals, clinics, schools, colleges, water supply and power stations to provide the ever increasing consumption needs.

The remaining sum was spent on industry. New cement and brick factories were constructed to cover the needs of the construction boom. Other modern industries such as textile, furniture, metal, leather goods as well as food, sugar and beverages were established to satisfy the local market. A bitumen refinery was constructed in the Qaiyarah field to provide the boom in the construction of roads while the Daura oil refinery was constructed in Baghdad to satisfy the ever increasing consumption of petroleum products.

Much has been written about the achievements and failures of the Development Board. However, it seems that the Development Board was most successful in the field of construction projects, most notably those for irrigation, flood control and communications while it was least successful in the field of industry.

Furthermore, and in spite of whatever had been said about how the Board could have managed the expenditure of the oil revenues in a more effective and efficient way, it could not be denied that many of its long term projects are still in existence and operating successfully until now.

This was money well spent compared with the enormous revenues which were wasted in later years on weapons and destructive wars.

IPC'S INDUSTRIAL RELATIONS

Gawer Baghi Massacre

No real trade union movement existed in the oil industry in Iraq in the 1920s and 1930s, since most of the middle and higher technical and clerical jobs in the Iraq Petroleum Company were held by expatriates. The Iraqi employees were mainly semi skilled or unskilled labourers who had basic school education if any at all and as such little or no knowledge or experience of trade union activities.

However by the 1940s more Iraqi school leavers began to join the Iraq Petroleum company replacing the lower and middle clerical, technical and artisan expatriates.

The spread of schools, radio broadcasting and the newspapers in the 1940s helped to further the awareness and understanding of the trade union movements in other parts of the world between the increasing literate Iraqi labour forces including those in the employment of the Iraq Petroleum Company in Kirkuk and the pipelines pump stations.

As a result an attempt was made in 1945 to establish a union for the oil workers in Kirkuk was met with objection from the Iraq Petroleum Company which instead permitted the formation of a toothless "Internal Labour Committee" in June 1946 under the watchful eye of one of its expatriate staff. This was not made possible until after the expulsion of a number of "trouble makers and undesirable persons" from the company. It is not clear as how the members of this committee were chosen.

All the same, some of the remaining "trouble makers and undesirable persons" succeeded in occupying five of the fifteen seats reserved for the oil workers.

These five immediately started to brand the committee as an imperialist tool in the hand of the IPC aimed at crippling the struggle of the workers and depriving them from their basic rights.

Soon after ,a meeting of some 500 workers, who have been suffering, as millions of other Iraqi citizens, from low wages, high level of inflation and shortage of necessities during and after the Second World War, was held in the evening of 13 June 1946. It was not very long before they agreed to support a list of demands including the following:-

1. The recognition of their right to form an independent union of their own.

2. The increase of the minimum basic daily wage from 80 to 250 fils, bearing in mind that 1,000 flls = I Dinar = £1.

3. The setting of an end to the company's practice of arbitrary and mass dismissal of its workers.

4. The introduction of a sickness, disability and old age pension scheme for the company workers.

The Iraq Petroleum Company became aware of the meeting and the workers excessive demands and as a result agreed on 1 July to increase the" High-Cost of Living Allowances" of the different grades of workers between 50 and 100 fils per day. However the company was adamant in rejecting any increase in the daily basic rates of pay as well as any of the other lesser benefits demanded by the workers.

This did not meet with the workers expectations and as a result a Higher Strike Committee as well as several other subcommittees representing the different trades and middle grade employees within the company were formed to coordinate the activities between themselves and all the workers and employees of the company.

Events were moving fast and a decision was made by the committees on 3 July to start a strike. The vast majority of the labour force and employees have been made aware of the recent events and had agreed in principle with the decision to go on strike.

It was estimated that about 5,000 people who represented most of the Company's Iraqi labour force and employees came out on strike on 4 July 1946 marching through the streets of Kirkuk holding the banners bearing their demands.

The strikers ended their march by holding a rally in the garden of Gawer Baghi at the outskirts of Kirkuk. From there on the strikers continued to assemble daily at Gawer Baghi chanting their slogans and listening to speeches demanding their rights.

In the meantime the management of the IPC wanted, out of regard for the company's prestige that the strikers should first return to work before their demands and grievances could be considered.

Meanwhile the government in Baghdad was uneasy about the continuing of the strike since it could seriously affect the flow of oil and subsequently the country's revenues. Hence commands were sent from Baghdad to the Governor of Kirkuk urging him to take the necessary measures to end the strike, by force if necessary. The Governor reported that the strikers and their rallies have been peaceful and have not resulted in any public disturbances in the city and did not deem it advisable to resort to force. By this he seemed to be intimating that the demands of the workers were not so unreasonable. The Governor was quickly replaced.

With the new governor in office, events soon took an ugly turn and on 12 July, mounted policemen appeared on the scene of the usual gathering of the strikers at Gawer Bhaghi. An order was given to the crowd to disperse and when this was ignored by the strikers the police charged from three sides into the crowd. At first they struck at heads and shoulders with their cudgels, trampling several under the hooves of their horses. As the crowd began to scatter the police started shooting indiscriminately at them. The result of this massacre was ten dead and twenty seven wounded. It became clear from the court proceedings later on that the dead were shot mainly from behind as they were running away.

As the news of the massacre spread, a wave of indignation ran through the country blaming the authorities and the IPC for such cruelty and heavy handedness, while the authorities went on the defensive and tried to put the blame on the "agitators and malicious elements".

The company too was put on the defensive and as a result announced its consolatory and belated decision to increase the minimum basic daily wage from 80 to 140 fils and raised the total minimum daily wage from 200 to 310 fils.

Thus the strike ended in such a tragic way and the labour force went back to work on 16 July 1946. They were defeated but not broken. They also started to reflect on the events that had shown them how the authorities who were supposed to support them against the "imperialist greedy oil company" had betrayed them and turned against them in such a brutal way.

There must have been sobering reflective thoughts by the IPC management as well about the unfortunate events and on ways of avoiding such ugly scenes in the future especially since the company's image in the Iraqi public eyes has been dragged in the mud.

THE AMAZING MARCH FROM K-3 PUMP STATION TO BAGHDAD

K-3 pump station near the town of Hadaitha on the western bank of the River Euphrates is the largest of the three other pump stations in Iraq, K-1, K-2 and T-1. The large number of workers and employees in the station had followed the events of the strike in Kirkuk and had been shocked by what had happened to their fellow workers and employees. They were also not impressed by the company's consolatory offer to raise the wages and wanted to improve their pay and working conditions in their remote station.

Hence it was during the early days of April 1948 that the two committees, one representing the workers and other representing the technical and clerical employees were considering the possibility of a strike action in support of their demand for better wages and working conditions. This was followed by a mass gathering held in the evening of 22 April outside K-3 station during which a motion was passed to go on strike.

 The strike began the day after and several subcommittees were hastily formed to supervise and coordinate the activities for ensuring the success of the strike. Members of these committees were posted throughout the station to ensure order, guards were posted to ensure the safety of assets and personal belonging and pickets were posted at the station gate to check the identities and materials entering or leaving the station.

The company had no idea of what was going on until the evening of 22 April and hence was taken by a complete surprise. There was little that the company could do except to accuse the strikers of acting unilaterally and as such denounced the strike as a breach of the law.

As the strike continued unabated, the company conceded a number of minor points but was adamant in rejecting the strikers claim for a 25 to 40 per cent increase in wages.

During this period the authorities had been patient and did not want to repeat the heavy handedness of the Gawer Baghi events which were still fresh in everybody's mind. However they were also uneasy about letting the strike continue for a long time since it could affect the export of oil and hence the country's revenues.

They finally decided to act decisively but even-handedly and on 5 May a strong mobile police force, supported by armoured vehicles arrived at the station. Machine guns were set up quickly in strategic points throughout the station including the workers living quarters and soon took full control of the station. Both the police and the strikers acted with restraint avoiding any provocation that may result in violence.

A situation of stalemate was created and since this could not be allowed to go on for long, the authorities took the initiative on 7 May by stopping the company's food ration of the workers and employees at first and followed it by cutting their electric and water supplies. This made the living conditions for strikers and the families living in the station very difficult indeed.

Thus the strikers were faced with the difficult choice of calling the strike off or continue to persevere under the intolerable conditions they have found themselves in. They finally came up with the bright face saving idea of taking their case to the public at large by marching to Baghdad which is lays some 250 kilometres away.

Thus they set out at sunrise on 12 May marching out of the station in a long orderly column carrying their huge banner "We the Oil Workers Have Come to Claim our Violated Rights". As the sun started to rise higher and the heat of the midday intensified all were very tired and stopped after covering a distance of about 30 kilometres.

The news of their amazing march had spread quickly to the surrounding towns and as a result several lorries were donated by the nearby town of Hit to bring them to town. They arrived there to spend the night in mosques and public places which did little to relieve their aching bodies.

On 13 May they left Hit on foot after the authorities had made sure that no other means of transport was made available to them. Needless to say the journey was more tiring than that of the previous day.

To avoid the scorching heat of the mid day sun they decided to make the next leg of their march by night. This proved to be a complete fiasco since they could neither see their way nor what is around them in the darkness in a region known to have wild animals.

They were finally able to enter the city of Ramadi, in an organised procession, tired but holding their banner high and shouting their slogans with the welcoming and cheering crowds along the way. They left Ramadi triumphantly in donated lorries and as they approached the bridge leading into the town of Fallujah they fell into a carefully laid police trap.

They were taken by a complete surprise and offered no resistance. Most of the leaders were quickly arrested and the remaining crowd was allowed to scatter to find their way back home.

Thus the strike and the famous March of the oil workers and employees of K-3 station ended in a complete failure to be followed later on by a mass dismissal of the activists and their main supporters.

It seems that the two events of Gawer Baghi and K-3 station, had taught all concerned, the IPC, the workers and the authorities a good lesson.

The IPC realised the need of professional public relation advisers and as a result created an Industrial Relation Department to handle the delicate affairs of the oil workers union before they got out of hand.

The Union learnt about how to present their claims and grievances in a businesslike manner without the need to resort to strikes

The authorities regretted their shameful extreme use of force in handling a peaceful rally of fellow citizen strikers and started to act with restraint.

There is no doubt that differences continued to come to the surface between the Company and the Union during the following 25 years leading to the nationalisation of the company in 1972, but these were always resolved one way or another without resorting to strikes or violence.

4

THE 1958 REVOLUTION
GENERAL QASSIM'S REGIME

As we have seen, the relationship between the Iraqi Government and the IPC up to 1958, despite their many differences remained cordial and fairly smooth. The main disputes between them as we have seen revolved around the level of oil production, the payment in gold, the fifty/fifty profit sharing, the students scholarships, the employees training and other minor issues. Many were ironed out fairly amicably though not always to the Government's satisfaction. It must be remembered that the Iraqi Government was until then still under the influence of the British Government through their bilateral treaty.

All this was to change soon after the 14 July 1958 revolution and the overthrow of the monarchy and its government and the establishment of the republican regime under the leadership of General Abdul Karim Qassim.

General Abdul Karim Qassim

I was one of the fortunate students who had been sent to the United Kingdom on what came to be known as the Ministry of Oil scholarship scheme in the autumn of 1954. After finishing my Advance Level, I went in 1956, to Sheffield University, which had many Iraqi and Arab students. There were, in those days hundreds of students either on scholarships or privately studying at different universities all over the United Kingdom, the United States and other western countries. Most of us belonged to societies, most prominent of which were the Iraqi and the Arab Student Societies. I remember the euphoria that gripped us all on hearing the news of the revolution. There were no satellite T.V. stations in these days and the radio reception of the Arab broadcasting stations was faint and crackling which made them difficult to understand what was actually going on in the country. Nonetheless we were young and optimistic and sincerely believed that the revolution will be good for our people and we supported it wholeheartedly.

One of the first statements made by the new republican government was to appease the oil companies in the country by broadcasting the following announcement on the Iraqi radio station as early as 19 July 1958.

> "In view of the importance of oil to the world's economy, the government of the Iraqi Republic wishes to declare its commitment to see the continuation of the production and flow of oil to the markets where it is sold, because of its importance to national wealth as well as the national and international economic and industrial interests. The Government of the Iraqi Republic respects its commitments with the parties concerned. It has taken all necessary steps to protect the oil wells, pumping stations, pipelines and all other installations within the borders of the Iraqi Republic. In the meantime the government of the Iraqi Republic will work for the preservation of its sublime national interests, and hopes that those concerned will respond to its desire to see the continual existence of this vital resource for the good of the national economy as well as the international economy."

Thus the new regime was cautious during its early days in dealing with the Iraq, Mosul and the Basra Petroleum Companies though it had its own grievances in addition to some of the old lingering ones inherited from the old regime. The failure of the drastic action of Mossadeq in nationalising the oil industry in Iran only five years earlier in 1953 was still fresh in the minds and nationalisation though always talked about as the best way of getting rid of the "imperialistic" and influential foreign oil companies, it could not be entertained at that time for the lack of resources, technical knowhow and marketing limitation.

However the new revolutionary regime could not accept the current dominant power of the companies that dictated their unfair terms of the concessions to the country when it was under the direct influence of Britain.

The new regime was particularly critical of the fact that the IPC Group through their three concessions had created a virtual monopoly by controlling the oil exploration rights of the whole country leaving no room for competition from other companies that may be willing to sign oil concession agreements on more favourable terms.

At the same time the government was in need of additional revenue and started to press the companies for new revisions to their concession agreements and as a result the companies agreed to enter into negotiations.

NEW GOVERNMENT/IPC NEGOTIATIONS

Hence, the new Minister of Economy, Ibrahim Kubba, wasted no time preparing for new negotiations with the IPC Group by asking for the preparation of a comprehensive internal report giving details of the previous negotiations and a summary of the previous outstanding disputes with the IPC Group in addition to new claims that had arisen since then.

The first session of these negotiations took place on 20 August 1958 in the presence of Ibrahim Kubba, Mohammad Hadid, Adib al-Jadir and Ibrahim al-Alousi. The negotiations were cordial during which the government side asked the IPC representatives to submit the studies they had promised to present to the previous government as soon as possible to enable the negotiations to go ahead without delay. They also asked that the BPC should relinquish its rights in the country's offshore territories.

Many of the old outstanding disputes were also discussed during the subsequent sessions without tangible results after which the negotiations were adjourned on 29 June 1959.

The negotiations were resumed on 27 September of that year but were disrupted by the attempted assassination of General Qassim in October 1959.

By this time I had obtained my university degree and returned to Iraq in September 1959. I was in Mosul at the time of the attempted assassination and was planning to travel to Baghdad to apply for a job with the Iraq Petroleum Company through the Ministry of Oil since I had been on their scholarship. The assassination attempt resulted in absolute chaos in the country and a travel restriction was imposed between Mosul and Baghdad as well as most of the other major cities. I had to go to the central police headquarters in Mosul, which was in a chaotic state and crowded with people desperately applying to get their Travel Permits for Baghdad! I had to wait a few days before I got my precious permit.

The overnight train journey to Baghdad, which was about 380 kilometres, took the usual time of about ten or eleven hours. The train was crowded and made its usual several prolonged stops on the way. It was also full of ordinary and secret police checking passengers' identities and travel permits. The travel restrictions did not last for long and were lifted soon after. I had to make two or three similar trips to Baghdad presenting my application form and other necessary documents to the newly established Ministry of Oil. I was them referred to the Baghdad office of the IPC where I was finally   offered a job with the Mosul Petroleum Company and by the end of December 1959 I was proudly working in the oil field of Ain Zalah.

New negotiations were held on 20 September 1960 which were led this time by General Qassim himself who had in July 1959 established the Ministry of Oil to provide the necessary expertise during his determined effort to extract the country's overdue rights from the oil companies. In the final stages of the negotiations, Qassim was assisted by Dr. Talaat al-Shaibami, acting Minister of Oil, Mohammad Hadid, Minister of Finance and Abdul Latif al-Shawaf, Governor of the Central Bank. Dr. Shaibani was replaced later on by Mohammad Salman, the Minister of Oil.

The IPC team was headed by Fisher of Standard Oil of New Jersey, Stephens, Chairman of Shell Transport, as well as Herridge, Bird and Stewart from the IPC.

The government's attitude during these negotiations seems to have hardened and became more bitter and demanding. This could be attributed, firstly to the sudden reduction in the BPC production from 12 million to 8 million tons per year, the minimum required under the terms of the concession agreement, in retaliation for the steep increases in the Fao port dues and secondly to the reduction in the posted prices in August 1960 as will be explained later. However some cynical views go further to allege that General Qassim had his suspicions that the international oil companies had been involved in the attempt to assassinate him.

IPC Group Office Building - Baghdad, 1960s
Courtesy of IPC Society Newsletters

Further top-level intermittent negotiations took place over the following months until October 1961 without tangible results.

The issues raised by the government included unresolved claims raised by the previous governments as well as these brought up during the various sessions of negotiations. They were numerous and new ones kept creeping up over the course of the negotiations. The most important of these complex issues could be summarised as follows:

1. The reduction in the Posted Prices and the demand for compensation.
2. The reduction of the Basra Petroleum Company crude oil export against the raising of the port dues.
3. The demand for an increase in the country's production and export of crude oil.
4. The demand for a 20 % participation in the ownership of the companies.
5. The demand for an increase in the percentage of profit sharing.
6. The utilisation of the associated gases.
7. A priority for the Iraqi tankers.
8. The status of the two Iraqi Directors.
9. Training and replacement of the foreign staff by Iraqis.

10. The expensing of the exploration and drilling costs

11. The recovery of the Dead Rents.

12. London Office expenses.

13. Contributions and Advertisement.

14. Interest on Bank Loans.

15. The 2% Discount as Marketing Costs.

16. Convertible Currency.

17. The return of the unexploited territories.

1 - THE REDUCTION IN THE POSTED PRICES AND THE DEMAND FOR COMPENSATION

As a result of the fifty/fifty profit sharing agreements between the producing countries and the major oil companies, the oil producing governments became increasingly interested in the profit calculations and the basis for the pricing of their crude oils. The oil companies came up in 1952 with the Posted Prices system at which they would offer their specified crude oils for sale at specified terminals and on such prices the calculations for the government's payments are then based. It was agreed that these posted prices for the different world crude oils would be published monthly. However these posted prices were, in fact artificial since they were being fixed by the major international oil companies themselves and therefore were subject to their own judgement as to what is a fair price as well as to their unilateral decision as to when and by how much such prices to be revised.

It was in February 1959 that the major oil companies decided to reduce their posted prices in the Middle East, a decision that was hotly disputed by the producing countries. In the case of Iraq this resulted in reducing the posted price of the Kirkuk crude at Tripoli from $2.51 in 1958 to $2.33 per barrel and that of the Basra crude at Foa from $1.98 to $1.82 per barrel. Iraq was in need of additional revenues after the revolution and this large reduction of more than seven per cent in her oil revenues was the last thing the government expected and hence it was met with protests which added to the uneasy atmosphere of the negotiations.

However when a second reduction was announced in August 1960, which resulted in reducing the posted price of the Kirkuk crude at Tripoli from

$$2.33 to $2.28 per barrel and that of the Basra crude at Foa from $1.82 to $1.78 per barrel it was met with disbelief and stronger protests from the Iraqi government as well as from the other governments of the other oil producing countries in the Middle East.

These unilateral actions by the companies, which resulted in the drastic reduction of Iraq's revenues of more than nine per cent over the two years period, came at a time when the Iraqi government was looking for additional revenues from its crude oil exports and added to the bitter and belligerent mood of the government against the IPC and BPC.

The IPC Group had argued that they had no hand in determining the posted prices since they were only operating companies and that these prices, were fixed by the major international oil companies. This argument was completely flawed and was rejected by the Iraqi government as well as by other oil producing governments since these international oil companies themselves were the owners of the operating companies such as the IPC and BPC. Furthermore, since these two companies were taking their instruction and guidance during their negations with the Iraqi government from some of these very international companies, they could not consider themselves as having no hand in fixing the posted prices.

In the meantime the international companies that set these posted prices, and, we must remember that four of them are the main shareholders of the IPC and BPC attributed the reduction in the posted prices to a glut of oil on the international markets. This they claimed had resulted in fierce competition between themselves in the refining and the marketing of their petroleum products which had resulted in losses and therefore they considered it necessary to reduce the posted prices. This explanation was rejected by Iraq and the oil producing countries. They countered by saying that the losses claimed by the companies occurred in other countries due to their greedy competition and hence their failure to maintain the product prices at some reasonable levels. They also claimed that other parts of these losses must also be blamed on the companies for their high costs of their downstream business which had nothing to do with the producing countries and as a result considered it unfair that these loses were in effect being transferred to them through the reduction in their posted prices.

As a result Iraq demanded that the total reduction in her revenues over the past period of time which resulted from the unilateral action of the IPC, MPC and BPC parent international companies in reducing the posted prices must be paid back to her.

The birth of the Organisation of Petroleum Exporting Countries, OPEC

This dispute had demonstrated the vulnerability of the oil producing countries and the dependency of their revenues on the unilateral decisions of the international oil companies. It had also shown the arrogance and strength of these few international companies in controlling and harming the economies and development of so many countries.

In the meantime, Venezuela had been proposing some sort of organisation which would encompass all the oil producing countries to counterbalance the monopolistic domination of the few international oil companies on the world crude oil market, she had not been able to persuade enough of them to come together to a conference to officially discuss this issue.

However it was these successive reductions in the posted prices and their catastrophic effects on the revenues of the producing countries that had finally brought home the necessity for the adoption of a collective bargaining power similar to that of the international companies.

Hence it was Iraq that was locking horns with these international companies at that time that took the initiative in calling the oil producing countries for a conference to discuss this important issue in Baghdad. As a result a conference was held during the period 10-14 September 1960 and attended by representatives from the governments of Saudi Arabia, Venezuela, Iran, Kuwait and Iraq, during which they succeeded in creating the famous Organisation of Petroleum Exporting Countries OPEC.

The official objective of OPEC was:

"To coordinate and unify petroleum policies among Member Countries, in order to secure fair and stable prices for petroleum producers; an efficient, economic and regular supply of petroleum to consuming nations; and a fair return on capital to those investing in the industry."

These five founding members were soon joined by many other member countries that enabled OPEC ultimately to succeed in wrestling the power from the international oil companies and become the world most powerful organisation in controlling the production, export and consequently the pricing of the world crude oils.

OPEC had its headquarters in Geneva for the first five years of its existence which was subsequently moved to Vienna on I September 1965.

2 - THE REDUCTION OF THE BASRA PETROLEUM COMPANY CRUDE OIL EXPORT AGAINST THE RAISING OF THE PORT DUES

The Iraqi Port Authority at the port of Fao was charging the Basra Petroleum Company (BPC) port dues at the rate of 23 fils per ton of crude oil, (one Iraqi Dinar = 1,000 fils). This rate was found to be much lower than rates charged at other ports in the Gulf and as a result the Iraqi dues were raised steeply in July 1960 as follows:-

Fils per ton	Quantity of oil exported
280	For the first 8.0 million tons
70	For the second 4.0 million tons
35	For the third 4.0 million tons
23	For the remaining quantities above 16.0. Million tons

The BPC protested angrily at these high dues, claiming that they were making the BPC crude oil expensive as compared with other crude oils in the Gulf and threatened to reduce its production and export as a result. When the dues were kept at the revised rates the BPC retaliated by reducing it current rate of export from some twelve million tons to eight million tons of crude oil per year which was the minimum rate specified under the terms of its concession agreement.

The Iraqi government reacted angrily at such drastic reduction in its crude oil export at the time when it was urging the company to increase it. It accused the company of using this as a mean of putting pressure on the government during its negotiations as well as an unacceptable interference in the government's sovereign right to impose taxes. As a result the company finally agreed to restore the crude export to previous levels subject to further discussions during the forthcoming negotiations though the BPC reserved its right in this respect.

This problem was not to last for long since the BPC had decided to build its own deep water terminal of Khor al-Amaya in the Gulf. The terminal was subsequently completed in 1964 and the problem was resolved permanently which allowed the BPC to abandon its crude oil lifting from the port of Fao and subsequently hand over its facilities there to the Iraqi Ports Authority.

The new deep water terminal also enabled the BPC to expand its production capacity and allowed much larger oil tankers to be able to load from there.

The oil export facilities at Fao were to be used again by Iraq National Oil Company during its first oil export in the early 1970s.

This at least resolved any further disputes regarding this issue from that date onwards.

3 - THE DEMAND FOR AN INCREASE IN THE COUNTRY'S PRODUCTION AND EXPORT OF CRUDE OIL

The demands by the government on both the IPC and BPC for an increase in the country's crude oil exports were becoming more intensified as the government was in need of additional revenues. The companies tried to appease the government by explaining that their ongoing expansion programme of their crude oil export capabilities was quite impressive. They pointed out that they had managed to increase their export capacity of the IPC fields from approximately 6.5 million tons of crude oil in 1949 to some 12.00 million tons in 1957 which was subsequently raised dramatically to some 27.00 million tons in 1959 through the construction of the 30/32 inch diameter pipeline to Banias.

The companies also explained that they had further plans to construct a second 30/32 inch diameter to Tripoli which would raise the export capacity to some 50 million tons per year within the follow few years.

4 - THE DEMAND FOR A 20 % PARTICIPATION IN THE OWNERSHIP OF THE COMPANIES

The subject of Iraq losing her right to participate in the ownership of the IPC which was given to her by the San Remo agreement and how she was deprived of that right when the country was under the mercy of the IPC through the mandate of the British government was never forgotten. It was felt by the new revolutionary regime that such injustice should not be allowed to continue and hence demanded the reinstitution of the government's right for the 20 %

participation in the companies. Furthermore it insisted that such participation should be based on the book value of the IPC, MPC and BPC assets.

The companies came up with the old hackneyed explanation by referring to the relevant clause in the 1931 concession agreement, which allowed participation for the Iraqis only if such offer of shares was made to the public and since no such offer has ever been made, it could not agree to the government demand.

When the government pointed out that the companies had been issuing new shares to their shareholders the companies were quick to repeat their old explanation that these were not offered to the public and hence none could be offered to the Iraqi public.

The government rejected this argument, and insisted on its right of participation in accordance with the San Remo agreement. The companies countered that they were not part of the San Remo agreement which was signed in 1925 while they obtained their concessions years later in 1931.

It was obvious, that no real compromise could be offered by the companies on this issue, since this would open the door for similar demands for participation by other producing countries which added to the government's frustration.

5 - THE DEMAND FOR AN INCREASE IN THE PERCENTAGE OF PROFIT SHARING

The government wanted to increase its share in the fifty / fifty arrangement since higher profit sharing crude oil concession agreements had been offered to some other neighbouring countries such as Iran, Kuwait and Saudi Arabia.

The companies argued that though this is true, no crude oil had been produced yet in any of these countries under such concession agreements that resulted in higher revenues per ton of oil paid by them. The companies pointed out further that in their view, this is due to the higher costs to be expected in some of these concessions.

In the meantime the Companies confirmed that they will be willing to consider the issue when any of the neighbouring countries receive such higher revenues for their oil than Iraq as required under the terms of their 1952 Agreement.

6 - THE UTILISATION OF THE ASSOCIATED GASES

Natural gas is produced in association with the production of crude oil, which is referred to as the Associated Gas. The amount of gas produced per one barrel of oil differs from one oilfield to another. This is referred to as the gas/oil ratio. These gases are normally rich in the valuable Liquid Petroleum Gas, LPG, and some condensates as well as the natural gas and other harmful gases such as hydrogen sulphide.

These associated gases could not be utilised during the early years of the oil industry and were normally flared. However demands for the LPG and natural gas had begun to grow, not only as clean fuel, but also for use in the chemical and fertilisers industry. As a result the government demanded that the companies should:-

• Make arrangement to utilise these associated gases, locally or for export.

• Offer them to the government for export or local consumption.

• Inject them back into the reservoirs which would help in maintaining their pressures and be ready when a market becomes available for their utilisation in the future.

• Pay for their flaring.

At the beginning the companies could not agree to any of these proposals. However when challenged by the government about such an unreasonable and unhelpful attitude, they suggested instead to make available to the government 150 million cubic feet per day of associated gas from Kirkuk's fields and 96 millions from the Basra fields pending further development, but they were not ready to give up their rights in the ownership of these gases. The companies suggested further that a mutual committee should be formed to examine the availability of further quantities in the future. This was considered by the government as a delaying tactic and was rejected.

When pressed further the companies finally suggested that the associated gases should be left to be available to both the government and the companies to be utilised by whoever could find a market for them first whether for the internal consumption or for export. However until such time, the companies refused any suggestion of paying for flaring them or giving up their right in their ownership in accordance with the terms of their concession.

This unreasonable attitude by the companies of refusing to make the associated gases, which they have been burning for years and had no plans for utilising them, or making them available to the government without conditions demonstrated the companies unreasonable attitude in their negotiations which added to the frustration of the government.

Hence no agreement could be reached on this important issue and the wasteful flaring of these valuable gases continued.

7 - A PRIORITY FOR THE IRAQI OIL TANKERS

The government wanted the companies to give priority in the shipment of Iraqi crude oil to its planned tanker fleet. The companies pointed out that their owners had their own fleets of tankers but did not reject the proposal outright since they saw this as a long term project that may not be realised for a long time to come.

8 - THE STATUS OF THE TWO IRAQI DIRECTORS

This was one of the longest outstanding disputes between the government and the companies and though the companies had accepted the appointment of two government directors as stipulated in the 1952 concession agreement, no real steps had been taken by the companies in implementing this in a meaningful manner.

The companies seem to have achieved this by arranging for all the important policy making decisions such as the budget, posted prices, planning and development to be taken by the representatives of the main shareholders, leaving the IPC Board of Directors in which the Iraqi directors can participate, to deal with the routine operational and administrative businesses. These usually included statistical information such as the number of wells drilled, total footage achieved, production figures, accounting reports and number of employees etc. which are normally sent to the Ministry of Oil regularly.

The companies argued that the Shareholders Board of Directors meetings deals not only with matters related to the IPC, MPC and BPC, but with those of the other sister companies such as Qatar and Abu Dhabi Petroleum Companies and as such could not be attended by the Iraqi representative and the issue remained unresolved

9 - TRAINING AND THE REPLACEMENT OF THE FOREIGN STAFF BY IRAQIS

During the 1930s and up to the middle of the 1950s, nearly all the managerial, engineering and higher technical positions in the Companies were held by expatriates. This was mainly due to the lack of suitably qualified Iraqis to fill in such positions.

As we have already have seen, the Scholarship programme adopted by the government and the IPC was very successful resulting in the return of early graduate students to join the IPC, MPC and BPC as well as the Ministry of Oil in the late 1950s.

Though the previous governments had urged the Companies to replace the expatriates by Iraqis, it was not until the establishment of the Ministry of Oil in 1959 that serious steps were taken to start planning to achieve this goal.

Serious negotiations took place between the Ministry of Oil and the IPC Group which resulted in the establishment of a mutual "Iraqiisation" committee to supervise the procedure for the appointment of Iraqi and expatriate employees. The procedure involved advertising in the local newspapers for vacancies to see if suitable Iraqi candidates are available before engaging expatriates.

It was also agreed to set up an intensive on the job training for the new Iraqi university graduates and a timetable for the replacement of the expatriate staff. This was one of the government points of view that was accepted without much fuss by the companies and which proved to be of a great benefit to both parties.

An intensive management training programme was also drawn up by the IPC Group themselves which was conducted by an outside Management Training Consultant to hold the following management training courses.

1. Staff Supervisory Courses for the new university graduate recruits which were held in Kirkuk and Basra.

   These condensed courses were designed to increase the knowledge of the candidates of the Company's organisation, the complexity of the Oil Industry and the responsibilities of the supervisor

2. Staff Development Courses for members of the staff who are earmarked for senior technical and administrative posts. These courses were residential and were usually held in one of the hotels in Baghdad.

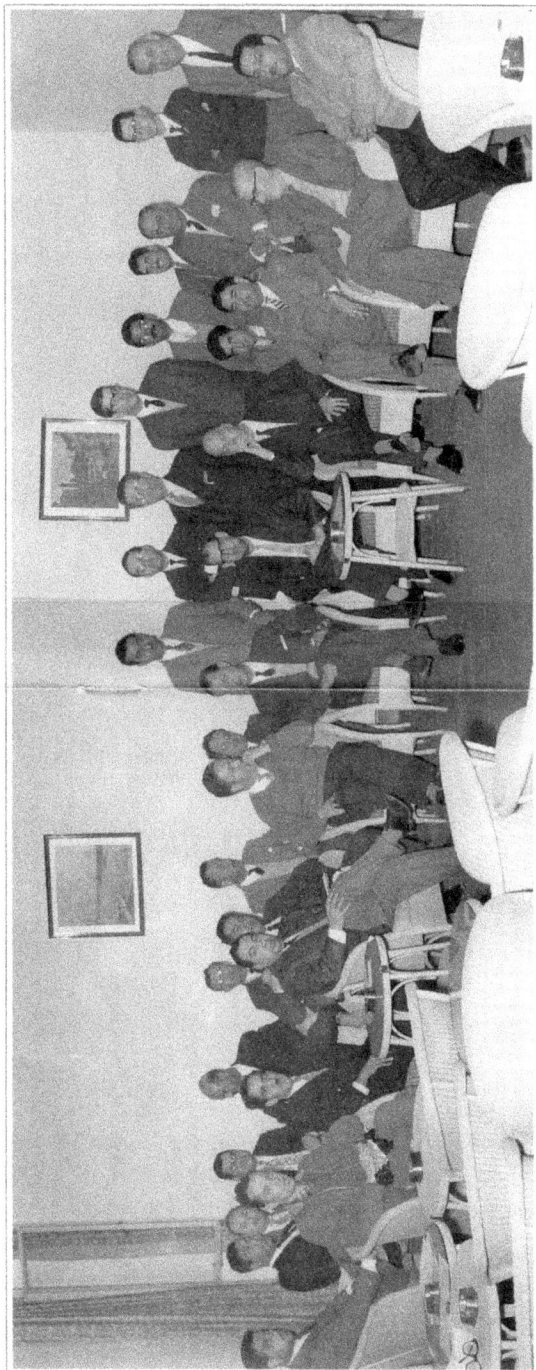

Dr. Harry Shearring the Management Training Consultant who was closely associated with the company in the 60's and 70's produced this photograph which will certainly stir lots of memories among those who were in Iraq at that time.

Staff Supervisory Training Courses Follow-up Session (10th January, 1962)

Sitting from left to right (first row)

Husam Arif, *Electrical Engineering* k-3 - Adnan Hamid Alkindi, *Process* - John Takavorian, *Staff* - G. R. McGeachie - G. Strobos - J. W. Macnab - Dr. H. A. Shearring - Fadhalalla Mohd, Hussain, *Production* - Karim Mohammed, *Estates & Commissariat* - J. Taylor - Adil Mohd, Saleh, *Production*.

Sitting from left to right (second row)

Khalid Amin Haidari, *Medical* - Faik Mohd. A. Aziz, *Elect Engineering* - Ah Abdul Razzaq Al-Dhahir, *Plant Survey* - Maurice Porter, *Estates & Commissariat* - Mohammed Saleh Qassab, *Estates & Commissariat* - L. E. Harrison - Hussam Aldhahi Dhahi, *M.P.C.* - P. J. Bawcutt - A. Ainscough.

Standing from left to right

Shakir Anani, *Mech. Engineering* - Awiya Karam, *Drilling* - Bulus Salman, *P.D.D.* - Sa'adoon Ibrahim Hilmi, *Employment* - Naji Muzher Abdul Rahman, *Communications* - Abdul Hamid Sadik, *Communications* - Youash Camber Iskender, *Geological* - Ala'a Kadhim Al-Khateeb, *Pet. Engineering* - Brimo Abraham, *Process.*

21

Courtesy of IPC Society Newsletters

20

3. Advance Development Courses for the grooming of the senior staff for higher managerial positions which were usually held in London.

The investment in this scholarship and training programme was one of the wisest decisions that were taken by the Iraqi government, since it enabled the country to nationalise the IPC with confidence in 1972. Many of these scholarship students went later on to fill some of the most senior posts in the Iraqi Government including that of the Ministry of Oil itself as well as many others ministries and directorates.

Staff Supervisory Course 1965

Photo Published in (Guide to Iraq Petroleum Company-Kirkuk-1966)

The Author First from the Right

Courtesy of IPC

At the same time an Industrial Training Centre equipped with all the necessary laboratories, workshops and other facilities was established in Kirkuk for the training of the company's much needed technicians and craftsmen. At the same time the Training Centre theoretical and practical training courses were augmented by on the job training. Some of the bright graduates were sent abroad to complete their studies at British colleges while others were sent for further training with some of the company's main equipment manufacturers and suppliers. This was one of the successful training programmes that were adopted by the IPC, which satisfied the company requirements, as well as these of the local markets with such excellent professional technicians and craftsmen.

From 1948 to October 1965, the Training Centre at Kirkuk trained and graduated (up to five-year courses) 729 technical, commercial, clerical and craft apprentices as well as skilled artisans for the various departments of the company.

10 - The expensing of the exploration and Drilling Costs

11 - The recovery of the Dead Rents.

12 - London Office expenses.

13 - Contributions and Advertisement.

14 - Interest on Bank Loans.

15 - The 2% Discount as Marketing Costs.

The above six items have already been discussed previously and though discussed again during these negotiations they remained unresolved.

16 - CONVERTIBLE CURRENCY

The terms of the 1952 concession agreement had stated that the oil revenues paid by the IPC Group to the government to be made in Pounds Sterling. The government had asked for this to be changed to convertible currencies to avoid any possible future depreciation in the value of the Pound Sterling.

The IPC Group could not agree to this claiming that the subject was beyond their authority since it is controlled by the British government.

17 - THE RETURN OF THE UNEXPLOITED TERRITORIES.

As we have seen this subject was discussed for the first time between the new regime and the IPC Group on 20 August 1958.

A subsequent meeting was held on 5 November 1958 during which the IPC Group's representatives presented the following proposal:-

1. Their readiness to relinquish with immediate effect 20% of their three concessions territories including the offshore areas.

2. A further 20% to be released after five years.

3. An additional 20% to be released after ten year.

The proposal was studied by the government which in turn put forward the following counter proposal during the meeting of 19 November 1958:-

1. The immediate release of 50% of the territories.

2. A further 20% after five years.

3. The remaining unexploited areas after ten years.

The IPC Group's representatives explained that it would be difficult for the companies to release 50% of their areas immediately and requested enough time to enable then to study the government proposal.

The Companies then presented a formal letter in which they qualified their previous proposal by explaining that the Companies themselves should have the right to determine the relinquished areas and that their commitments in the IPC and MPC concessions to be amalgamated

The negotiations were resumed on 13 December 1958 when the Representatives presented their amended proposal as follows:-

1. The immediate release of 25% of their territories.

2. The release of 25% after seven years.

This was rejected by the government which insisted on their proposal.

It was not until 21 June 1959 that the IPC Group sent an unofficial memorandum expressing their willingness for:-

- The immediate release of 50% of their territories.

- To consider the release of further areas after five years

The Companies then sent another unofficial memorandum dated 9 July 1959 qualifying their offer as follows:-

- They should have the right to determine the relinquished areas.

- Their commitments in the IPC and MPC concessions to be amalgamated

- That the agreement should be ratified by a Law.

During the meeting held 27 September 1959, in the presence of General Qassim, the government brought up a new principle, by proposing that any percentage agreed must apply separately to each individual concession.

The Companies were taken aback by this new principle which they explained would render their current studies obsolete and require new studies to be made which could take time.

The question of who has the right to select the relinquished areas was raised during the meeting held on 19 October 1959 during which the Companies insisted on the right to do so.

The government could not agree to this and proposed the following:-

- Offer to let the Companies keep their current production areas in addition to those in which they had discovered oil.

- The remaining areas to be divided between the two sides by mutual agreement.

This was not acceptable to the Companies.

During a subsequent meeting the government showed its readiness to:-

1. Accept 60% of the area of each concession, equivalent to 100,000 square miles.

2. Give the Companies the right to select 10% of the 60%.

3. Agree on the division of the remaining 40%.

Again this was not acceptable to the Companies.

The IPC Group then sent their memorandum of 4 November 1959 advising that they had reconsidered the government's recent proposal and would like to present their new proposal as follows:

1.   The IPC Group would select 90,000 square miles, representing 50% of their total concessions, that would be relinquish from their three concessions as follows:-

    -    9,500 square miles from the IPC concession.

    -    23,000 square miles from the BPC concession.

    -    12,000 square miles from the MPC concession.

    -    The remaining 45,500 square miles to remain open for release by the companies.

2.   The commitments in the IPC and MPC concessions to be amalgamated

3.   The Companies will release further areas after five years from the date of the first relinquishment.

This again was unacceptable to the government.

A new government committee was formed on 13 June 1960, to report on the negotiations and present their recommendations. It included Taha al-Sheikh Ahmad, Abdul Fattah Ibrahim, Nadhim al-Zahawi, Zaki Abdul Wahab and Fathallah Luqa.

The committee presented its report on 2 July 1960 with the following recommendations:-

1.   The Companies to select 20% from their producing and discovered areas.

2.   The remaining 80% to be relinquished immediately.

3.   25% of the remaining 20% to be released in each of the following three years.

4.   The release of the remaining unexploited area in the fourth year.

The subject was discussed further between the two sides without any tangible progress.

During the meeting of 20 September 1960, which was headed by General Qassim, the government advised the Companies that they would be ready to:-

1. Accept the immediate release of 90% of the concessions areas.

2. The Companies will have the right to select 10% of such areas with the remaining 80% to be decided by both parties.

This proposal was countered by a proposal by the IPC Group's representatives during a meeting held on 22 September 1960 as follows:-

1. The Companies to keep 40% of the area of each concession and release the remaining 60% to the government.

2. The Companies to have the right to select 50% of the above 40% areas.

The government accepted the relinquishment of the 60% of the areas on the condition that:-

1. The Companies to select the first 10% of the areas which they want to retain and 20% of the areas that they want to release.

2. The government will select the first 10% of the areas they want to retain.

3. The remaining 60% to be divided by the mutual agreement of both sides.

This was not acceptable to the Companies and as a result the government proposed that the Companies and the government be allowed to select 10% each at the same time and this procedure to be repeated four times by which the Companies would have selected their 40% and thereby release the 60%.

The IPC Group's representatives requested some time to study this proposal and during the meeting of 28 September 1960 they offered to:-

1. Release 60% of their territories.

2. The Companies should have the right in choosing the areas to be released.

3. Their commitments in the IPC and MPC concessions to be amalgamated.

This was rejected by the government which presented its final proposal:-

1. The companies to select 20%-25% of the area of each concession.

2. The government to select 5% of the area of each concession.

3. The companies to release 50% of the unexploited areas after 5 years and all the remaining unexploited areas after the subsequent 5 years.

This was not accepted by the companies.

During the meeting of 15 October 1960, and as a result of the rejection of its previous final offer the government increase the areas to be release from 70% to 75%.

As a result, the IPC Group addressed their letter of 17 October 1960 to the prime minister presenting the following proposal:-

1. Their agreement to release 75% of the area of each concession within 30 days of signing the proposed agreement..
2. To release 50% of the unexploited area at a later stage by mutual agreement with the government.
3. The companies to keep the final 10% of the area of each concession.

This proposal was not acceptable to the government.

During the meeting of 7 November 1960, General Qassim dictated the draft of five letters to the IPC Group's representatives adding that if the contents of these letters are accepted he will consider the first stage of the negotiations as being successful. The main contents of these letters included the following:-

1. The immediate relinquishment of 75% of the area of each concession.
2. No more than 5 plots should be selected for each of the remaining 25% area of each concession with the area of each plot not to be less than 3,000 square kilometres.
3. To release 60% of the areas of these plots after 7 years with the area of each plot not to be less than 1,500 square kilometres.
4. The companies to make available to the government all the geological and technical data relating to the relinquished areas.

This was finally accepted by the IPC Group as dictated to them by their memorandum and its attachments, which was presented to the government during the meeting of 4 April 1961. General Qassim checked the documents and after he found them in accordance with the government's draft he declared that he was pleased with the companies' acceptance and intends to declare to the Iraqi people the successful conclusions of the first stage of the negotiations.

This happy atmosphere was not to last for long when Mohammad Hadid reminded General Qassim that there was still the other outstanding issues to be resolved such as the 20% participation by the government, the Dead Rent etc. General Qassin agreed with Hadid's comments and asked the IPC representatives to accept Iraq's 20% participation.

The IPC team were taken aback and expressed their surprise since they have accepted the government conditions without any change and added that every time they seem to come nearer to an agreement the government seem to come up with new demands.

Further negotiations took place which by then had become more difficult and bitter with the Iraqi government accusing the companies of their delaying tactics by sending low-level delegations with limited authorities, which resulted in their frequent requests for adjournment to enable them to go back to London for consultation with their shareholders.

As a result, the government issued a warning to the companies to suspend their exploration and drilling activities until further notice.

The negotiations were resumed on 24 August 1961, led this time by a new high level IPC team armed with more authority in a final effort to reach an agreement.

During this period the national press as well as the government broadcasting station had been attacking the companies for refusing what they saw as Iraq's legitimate rights. By leading the negotiations personally, and by publishing as well as broadcasting some of the proceedings of the negotiations, which the author remembers listening to, General Qassim had committed himself publicly to extract these rights from the companies either through negotiations or through the expropriation of some of the unexploited areas of their vast concession territories.

The negotiations continue during subsequent meetings when the negotiations finally reached their final stage with each side stretching their offers to their limits.

The Companies final proposal which was on offer during the last meeting of 11 October 1961 was as follows:-

1. The immediate relinquishment of 75% of their concession territories.

2. The retention of 10% by the IPC Group.

3. The establishment of a joint venture company for exploiting the remaining areas of 15% with 20% government and 80% IPC participations.

The government's counter final offer was:-

1. The retention of 2% of the total territories by the Companies.

2. The immediate relinquishment of 90% of the concession territories.

3. The establishment of a joint venture company for exploiting the remaining areas of 8% with 20% government and 80% IPC participations.

4. The government to forego its demands for the 20 % participation in the ownership of the companies and for the increase in the percentage of profit sharing.

This was not acceptable to the IPC Group and an impasse seem to have been reached. As a result both sides expressed their regret for being unable to reach an acceptable compromise after three years of intensive and difficult negotiations.

When there was nothing more to add by either side, General Qassim thanked the IPC Group's representatives but added that a suitable legislation will be forthcoming to protect the legitimate right of the Iraqi people and ensure the return of their territories.

The Representatives in turn thanked General Qassim and the lengthy and hectic negotiations finally came to a close.

With the complete collapse of the negotiations, the companies could do nothing more, and it was therefore up to the government to take whatever action it deemed necessary.

It is reasonable to conclude that the government's final offer was not attractive enough to be acceptable to the international oil companies since it included fundamental changes to the terms of their concessions policy in the Middle

East and beyond that would have wider implications and consequences and as a result they had to reject it for the following reasons:-

1. The immediate relinquishment of 90% of their territories meant that they would be deprived from some of the most lucrative oil rich regions in the world and this would set a precedent to be followed by the other oil producing countries.

2. The government's participation in the ownership of the companies would set a precedent and open the door for other oil producing countries to follow.

3. The restriction of the operations to the limited area of 2% of their original territories, though would have included the highly prized North Rumaila field, it was considered not worth the risk of changing the fundamental global policies of the major international oil companies.

A communiqué was issued on 17 October 1961 by the Ministry of Oil giving a brief history of the negotiations and blaming the Oil Companies for their failure to accept the legitimate demands of Iraq which resulted in the collapse of the negotiations.

Furthermore, it declared that the government of Iraq will continue to defend the rights of the Iraqi people and take whatever legitimate steps it deemed necessary to safeguard them in accordance with the current laws.

THE FAMOUS LAW NO 80

A high level ministerial committee was formed after the collapse of the negotiations from Mohammad Hadid, Modhaffar Hussain Ali, Abdul Latif al-Shawaf, Hashim Jawad, Mohammad Salman and Taha al-Sheikh Ali to evaluate the situation.

Two points of view prevailed regarding the areas that would be allocated to each of the IPC, BPC and MPC. The first point of view suggested the allocation of the areas currently being exploited plus the areas in which oil had been discovered by the companies. The second recommended the allocation of the producing areas only. Finally the committee agreed to adopt the second point of view and to formulate the necessary draft law based on this which resulted in the famous law 80, however, without the equally famous article three which was added later on by General Qassim himself.

It is said that by adding article 3 to law 80, which permits the return of an area equal to the area, which had been left to the companies, General Qassim wanted to tempt the Companies to accept the Law and Iraq's points of view regarding the other outstanding disputes with the Companies.

It was not until 12 December 1961 that the government announced, that after three years of unsuccessful negotiations with the oil companies, it finds itself obliged to follow the other legitimate and just methods for protecting the rights of the Iraqi people and their oil wealth by issuing the famous Law 80.

The Law resulted in the unilateral expropriation of 99.5 per cent of the IPC, MPC and BPC concessions areas, including the rich but non-producing northern part of the Rumaila field and all the discovered but undeveloped oil and gas fields. Thus the law basically restricted the three companies' activities to their operation regions only, presumably in line with one of their worst predictions.

As a result, the exact area which was allocated for operation to each of the three oil companies was detailed in a table attached to law 80 as follow:-

Oil Company	*Allocated Area (km²)*
Iraq Petroleum Company	747.75
Mosul Petroleum Company	62.00
Basra Petroleum Company	1,128.00
Total Area	**1,937.75**

The companies protested against such unilateral action and demanded arbitration as provided for under the terms of their concession agreements, a demand, which was completely ignored by the government.

It is important to highlight that in passing law 80 the government had been careful in leaving the door open for a possible return of an area equal to the area which had been left to the companies if it saw fit to do so.

This opportunity of the return of such unspecified area, which could have included the lucrative North Rumaila field, was very tempting to the companies but the prospect for reaching such an agreement was to prove far from straightforward.

Law 80 was hailed as a triumph for the Iraqi people and was supported by the national press as well as the public at large and hence as we shall see, no subsequent government dared to rescind it or modify any part of it.

I was at that time working in Kirkuk and I could say with complete confidence that there was a genuine and enthusiastic support for Law 80 amongst all the Iraqis working in the IPC.

Law 80 was seen by most as the beginning of the freeing of the Iraqi economy from the control of the foreign oil companies, which were seen as the hidden arm of the western colonial powers.

It also freed almost all the Iraqi territories from dominance of one group of oil companies, which were reluctant to explore and develop them for the good of the country.

The government also had the wisdom of avoiding nationalisation which could have resulted in extreme confrontation with the companies and possible embargo as had happened in Iran a few years earlier.

Instead it put the oil companies on the defensive and the difficult situation of not daring to take any drastic action such as stopping their operations since that would have harmed them as much as Iraq.

As a result the oil companies had no option but to adopt the legal position of reserving their rights to claim ownership of any oil that may be produced from their expropriated territories which was to result in serious marketing difficulties to the Iraq National Oil Company when it started to develop some of the oil fields in the late 1960s and early 1970s as we shall see later on.

In the meantime Iraq seems to have lost little except a freeze on the expansion of her production capacity, since she had managed to keep the export of the crude oil flowing from the existing fields at near maximum capacity, to maintain the required revenues

Meanwhile the relationship between the government and the IPC Group remained uneventful though tense, until the overthrow of General Qassim by a coup on 8 February 1963 and his death the next day, the ninth.

It was on 7 February 1963 that I had made my way to Baghdad in readiness to catch my plane the next morning to London. It had taken me months of preparation to arrange my leave, get my passport and visa and was looking forward to join my family that had travelled before me. My journey to the old Baghdad airport on 8 February was uneventful; the roads were empty and the city was still asleep at that early hour of 5.00am. The formalities at the airport were normal and the Iraqi Airways plane took off on time for our stopover at Istanbul. The morning was crisp, the sky was blue and the sun was just rising. At that time of the morning I was able to spot the large flares of Kirkuk oil field, which I had left the day before. Everything looked peaceful and normal until just before we reached Istanbul that we could see an unusual and uneasy circulation between the stewardesses accompanied by that unmistakable whispering. I could see that a strange feeling had started to grip the passengers who did not know and were not being told of what was going on. It seemed that the pilot had lost contact with Baghdad for some reason and was uneasy about the cause of that.

It was however not until we landed at Istanbul airport that we were surrounded by reporters, who, wanted to know what was happening in Baghdad? When we informed them of our ignorance they in turn informed us that a coup d'état had taken place, which must have started soon after our departure! The pilot was worried in case our plane is ordered to return to Baghdad and he only advised us of his worry after leaving Istanbul.

I arrived at home in the U.K. to see on television that the famous building of the Ministry of Defence in Baghdad had been bombed and to hear the next morning of the execution of General Qassim. The coup was masterminded and led by Qassim's old friend Abdul Salam Arif.

APPRAISAL OF GENERAL QASSIM'S OIL POLICY

We have seen that during the pre-revolution decades, the government's oil policy and the coordination of its business with the oil companies had been conducted mainly by the politicians with the help of a very limited professional technical support. The small Oil Affairs department which was attached at first to the Ministry of Communications and Works and later on to the Ministry of Economy was not staffed with enough experienced oilmen and other experts to deal effectively with the vast and complicated crude oil business of the country.

This was to change by the new government under General Qassim by the introduction of the following new measures:-

1. The establishment of the county's first Ministry of Oil on 14 July 1959 which was strengthened to include all the necessary dedicated experts required to deal effectively with the country's vast crude oil operations.

2. The participation in the establishment of the Organisation of Petroleum Exporting Countries, OPEC in September 1960 which wrestled the power of setting the policies of the world oil industry from the domination of the international companies. OPEC was ultimately able to set its own oil policies especially those concerning its member's rates of production and export and consequently was able to dictate the levels of the international crude oil prices which resulted in a more balanced and fairer oil prices than the artificially low ones dictated by the oil companies during the previous decades. This at long last raised the revenues of the governments of OPEC as well as the other non OPEC oil exporting governments to reasonable levels to allow them to develop their impoverished countries.

3. The issue of Law 80 in December 1961 which freed 99.5% of Iraq's territories and subsequently the country's enormous oil and gas fields from the control of the international oil companies and opened new opportunities for the Iraqi oilmen of different disciplines to engage directly in the oil exploration, drilling, production, marketing and all the other activities relating to the oil industry.

4. Setting the foundation for the establishment of the Iraq National Oil Company, INOC in February 1964 which grew with time to be able to explore, develop and operate new oilfields, which resulted in the creation of a large group of professional oil experts capable of managing the complex business of the country's oil and gas industry.

The Arif Brothers Regime

The government of the new regime which took over on 8 February 1963 included Abdul Aziz al-Wattari, as Minister of Oil, a technocrat who had good experience in the oil industry. The government recognised the difficulties in exploiting the vast expropriated territories on its own and decided to avoid further confrontational policies with the IPC Group and to seek instead some sort of cooperation with them within the framework of Law 80.

As a result the Ministry of Oil wanted to create an organisation that could develop, albeit in association with others, these territories and decided to form the Iraq National Oil Company, INOC which was established by Law 11 of 8

February 1964. This law permitted INOC to associate with foreign companies including those operating in the country, subject to the approval of the Cabinet.

Since Law 80 has also permitted the possible allocation to the IPC Group an area equal to the area left to them of about half per cent, they were eager to enter into new negotiations to at least recover such area, through some form of association with INOC, bearing in mind that the area in question would be large enough to include the lucrative North Rumaila field as well as most of the other proven fields.

President Abdul Salam Arif   President Abdul Rahman Arif

Hence fresh serious negotiations were initiated between the Ministry of Oil and the IPC Group in1964 revolving around the possible association between INOC and the IPC Group as well as the settlement of all the outstanding disputes.

The subsequent lengthy negotiations resulted in June 1965 in a two parts agreement, a joint venture agreement between INOC and the IPC Group and a settlement agreement with the government of all the outstanding disputes.

The terms of the joint venture agreement which are detailed under the INOC in Chapter 7, provided for the establishment of the new company by the name Baghdad Oil Company, BOCO, which would be 33.33 per cent owned by INOC and 66.7 per cent by the IPC Group. While the settlement agreement provided for certain payments by the IPC Group to the government in settlement of the outstanding issues between them, as will be described in more detail in Chapter 7.

The agreements were presented to the Cabinet and were met with strong opposition which split the Cabinet and prompted the resignation of six ministers.

A new government was formed on 3 September 1965 which resulted in the ousting of al-Wattari and the postponement of any serious attempts to deal with the two agreements.

However the new government which was formed on 1 July 1967 had decided to keep the lucrative North Rumaila field and as a result issued Law 97 of 16 August 1967 which gave exclusive rights to INOC to develop the expropriated territories and prohibited the offering of any oil exploration concessions to foreign companies. Furthermore the Law also prohibited the restoration of the North Rumaila field to the IPC Group.

The IPC Group protested claiming that Law 97 was a further breach of the international law and reserved the right to take whatever legal action it deemed necessary to prevent its concession territories falling into the hands of other parties. Though Law 97 did not specifically prohibit a possible association with the IPC group in developing territories other than North Rumaila field, such association was politically near impossible.

Meanwhile new disputes had come up during this period in addition to the previous unresolved one from General Qassim's regime as follows:-

1 - THE EXPENSING OF ROYALTIES

In the fifty/fifty agreements, the royalties during the years of the 1950s were included in the profits received by the governments in the form of an income tax.

However, by the early 1960s, OPEC began to argue that the royalties are payments for the depletion of their oil reserves and therefore should be treated as costs in calculating the governments' share of their fifty per cent profit.

The new method of expensing the royalties as cost of production would result in increasing the revenues of the governments by fifty per cent of the 12.5% royalties payable and thereby increase the government share of the profit from 50% to 56.25%. Therefore it is easy to see why the principle of the expensing of royalties was to become a demand on which all OPEC member governments agreed and began to insist upon.

It was under the intensified collective demands of OPEC, that the companies finally accepted the principle of expensing the royalties but they were unwilling to base the calculation of royalties on the current posted prices since these were in their opinion higher that the market prices at that time. As a result the oil companies proposed to use lower posted prices in the calculation for the purpose of determining the royalties.

The initial offers made by the companies were considered too low and after some lengthy negotiations the oil companies proposed at the end of 1964, a discount to the posted prices which was acceptable to the majority of OPEC members but not to Iraq, Venezuela and Indonesia. As a result OPEC decided to leave it up to the individual countries themselves to decide whether to accept the proposed offer or not. Iraq opted not to accept it and this proved to become one of the major disputes between the government and the IPC Group for a long time to come.

2 - SYRIA AND THE PIPELINES

The IPC had signed agreements with Syria and Lebanon in 1931 to secure the transit route of its crude oil from Kirkuk to the Mediterranean. The fees paid by the IPC were the subjects of revisions over the years. After the introduction of the fifty/fifty profit sharing agreement between Iraq and the IPC in 1952, both Syria and Lebanon demanded a similar arrangement. This principle was finally accepted by the IPC, which resulted in a substantial increase in the revenues of both countries.

In 1966 the Syrians, demanded a further increase in the transit dues of the IPC oil. As a result negotiations were conducted between the Syrian government and the IPC. The IPC had accepted in principle to increase the transit fees but the government's demands were far too high as well as they should be backdated. The dispute escalated with the government threatening the closure of the pipelines.

Meanwhile the Iraqi government had kept away from getting involved in the dispute. A stalemate was reached and in November 1966 the Syrian government broke the negotiations. The problem became very acute with the Syrian government bargaining from a position of strength basically holding the IPC to ransom. The government finally raised the fees to a much higher level and in mid December stopped the oil going to its port at Banias pending the IPC agreeing to its demands.

Meanwhile the Iraqi government remained neutral by informing the IPC that it considered the dispute to be between the company and Syria and hoped for an early settlement, in the meantime it reserved its right to receive its full crude oil revenues despite the closure of the pipelines.

Meanwhile the IPC Group had other sources of crude oil to compensate the losses through Syria and refused the unilateral action taken by the Syrian government. In the face of this stalemate and the refusal of the Iraqi government to interfere in the dispute, the Syrian position became weaker and in March 1967 a more amicable settlement was reached between the Syrian government and the IPC and the Iraqi oil started to flow again to Banias.

After this settlement the Iraqi government started to press its claim for the three-month loss of revenue as a result of the stoppage of the export of its crude oil from Banias arguing that its loss of revenue was due to the IPC's inability to settle its problems with Syria. The IPC pleaded force majeure and the dispute was finally resolved by the advancement of a £14 million loan to be repaid out of future revenues.

3 - THE PRICE DIFFERENTIAL BETWEEN THE MEDITERRANEAN AND THE GULF CRUDE OILS

Iraq started to demand higher prices for her Mediterranean crude oil resulting from higher freight charges from the Gulf following the closure of the Suez Canal in mid 1967. During subsequent negotiations, the IPC Group agreed to settle the Mediterranean- Gulf price differential issue by paying a lump sum of £10 million for the period June 1967 to May 1968 and thereafter to pay an extra US 7 Cents per barrel as long as the Suez Canal remained closed.

4 - THE EXPORT OF GAS TO SYRIA

The installation of gas turbines to replace the old diesel engines at the Syrian crude oil pumping stations along the IPC's export pipelines in the early 1960s necessitated the conversion of one of the 16 inch diameter crude oil pipelines to gas to deliver the required fuel for these new gas turbines.

Iraq is not required by the terms of concession to supply free gas outside the country and a claim was made for the cost of such gas.

No agreement could be reached and this dispute remained unresolved.

5 - THE LOW PRICE OF THE JAMBUR/BAI HASSAN CRUDE OIL BLEND

The API gravity of the crude oil produced from the IPC Jumbur field at that time was about 39-41 degrees and that of the Bai Hassan field was about 33-34 degrees. The IPC mixed the two crudes to market the mixture as the Jambur/ Bai Hassan blend which had an API gravity of about 35.0 to 35.5 degrees.

It was the accepted practice at that time that each API degree difference between two different crudes represented US2.0 Cents per barrel. Based on this rule the Jambur/ Bai Hassan blend should be priced at US2.0 Cents per barrel lower than that of the Kirkuk crude.

However the price of the Jambur/Bai Hassan blend was set by the companies at a discount of US10.0 Cents to that of Kirkuk.

The government considered this difference in the prices of the two crudes as excessive as evident from the accepted practice and demanded a correction to the price and a refund of the all the previous underpayments.

The IPC claimed that the products of the Jambur/Bai Hassan blend had undesirable colours which necessitated the additional discount to market them.

Again no agreement could be reached and the dispute remained unresolved

6 - BASRA CRUDE OIL PRICE DEFERENTIAL

The price of the Basra crude oil from Fao was agreed in the 1952 concession agreement to be sold at US5.0 Cent discount to that of the Saudi crude oil from Ras Tannorah. However, in 1956 the BPC began to sell its crude oil at a discount of US10.0-12.0 Cents.

The government objected to this practice and demanded compensation for all the quantities of oil that were sold at such a discount.

The BPC claimed that this discount became necessary to make its crude oil competitive with the other Gulf crude oils.

The dispute remained unresolved

7 - CRUDE OIL SUPPLY FOR IRAQI REFINERIES

In the 1952 concession agreement, the IPC had accepted so supply the Daura refinery in Baghdad with its requirement of Kirkuk crude oil at cost.

The BPC had also agreed at a later date to supply the Muftiyah refinery at Basra with its requirement of crude oil at cost.

With time Iraq's requirement for petroleum products increased enormously and as a result new refineries were needed to satisfy the local market.

As a result the government asked the IPC Group to supply the necessary crude oil for current and planned refineries at cost.

The Companies for a change agreed to this request without the usual hassle.

8 - CRUDE OIL MEASUREMENT

The custody measurements of the IPC, MPC and BPC had been based until the early 1960s on the height or weight of the oil in the previously calibrated tanks as detailed later on. Occasional errors had occurred over the years in the calculation of these quantities

In the meantime, new modern crude oil meters were installed by the BPC on its new Khore al-Amayah deep water terminal which proved to be accurate and as a result the government had asked the IPC to install similar meters for the Kirkuk and Ain Zahah fields.

The IPC and MPC accepted the proposal and promised to carry out the necessary study for its implementation. However, this was delayed and the meters were never installed.

9 - EXPORT OF NAFTKHANAH CRUDE OIL

The crude oil from the Naftkhanah field which belonged to the Khaniqin Oil Company (KOC) had previously been delivered to the local al-Wand refinery which was supplying the northern regions of Iraq with their petroleum products.

However the concession of Khaniqin Oil Company was terminated in 1958 and the Naftkhanah field was returned to the government.

It was proposed to export some of the Naftkhanah crude oil and as a result the government approached the IPC about the subject.

The IPC agreed to help in exporting such crude which should be delivered by a new pipeline to its K-2 pumping station near the town of Baiji.

Hence a new pipeline 138 kilometres in length and 12 inch in diameter was constructed and commissioned in 1963 between the Naftkhana oil field and Daura refinery as a first stage of this project.

However the delivery point for the crude oil was changed by the IPC from K-2 to K-3 pumping station near the town of Haditha on the river Euphrates.

A study which was conducted by the ministry of oil at a later date proved that the project was uneconomical for the following reasons:-

1. The proven reserves of the field were not enough to sustain export for a long time.

2. The reserves were needed to maintain the al-Wand refinery with its needs of crude oil.

3. The high cost of the project due to the longer pipeline to K-3 and the necessary additional storage tanks at both K-3 and the terminal at Tripoli.

The new Naftkhana - Daura pipeline was, however, subsequently utilised to supply the Daura refinery with crude oil from the Naftkhana field which is in excess of the requirement of al-Wand refinery as well as any surplus quantities of fuel oil from that refinery.

5

THE 1968 REVOLUTION - THE BAATH'S PARTY REGIME

A new regime led by the Baath Party came to power on 17 July 1968 with Ahmad Hasan al-Bakr as president. The regime was too occupied during its early days in consolidating its power base and purging its opponents to pay serious attention to the oil companies and the outstanding disputes with them, though not forgetting to stress its criticisms of their monopolistic natures. Statements were made that the government will follow up Iraq's legitimate rights with the companies, stressing that there would be no compromise on the provisions of Law 80. The Ministry of Oil issued a similar warning, in January 1969, stressing that the government resolve to exploit the expropriated areas of Law 80 directly.

President Ahmad Hasan al-Bakr

However, despite the extreme nationalistic rhetoric of the new government, it was in no better position at that stage than the previous governments in dealing with the much criticised oil companies.

Early Tension

One of the early actions taken by the government to express it displeasure and frustration with the IPC was to come in 1969. It unleashed its wrath by arresting the IPC's Iraqi General Manager in Kirkuk, Dr Hilmi Samara. The Government was able to do that only because Dr Samara happened to be an Iraqi citizen. He was the first Iraqi to occupy that post and the last for that matter. His arrest sent shock waves throughout the company's management and employees in Kirkuk and beyond and resulted in an atmosphere of disbelief, intimidation and fear amongst the rest of the Iraqi staff. This particularly was so since Dr Samara, though of Palestinian origin, loved Iraq and was very sincere in trying to do his best for the welfare of the company's employees.

He extended a lot of assistance to the city of Kirkuk in the expansion of its water supply. The author, who was Development Engineering Superintendent, remembers well his personal interest and follow up of the completion of the drawings and specification which were being prepared by the IPC on behalf of the Kirkuk municipality for of the expansion of its water supply by up grading the pumping equipments at the river Zab and the laying of a new pipeline 24 inch in diameter and some 45 kilometres in length.

He was also able to extend a helping hand to Kirkuk's general hospital by building an extension which included a modern laboratory.

He was finally freed after a few months only to leave Iraq for good and to become one of the early cases of the brain drain of the company, as we shall see later on. It was not until the 1990s, when Dr Samara and the author used to meet regularly in Sharjah, United Arab Emirates again, while they were working there; that he was able to tell of his ordeal. He was held in a very small solitary cell, and subjected to continuous interrogations about his motives and relations with the IPC.

Other senior members of the IPC management in Kirkuk were to face similar fates as to that of Dr Samara, by being arrested and accused of being agents of the IPC.

The Shelling of the Process Plant

The IPC had a cinema opposite the company's main club in the Baba residential area that showed films at 8.30 pm on certain nights of the week as well as the weekends. It was on such a night on 1ˢᵗ March 1969 that the author and his wife were watching a film at the cinema when the film was stopped and an announcement was made advising the audience that they should go home without explaining a reason for such an unusual advice. The author lived in Arrapha residential area in Kirkuk and the road back home passes in front of the Central Process Plant. We found that the road had been closed and we were diverted to a parallel road from K-1 area to Arrapha. It was while we were driving on this road that we saw flashes of light in the sky coming from behind the Process Plant followed by loud bangs without realising fully what they were. It was not until the next day that we learned that these flashes of lights were 20 millimetre mortar shells. Apparently, 117 of them had been fired that night, with some 50 of them landing in the Process Plant Area. The largest process unit No 12, with a capacity of 250,000 barrels per day of crude oil was set on fire with other equipment around it.

Miraculously, there was no loss of life or injuries, but the damage was extensive and affected unit twelve's column, its pump house, the petroleum engineering store and the adjacent transfer lines. as shown in the photographs.

The events of that night were related to the author recently by the veteran head of the Process Plant Abdul Karim Mohammad as follows:

"The shelling of the Process Plant started around 9.30 pm on 1ˢᵗ March 1969. The Plant, which had 12 units, nine of which were in operation at that time was processing crude oil at the rate of nearly one million barrels per day. Each of these units consisted of a huge one or two vertical columns, a pump house with powerful electrically driven pumps circulating very hot crude oil, a gigantic vertical crude oil heater and numerous other ancillary equipment in addition to the usual tangle of crude oil, fuel gas, water and air piping.

It was, as usual, manned entirely by an Iraqi team of about 65 shift operators. The Plant emergency shutdown procedure was immediately set into action for the shutting down of the entire Process Plant through the emergency shutdown button. This in turn triggered similar shut down procedures at several degassing stations, which resulted in turn in the closure of tens of oil wells across all the oil fields that stretch over a huge area of nearly 200 kilometres in length and three kilometres in width.

The Company's fire brigade, which was stationed nearby, was summoned, and was on the scene within minutes of the shelling.

The arrival of the General Manager Allan Gillan and the Fields Manager Fadhil Khan immediately after the start of the shelling and their stay overnight at the Process Plant had a profound effect in lifting the morals of all those who were at the scene.

The shelling lasted for a few hours, during which process unit 12, which was operating at its full capacity of 250,000 barrels per day, received a direct hit and was set on fire.

Fire fighting efforts were started immediately, going hand in hand with the risky endeavour of isolating the burning equipment. The initial aim was to contain the huge fires from spreading and ultimately to extinguish them. It is to be recorded, that this very dangerous work, was being carried out by, these courageous men, under continuous bombardment. Their brave efforts finally paid off and the last of the fires was completely extinguished the next morning at about 7.00 am which no doubt limited the extent of the damage which could have been catastrophic in destroying the entire Plant.

While the inspection of the damage was being assessed, the operators identified the units that had escaped damage and in a daring gesture, the first of these units was started up within a few hours and was in full operation by that evening of 2 March. As a result the flares were lit again to the cheering and chanting of all those present.

Meanwhile the medical team at the nearby Company's hospital at K-1 was put on alert in anticipation of the worst but miraculously there were no injuries and the emergency plan was thankfully called off.

Actions were immediately taken to order replacements for the damaged upper section of the column, the main pumps and the motors that were long delivery items since they had to be manufactured by the original supplies on an emergency basis. Since unit 12 was the most important unit in the Process Plant, it was decided to air freight these very heavy and bulky replacement equipment. The upper section of the column measured 14 foot in diameter by 60 feet in length and weighed about one hundred tons and hence required a special large aircraft.

During this period all the preparatory work had been completed on site and the installation work of these large equipments were carried out at full speed.

Unit 12 was finally completed and commission and a ceremony took place for its inauguration on the Iraqi Army Day on 6 January 1970, almost exactly ten months after its damage. The ceremony was attended by the Governor of the Province of Kirkuk and dignitaries."

Crude Oil Process Unit No. 12

Courtesy of IPC Society Newsletters

It is to be recorded that Abdul Karim must be the longest serving staff in the history of the IPC and later on with the North Oil Company. He originally joined the company in 1942, retired officially in 1989 and continued to work on contract basis until 1992. All these long years were entirely spent in the Process Plant and no wonder his name became associated with it. He received two letters of appreciation for his excellent efforts in managing the emergency work during and after the shelling, the first from the IPC Chief Representative in Baghdad and the second from the General Manager in Kirkuk.

In a comment in the IPC Society Newsletter issue 146 of April 2010 the general manager of the time, Allan Gillan praised the efforts of his staff and employees who were at the scene during the shelling as follows:

"The performance of all-Iraqi Process and Production staff as well as the Fire Brigade was exemplary. By their courage and discipline under bombardment and their professionalism, they contained the conflagration, brought the system under control and prevented much more serious consequences."

Meanwhile, Allan Gillan was subsequently awarded the honour of O.B.E. for "Services to the oil industry in Iraq".

Crude Oil Process Unit No. 12-After Shelling

Courtesy of IPC Society Newsletters

New Negotiations

In February 1970 the government affirmed the cancellation of the provision in Law 80, which permitted the allocation of additional areas to the IPC Group. Moreover on the second anniversary of the revolution in July 1970, the government attacked the IPC Group and warned the Basra Petroleum Company that if it did not increase its crude oil production which had been limited to 16 million tons per year (320,000 barrels per day), against the combined available export capacity of the Fao and Khor Al-Amaya terminals of 35 million tons per year (700,000 barrels per day), the government will take over the spare capacity and use it for the export of its own INOC crude oil. The BPC argued that the low throughput was due to its crude becoming uncompetitive due to the government high costing policies. Meanwhile the refusal of the IPC Group to settle the long outstanding dispute with the government for the expensing of royalties amongst the other outstanding issues did not help the growing tense relationship between them.

Meanwhile during this time the demand for oil from the Mediterranean had increased as a result of the continuing closure of the Suez Canal. This together with the high freight charges from the Gulf had raised the price differential between the Gulf and the Mediterranean crude oils. As a result the posted price of the Iraqi oil from the Mediterranean was increased at the end of September 1970 by US20 Cents per barrel.

The IPC Group's Conciliatory Attitude

It was not until June 1971 that the IPC Group's attitude became more conciliatory when it decided to compensate Iraq for the royalty expensing with effect from January 1971. The government accepted this but reserved its rights for further compensations for the period from 1964 to 1970.

Moreover the BPC had agreed to raise its annual production rate from 16 million tons (320,000 barrels per day) to an annual rate of 21 million tons (420,000 barrels per day) for the remaining period of 1971. It also offered to raise it further to 28 million tons (560,000 barrels per day) during the following year.

At the same time a number of the other minor issues such as the accounting treatment of the Dead Rent, production costs, drilling and exploration expenditures and head office expenses were ironed out and resulted in substantial payments and loans to the government.

However two of the main outstanding disputes remained unsolved. These were the government's demand for back payments for the royalty expensing between 1964 and 1970 and the IPC Group's demand for compensation for the expropriation of their concessions territories as result of Law 80.

The Souring Of Relations Again

This atmosphere of fairly amicable negotiations and understanding which the IPC Group had hoped to lead to a comprehensive settlement was soon to be shattered in the autumn of 1971, by the sharp drop in the Gulf freight charges which changed the posted prices differentials and made the Mediterranean crude oils too expensive as compared with those from the Gulf. As a result the IPC reduced its crude oil export from Banias and Tripoli at the Mediterranean, which brought in strong protests from the Iraqi government, which demanded the immediate restoration of the exports rates back to their previous levels.

During this period Saddam Hussain had become Vice President and as a result the government attitude towards the IPC Group had become more critical, acrimonious and quite inflexible.

New negotiations began in mid January 1972 in which the government put its demands as follows: -

1. The settlement of the long outstanding issue of the expensing of royalties for the period 1964 to 1970, bearing in mind that the IPC Group had already accepted the principle with effect from 1st January 1971.

2. The participation in the ownership of the IPC, a right that was given to Iraq by the San Remo agreement in 1920, only to be refused by the IPC Group under the protection of the mandated British government and which had been raised repeatedly over the previous forty years, bearing in mind that the issue of participation had become in recent years a frequent demand from the other oil producing countries.

3. The effective participation in the strategy for the future development and production levels of the IPC Group's oil fields.

4. A procedure for the continuous auditing and costing.

5. A demand for the transfer of the IPC Group's Head Office from London to Baghdad.

The IPC Group responded on 1st February with the following indivisible package: -

a   To increase the export current capacity of the BPC from 600,000 barrels per day to one million barrels per day in mid 1976 and to one and a half million barrels per day by 1980.

b   To accept backdating the royalties expensing principle to 1st January 1968 instead 1st January 1971.

c   To purchase 8,000 million barrels of INOC crude oil over 20 years at a discount of 20 cents per barrel below the current price at that time.

d   To pay a lump sum of £10 million in settlement of a variety of other financial outstanding issues.

e   To make oil available to the government for certain barter deals.

f   To receive, from the government 12.5 per cent of crude oil produced by INOC delivered free of royalties, taxes and costs as a compensation for the effects of Law 80.

Not surprisingly, this offer was rejected outright by the government, as completely inadequate since it clearly included the principle of compensation for the effects of Law 80 though without explicitly expressing it.

The IPC Group then made things worse by reducing their crude oil export from the Mediterranean again to the level of 600,000 barrels per day citing the same old reason that it had become uncompetitive in comparison with other Gulf oils.

This enraged the Iraqi government by prompting the Ministry of Oil to demanded that the IPC Group should either: -

1.   Raise the oil export from 600,000 barrels per day to the previous level and hand over the difference to the government at cost to market as its own.

Or

2.   Relinquish the excess production and export capacity to the government.

Or

3.   Hand over the northern fields to the government and concentrate on production from the south.

Meanwhile Zaki Al-Yamani the Saudi Minister of Oil had been authorised by the OPEC governments to conduct negotiations with the major oil companies on the principle of participation. Following some prolonged negotiation and a very intense pressure, the major oil company by March 1972 accepted the principle of 20 per cent participation, which was subsequently offered by the IPC Group to Iraq. But this offer for which Iraq had been demanding during the past four decades was considered as too little too late to impress the government.

The Government's Ultimatum

The Revolutionary Command Council, the highest authority in the country, then stepped in to give the IPC Group an ultimatum within two weeks ending on 31 May 1972 that they should respond to the government's demand to raise production and take steps to do so; draw up a definite long term production programme; and submit a positive offer in response to the government's demands to resolve the outstanding disputes.

The Government's Preparation for the Worst

Obviously the government had by this time decided on nationalisation, encouraged by the prevailing favourable international circumstances and as such began to take precautionary measures to reduce its possible harsh consequences as follows: -

1. Since the country was still heavily dependent on the revenues from the export of its crude oil, the government had thought it wise to nationalise the Iraq Petroleum Company only and to leave the Basra Petroleum Company operating as usual. Although the revenue from the BPC was much lower than that of the IPC, it was large enough to keep the country going for some time. In the meantime the argument that the IPC Group may stop lifting the BPC crude in retaliation had been considered and rejected as unlikely.

2. Still the government could not rule out completely the worst, which is a total embargo on the export of all its crude oil as had happened with the Iranians during the nationalisation of their oil in the early 1950s. As a result the government announced austerity measures such as the freezing of all public work projects, a restriction on the foreign exchange and the withdrawal of its deposits from foreign banks of countries, which it feared might freeze them in the event of nationalisation.

3. The fact that Algeria had already acted unilaterally by nationalising a number of the foreign oil companies and taken 51 per cent of the assets of some of the major French oil companies without major retaliation by the oil companies had set a recent precedent and encouraged Iraq to press ahead with nationalisation.

4. Also the fact that OPEC itself had become a major force and had finally succeeded in wrestling the principle of participation from the major international crude oil companies was considered as an opportune time for the government to go ahead with its decision to nationalise the IPC.

5. The government also pressed ahead in intensifying its campaign to gain international support from OPEC, the Arab countries as well as the other friendly countries such as the Soviet Bloc countries, Italy and in particular the French government which had companies such as ERAP already operating in the country.

6. In a shrewd move to split the shareholders of the IPC and to contribute to supplementing Iraq's expected dwindling revenues, the government was quick to offer to discuss with France the future of her 23 ¾ per cent shareholding in the IPC. A high level delegation led by Saddam Hassain went on an official visit to Paris and on 18 June 1972 an agreement was announced under which CFP would be able to contract to buy 23.75 per cent of the production of the former IPC fields on terms prevailing before the nationalisation, plus any further increases in fiscal revenues that the OPEC countries might obtain as will be detailed in Chapter 7 dealing with Iraq National Oil Company. By this it was also hoped that France would not support any embargo that may be imposed on the sale of the nationalised crude oil.

7. On the home front the government started an intensive campaign against the monopolistic and imperialist oil companies through the government controlled press, radio and television broadcasting stations.

8. The Iraqi members of the top management and the other senior staff of the IPC in Kirkuk, were individually approached by senior members of the Baath ruling party, and briefed on the possible nationalisation of the IPC and asked for their support and to be prepared to assume responsibility when the time comes.

9. At the same time the government through its party organisation and Oil Workers Trade Union in the oil fields and the pipeline pumping stations, conducted a similar campaign to ensure the smooth takeover of the IPC operations.

The IPC Group's Final Offer

In response to the government's ultimatum, the IPC Group submitted its revised proposal, which was conciliatory in some respects and went further towards meeting some of the government demands but it failed to cancel its previous demand for compensation for the effect of Law 80. However it did propose to reduce its previous demand for compensation from 12.5 per cent of the crude oil produced by INOC to 7.0 per cent.

Clearly the subject of compensation for the effect of Law 80 had become a vital issue of principle for both the government and the IPC Group.

The IPC Group could not accept the expropriation of its concessions territories without compensation since this would have set a precedent and undermined the position of the major international oil companies' worldwide in similar future circumstances.

As for the government, it was impossible to accept the principle of compensation after so many years of its rhetoric of claiming a total victory in the repossession of its territories. Furthermore it would have constituted a total political defeat and capitulation to the so-called greedy foreign companies.

Both the government and the IPC Group knew that an impasse had been reached and none of them could do more and it was up to the government to make the final move.

The Nationalisation of the Iraq Petroleum Company

The Revolutionary Command Council wasted no time and on 1st June 1972 issued Law 69 nationalising the Iraq Petroleum Company and the transfer of all its assets, rights, operations, production and all other activities to the a newly established organisation by the name the Iraqi Company for Oil Operations (ICOO), which would be managed and operated by the existing Iraqi staff and employees of the IPC.

The reaction of the IPC was swift by stating that the Iraqi government's action in nationalising its assets was a breach of the Company's Concession Agreement and of international law and reserved its rights to take legal action against anybody buying its nationalised oil.

On the other hand, the government had announced its willingness to enter into negotiations with the IPC to settle their difference but made it clear that neither Law 80 nor the principle of nationalisation could be discussed during such negotiations.

Mediation

In the meantime the government had sought the support of OPEC in its dispute with the IPC and as a result a statement, was issued by Nadim Al-Pachachi, the Secretary General of OPEC supporting Iraq's action and condemning the IPC for reducing its export of the Iraqi crude oil from the Mediterranean as a deliberate and premeditated measure aimed at punishing Iraq and exerting pressure on her.

Furthermore OPEC at its extraordinary conference in Beirut on 9 June 1972 approved Iraq's nationalisation and agreed that no member country would permit increase in its own output, which is designed to replace any reduction in Iraq's output. At the same time it delegated its Secretary General to mediate between the government of Iraq and IPC.

OPEC had stipulated that the mediation should be conducted within the framework of Iraq's nationalisation law and that during the mediation period the IPC should take no legal action to hamper Iraq's crude oil export from the Mediterranean ports.

The IPC agreed to the mediation under the auspices of OPEC and proposed that the period for the negotiations should be 90 days and proposed further that Jean Ducoc Danner of CFP should act as a co-mediator with OPEC's Secretary General Nadim Al-Pachachi.

Meanwhile since France had very little crude oil supply of its own, CFP did not contest Iraq's right to nationalise its oil. This was quickly followed by an official visit by a high level Iraqi ministerial delegation to Paris on 14 June 1972, lead by Vice President Saddam Hussain himself. The visit lasted until 18 June during which a ten-year agreement of cooperation between the two countries was announced as has already been mentioned. Under the terms of this agreement, CFP would be able to contract to buy 23.75 per cent of the production of the former nationalised fields, which was exactly equal to its previous shareholding in the IPC. The price of this oil will be based on the previous prevailing terms of the IPC plus any further increases in fiscal revenues that the OPEC countries might obtain, plus the option to buy additional Iraqi crude at market prices. At the same time France, in its support for the principle of nationalisation, did not want to upset its previous partners too much, had made provisions in that the implementation of the agreement would be subject to the conclusion of a satisfactory compensation arrangement for the IPC's shareholders. This amounted to exempting CFP from the nationalisation Law 69 without explicitly announcing it as such. By this the Iraqi government had succeeded in sowing descent between the IPC's shareholders, gained a safe market for large quantities of the nationalised oil and secured the support of the French government which had its other company ERAP busy working in cooperation with INOC in areas in the south of Iraq. This no doubt strengthened the position of the government in the mediations.

Meanwhile the mediators continued their tedious work in narrowing the differences, which was becoming clear that it would drag on much longer than the 90 days limit set by the IPC and to which the Iraqi government had objected as an unacceptable precondition. As a result the IPC issued a long statement on 14 July 1972, which included the following: -

> "It (the IPC) will, without prejudice to its rights, abstain from commencing legal proceedings …prior to any declaration by one or both of the mediators regarding the status of the mediation ... A declaration will be made not later than the 12th October, 1972. If this or any other declaration states that the mediation has failed, the Company will be free to exercise its full legal rights."

Meanwhile the mediation talks continued and the IPC went to extend its deadline two more times, to the end of January and finally to the end of February 1973.

Final Settlement

It was finally announced on 28 February 1973 that an agreement had been reached between the government and the IPC on the following terms: -

1   The Iraqi government to provide 15 million tons, equivalent to some 110 million barrels of Kirkuk crude free of all costs and charges in final settlement of all claims of the IPC Group on the government at the rate of one million tons (7.5 million barrels) per month or faster if agreed.

2.   The IPC Group was to pay the government £141 million (equivalent to some $345 million at the prevailing exchange rate of £1 = $2.45) in settlement of all the government's claims against the IPC Group.

Based on the prevailing and expected crude oil prices during the period of fifteen months, it was estimated that the value of the 15 million tons of crude oil offered to the IPC would be equivalent to over $300 million.

Meanwhile, the Middle East Economic Service (MEES) had reported in May 1972, that, the value of the net fixed assets of the IPC Group at the end of 1970, which would be taken over by the government, had been estimated by the Petroleum Industry at $104 million

This settlement was hailed as a final triumph for the government over the IPC since no mention was made of the word compensation nor any reference was made to the expropriation effects of Law 80 or the nationalisation Law 69, in conformity with the long held government policy. There was also a genuine relief and euphoria in the country at the news of the historic emancipation of the country's oil wealth from the clutches of the foreign companies, which have been portrayed over the previous four decades as the ugly face of the foreign monopolies.

The Abandonment of the Mosul Petroleum Company

Though Mosul Petroleum Company was not nationalised, it had lost its export pipeline outlet to the Mediterranean as a result of the nationalisation of the IPC and since it was only producing just over one million tons of crude oil per year it was not worth keeping and was simply abandoned by the IPC Group to be taken over by to the government.

The Nationalisation of the Basra Petroleum Company

Meanwhile the Basra Petroleum Company was left alone to operate as usual for the time being, though it was agreed that:-

1. The IPC Group would expand the output of BPC from an average of some 35 million tons in 1973 (700,000 barrels per day) to 80 million tons of crude oil in 1976 (1.6 million barrels per day).

2. The government agreed to provide all reasonable facilities to enable the BPC to carry out the expansion.

However this apparent calm was to be shattered within a few months following the Arab-Israeli war in October 1973, when the government announced the nationalisation of the American Near East Development Corporation share of 23.75 per cent and the 60 per cent Dutch portion of the 23.75 per cent share of the of the Royal Dutch Shell in the BPC. This action was taken in retaliation for the support given to Israel by the American and the Dutch governments during that war.

The five per cent of Gulbenkian, who had his foundation based in Portugal was also nationalised in December 1973 due to Portugal's similar attitude in that war.

Finally the government having gained confidence in the control and operation of its oil industry took the final step to free the whole oil industry of the country from any foreign ownership and nationalised the 23.75 per cent shareholding of both the French company, CFP and the British company, BP, as well as the and the remaining 60 per cent British portion of the 23.75 per cent shareholding of the Royal Dutch Shell in December 1975.

Hence the much disputed right for the participation of Iraq in the ownership of its oil wealth, a right which was given to her by the San Remo conference more than half a century ago in 1921, came at last to the fruitful end of full ownership, though after four decades and a lot of arm twisting and much resentment and bitterness that were felt by the Iraqis at large.

The IPC Group's Total Production

It is of interest to record that the total accumulated quantities of crude oil produced by the IPC, MPC and BPC over the period of approximately 41 years from 1934 to 1975 was a staggering 1,185.3 million tons of crude oil equivalent to approximately 8,890 million barrels.

The Nationalisation Law No. 69

The nationalisation of the Iraq Petroleum Company was executed through Law No. 69, which included the following:

•   The establishment of the Iraqi Company for Oil Operations (ICOO), which was to become the current North OIL Company (NOC).

•   The transfer of all the IPC's rights and assets including all its oil and gas fields together with all its production, processing, tank farms, pipelines, pumping stations, and all other facilities and properties to ICOO.

- The confirmation of the IPC's organisation structure and the transfer of all its staff and employees to ICOO.

- The confirmation of all the IPC's Iraqi staff in their previous posts without any change to their previous salaries and benefits.

- The restriction of the resignation or the transfer of any of the ICOO staff to other government or private organisations without the explicit approval of the higher authority.

NEW MANAGEMENT

One of the immediate changes at Kirkuk was the appointment of Ghanim Abdul Jalil, a former Governor of the Province of Kirkuk and a high ranking member of the leadership of the Iraqi Ruling Baath Party, the highest authority in the land, to the post of the General Manager of ICOO. The appointment of such high political figure, with wide-ranging authorities, was to ensure open channels with the highest authorities in the country to enable the quick takeover of the IPC's operational activities, the smooth running of the ICOO business and the ease and swiftness to resolve any serious oil operation problem that may arise as a result of the nationalisation.

It is to be recorded that this man together with a subsequent ICOO General Manager, another high ranking member of the Baath Party, were to be accused of the alleged conspiracy to overthrow the newly appointed President Saddam Hussain in 1979, as will be mentioned later on.

SMOOTH TRANSFER

With the departure of the small number of expatriate staff, the remaining national staff, who were holding nearly all the sensitive and managerial posts by then and were virtually running all the IPC's vast fields and export operations, continued to run them with their business as usual attitude without any interruption.

However the main areas of concern at the early days of nationalisation can be summarised as follows:

- That the IPC's and its shareholders with the support of their governments may impose an embargo on the export of the ICOO oil as they did during the nationalisation of the Iranian crude oil in 1951.

- The IPC threat of taking legal action against any buyer of crude oil from its oil fields in northern Iraq may result in deterring such interested buyers from attempting to purchase such crude oil. This concern did not last for long, since the Ministry of Oil by that time had already established its crude oil marketing organisation and was able to sign some barter contracts with some of the Eastern Bloc countries in addition to the willingness of CFP to continue to lift its previous share of 23.75 % of the nationalised crude oil.

- The other big concern was to ensure the continued supply of the necessary spare parts for the vital operational equipments such as the numerous drilling rigs and associated equipment, pumps, motors, valves etc. as well as the other necessary new operational, maintenance, and construction equipment. As a result a high level committee from the involved departments of ICOO was formed to identify such spare parts and equipment. At the same time contacts were maintained with the main foreign suppliers for the possibility of their readiness to continue supplying these items. No real resistance was shown by these suppliers to deal with ICOO and quotations were readily forthcoming. A high level ICOO delegation, armed with the necessary authority, was then sent to visit these suppliers in order to negotiate the final prices, terms and conditions and to sign the relevant contracts and purchase orders for the required equipment and spare parts.

The above three main concerns were to disappear completely within exactly nine months of the date of the nationalisation following the final settlement agreement between the Iraqi Government and the IPC on 28 February 1973.

ICOO'S FIRST ANNIVERSARY

ICOO finished its first year full of confidence having proved itself capable of overcoming all its teething problems and the successful running of its operations and went to hold two memorable first anniversary celebrations one at its Employees club in Kirkuk and the second at the main Staff club in the Baba area. These celebrations were attended by the staff and employees with their families and some government dignitaries from the Oil Ministry as well as those from Kirkuk. The party at the Staff club was held in the club's gardens with an elaborate floating stage in the middle of the swimming pool under the blue sky of June 1973. Many artists were invited to join in the celebration including the famous singers Fadhil Awwad and Dalal Shamali who entertained and thrilled the audience with many of their popular songs. The party was truly memorable and went on until the early hours of the next morning.

In another sign of appreciation of the excellent performance of ICOO's staff and employees a delegation from the ICOO management was invited to visit Vice President Saddam Hussain in Baghdad. He was briefed at first hand of the company's vast operations and of the great effort made by all to overcome all the difficulties they faced. He thanked the members of the delegation and expressed his personal appreciation of their valuable and vital participation in the successful nationalisation of the IPC.

In the meantime many television and radio programmes were also broadcasted to celebrate and highlight the significance of the freeing of the Iraqi oil from the control of the foreign companies by the historic nationalisation of the IPC, which had been talked about and dreamt of over decades.

The 1973 Oil Embargo and the Explosion Of Prices

Throughout the 1960s there had been more and more crude oils coming on the international markets including those from the Arctic after the discovery of the Prudhoe Bay field which proved to be enormous. As a result the supplies exceeded demands and depressed the prices. However by 1970 the international demand for crude had increased beyond expectations and the United States was by then importing nearly 28 per cent of its consumption. This tight supply of crude oil started to push the free market prices higher and higher.

Meanwhile King Faisal of Saudi Arabia was unhappy with the United States policy of supporting Israel in continuing to occupy the Arab lands after the 1967 war, and had warned of restricting the increase in the future oil production of the Kingdom to 10 per cent, which was much lower than Aramco's projections.

It was by September 1973 that the free market crude oil prices had risen, for the first time, above the major oil companies posted prices of around $3.0 per barrel, which prompted OPEC to demand higher prices. As a result negotiations between the major oil companies and OPEC were planned for early October 1973 to discuss the prices.

However the 1973 Arab Israeli war broke out on 10 October and the United States began supplying Israel with large quantities of weapons and sensitive intelegance information. A delegation of four Arab foreign ministers led by the Saudi foreign minister Omar Saqqaf, arrived in the United States on 16 October, to convey the concerns of the Arab world about the unconditional support of the United States to Israel. Their visit was in vain and as a result, after Saqqaf's return home, Saudi Arabia announced an immediate cutback of its crude oil production by 10 per cent and imposed an embargo of its oil to the United States and the Netherlands for their active support of Israel. This was to be followed by similar embargos to be taken by the other Arab oil producing countries.

Meanwhile members of OPEC had assembled in Kuwait and decided unilaterally to increase the price of their crude oil from $3.0 to $5.12 per barrel.

Though the Israelis had agreed a cease-fire on 21 October 1973 and the U.N. Security Council had also called for a cease-fire the embargo continued.

The embargo was soon to result in an acute worldwide shortage of oil and as a result the free market prices jumped beyond any expectation. The oil producing countries, through their participation agreements with the oil companies, began selling their 50/50 share of crude oil and on 16 December 1973 the Iranian National Oil Company auctioned some of its oil and received a bid of $17.0 per barrel. Most of the bids came from the independent companies but it is said that a bid of $12.0 per barrel was submitted by an affiliate of Royal Dutch Shell.

Events were moving very fast and on 22 December 1973 six Gulf members of OPEC met in Teheran to discuss their oil price policy. The main member countries Iran and Saudi Arabia were at the two extreme ends of the negotiations. The Iranians wanted high prices while the Saudis preferred much lower reasonable figures; each one of them was armed with a convincing argument.

The Shah of Iran then took the initiative and went to announce at a press conference that the price of oil would be set at $11.65 per barrel. This was more than double the $5.12 per barrel, which was set in Kuwait weeks earlier and almost quadrupled the posted prices of the major oil companies in less than three months.

All of a sudden the OPEC countries found themselves in control of their own crude oil prices with the major oil companies looking on helplessly.

The quadrupling of the revenues of the producing countries brought wealth at last and enabled Iraq to embark on expanding her oil industry. Major crude oil projects such as the expansion of the northern export capacity to 1.4 million barrels per day, the Strategic Pipeline and the Iraq Turkey Pipeline could now go ahead with confidence.

Michel Aflaq -An Unusual Encounter

The author had been invited by the French Company, Entopose to follow up the progress of the manufacturing of some of the major equipment for the 1.2 million barrels per day expansion project in France and an official visit had been arranged for that. A first class reservation had been made by ICOO on Iraqi Airways to Paris and I found myself finally occupying my seat in the plane. There were only another three or four people in the first class and we were waiting for the plane to take off.

All of a sudden a new huge black car came rushing towards our plane followed by two or three army escorts vehicles full of soldiers with machine guns at the ready. Panic gripped the passengers for a brief duration as to what was going to happen next. The cars suddenly stopped near the plane's stairs and a man with a well-known and recognisable face from the TV news and the local newspapers, stepped out. It was Ezzat Al-Douri, the member of the Revolutionary Command Council, a minister and a member of the leadership of the Baath ruling party in Iraq. A sigh of relief must have been uttered, by all the passengers who were watching from their windows, as by then every body must have realised that he had come in peace and would probably be travelling with us. It must be remembered that this man was to become later on the Vice President of the Republic of Iraq and hence the second powerful man in the country He became one of the most wanted men by the Americans after their invasion of Iraq in 2003. However he was never caught despite the big bounty for any information that could lead to his capture and even at this time in 2011 no one knows for sure whether he is alive or dead.

Anyway he stood there chatting to his few companions without boarding the plane. This went on for a few minutes before another black car arrived with its army escort. The door was opened and a small built man in his mid sixties stepped out and was soon greeted with embraces by all those waiting. It soon became clear to me that the man was none other than Michel Aflaq, one of the founding members of the Baath Party and its Pan Arab Secretary General at that time.

After another few minutes of chatting, more embraces were exchanged before Aflaq boarded the plane and took his seat across the aisle only a few metres in front of me. The engines were started and as the plane started to move he and the party on the ground exchanged vigorous farewell waving of hands before all those on board must have uttered their final sighs of relief.

The flight to Paris was uneventful as the man sat quietly and as I too sat quietly thinking about the frail man ahead of me who had co-founded the famous Baath Party in 1944 that had spread its ideology throughout the Arab word. It had also been involved in countless demonstrations, uprisings, coups and revolutions before finally seizing power in Iraq as well as Syria. I also could not stop wondering about what he must have been thinking of it all himself now that his party had achieved one of its aims of seizing power but had a long way to go in achieving its other fundamental ideological aims of Arab Unity, Freedom and Socialism.

The Brain Drain

It must be recorded that the nationalisation of the IPC was supported at the national level and more so by the Iraqi staff and employees of the IPC itself. A state of euphoria swept throughout the Company at the news and everybody was more than happy and willing to do what could be done to make it a success. All worked very hard and long hours during the following months and years to resolve the problems that had arisen , as mentioned previously.

It must be highlighted as well that the Company's staff and employees were praised by Vice President Saddam Hussian himself for their hard and sincere work and consequently held in high esteem.

We have also seen that the young students who were sent on the Ministry of Oil scholarships since the early 1950s had been returning back to Iraq to join the Ministry of oil itself and some of its organisations such as the Iraq National Oil Company, INOC, the Refineries, the Petroleum Products Distribution as well as the IPC, MPC and the BPC and have been able to gain enough experience to be able ultimately to hold most of the key positions in the oil industry in the country. These highly qualified and experienced people were to become instrumental in emboldening the government to make the critical decision of nationalising the IPC.

It is also to be noted that many of these scholarship students had got married during their university years and had brought their foreign wives back home with them. With time these families had settled well and had their children at schools and colleges. By the time of the nationalisation in 1972 many of these people were holding most of the top posts in the IPC and went to play an essential and pivotal role in ensuring its success. Hundreds of other ex government scholarship and private students with foreign wives were similarly holding sensitive government jobs including ministerial and top departmental posts all over the country.

These people were running the Country with a steady hand based on their experience of living in the western democratic societies during their university years. Hence, by the mid of the 1970s, the economy was doing well and life was in general peaceful and normal. The travel restriction in these days was bearable and people were in general able to travel abroad on business and holidays.

However by the late 1970s these travel restrictions became harsher especially for the ex Iraq Petroleum Company staff with higher qualifications and experiences. Two reasons could be cited for this change: -

1. That the nationalisation Law had included the article regarding the restriction on the resignation and the transfer of the ex IPC staff outside the Company. Although the article was meant to be temporary to ensure the smooth takeover and the ultimate success of the nationalisation, it was never repealed. This very article was to be seizes upon later on by the Security and the Passport Departments to impose increasing restriction on the travelling abroad of the Company staff.

2. That such highly qualified people in the country as a whole were essential for the success of the government's ambitious development programme and as a result they were increasingly discouraged from travelling abroad in order to minimise the possibility of their not coming back.

One of the early travel restriction tactics adopted by the security and passport departments was the introduction of the principle of surety where by such people were required to present a surety of 3,000 Iraqi Dinars, equivalent to about US$10,000 at the official rate of exchange or some US$6,000 at the black market rate to ensure their return to the country after their trips abroad.

That was a large sum of money for the average salaried person but still was affordable and hence this was raised to 5,000 Iraqi Dinars. With time this sum was to become the minimum standard surety but was open to be raised much higher depending on the "risk factor" of the individual and hence subject to the interpretations and whims of the security and passport departments. The highest such surety was that demanded from (and paid by) the author in 1984, was the crippling sum of 30,000 Iraqi dinars equivalent to some US$100,000 at the official rate as will be detailed later on.

This very harsh treatment of the very people who had served their country so well and were instrumental in making the nationalisation of the IPC a success resulted in an atmosphere of disbelief, resentment and suspicion amongst the Company staff. The effect of this treacherous treatment was to result in forcing many such people to flee the country at the first opportunity since they felt that they were discriminated against and their freedom restricted. As the treatment became harsher it became intolerable and as a result they began to leave the country in larger numbers, even though by doing so they would be losing their lifelong savings to pay for the surety as well as *forfeiting* their well earned pensions.

Another thoughtless if not spiteful law was issued in the autumn of 1977 banning all university professors from practicing their professions outside the universities. The law was aimed at the medical doctors most of whom were specialists with highly successful private practices. The Law was simple and clear, abandon your private practice or leave the university. The Law also affected engineers, architects etc who had consulting firms.

This Law resulted in depriving the universities of these highly qualified and experienced professors and lecturers who had to abandon their university posts since their private practices were their main source of incomes. Others just simply left the country to find attractive and well paid jobs at foreign universities or private companies.

A similar harsh and unnecessary law was issued in January 1978 which had an article specifically aimed this time at the engineers. The article stated that engineers in the civil service are not allowed to resign or leave their posts for any reason and if they do, they would be deprived from practicing their professions or any other profession for that matter.

This meant that an engineer, who leaves or resigns his government post even though for some private necessity, could find himself unable to earn a living.

If we assume that the law was intended, as its sounds, to keep the engineers in the service of the government, it defeated the object since many of the capable engineers felt trapped in their posts and as a result many decided to leave the country to be free and find more attractive jobs abroad.

These thoughtless and harmful laws kept coming, when the government, in the late 1970s issued its notorious amendment to the Iraqi Nationality Law, which required foreign wives and husbands of Iraqi citizens to either:-

- Renounce their own nationality, hand over their foreign passports and become Iraqi citizens in order to continue to live in the country.

- Or leave Iraq within six months.

This was one of the most unreasonable and thoughtless laws imaginable which affected thousands of law abiding families of all walks of life all over the country. These foreign spouses had their own immediate families and relatives back home in their countries and were free to travel to visit them on holidays and in cases of emergencies. By becoming Iraqi nationals they would be subjected to the harsh travel restrictions and be deprived of their freedom to visit their families and hence this could not be accepted by the majority of such people.

This cruel law presented the foreign spouses of these mixed marriage families with one of the following extremely difficult and unpleasant choices:-

- To accept to be naturalised as an Iraqi citizens and thereby, lose their foreign passport and become liable the travel restriction and subject to the whims of the ever suspicious security and passport departments.

- To arrange for the foreign spouse to leave Iraq as required by this law and leave behind the Iraqi spouse and their own children.

- To arrange for the whole family to leave together, which was not easy since this would raise suspicions and could result in harsher travel restrictions.

- Arrange for the foreign spouse to leave Iraq with the children, if possible, first to be followed by the Iraqi spouse later on.

The last choice was the most practical solution that was adopted by thousands of families, which resulted in a real brain drain when the country was in desperate need of the skills and knowhow of these experienced people.

It was said that this problem was brought to the attention of President Saddam Hussain who had apparently advised that such husbands should divorce their foreign wives and marry Iraqi women instead; after all there were plenty of beautiful Iraqi women around.

It may be of interest to record that Allan Gillan, the expatriate general manager of the IPC at the time of the nationalisation was transferred to Basra Petroleum Company as a general manager. After the nationalisation of the BPC, he was transferred again as general manager, to Abu Dhabi Petroleum Company, ADPC, the last surviving daughter of the IPC. In the meantime many of the expatriate staff from both the IPC and BPC had also been transferred after nationalisation to the ADPC. This meant that the general manager as well as these staff had worked and known most of the IPC and BPC Iraqi staff. Furthermore they knew their capabilities and experiences in the oil industry and were soon offering those who had managed to leave Iraq the opportunity to join the ADPC. It was ironic to hear later on the Iraqi authorities complaining that the ADPC had been pinching Iraq's top oilmen when they themselves had forced them to flee the country in the first place.

The Fate of Three General Managers of ICOO

We have already mentioned that to ensure the success of the nationalisation and the smooth takeover of the IPC's vast oil operations, Ghanim Abdul Jalil, a previous Governor of the Province of Kirkuk and a high ranking member of the Baath Party was appointed as the first general manager of the Iraqi Company for Oil Operations, ICOO.

He was to be followed by Abdul Fattah al-Yasin, Abdul Sattar al-Raw and Ismail al-Najjar all of whom were high-ranking members of the Baath ruling party.

The fifth man to hold the post of general manager was Majid al-Hamdani, the elder brother of Adnam Al-Hamdani, the rising star in the Baath Party at that time and a close friend of Saddam Hussain himself. Majid was a U.K. graduate engineer whom the author had known from the early 1960s and worked closely with him during the execution of the 1.2 and 1.4 million barrels per day expansion projects in the 1970s. He had progressed over the years and was holding the post of the general manager of the Company in July 1979.

It was on 16 July 1979 that president Ahmad Hassan al-Bakr resigned and Vice President Saddam Hussain took over as the president of Iraq.

Meanwhile an alleged plot to over throw President Saddam Hussain had been discovered a few days earlier and Muhyiddin Abdul Hussain, a member of both the Revolutionary Command Council and the Baath Party's Regional Command Council was arrested. It has been said that the scorching heat of July in Iraq seems to make it the preferred month for coups and revolutions as has often happened since the first revolution of 14 July 1958.

As a result an extraordinary session of the Regional Command Council of the Baath Party was held on 22 July during which Muhyiddin Abdul Hussain made a public confession and named those involved in the alleged plot. Following the pronouncement of each name, the accused was immediately arrested and led out of the conference hall protesting his innocence.

The main alleged plotters were five key members, Muhyiddin Abdul Hussain himself, Mohammad Ayish, Adnan al-Hamdani, Mohammad Mahjub and Ghanim Abdul Jalil the first general manager of ICOO in Kirkuk.

President Saddam Hussain

The remainder of those accused were other senior members of the Baath party including Ismail al-Najjar the forth general manager of ICOO.

An investigation committee and a court, composed of members of the Revolutionary Command Council, were set up and soon after death sentences were issued for the five main conspirators and many others including Ismail al-Najjar with the actual execution being carried out soon after.

Though Adnan al-Hamdani was amongst those executed, mercifully his brother, Majid, the general manager of ICOO at that time, was not harmed but of course was immediately dismissed from his post.

The 1980s – Years of War

As we have seen the 1970s had been years of expansion for the oil industry in Iraq and years of growth for the economy as a whole. By 1980 Iraq was producing 3.4 million barrels of oil per day which was generating corresponding annual revenues of over twenty six billion Dollars and raising the country's reserves to some thirty five billion dollars.

Unfortunately the bilateral relationships between Iraq and Iran started to deteriorate after the Islamic revolution in Iran in 1979. The bitter deputes between the two countries continued to worsen as time went on and by September 1980 the hostilities intensified and escalated into a full scale war which lasted for eight years. The causes and the actual course of the war are beyond the scope of this book, however their catastrophic effect on the crude oil industry in Iraq and to some extent in Iran are.

IRAQ'S SOUTHERN OIL FIELDS

The crude oil installations in both countries became the immediate prime targets of the war and within a short period of time most of the oil production export and refining facilities in the south of Iraq were either destroyed or damaged including the two deep water terminals of Khor al-Amayah and Mina al-Bakr which resulted in a complete stoppage of Iraq's oil export from the Gulf.

Similarly the Iranian crude oil production, export and refining installations were bombed resulting in severe damage to the Abadan oil refinery and other less severe damage to the production and terminal facilities, nonetheless Iran managed to continued to export its oil from the Gulf.

IRAQ'S NORTHERN OIL FIELDS

The oilfields production and export installations of the North Petroleum Organisation, NPO, (the new name adopted instead of the Iraq Company for Oil Operations ICOO) were beyond the reach of the Iranian artillery bombardment and were hence subjected to bombing from the air only. Hence intensive precautions were taken to safeguard these vital oil installations since they represented the only lifeline left for the export of Iraq's crude oil.

The author was given the task of coordinating the protection of these oil installations with the Army, Air Force, Fire Brigades and the local police.

Some of the most effective measures were immediately put in hand as follows: -

1. Millions of sand bags were provided by the NPO while the Army provided hundreds of soldiers to fill in these bags with sand and build protective walls around the thousands of oil installations, such as wellheads, separators, vessels, process columns, storage tanks, manifolds, valves, pumps, machinery, electric power equipment, etc. The volume of work was enormous but was carried out in the order of priority and resulted in saving this equipment from the bomb shrapnel.

2. Equipment which could be spared were drained of oil and ventilated to eliminate their risk of catching fire which could be spread to other operating equipment.

3. The painting of all the oil and gas equipment as well as the corrugated sheeting of all pumps houses and other similar building with khaki colour. Again the NPO provided all the paint and necessary equipment and the Army provided the soldiers to carry out the work.

4. Most of the 28 huge export oil tanks at the K-1 tank farm were emptied and filled with water and the remaining few tanks in operation were located amongst these filled with water in order to minimise the chances of their receiving a direct hit and the spread of fire to the other oil tanks in operation.

5. Personnel air raid shelters were provided by converting suitable existing underground stores or suitable buildings through strengthening and additional protection means

6.   Anti aircraft guns as well as Surface to Air Missiles (SAM) were installed at suitable positions around all the vital oil and gas installations.

7.   Additional fire fighting equipment was brought from the less vulnerable nearby areas to enhance the NPO equipment.

8.   Air raid sirens were installed at strategic positions throughout the oil fields, personnel concentration centres and the nearby residential areas.

Meanwhile very strict security measures were adopted for access to all the oil and gas installation areas.

ACTUAL AIR RAIDS

The actual air raids on the oil installations in the Kirkuk fields were quite often in the first few weeks but became less frequent as the war was prolonged and finally ceased. The actual damage to the oil installation was minimal and did not seriously affect the actual production and export capabilities of the NPO.

However there were near miss incidents such as the bombs that hit the Fields Power station but luckily failed to explode which could have resulted in a drastic reduction of the production and export capacity since it would have affected the operation of some of the vital crude oil electrical equipment in the main process plants, production and export oil pumps and the numerous other production equipment throughout the oil fields.

As a result of this near miss incident, two Swedish Stal Laval gas turbine generating sets, each with a rating of some 8,000 megawatts were acquired quickly and installed in separate deep earth pits in the vicinity of the Fields Power Station and connected to its switch gears as a standby power supply.

In another air raid, one of the Water Injection storage tanks received a direct hit which resulted in the destruction of the tank and the flooding of the area around it. This, however, had very little effect on the production and export of oil.

A third raid was made on the Bai Hassan degassing station which resulted in the destruction of its electric substation and the shutdown of the entire Bai Hassan field for some weeks.

The old Process Plant was lucky to escape real damage during another air raid which resulted in a limited damage confined to the electric substation of process unit 12.

THE FAILED AIR RAID ON THE PROCESS PLANT

The NPO golf club is located in the vicinity of the main Process Plant and the Baba Degassing Station. It was normal for the NPO staff to have a game of golf during the weekends as it was considered quite safe to be in the open air despite the proximity of the oil installations. It was on such a sunny day while the author was enjoying a game of golf that the air raids sirens were sounded to be followed immediately by a barrage of anti aircraft gun fire and missiles. These weapons were positioned on the hills surrounding the old Process Plant and they were all firing at the same time. We the players could do nothing but lay face down with hands covering our heads and hope for the best. The danger for us was not from the enemy aircraft but from the possible shrapnel from our own anti air craft guns. This lasted for no more than two or three minutes when the guns suddenly fell silent and the soldiers from the nearby position were celebrating with their usual war victory chants and dance. They shouted to us that they had shot down the enemy aircraft well before it could reach its target. We heaved a sigh of relief and looked towards the direction the soldiers were pointing and saw a column of smoke rising in the air. The plane seemed to have been shot down a short distance of its target, the vital Process Plant.

THE RETURN TO NORMAL OPERATIONS

Though the NPO crude oil production was shutdown during the early weeks of the war, it was gradually restored back to normal soon after since it represented the only crude oil available in the county for export and as such the main source of revenue to the government to finance the costly and prolonged war. It took much longer to restore part of the crude oil production from the southern fields but such oil had no outlet through the Gulf and had to be pumped through the strategic pipeline to the K-3 pumping station to join the northern export pipelines system.

IRAQ'S OIL NORTHERN LIFELINE

The loss of Iraq's oil export capabilities from the Gulf left Iraq with its Mediterranean pipelines through Syria and Turkey. The Syrian pipeline system had a capacity of 1.4 million barrels per day while the initial single 40 inch diameter pipeline through Turkey which was available at that time had a capacity of 750,000 barrels per day. Hence the total export capacity available for the whole country was 2.15 million barrels per day.

The maximum production capacity of the northern oil fields was 1.4 million barrel per day, which if it could be utilised fully for export would leave a spare capacity of 750,000 barrels per day for the southern fields. This is well within the Strategic Pipeline South-North capacity of 880,000 barrels per day.

However disaster struck in April 1982, when the Syrian government decided to close all Iraq export pipelines passing through its territory. This unexpected action left Iraq with one single outlet for its oil export, through the single Iraq-Turkey Pipeline, with the modest capacity of 750,000 barrel per day. This drastically curtailed the government's much needed revenue to finance the mounting cost of the war and as a result, Iraq had no option but increase its oil export capabilities through the construction of new pipelines.

The outlets to such pipelines were limited, either to the Mediterranean through Turkey, or to the Red Sea through Jordan and Saudi Arabia. It was finally decided to adopt the Turkish and the Saudi options. The contracts documents for these two projects were completed quickly and contracts were awarded as follows:-

1. The second Iraq-Turkey Pipeline- This was completed in two phases, it had a 46-inch diameter and was laid parallel to the first 40 inch diameter pipeline and had a similar throughput capacity of 750,000 barrels per day. The contract for the project was awarded in December 1985 and the pipeline was completed and commissioned in July 1987.

2. The first phase of the Iraq Trans-Saudi Arabia Pipeline was 48 inch in diameter, 465 km long and a design capacity of 500,000 barrels per day.

    The pipeline starts at Zubair in southern Iraq and ends by joining the existing Saudi Arabian's (ARAMCO's) east –west or Abqueeq-Yanbu, 48 inch diameter pipeline (Petroline) at IPS-5 Pump station near the town of Khurais.

    The construction of this phase started in early 1984 and the project was completed in mid 1986.

The second phase of this pipeline involved the construction of 953km pipeline between Khrais and Yanbu, the first 863km of which having a 56 inch diameter with the final 90km before Yanbu having a diameter of 42 inches. This brought the total length of the entire pipeline between Zubair and Yanbu to 1,568km and created an entirely independent pipeline for the sole export of the Iraqi crude.

This phase was completed in early 1990 and raised the capacity of the independent pipeline to a massive 1.6 million barrels per day and Iraq's crude oil export capacity to a total of 3.2 million barrels per day through both Turkey and Saudi Arabia.

Sadly this entire pipeline through Saudi Arabia was shutdown only a few months after the completion of the second phase in August 1990 after the invasion of Kuwaiti.

Full details of these two pipelines can be found in Chapter 10 of this book.

1990s - Years of Embargo and Sanctions

Iraq's crude oil production peaked in December 1979 at 3.7 million barrels per day only to be reduced suddenly and drastically during the Iraq-Iran war.

In July 1990, just prior to the Kuwaiti crisis it was brought gradually back to 3.5 barrels per day.

With the closure of the Saudi pipeline after the invasion of Kuwait and the subsequent Gulf War, the country's total production then crashed suddenly and dramatically to as low as 75,000 bpd by the middle of 1991.

The notorious UN sanctions that were enforced against Iraq after the Gulf War kept the total production during the period 1991 and 1996 to around 600 to 700 bpd most of which was used to supply the country's oil refineries with virtually no export except through smuggling.

It was not until late 1996 when Iraq accepted the United Nations Resolution No 986, which allowed limited oil exports in exchange for food and other humanitarian supplies (The so called Oil for Food Programme) that the country's crude oil output began to increasing. It reached 1.20 million barrels per day in 1997, 2.20 mm bpd in 1998 and around 2.50 million barrels per day by the end of the century.

Such were the misfortunes of wars, will we ever learn?

IRAQ'S MINISTRY OF OIL

Iraq's oil affairs during the 1920s were limited and basically confined to the negotiations on the oil concession with the Turkish Petroleum Company, TPC and later on with the Iraq Petroleum Company, IPC, as it became known in 1928. During this decade the Ministry of Communications and Works was responsible for the oil affairs though the actual negotiations with the TPC/IPC were conducted by different Ministerial Committees which normally included senior staff concerned with the oil affairs from this Ministry as well as the Ministry of Finance.

In January 1930 the name of the Ministry of Communications and Works was changed to the Ministry of Economy and Communications.

This Ministry was then split in August 1939 into two, the Ministry of Communications and Works and the Ministry of Economy. As a result the section dealing with the Oil Affairs was transferred to the newly established Ministry of Economy.

The General Directorate of Oil Affairs

Due to the vast expansion of the operations of the Iraq Petroleum Company after the Second World War, a new department was established in 1950 within the Ministry of Economy by the name of the General Directorate of Oil Affairs.

This Directorate, became responsible for dealing with the three main oil companies, the Iraq Petroleum Company, the Mosul Petroleum Company and the Basra Petroleum Company as well as the Khaniqin Oil Company and its subsidiary the Rafidain Oil Company responsible for the distribution of petroleum products throughout the country.

These responsibilities covered all matters concerning the Companies contractual, financial, legal, and all other related obligations as well as disputes arising in connection with their Concession Agreements.

They also covered all the relevant technical aspects of these Concession Agreements such as, exploration, drilling, production, export and other operational matters.

Soon after, the Directorate, became involved with following-up of the training of the Iraqi staff and employees of these companies, the replacement of the companies expatriate staff and employees by Iraqis, the selection of students for scholarships, and numerous other routine matters between the Government and these Oil Companies.

As a result, the Directorate grow over the years to gain enough experience in the various fields of oil industry to present itself as a good foundation for a future Ministry of Oil

The General Administration of Oil Refineries

In March 1952, the General Administration of Oil Refineries was established after the purchase of Al-Wand refinery by the government. Though the actual operations of the this refinery as well as the marketing of its products were handled, under service contracts, by the previous owners, the Khaniqin Oil Company, KOC, and it subsidiary and the Rafidain Oil Company respectively, and the new Administration became directly involved not only in the refinery operations and marketing activities but also in the operations of the Naftkhanah oilfield itself, which supplies the refinery with its requirement of crude oil.

In the meantime, the Administration became directly involved in the planning, construction and finally the commissioning of the Daura refinery in 1955.

Though the operations of the Daura refinery were initially carried out by a foreign company under a service contract, the Iraqi engineers and operators became increasingly involved with them and were finally able to assume full responsibility.

By 1958, this young Administration had gained enough experience and confidence to be able to take over the direct operations of the Al-Wand refinery after the termination of the operations service contract of the KOC .

At the same time it was also able to take over the operations of the Naftkhanah oilfield in December 1958 after it was taken over by the government as a result of the failure of the KOC to abide by the terms of their Concession Agreement.

Hence by this time, this Administration had grown enough in size and confidence to present itself as another solid foundation for the future Ministry of Oil.

The General Administration for the Distribution of Petroleum Products

This General Administration was established on the first of July 1959 the same day as that of the termination of the marketing and distribution service contract of the Rafidain Oil Company.

Its original activities were the distribution and marketing of the various petroleum products including that of the Liquid Petroleum Gas (LPG) throughout Iraq. However the distribution of LPG was transferred to the new Establishment of Gas (LPG) Distribution on 25 June 1964.

Apart from its operations of hundreds of petrol stations all over the country, this Administration was involved in the construction and operations of many petroleum products depots, numerous products pipelines and a large fleet of road tankers.

With the sudden increase in the consumption of petroleum products in the country, it soon grew quite rapidly to become one of the biggest petroleum organisations in the country, in terms of its number of employees and geographical spheres of activities.

The Ministry of Oil

It was not until 14 July 1959, the first anniversary of the 1958 revolution, that the Ministry of Oil was established. This was mainly due the vast expansion in the operations of the three oil companies, the Iraq Petroleum Company IPC, the Basra Iraq Petroleum Company, BPC and the Mosul Petroleum Company, MPC. Their production of crude oil had reached hundreds of thousands of barrels per day and the Iraqi crude oil was being exported through the Gulf as well as the Mediterranean.

In the meantime, the number of employees of these companies had grown to over ten thousand and had become unionised and hence needed careful administration.

Furthermore, numerous complicated disputes had arisen between the government and these Oil Companies which needed urgent attention by a well trained and experienced staff in the many aspects of the oil industry.

In the meantime the activities of the Administrations of Refineries and Distribution of Petroleum Products had expanded greatly throughout the county and their business had become quite specialised and complex to be handled efficiently by the Ministry of Economy, which lacked the necessary experience in the oil industry..

Meanwhile, in addition to the ever growing responsibilities resulting from the rapidly expanding oil industry, the activities of the Ministry of Economy itself had expanded enormously, and as a result of the inflow of the additional oil revenues which resulted in stretching its human resources to the limit.

It was for all these reasons, as well as that the government's revenues had continued to become more and more dependent on the incomes from the exports of crude oil, that the establishment of an independent and specialised Ministry of Oil had become a necessity.

In the meantime a viable organisation could be made readily available to shoulder the responsibly by bringing the General Directorate of Oil Affairs, General Administration of Oil Refineries and General Administration for the Distribution of Petroleum Products under its umbrella.

Based on this, the new Ministry was established and its responsibilities and organisation were subsequently defined by Law Number 13 of 1961.

The Ministry then went to gain prominence during the important and difficult negations with the IPC Group under the leadership of General Qassim in the early 1960s which ended in failure and the issue of the famous Law 80 which expropriated 99.5% of the Group's territories as detailed under chapter 4.

The Ministry came to the limelight again under the new Minister of Oil, Abdul Aziz al-Wattari, when it became directly involved with the equally important and controversial negotiations with the IPC Group during 1964/1965. These negotiations resulted in what was to become known as al-Wattari two parts agreement, which though initialled by the Minister of Oil, was met with fierce opposition from within the Cabinet and the subsequent resignation of five ministers and ended with the ultimate exclusion of al-Wattai from the subsequent new Cabinet as detailed in chapter 4.

The other big role played by the Ministry of Oil was during the nationalisation of the Iraq Petroleum Company in 1972 and the subsequent negotiations which resulted in the signing of the Settlement Agreement between the Government and the IPC Group . This opened the way for the subsequent nationalisation of the Basra Petroleum Company in 1975 which realised the decades sought after dream of the ultimate liberation of Iraq's oil resources from the monopoly of the international oil companies.

One of the most important international roles played by the Ministry was the establishment of the Organisation of Petroleum Exporting Countries, the famous OPEC, which wrenched the dictation of the international crude oil prices from the clutches of the International Oil Companies.

In the meantime the Ministry continued to grow rapidly over the years and

by 1976 it had the following organisations under its umbrella.

1.   The General Directorate of Oil Affairs, 1950.

2.   The General Administration of Oil Refineries, 1952.

3.   The General Administration for the Distribution of Petroleum Products, 1959.

4.   The Department of Economy, 1963.

5.   The Technical Department, 1963.

6.   The Organisation for Oil Projects, 1964.

7.   The General Administration for the Distribution of Liquid Petroleum Gas (LPG), 1964.

8.   The Iraq National Oil Company, INOC 1964

9.   The Iraqi Oil Tanker Establishment 1972

10. The Iraqi Company for Oil Operations, subsequent to the nationalisation of the Iraq Petroleum Company, IPC in 1972.

11. The Establishment for crude oil marketing.

12. The South Oil Organisation, subsequent to the nationalisation of the Basra Petroleum Company in 1975.

It is to be noted that though the Iraq National Oil Company INOC was established and attached to the Ministry in 1964, it was detached from the Ministry and attached directly to the Office of the President of the Republic in 1967 vide Law No. 127 of 16 August 1967. This was mainly due to the controversial possible role of INOC's association in a joint venture with the Iraq Petroleum Company Group for the development of some of the expropriated concession areas and in particular the North Rumaila Field, through the proposed Baghdad Oil Company, BOCO, which raised some fierce opposition and split the Cabinet.

In March 1970, a special committee of Ministers directly responsible to the Revolutionary Command Council was established to supervise the commercial contracts and foreign agreements and particularly oil matters affecting INOC. In September 1971 Vice President Saddam Hussain became the chairman of this committee and its name was changed to the Follow-up Committee of Oil Affairs and Implementation of Agreements, which curtailed the authorities of the Ministry leaving it to concentrate on the exploration and operational matters.

The 1976 Reorganisation of the Ministry of Oil

By early 1976, the activities of the Iraq National Oil Company, the Iraqi Company for Oil operations and the newly created South Petroleum Organisation, subsequent to the nationalisation of the Basra Petroleum Company, suddenly became complex and a revision to the organisational structure of the Ministry of Oil had become a necessity. As a result Law number 101of 1976 was subsequently issued for the reorganisation of the vast responsibilities of exploration, drilling, oil fields operations, refining, local marketing, oil tankers, petroleum projects , crude oil marketing, training etc as shown in the following organisation chart.

The 1987 Reorganisation of the Ministry of Oil

Over the years the Iraq National Oil Company became increasingly involved in its own spheres of activities such as exploration, drilling, and the discovery and development of new oil and gas fields all over the country etc, whether on its own or in association with the many foreign companies. All these responsibilities together with the management of the three huge operating companies namely the North, the South and the Midland Oil Organisations, each of which having its own complex operation had made INOC grow into a mammoth, cumbersome and very difficult to manage company. Furthermore there was no clear line of responsibilities in many spheres of its activities resulting in confusion and overlapping layers of authority between it and the Ministry of Oil.

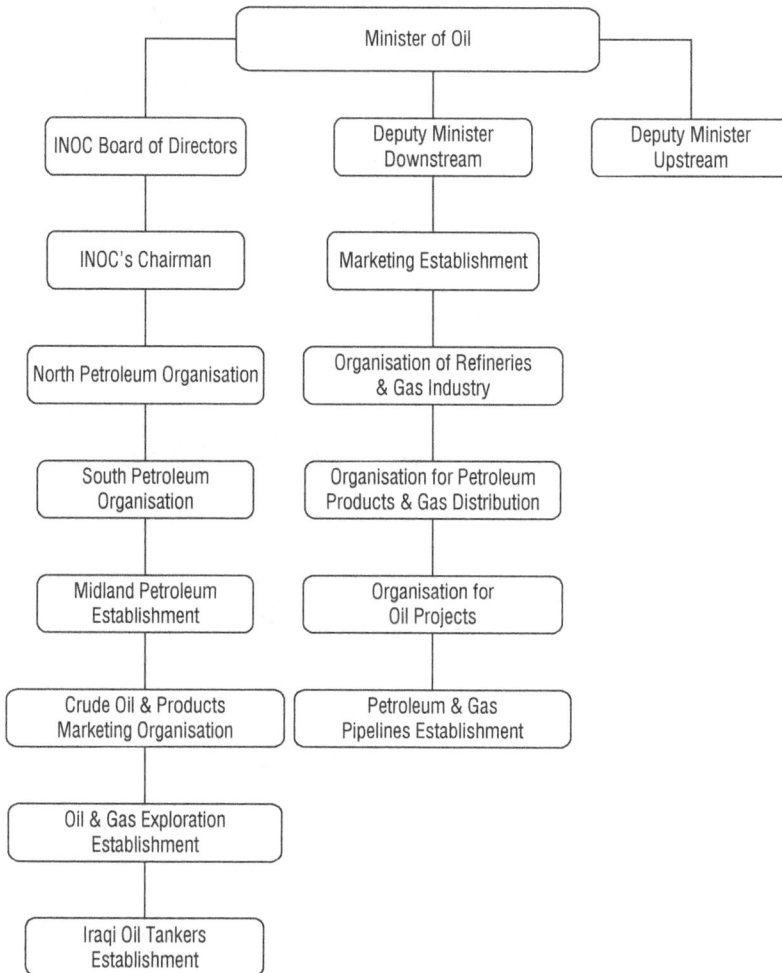

Ministry of oil Organisation Chart 1976

This together with the fact that the number of employees of the Ministry had reached over 65,000 by the mid 1980s had called for the urgent need for a drastic restructuring of the Ministry of Oil again which finally took place in April 1987.

The main outcome of this restructuring was the break up and dissolution of the Iraq National Oil Company and the creation of a number of independent State owned companies directly under the control of the Minister of Oil as shown in the following organisation chart. It is worth highlighting that the old North Petroleum Organisation, South Petroleum Organisation and Midland Petroleum Establishment were renamed North, South and Midland Oil Companies respectively and were given the same authorities as those of INOC.

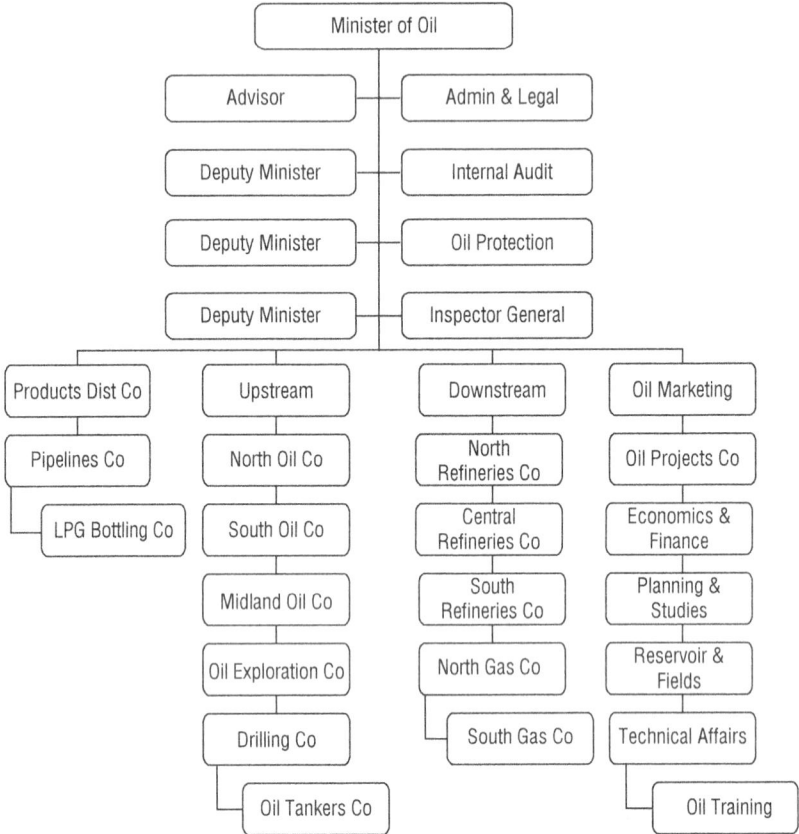

Ministry of oil Organisation Chart 1987

Iraq's Oil Ministers During The Twentieth Century

The following table shows the names and duration of the all the Oil Ministers in the twentieth century.

Name	From	To
Dr Ibrahim Kubba	14/7/1959	16/2/1960
Dr. Talat al-Shaibani	17/2/1960	8/12/1960
Mohammad Salman	9/12/1960	7/2/1963
Abdul Aziz al-Wattari	8/2/1963	3/9/1965
Abdul Rahman al-Bazzaz	6/9/1965	16/9/1965
Shukri Saleh Zaki	18/9/1965	11/8/1966
Naji Talib	12/8/1966	2/5/1967
Abdul Sattar Ali al-Hussain	2/5/1967	16/7/1968
Dr Mohammad Yagoub al-Seaidi	17/7/1968	30/7/1968
Dr Rasheed al-Refaee	30/7/1968	30/12/1969
Dr Sadoun Hummadi	31/12/1969	4/11/1974
Tayeh Abdul Karim	4/11/1974	28/6/1982
Qasim al-Oraibi	28/6/1982	22/3/1987
Issam al-Chalabi	23/3/1987	23/10/1990
Osama al-Heeti	1991	1992
Safaa al-Haboobi	1992	1995
Dr Amir Rasheed	1995	2003

7

IRAQ NATIONAL OIL COMPANY - INOC

As we have seen the relations between the Iraqi government and the Iraq Petroleum Company Group deteriorated after the 1958 revolution and an impasse was reached which resulted in the promulgation of Law No 80 on 12 December 1961. The Law resulted in the expropriation of 99.5 per cent of the IPC Group's concession areas, and restricted their activities to their existing operation regions only

However in passing Law 80 the government had been careful in leaving the door open for a possible return of an area equal to the area which had been left to the IPC Group if it saw fit to do so. This opportunity of the return of such unspecified area, which would be large enough to include the lucrative North Rumaila field, was very tempting to the distressed IPC Group and they were determined to at least regain it since it became clear later on that the return of all their concession areas was becoming more and more remote.

In the meantime the Government had no plans as what to do with the expropriated territories and the idea of creating a national oil company similar to those of Venezuela, Iran and Kuwait began to emerge as a possible vehicle for exploiting them. But the establishment of a national oil company which would be competent enough to exploit such vast expropriated territories would require financing, experienced engineers, technician and a skilled labour force which were not readily available at that time.

The revolution of 8 February 1963 brought in a new government in which Abdul Aziz al-Wattari was appointed as Minister of Oil. Al-Wattari, was an American university graduate engineer who had previous good experience in the oil industry and was holding the post of the Director General of the Administration of Iraq's Oil Refineries before his ministerial appointment. He remained in office for over two and a half years from 8th February 1963 to 3rd September 1965, during which he recognised the difficulties Iraq was facing in exploiting the expropriated territories directly.

Hence the new Ministry of Oil wasted no time in preparing a draft law for the establishment of a national oil company and as a result Law 11 was issued a year later on 8th February 1964 under which the Iraq National Oil Company, INOC, was created.

The Law authorised INOC to engage both inside and outside Iraq in any or all of the upstream aspects of the petroleum industry including exploration, drilling, operation, development of oil and gas fields, production, transport, and export of crude oil and petroleum products, but not in the downstream aspects of the industry which included the refining and internal distribution of petroleum products.

INOC was permitted by Law to form subsidiaries and to associate with other companies, including foreign companies operating in Iraq subject to the approval of the cabinet.

INOC was also directed to select the areas where it prefers to operate and to submit within six months its application for the selected areas to the cabinet for approval.

A modest capital of 25.0 million Iraqi Dinar, (Approximately $84.0 million), was allocated to INOC which was also authorised to borrow within certain limits subject to the approval of the cabinet.

The company was to be managed by a board of directors, with one third of its members were to be government officials.

Though INOC was attached to the Ministry of Oil, it was fairly independent as it had its own separate budget which was subject to the approval of the cabinet as well as that any dispute or disagreement on serious issues between the Ministry and INOC were to be referred to the cabinet for a final decision. The full text of Law 11 is shown at the end of this chapter.

New Negotiations

It must be highlighted that the attempts made by the previous as well as the new government to tempt the other various foreign oil companied to participate in the development of the expropriated areas including some of the rich proven fields such as North Rumaila were fruitless for the following reasons:-

1. The terms presented by some of the companies were no better, if not worse than those of the old concessions since these companies were taking into account the possible high risk of being sued by the IPC Group.

2. Better terms were offered by other companies on the condition that the government itself would accept the consequences of any legal action taken against them by the IPC Group.

The new government of Tahir Yahya realised that the prolonged state of stalemate and the stagnation of the country's oil industry could not continue for much longer. As a result a committee was formed to study the situation and the outstanding disputes with the IPC in an effort to find a possible solution and to present its recommendations.

The committee included Abdul Aziz al-Wattari, Adib al-Jadir, Khair al-deen Hasib, Abdul Karim al-Ali, and Mustafa Abdullah.

The committee submitted its report and recommendations, and as a result the Cabinet during its meeting of 27 February 1964 decided to enter into new negotiations with the IPC Group.

It was also decided to form a committee to conduct the new negotiations with the oil Companies which included:-

- Abdul Aziz al-Wattari, Minister of Oil.

- Saleh Kubba, Chairman of INOC.

- Ghanim al-Uqaili, General Manager of INOC.

- Abdullah Ismail, Director General of Oil Affairs.

A second ministerial committee was formed at the same to supervise and direct the negotiations consisting of:-

- Tahir Yahya, Prime Minister.

- Abdul Aziz al-Wattari, Minister of Oil.

- Mohammad al-Oboosy, Minister of Finance.

- Abdul Aziz al-Hafidh, Minister of Economy.

Meanwhile the IPC Group had gained nothing over the past years from their insistence on arbitration over Law 80 and had began to look for a way to come to some sort of an agreement with the government to settle their long outstanding disputes and regain part of their expropriated territories.

The establishment of INOC presented both a threat and an opportunity for the IPC Group.

A threat in that INOC which has been given the right to select and develop parts of the expropriated territories including the North Rumaila field either on its own or in association with other foreign companies may result in the IPC Group losing it for good.

Here is then an opportunity to regain the North Rumaila field in accordance with Provisions of Law 80 which had permitted the return of an area equal to that left to them in addition to some of the other proven fields and promising structures through the association with INOC before such fields could be offered to outsiders.

Hence both parties were ready to enter into serious negotiations that started in earnest on 2 May 1964 with each side hoping to settle the long outstanding and bitter disputes.

The government's team was directed to reach a settlement agreement with the IPC Group within the framework of:-

- Law 80 of 1961, which had permitted the government, if it saw fit to do so, to allocate additional areas of land to the IPC Group equal to the areas left to them of about half percent of their total original concession territories.

- Law 11 of 1964 which had permitted INOC to form subsidiaries and to associate with other companies, including foreign companies operating in Iraq (which included the IPC Group), subject to the approval of the cabinet.

The aim of the IPC team was to recover as much as possible of their expropriated territories including all their proven oil fields especially the most sought after, the North Rumaila field.

It was soon to become clear to the government team that the IPC Group were not ready to continue the negotiations unless they are allocated territories large enough to cover the North Rumaila and at least some of the other proven fields. The areas initially requested by the IPC Group were to be not less than 100,000 square kilometres, equivalent to more than 22% of the original total area of their three concessions.

The government team explained that the maximum area that could be returned to the IPC Group is that specified in article 3 of law 80 which is equal to the total area left to them of 1,937,750 square kilometres.

It was however pointed out by the government's team to the Companies that they could make use of INOC's ability to associate with foreign companies operating in Iraq and to enter into a joint venture agreement with it to explore and develop additional areas.

The IPC Group finally accepted to negotiate on this basis, but insisted on the following:-

- That any joint venture agreement reached with INOC must be made an integral part of the settlement agreement to be concluded with the government.

- That no territories should be allocated to other companies before these are offered to the IPC Group on the same terms.

- That the IPC parent companies should be given priority for entering into any future joint ventures that INOC may offer to other companies.

The first item of the above requests was accepted by the government but the other two were rejected.

The Companies then raised the question of the nature of the areas that would be returned to them in accordance with article 3 of law 80. They wanted to be given the opportunity to select such areas which meant that they will be able to choose the proven fields and the most promising structures.

This was rejected by the government team except for the return of the natural extensions of the fields being produced by the companies in accordance with the safe production practices and the return of these wells which were taken over within the expropriated areas.

The negotiations continued in earnest for more than a year before a draft settlement agreement consisting of two parts was finally concluded.

The first part of the draft agreement dealt with the settlement of all the previous and some of the recent outstanding disputes between the government and the IPC Group.

The second part of the draft agreement provided for the establishment of a joint venture company, the Baghdad Oil Company (BOCO), which would be jointly owned by INOC and the IPC Group.

Thus these difficult negotiations that had lasted for 13 months were finally and for a change successfully concluded 3 June 1965.

The First Part of the Agreement - Settlement of Disputes

This covered the settlement of the old outstanding disputes which have been inherited from General Qassim's regime as follows:-

MATTERS RELATED TO LAW 80

The government agrees to return additional areas to each of the IPC, MPC and BPC in accordance with article 3 of law 80 with such areas not exceeding these of their current operation areas as shown in the following table.

Company	Previous Allocation Square Kilometre	New Allocation Square Kilometre
IPC	747.750	747.160
MPC	62.000	61.330
BPC	1,128.000	1,127.800
Total	**1,937.750**	**1,936.290**

It is of interest to highlight that the grand total of the previous and the new areas represented slightly less than 1% of the old three concession areas of the IPC Group.

In return The IPC Group:

- Agreed to increase Iraq's minimum production rate stipulated in the 1952 concession agreements by 50% from 30 to 45 million tons per year.

- Agreed to endeavour to export the quantities shown below during each of the three consecutive years.

Year	Million Tons
1965	63
1966	66
1967	70

- Agreed to withdraw their notice of arbitration to the government concerning Law 80, in acknowledgement of the acceptance of it validity.

- Agreed to enter into a joint venture agreement with INOC for the establishment of an Iraqi company by the name of Baghdad Oil Company.

SETTLEMENT OF THE PRODUCTION COSTS DISPUTES

Dead Rent

The IPC Group agreed to return half of the dead rents for the years 1951, 1952, 1953, 1954 and 1955. As for the ten years period between 1956 and 1965 it agreed to return the dead rents in full. It was estimated that the total sum involved was about £9.5 million.

Exploration and Drilling Costs

Agreement was reached to discontinue expensing these costs but to depreciate these costs over 20 years if they are capital costs and over 10 years if they are equipment. All other operating costs to be expensed during the same year.

Based on this it was agreed to re-examine the accounts of the ten years between 1955 and 1965 in accordance with these rules and refund the differences to the government.

LONDON OFFICE EXPENSES

This subject was not pursued further by the government since it was examined by the auditors who found the 49% charged to Iraq as fair.

COSTS OF CONTRIBUTIONS AND ADVERTISEMENT

It was agreed to limit these expenses outside Iraq to a maximum of £10,000. Similar expenses inside Iraq are to be made with the agreement of the government.

COSTS OF THE STUDENTS' SCHOLARSHIPS

The IPC Group agreed to bear these costs with effect from 1955 and to refund the differences to the government.

THE 2% DISCOUNT AS MARKETING COST

The government accepted the discount of 0.5 Cent per barrel which had originally rejected.

THE UTILISATION OF THE ASSOCIATED GASES

The IPC Group agreed to supply the government with its requirements of these gases free of charge except the costs of gathering and compression. However, any remaining quantities could be exported by the party that could do so first.

THE PORT DUES

The IPC Group agree to the following rates which they had objected to before:

Fils per ton	Quantity of oil exported
280	For the first 8.0 million tons
70	For the second 4.0 million tons
35	For the third 4.0 million tons
23	For the remaining quantities above 16.0. Million tons

BASRA CRUDE OIL PRICE DEFERENTIAL

The IPC Group agreed to give the government £4.50 million as compensation for discounting the price of the BPC crude oil at a rate exceeding the US5.0 Cents per barrel to that of the Saudi crude oil at Ras Tannurah over the previous years.

THE EXPORT OF GAS TO SYRIA

The IPC Group agree to pay £50,000 per annum for the fuel gas exported to Syria with effect from 1962 provided that the quantity exported does not exceed 20 million standard cubic feet per day.

THE EXPENSING OF ROYALTIES

The principle of expensing the royalties had already been agreed which brings the government's share in the profit sharing agreement to 56.25 for the previous period pending agreement on some minor details.

It was agreed further that the IPC Group would make within 14 days from the date of the agreement, an advance payment of £20 million to the government in settlement of some of the outstanding issues. Included in this is a payment of £2,652,750 by the IPC Group for the unpaid port due by the BPC prior to 1960 and a payment by the government of £3,050,000 for the unpaid costs of crude oil supplied to the Iraqi refineries.

It was estimated that the total final payment due to the government as a result of this settlement could exceed £100 million after recalculating the exact sum due for each of the above outstanding issues.

The Second Part of the Agreement
Baghdad Oil Company, BOCO

This part of the agreement dealt with the establishment of a joint venture company based in Iraq, the Baghdad Oil Company (BOCO), which would be jointly owned by INOC and the IPC Group.

The main terms of this joint venture agreement were:-

- INOC would own 33.33% of BOCO while the remaining 66.67 would be divided between the four main shareholders of the IPC Group namely, Bp, Shell, CFP and Middle East Development with 15 5/6% each and the remaining 3 1/3% for Gulbenkian.

- The Company is authorised to engage in all of the upstream aspects of the petroleum industry including exploration, drilling, development, production, transport and export of crude oil.

- The shareholders would be responsible for setting the annual operating and capital expenditure budgets of the company as well as the long term planning for its development and production programmes.

- The board of directors would consist of three directors from INOC and one director from each of its other five shareholders, with one of the INOC directors to serve as a chairman.

  (This gave the IPC Group a majority vote in the board of directors and hence control in decision making especially when difference of opinions arise on serious issues).

- The Company's concession consisted of two plots, the first in the middle and the second in the south east of the country, with the total area of the concession being 32,000 square kilometres representing 7.36% of the total area of Iraq.

- The first 25% of the total area of the concession to be returned to the government after six years from the date of the concession.

- The second 25% of the total area of the concession to be returned to the government after nine years from the date of the concession.

- The third 25% of the total area of the concession to be returned to the government after twelve years from the date of the concession.

- The concession period is 46 years.

- The Company is to spend $30.0 million on its exploration work during the first six years at an average annual rate of expenditure of $5.0 million.

- The Company is to spend $20.0 million on its exploration during the second six years at an average annual expenditure rate of $3.33 million.

- INOC will be exempt from participating in the exploration expenditure until oil is discovered in commercial quantities.

- INOC will start to repay its share of the exploration expenditure in six equal annual payments one year after the export of oil.

- INOC will be exempt from paying any of the exploration expenditure if oil is not discovered in commercial quantities.

- The royalties would be expensed at 12.5%.

- The taxation regime is fixed at 50%.

- BOCO accept the responsibility of supplying the Iraqi refineries with any shortfall of oil that could not be supplied from other sources at cost price.

- The government shall have priority in utilising the surplus gas from BOCO's fields.

- The five foreign shareholders agree to buy INOC's share of the oil produced, if requested by INOC, at agreed prices.

- Other articles deal with accounting procedures, training etc.

Thus, with this agreement, the IPC Group was basically able to reach its objective to recover the North Rumaila field together with many of the other proven fields and promising structures. At the same time this represented a bitter pill for the IPC Group to swallow since it would have set a precedent that could be followed by other producing countries in the expropriation of their concession areas. This risk was obviously weighed against the prize of the recovery of the huge crude oil reserves that they knew existed in the giant North Rumaila field as well as those in the other proven fields and as a result they decided at long last and after missing their previous opportunities, that it was a risk worth taking.

The government's team had also achieved the objective set for them by reaching an agreement within the framework of the old Law 80 of 1961 and the new Law 11 of 1964.

However when the agreement was presented to the cabinet, it was met with a fierce opposition which split the cabinet in two. It was claimed that the negotiations were conducted in secrecy and without proper and regular advice to the cabinet and as a result six of the ministers submitted their resignation as a sign of their protest. The most prominent amongst them was the powerful Adib al-Jadir, the Minister of Industry who as we shall see later; put the final nail in the coffin of the BOCO agreement.

A violent campaign against the agreement followed in the national press which resulted in the resignation of the government on 3 September 1965. A new government was subsequently formed which did not include al-Wattari. However, the new government became increasingly preoccupied with other political and internal issues and finally with the tragic death of President Abdul Salam Arif in a helicopter accident on 13 April 1966.

The Agreement was considered by the subsequent governments without any decisions being taken until the relations between the government and the IPC deteriorated again as a result of the dispute between the Syrian Government and the IPC which resulted in the closure of the Mediterranean pipelines by the Syrian government in the middle of December 1966 which lasted for about three months until March 1967. The Iraqi government had claimed that the closure of the pipelines was solely due to the failure of the IPC to resolve its commercial dispute with the Syrian government and expected normal full revenues to be paid by the IPC for the period of closure to which the IPC pleaded force majeure. This, together with the continued press campaign against the IPC Group and the increasing opposition within the government circles reduced the chances of any decision being made regarding the Agreement. Finally, whatever little chance there was to salvage the ill fated Agreement was completely dashed by the outbreak of the Arab Israeli war in early June 1967.

The IPC Group's Missed Opportunity

It is not clear as to why the IPC Group had decided to accept the much less attractive Al-Wattari two part agreements less than four years after rejecting the much more generous final offer of General Qassim in October 1961.

Let us examine what was on offer by the Iraqi government to the IPC Group in each of these two cases.

	General Qassim's Offer	Al-Wattari Two Part Agreements
Date	11 October 1961	3 June 1965
ORIGINAL CONCESSIONS		
Area to be retained by the IPC Group as % of their Original Concessions Area	2%	1%
JOINT VENTURE AGREEMENTS		
New Concession Area as % of the Original IPC Group Concessions Area	8%	7.36% to be reduced to 1.84% after 12 years
Government Shareholding	20%	33.33%

One explanation could be that the IPC Group must have underestimated General Qassim's determination to expropriate such a vast area of their concessions of some 99.5% and the swiftness of issuing Law No. 80. Furthermore the Law had become very popular and was considered as a triumph over the oil companies and the IPC Group must have realised by then that it would be very difficult for any subsequent government to repeal or amend it and hence it would be better to come to terms with accepting.

In the meantime it remains to be seen if the IPC archives could shed further lights on this issue when they become open to the public in the future.

Law 97 of 16 August 1967

A new government was formed in July 1967 which included Adib al-Jadir as Minister of Economy. He was one of the main opponents of the formation of the Baghdad Oil Company and as we have seen had resigned in protest against it. His appointment then was a sure sign that the Agreement is now truly dead and buried. The new government was quick to confirm this a month later, by issuing Law 97 of 16 August 1967. The law gave exclusive rights to INOC to develop the expropriated territories and strictly prohibited the offering of any exploration concessions of such territories to foreign companies. The Law also included the prohibition of the restoration of the North Rumaila field to the IPC Group. The IPC Group protested claiming that Law 97 was a further breach of the International Law and reserved the right to take whatever legal action necessary to prevent its concessions territories falling into the hands of other parties. Though Law 97 did not specifically prohibited a possible association with the IPC Group in developing territories other than North Rumaila field, such association was politically near impossible.

Law 123 of 21 September 1967

With all these developments it was considered time to re-examine the outdated INOC organisation, its policies and finances. As a result Law 123 was issued a month later on 21 September 1967. This law restructured INOC on new basis by abolishing the post of the managing director and strengthening the power of the chairman. The chairman was to be appointed by a Presidential decree and would have the rank of a minister. As a result the obvious choice was made by appointing Adib al-Jadir as the new president of INOC and chairman of the newly formed board of directors.

In the meantime, it was recognised that INOC would not be able to develop the North Rumaila field and the other promising areas on its own and that technical, financial and managerial assistance will have to be sought from friendly countries. As a result a policy was formulated on the following basis:-

1. Areas with proven reserves which need no further exploration expenditures such as the North Rumaila field would be developed directly by INOC albeit with the help of some foreign companies as necessary.

2. Promising areas where reserves have not been proven and required further studies, exploration work and expenditure could be developed by INOC in association with foreign companies on service contracts basis.

Such assistance and association were envisaged to come from friendly countries such as the Soviet Union, France, Italy as well as Spain and Japan as will be detailed later on. Negotiations had already been going on with the French company CFP and the Soviet Union for possible association in developing parts of the expropriated territories. As a result a Soviet delegation visited Baghdad in December 1967 and a letter of intent was signed by the chairman of INOC and the head of the Soviet delegation for extending assistance to INOC in the exploration, production, management and marketing of crude oil as well as in the training of the Iraqi engineers and technicians.

This was followed by a final declaration on 10 April 1968 by the chairman of INOC confirming that the North Rumaila field will be developed directly by

INOC on its own account. This represented an ultimate triumph over the IPC Group and closed the door for any little hope that it might have had for regaining the North Rumaila field. It was however made clear that foreign companies would still be able to work as contractors for INOC to explore and develop other promising areas in the country which did not appeal to the IPC Group even if they wanted to do so since it would compromise their legal position.

The 1968 Revolution

The 17 July 1968 revolution brought in a new government led by the Baath party and with it came a new Oil Minister and a new management for INOC. The new regime had no specific oil policy of its own and hence had no choice except to continue for the time being anyway with the inherited policy though it was quick to declared that there will be no compromise whatsoever over the provisions of Law 80 of 12 December 1961, Law 97 of 16 August 1967 and Law 123 of 21 September 1967. This was to be followed by a public warning to the IPC Group issued by the Minister of Oil in January 1969 that there will be no compromise over Iraq's determination to exploit her oil wealth. Again in February 1970 the government declared the cancellation of the last provision in Law 80 which permitted the allocation of any new territory to the IPC Group.

As a result of the anticipated important oil related agreements to be signed by INOC, a special committee of ministers, responsible to the Revolutionary Command Council, was established in March 1970 to supervise all the commercial contracts and foreign agreements and in particular those affecting the oil industry and INOC. Meanwhile Saddam Hussain who had become Vice President of the republic in September 1971 also assumed the chairmanship of this ministerial committee. Soon after in November the committee became to be known as the Follow-Up Committee of Oil Affairs and Implementation of Agreement and as a result took direct control of the country's oil production and marketing policy.

The Restructuring of the Ministry of Oil and INOC

The nationalisation of the Iraq Petroleum Company and the creation of the Iraq Company for Oil Operations, ICOO (later on the North Petroleum Organisation, NPO) in June 1972 and the nationalisation of the Basrah Petroleum Company in December 1975 and its replacement by the national South Petroleum Organisation, SPO put the management and operations of the whole of Iraq's upstream oil industry in the hands of three organisations, NPO,SPO and INOC.

Over the period of ten years from 1967 and 1976, INOC had expanded its operations enormously. It had its own experienced teams in the fields of exploration, drilling, production and operations. It explored and drilled in several old and new locations all over Iraq such as Nahr Omar (1971), Rattawi (1971), Luhais (1973), West Qurnah (1973), Sufaiya (1974), Suba (1974), Jabbal Fakka (1974), Khabbaz (1976), Mansuria (mid 70s), East Bagdad (mid 70s) and Halfaya (1977).

It was involved in the development and construction of some of the giant projects such as the Iraq-Turkey pipeline, the strategic pipeline, the Rumaila/ Fao pipeline, the rehabilitation of the oil terminal at Fao, the new deep sea water terminal, Mina al-Bakr, which had a design capacity of 80 million tons per year together with the onshore and marine pipelines connecting it with the Rumaila field, and all the development and construction work of the different newly discovered oilfields including the North Rumaila field itself.

As a result of the rapid growth of its vast activities, INOC's organisation had been developed more on the basis of what was dictated by the circumstances rather than by a detailed and long term planning. Furthermore, during this period, INOC had been attached to the office of the President of the Republic and later on to the Follow-Up Committee; it has had the Minister of Oil as its chairman for certain periods as well as others. All this resulted in confused lines of communications; vague spheres of responsibly and at times overlap of authorities and cumbersome relationship between it and the Ministry of Oil.

Hence it was decided to reorganise the whole of the oil and gas industry on a more modern industry footing and as a result a committee was set up headed by the Deputy Minister of Oil, Deputy Chairman of INOC and other senior experts from within the oil industry to restructure the organisation of the country's vast oil and gas industry. This effort was culminated in the issue of Law 101 of 1976 which brought back the whole of the oil and gas industry under the umbrella of the Ministry of Oil. The resultant organisation chart of the restructured Ministry of Oil is shown in Chapter 6 of this book.

In the meantime INOC itself emerged from this restructuring much bigger and more powerful than before retaining its full control of the upstream side of the county's oil and gas industry. This included not only the management and operations of its own modest newly discovered oil fields but all the country's other major and well developed fields of the recently nationalised oil companies the IPC, BPC and MPC.

Other centralised activities such as planning, exploration, drilling, reservoir engineering as well as crude and products marketing and the ownership and operation of an oil tankers fleet were also retained under its umbrella which resulted in a truly gigantic company as shown by the organisation chart hereunder.

Unfortunately this sudden and great expansion of the spheres of activity of INOC was to lead to greater trouble for it as we shall see later on.

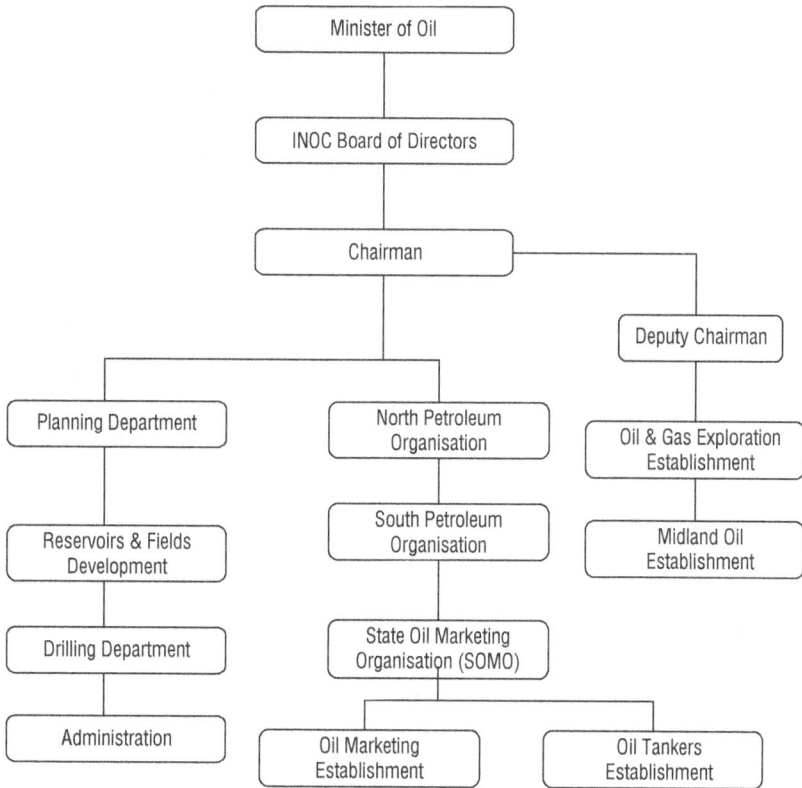

```
                        ┌──────────────────┐
                        │  Minister of Oil │
                        └──────────────────┘
                                 │
                        ┌──────────────────────┐
                        │ INOC Board of Directors │
                        └──────────────────────┘
                                 │
                        ┌──────────────────┐
                        │     Chairman     │──────────────┐
                        └──────────────────┘              │
                                                   ┌──────────────────┐
                                                   │ Deputy Chairman  │
                                                   └──────────────────┘
  ┌──────────────────┐    ┌──────────────────┐    ┌──────────────────────┐
  │Planning Department│    │ North Petroleum  │    │ Oil & Gas Exploration│
  └──────────────────┘    │   Organisation   │    │   Establishment      │
                          └──────────────────┘    └──────────────────────┘
  ┌──────────────────┐    ┌──────────────────┐    ┌──────────────────┐
  │Reservoirs & Fields│    │ South Petroleum  │    │   Midland Oil    │
  │   Development     │    │   Organisation   │    │  Establishment   │
  └──────────────────┘    └──────────────────┘    └──────────────────┘
  ┌──────────────────┐    ┌──────────────────────┐
  │Drilling Department│    │ State Oil Marketing  │
  └──────────────────┘    │ Organisation (SOMO)  │
                          └──────────────────────┘
  ┌──────────────────┐   ┌──────────────────┐  ┌──────────────────┐
  │  Administration  │   │  Oil Marketing   │  │   Oil Tankers    │
  └──────────────────┘   │  Establishment   │  │  Establishment   │
                         └──────────────────┘  └──────────────────┘
```

ERAP (Enterprise de Recherches et d'Activites Petrolieres)

The negotiations with CFP for assistance in the exploration and development of INOC's oil activities did not come to a fruitful conclusion and it was decided that a service contract with the other French state oil company ERAP, similar to the one signed with Iran, was more favourable. Negotiations between INOC and ERAP went ahead and a service contract was initialled by the end of November

1967. The contract covered some 11,000 square kilometres of four separate blocks in the south and south eastern parts of Iraq under which ERAP would carry out exploration work in these blocks and would bear the full cost of the exploration work if oil was not discovered. These costs would however be repaid by INOC if oil was discovered in commercial quantities. ERAP would also finance the cost of the development of the new fields by loans which would be repaid without interest after the production was achieved. Fifty per cent of the discovered reserves would be set aside by INOC as a national reserve when production reached 75,000 barrels per day. In the meantime ERAP would be entitled to purchase a large proportion of the other half of the oil produced. ERAP would pay 50 per cent income tax on the profit. In the meantime INOC would bear the capital cost of the development of the fields.

This agreement was hailed as a complete triumph since it will be the first time in the history of the oil industry in Iraq that the country had full control of its crude oil with a foreign company acting under a service contract only. The INOC/ERAP agreement was formally sanctioned on third February 1968 vide law 5 of 1968. It also was considered as an important political achievement in that a well-known French company has agreed to operate in the expropriated concession areas of the IPC Group without fearing the back lash of the threatened legal action against it.

Relations between INOC and ERAP did not go smoothly mainly as a result of the insistence of INOC on the employment of Iraqi engineers and local contractors. Nonetheless ERAP was able to announce in January 1969 encouraging signs from its first wildcat well and a year later in January 1970 to declare the Buzurgan as a commercial field though the oil was of disappointing quality. After that ERAP went to drill its first well in the Abu Ghrab field on 18 January 1971 and on the first of February 1971 it agreed to relinquish some 65 per cent of its original allocated area.

A separate contract was signed on 20 April 1971 between INOC and ERAP for the preparation of a feasibility study for the construction of a new deep sea water terminal and the export pipeline connecting it with the North Rumaila field

Soon after the discovery of the Buzurgan field, serious disagreements regarding the interpretation of the commercial and financial terms of the original agreement began to appear between INOC and ERAP such as the provision for the fifty per cent national reserve since it was very difficult to determine the quantity of the recoverable reserves, and INOC's demand to go back on the repayment of the exploration costs to ERAP on the ground that the actual costs proved to be very low which would result in excessive profits for ERAP. It is to be noted that by then the two French state companies ERAP and ELF had merged by then to form the ELF/ERAP group.

Negotiations continued in an effort to resolve these disputes when finally a supplementary agreement was signed between INOC and ERAP in which INOC dropped its demand for retaining the fifty per cent national reserve provision and agreeing for the field to be produced as one unit. The financial disputes were also ironed out with ELF/ERAP being granted approval for the assignment of 40 per cent of its interest to a Japanese consortium. The supplementary agreement was finally ratified by the Revolution Command Council in February 1974 and as a result construction work went ahead in earnest and by the third quarter of 1976 the development of two fields of Buzergan and Abu Ghrab had been completed and finally came on stream, though the crude was somewhat heavier and more sour as compared with the much sought after Rumaila crude.

Some financial and expenditure issues started to come to the surface again as INOC thought the price of the crude was still low and the cost of operation and management too high and as a result the profit margin of ELF/ERAP was considered to be too high. By July 1977 INOC had gained enough experience and decided to take over the operation and management of both the Buzurgan and Abu Ghrab fields and the Misan Oilfields Directorate was established to take over these duties. In the meantime ELF/ERAP's crude oil supply from these two fields continued as before without any interruption.

The Soviet Companies

As we have seen a letter of intent was signed in December 1967 in Bagdad by the head of the Soviet delegation and the chairman of INOC for the Soviet assistance in the various fields of the crude oil industry including amongst many others areas, exploration, production marketing, management and training.

The letter itself summarised the scope of the assistance as follows:

> "The Government of the Soviet Socialist Republics has agreed to provide assistance to the Government of the Republic of Iraq in the direct development of its oil industry. Such assistance can be provided by the Soviet organisations in the following fields: drilling producing wells in southern Iraq, and supplying the equipment and services required for this purpose; carrying out geological

and exploratory surveys in connection with the search for oil in the northern areas of Iraq; and determining well locations in areas with proven reserves in southern Iraq, as well as in the areas where geological surveys and exploration operations are to be carried out in northern Iraq.

The scope, terms and conditions of the assistance to be made available in the above-mentioned fields will all be determined in the course of the subsequent negotiations between the delegated representatives of the two parties. It is understood that the expenses incurred by the Soviet organisations in the supply of the equipment and provision of technical assistance for geological surveys and exploration and development drilling, together with expenditure on other operations connected with assistance required for the direct development of Iraq's national oil industry, will be reimbursed by the Iraqi side in the form of deliveries to the Soviet Union of crude oil produced by the Iraq National Oil Company. The terms and conditions applicable to such deliveries will be determined at the same time as those governing the provision of assistance mentioned earlier."

In the meantime INOC, with its management attached directly to the President of the Republic's Office and with such support at the highest level, began work in earnest on setting the required organisation for the development of the North Rumaila and the other fields. A recruitment programme of engineers and technicians was initiated and a vigorous training programme was set up for them both inside the county and abroad. Another programme was also drawn up for the procurement of some of the essential exploration, drilling, and other equipment. As a result, by April 1968 INOC had managed to establish some of its first core technical organisations such as the exploration and the drilling departments.

The programme set up for the development of the North Rumaila field in conjunction with the Soviet assistance was envisaged to be carried out in two phases as follows:-

FIRST PHASE

This phase envisaged bringing the production capacity of the Field to 100,000 barrels per day at an estimated cost of six million Iraqi Dinars or approximately US $20,000 million and will involve the completion of the following major works:-

1.   Construction of all the necessary infrastructures and the supply of services.

2. Drilling of the necessary production and observation wells.

3. Construction of flow lines, degassing stations, tank farm and pumping stations.

4. Construction of a pipeline from North Rumaila field to the port of Fao.

5. The rehabilitation of the port of Fao which was used by the Basrah Petroleum Company prior to the construction of its deep seawater terminal at Khor al-Amaya in 1964. Though the facilities at Fao were limited and could only handle tankers of up to 50,000 tons, it had an annual capacity of some 10 million tons equivalent to 200,000 barrels of oil per day which would be enough for this phase.

SECOND PHASE

This phase envisaged the expansion of the production capacity of the North Rumaila Field to 360,000 barrels per day which would involve the following major works:-

1. Drilling of additional production and observation wells, flow lines, degassing facilities, storage tanks and pumping units.

2. Construction of onshore and marine large diameter pipeline system for the delivery of the export crude to a new deep-sea water terminal.

3. Construction of a new deep seawater terminal with a capacity of some 80 million tons of crude oil per year equivalent to some 1.6 million barrels per day which was to become known later on as Mina al-Bakr.

Work progressed at a fairly good pace in the first half of 1968 until July of that year when the 17 July revolution brought in the new government of the Baath party. The internal struggle within the party and the government's involvement in other political issues as well as the introduction of a new Minister of Oil and a new management at INOC slowed the pace of progress of the implementation of the whole programme. It was not until a year later that a general agreement was signed on 4 July 1969 between INOC and the Soviet firm Machinoexport. The agreement was for a loan of 25 million Iraqi Dinars equivalent to US $72 million which would be used for the provision of drilling rigs, survey teams, the preparation of studies, specification, design work and the training of

INOC personnel. Other similar agreements were made later on to ensure the completion of the first phase of the development programme on time.

The actual drilling of the first well in the North Rumaila field began on 12 July 1970 by an INOC drilling team with the help of the Hungarian company Kemocomplex. This was followed by the drilling of the second well by an INOC's team alone. Extensive on the job training followed and efficiency increased dramatically and soon after new all Iraqi drilling teams were created and were able to join in the drilling operations all over the country.

However the progress of work by the Machinoexport and other Soviet organisations was falling behind schedule and INOC urged the Soviet Union to take action to bring it back on schedule since it was important for INOC to make its first large scale project a success and since it was politically vital for the government as matter of national pride to ensure the production and flow of its own crude oil to world market on time. Intensive discussions followed with the signing of additional protocols in September 1971 under which the Soviet government agreed to urge the various Soviet organisations to speed up the supply of equipment and the provision of additional experts and technicians to meet the completion date.

In the meantime work had already started on 10 February 1971 for the construction of the 138 kilometre long and 28 inch diameter pipeline between the North Rumaila and Fao which had a design capacity of 360,000 barrel per day.

Hence it was a proud moment for the Iraqi and the Soviet governments as well as for INOC and the Soviet organisations when the inauguration of the North Rumaila field was announced. Alexei Kosygin, Chairman of the Council of Ministers of the Soviet Union joined Saddam Hussain, Vice President of the Republic of Iraq together with oil ministers and other high ranking foreign dignitaries attended the inauguration ceremony on 7 April 1972. This date was significant since it was less than two months before the nationalisation of the Iraq Petroleum Company on first June 1972.

The first shipment of 21,000 tons of North Rumaila crude oil was loaded on a Soviet tanker under charter by INOC in early April 1972 only to be followed a week later on 14 April by a second shipment which was proudly loaded this time on Iraq's first crude oil tanker the Rumaila.

A separate agreement was signed on 28 April 1973 between the Iraqi State Organisation for Oil Projects and the Soviet organisation Technoexport for the development the of the newly discovered Nahr Omar field. The initial production capacity of this field was estimated between 10,000 and 30,000 barrels per day bearing in mind that the drilling in this field was started by INOC in October 1971 and oil was discovered in commercial quantities on 15 June 1972. The field was finally developed and went on stream during the late 1970s.

Petrobras

A service contract was signed on 6 August 1972 between INOC and the Brazilian oil company, Petrobras, under the terms of which Petrobras was granted an area of 7,900 square kilometres in three separate blocks for exploration. The first block was between the city of Falluja and Baghdad, the second in the Ali al-Gharbi region and the third east of the town of Qurna towards the Iranian border. Petrobras was to provide technical, financial and marketing services against which it was entitled to purchase crude oil on special terms.

Petrobras began its exploration work on 15 December 1972 and its long searches were finally rewarded in 1977 by its discovery in the third block of the now famous Majnoon oil field.

Subsequent appraisal drilling had proved the field to be gigantic with its enormous recoverable reserves being estimated between 7 to 11 billion barrels of oil.

India Oil and National Gas Corporation

A service contract was signed 8 April 1973 between INOC and India Oil and National Gas Corporation, for providing exploration and development services in the south of Iraq similar to that of Petrobras. The Company started its operations by drilling its first well in August 1975. The well proved to be dry and after spending US $9.0 million, it relinquished its rights in early 1977. However other agreements in the fields of oil exploration, development and technical co-operations as well as training, were not affected.

The Japanese Companies

A 15 year agreement was signed between INOC and Mitsubishi Corporation for the purchase of liquid petroleum gas (LPG) to begin as soon as INOC's

LPG was in production. Mitsubishi was also participating in the Japanese consortium which in 1973 acquired the 40 per cent interest in the ELF/ERAP contract as mentioned before.

At the beginning of 1974 an economic and technical agreement was signed between the Japanese Minister of Trade and Industry and the Iraqi Minister of Industry, under which Japan was to lend Iraq US $1,000 million to be used to finance the construction of a variety of projects including chemical, gas liquefaction, an export refinery and other plants. The loan was for 15 years and would be repaid in crude oil, refined products, and LPG.

The first of the contracts to be financed by this loan was signed in September 1975 with Mitsubishi for the construction of a chemical fertilizer plant. A second contract was signed a month later for the construction of a pipeline for the supply of natural gas from the south Rumaila field to the industrial complex at Khor al-Zubair. A third contract was awarded to another Japanese company to build oil tankers for INOC.

The Spanish Companies

The Iraqi government realised that the major oil companies controlled most of the world's crude oil tankers and could make it very difficult for Iraq to export its nationalised oil in the future if and when the occasion arises. As a result a loan agreement was negotiated at the end of 1969 with a Spanish company for the construction of crude oil tankers. Seven such tankers were constructed and delivered to INOC during the period 1972 and 1973. Each tanker had a capacity of some 35,000 tons and a subsidiary of INOC by the name of Iraqi Oil Tankers Company was establishes to operate the fleet. The seven tankers were named Rumaila, Kirkuk, Ain Zalah, Jambur, Khaniqin, Baba Gurgur and Buzergan. Rumaila was the first tanker to be built and its completion coincided with the inauguration of the North Rumaila field and as such she was able to lift the second shipment from this field on 14 April 1972.

The Italian Companies

A contract was signed on 9 March 1972 between INOC and ENI, a subsidiary of the Italian company Snam-Progetti, for the sale of 20 million tons of oil over a period of ten years.

A second contract was signed on 16 December 1972 with Snam-Progetti for the construction of the first Iraq-Turkey pipeline for the export of the Kirkuk crude. The 1005 kilometre long and 40-inch in diameter pipeline from Kirkuk to the Mediterranean port of Ceyhan had a design throughput capacity of 750,000 barrel of crude oil per day and was commissioned in 1977.

A third contract was signed in 1973 with ENI for the preparation of the study and the construction of the Strategic Pipeline system which stretches over a distance of 730 kilometres between K-3 pumping station on the river Euphrates and the southern oil fields. It consists of two pipelines, a 42 inch diameter crude oil pipeline and a 16 inch diameter fuel gas pipeline as detailed in Chapter 11 of this book.

The Breakup of INOC

As described under the Ministry of Oil in Chapter 6, INOC over the following eleven years grew into a mammoth, cumbersome and very difficult to manage company with no clear line of responsibilities in many spheres of its activities resulting in confusion and overlapping layers of authority between some of its own subsidiaries and at times with the Ministry of Oil. This led to the second drastic restructuring of the Ministry of Oil which finally took place in March 1987. The main outcome of this restructuring was the complete breakup and final dissolution of the once powerful Iraq National Oil Company and the creation of a number of independent State owned companies under the direct control the Ministry of Oil as shown by the relevant Ministry of Oil organisation chart.

PREAMBLE
to the
LAW ESTABLISHING THE IRAQ NATIONAL OIL COMPANY

The most important objective of The oil policy of the Government of the Republic of Iraq as portrayed in the Government's programme announced on December 24, 1963 is the establishment of a national oil industry that would serve as basis for future oil exploitation activities in the areas of which the rights of exploitation have been restored to the State by Law No. 80 of 1961, and the laying down of the groundwork necessary for the growth and development of the industry so as to create an advanced oil economy not limited in scope to exportation of crude oil but extending to effective engagement in the various phases of the oil industry with a view to bringing about interaction on a larger scale between the oil economy and the national economy.

In view of the importance of the oil reserves of which the rights of exploitation are expected to be granted to the National Oil Company, and of the significance of those reserves for the future of the country's economy, the law has stipulated that the Company's capital shall be purely governmental, in keeping with the principle of sovereignty over mineral resources of the State that are natural monopolies.

This, however, shall not preclude the Company, acting within its statutory framework, from making use of other capital, domestic or foreign, through loans or through partnership of various forms of business cooperation with concerns or organisations concerned with oil development, should this be warranted by the magnitude of the capital needed, marketing exigencies or the technological requirements of construction.

Further, since it is necessary that the Company enjoys financial and administrative independence for it to be able to perform most efficiently its diverse and steadily-growing tasks so as to achieve the purposes for which it is established, the law has stressed the Company's independence in those spheres and stipulated that the decisions of the Company's Board of Directors shall be implemented immediately upon their issue, with the exception of such decisions as may involve matters regarded as pertaining to the country's supreme oil policy. The law stipulates that such matters shall be dealt with by the Council of Ministers.

1

In the Name of the People

The Presidency of the Republic

In accordance with Proclamation No. 1 issued by the National Council of the Revolutionary Command, pursuant to the proposal of the Minister of Oil and with the approval of the Council of Ministers, do hereby order the promulgation of the following Law :-

Article 1. — A company shall be established in accordance with this law under the name of the "Iraq National Oil Company" (hereinafter referred to as the "Company") having corporate status and full capacity to act for achieving its objectives.

Article 2. — (1) The Company's objectives shall be to engage both inside and outside Iraq in the oil industry in any or all of its phases including exploration and prospecting for oil and natural hydrocarbons, production, transportation, refining, storage, and distribution of said substances or of their products or derivatives (prtrochemicals) and the manufacture of relevant equipment. The Company shall have the right to trade in all these substances.

(2) The Company for the purpose of achieving its objectives shall have the right to establish companies, singly or jointly with other parties, or participate in existing companies.

(3) The Company shall have the right to enter into contracts, for cooperation in various forms, with companies or organisations engaged in activities related to its objectives, also to purchase or affiliate such companies or organisations.

(4) The Company within the scope of its objectives shall have the right to establish, singly, companies with capital wholly owned by it in accordance with articles of association to be issued by the Company.

(5) The Company shall not exercise the operation of refining and distribution of oil products for the purposes of local

2

consumption within Iraq so long as there exist other Government organisations having legal monopolistic control over said operation.

Article 3. — (1) The Company shall have the right to perform the functions prescribed in Article 2 hereof in all Iraqi territory with the exception of areas covered by Article 2 of Law No. 80 of 1961 Defining the Areas for Exploitation by the Oil Companies and of such areas as the Government may allocate to these Companies under Article 3 of the said Law.

(2) The Company shall select the areas wherein it may desire to carry out its operations. Such areas shall be allocated to the Company by the Council of Ministers upon recommendation by the Minister of Oil.

(3) The Company shall within a period not exceeding six months from the date of this Law submit an initial application for defining the areas wherein it desires to carry out its operations.

Article 4. — (1) The Company's capital shall be twenty-five million Dinars payable by the Government upon request from the Company's Board of Directors and with the approval of the Council of Ministers, which capital may be increased as required up to such limit as may be decided by the Council of Ministers upon the proposal of the Board of Directors,

(2) The Government may hand over the capital to the Company wholly or in part in the form of materials valued in cash.

(3) The liability of the Company shall be limited to its capital.

Article 5 — (1) The Company shall have the right to secure loans or borrow from any party inside or outside Iraq for financing its projects.

3

(2) The Company shall have the right to secure loans or borrow against Government guarantee on such conditions as may be decided by the Council of Ministers. Where loans are secured through the issue of domestic bearer-bonds, such loans and the interest thereon shall be exempt from all current and future taxes and duties, and the bonds together with the relative coupons and receipt vouchers shall be exempt from stamp duty. The Company's bonds shall be regarded as cash for the purposes of tenders, sureties and bids concerning official and semi-official departments and institutions.

(3) The total of standing loans owned by the Company shall not exceed a sum three times its capital as prescribed.

The Company shall keep its deposits with the Central Bank of Iraq or with such party as may be designated by said Bank and shall have the right to deal with all banks inside or outside Iraq.

1) Oil and hydrocarbon resources in areas allocated to the Company under Article 3 hereof shall remain to be inalienable and imprescriptible property of the State.

2) The Company shall pay to the Government, as Government share, 50% (fifty per cent) of its annual net profits, which share shall, for income tax purposes, be treated as part of the operating expenses.

The Company and the companies wholly owned by it shall enjoy the following privileges :-

) Their profits shall be exempt from the provisions of Income Tax Law No. 95 of 1959 for a period of five years as from the year in which the Company realises its first profit. Subsequently, there shall be exemption of all reserve funds which the Company allocates out of its profits for reinvestment in connec-

4

tion with its objectives prescribed in this Law, provided that such funds are invested within a period not exceeding five years. If they are not invested within the said period they shall be subject to the provisions of the Income Tax Law in that they will be regarded profits in respect of the year following the five-year period.

2) The Company shall be exempt from all taxes and duties in respect of the performance of its functions prescribed in Article 2 of this Law.

3) The Company shall be regarded as a public utility institution for the purposes of expropriation.

1) The Company shall be administered by a Board of Directors which shall be financially and administratively independent and composed of nine members, including the Chairman and the Deputy Chairman, as shown hereunder :-

(a) Three members, who shall be senior Government officials. These shall be appointed by a Council of Ministers decision upon recommendation by the Minister of Oil, provided that the status of each such official shall not be below that of Director General.

(b) Six full-time members who shall be appointed and their salaries determined by a Council of Ministers decision and a Republican Ordinance upon recommendation by the Minister of Oil, provided they are experts specialised in oil, economic, legal, or technical affairs. These members shall include the Managing Director.

(c) The Council of Ministers shall select the Chairman of the Board of Directors from among the full-time members mentioned in Para. (b) above. The posts of Chairman of the Board of Directors and that of Managing Director shall not be held by the same person.

5

(b) The board shall elect from among its members a Deputy Chairman to act as Chairman in the absence of the latter.

(2) Three alternate members shall be appointed on the line prescribed in Para. (1) (a) of this Article.

(3) Board membership shall be for a renewable period of three years.

Article 10. —(1) The Managing Director shall be appointed and his salary determined by a Council of Ministers decision and a Republican Ordinance upon recommendation by the Minister of Oil.

(2) The Managing Director shall represent the Company before official and other quarters and shall implement the decisions of the Board of Directors. The Board may entrust him with such powers as it may deem appropriate.

Article 11. —The decisions of the Company's Board of Directors shall be implemented upon the issue thereof, with the following exceptions :-

(1) Any partnership or participation into which the Company may enter with another party shall not be implemented prior to approval by the Council of Ministers.

(1) A Company established in accordance with the provisions of Para. (3) of Article 2 shall not be regarded as existing unless the Council of Ministers has approved its establishment and its articles of association and unless same has been published if the Official Gazette.

(3) No external or domestic loan Shall be concluded before the approval of the Council of Ministers.

Article 12. —(1) The Company shall adhere to the general oil policy of the State and shall be attached to the Minister of Oil in respect to the implementation thereof. In the event of a difference between the Minister and the Company in regard to said policy, such difference shall be brought before the Council of Ministers for a decision.

6

(2) The Chairman of the Board of Directors may upon the approval of the Prime Minister attend the discussions of the Council of Ministers on matters pertaining to the Company in a consultative capacity.

Article 13—(1) The Company shall prepare its annual budget and shall submit same to the Council of Ministers for approval. In case the approval is delayed and the relative fiscal year sets in, recourse shall be had to the previous budget which shall be taken as basis and applied at the rate of 1/12 per month until the approval is given.

(2) The Company shall prepare its closing accounts within a year as from the end of its fiscal year, provided that said accounts shall be certified by a chartered accountant by the Board of Directors. The closing accounts shall be published in the Official Gazette.

(3) The Board of Directors shall submit an annual report to the Council of Ministers together with the Company's closing accounts.

Article 14—The Company shall be administered in accordance with articles of association to be laid down by the Board of Directors.

Article 15.—The Company shall not be dissolved nor liquidated except by law.

Article 16.—No legal stipulations shall apply which are incompatible with the provisions of this Law.

Article 17.—This Law shall come into force after thirty days from the date of its publication in the Official Gazette.

Article 18.—The Ministers are charged with the execution of this Law.
   Made at Baghdad this 25th day of Ramadhan, 1383, and 8th day of Febrawary of 1964.

7

Staff Field-Marshal
Abdul Salam Mohammed Arif,
President of the Republic.

Tahir Yahya,
Prime Minister and
Ag. Minister of Defence.

Subhi Abdul Hameed,
Minister of Foreign Affairs.

Rasheed Muslih,
Minister of Interior.

Abdul Kerim Farhan,
Minister of Guidance.

Abdul Kereem Kannouna,
Minister of Industry.

Abdul Aziz al-Wattari'
Minister of Oil.

Abdul Kereem al-Ali,
Minister of Planning.

Mahmoud Sheet Khattab,
Minister of Municipal and
Rural Affairs.

Kamil al-Khateeb,
Minister of Justice.

Mohamed Jawad al-Oboosy,
Minister of Finance.

Mohamed Nasir,
Minister of Education.

Abdul Kereem Hani,
Minister of Labour and
Social Affairs.

Abdul Fattah al-Alousi,
Minister of Works and Housing

Abdul Sahib al-Alwan,
Minister of Agrarian Reform and
Ag. Minister of Agriculture.

Abdul Aziz al-Hafidh,
Minister of Economics.

Shamil al-Samarrrai,
Minister of Health.

Abdul Razzaq Muhyi al-Din,
Minister of State for Unity Affairs.

Hassan Majeed al-Dujaili,
Minister of Communications'

Muslih al-Naqshabandi,
Minister of State for Awqaf,
(Published in the Waqayi' al-Iraqiya No. 912 of 8/2/1964).

8

IRAQ'S OIL AND GAS FIELDS

The following eighty four oil and gas fields have been discovered in Iraq. Six of them are deemed giants, each containing more than five billion barrels of oil. Another 16 fields are classified as large each containing between 500 million and five billion barrels of oil. The total recoverable reserves in these fields at the end of the twentieth century was estimated at 112 billion barrels of oil while their gas reserves were estimated at 110 trillion standard cubic feet of associated and dome natural gas. However more recent estimates put the recoverable oil reserves at 143 billion barrels which ranks Iraq in terms of recoverable reserves as the third country in the world after Saudi Arabia and Iran.

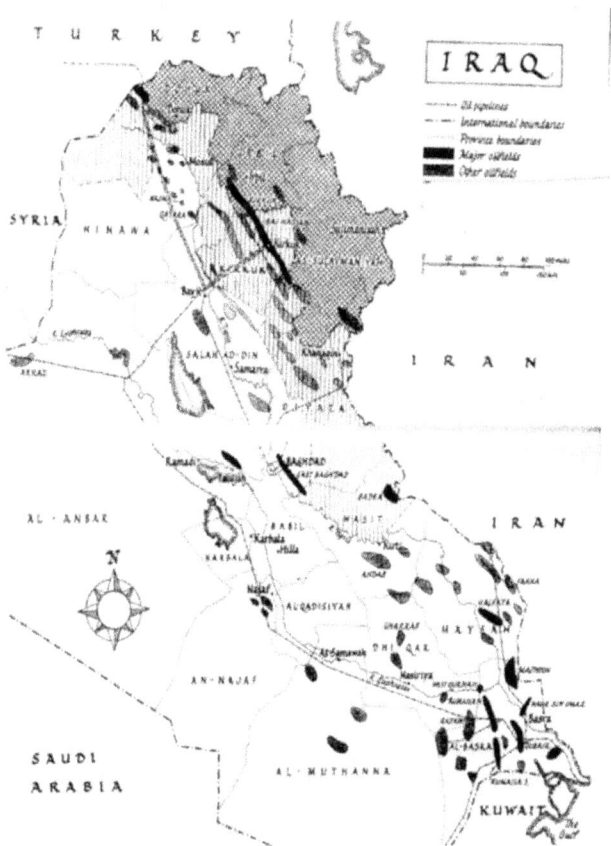

Map of Most of Iraq's Oil & Gas Fields

Current Oil and Gas Affairs

It is to be highlighted that though this book deals with oil and gas related events that took place during the twentieth century, certain important and controversial other events have taken place during the first decade of the twenty first century. These include the award of several Production Service Contracts by the Ministry of Oil of the Central Government in Baghdad to a number of the international oil companies and the signing of numerous Exploration and Production Sharing Agreements by the Kurdistan Regional Government for a large number of oil and gas fields to some other companies. It is therefore considered appropriate to briefly comment on these much debated topics and to include the newly discovered oil and gas fields in this book.

THE PRODUCTION SERVICE CONTRACTS

While some of the Production Service Contracts relate to the further development of some of the currently producing giant and large fields, others relate to the development of a number of similar proven but undeveloped oil and gas fields.

These Contracts are based on paying the oil companies fixed fees for each new barrel of oil produced by them, in addition to reimbursing them with their actual costs. The Contracts have attracted criticism from some of the political parties, parliamentarians, prominent independent politicians, a wide circle of experienced oil industry technocrats, legal experts, intellectuals and the Federation of the Oil Unions.

The main criticisms directed towards these Contracts refer to:

- The extent of the control that the International Oil Companies have over these oil and gas fields which is considered by many to infringe on the sovereignty of the state.

- The lengthy terms of these Contracts of 20 years with some of them renewable for a second term, since the usual term for a typical Service Contract is much shorter than that.

- The excessive number of mainly giant and large fields involved in these Contracts which resulted in putting a very high percentage of the country's oil and gas resources under some control of these international oil companies.

- That they were awarded in the absence of clearly defined articles in the Constitution regarding the national hydrocarbon resources as well as the absence of an approved Hydrocarbon Law.

Other criticism questions the wisdom of the latest Contracts for the development of the three gas fields, Akkas, **Mansuriyah and Siba** for a combined total production rate of some 800 million standard cubic feet per day of gas at the time when 700 MMSCFD out of the country's 1,500 MMSCFD of associatesd gases are currently being flared.

Further criticisms are directed towards the Central Government's over-ambitious future production policy which is expected to raise the country's crude oil production from the current level of 2.5 million barrels per day to the staggering figure of 12.0 million barrels per day by the year 2017. This seems to be grossly unrealistic, difficult to attain, unnecessary as well as being a likely cause for future friction or even a possible confrontation with the Organisation of Oil Producing Countries (OPEC), the very organisation that Iraq was one of its champions and founders in 1961. It seems that a more reasonable and realistic rate of production of six to eight million barrels per day is considered to be more acceptable to most Iraqi reservoir engineers, industry experts, economists, and the mainstream independent politicians.

All that said, it must also be added that the Production Service Contract is a much more advantageous method for the Government than the originally proposes method of Production Sharing Agreement. This is so because the fee per new barrel produced is fixed during the term of the Contract . For instance the fee for British Petroleum for its contract for the Ramaila field is $2.00 per barrel, that for the ExxonMobil for its contract for the West Qurna Phase One is $1.90 per barrel, while that for Eni, Occidental and Korea Gas Corporation for the Zubair field is also $2.00 per barrel.

Such fees represent about 2% of the price of a barrel of oil, based on current average international crude oil prices of around $100 per barrel, equivalent to 2% of the quantity of the oil produced, which appears to be reasonable if no other undeclared strings are attached to it.

In the meantime, since the crude oil prices are expected to rise during the 20 years term of such contracts due to normal inflation if not for other reasons, the $2.00 per barrel fee will represent a much lower percentage than the currently calculated 2%, making them even more advantageous for the Central

Government as compared with the Production Sharing Agreements signed by the Kurdistan Regional Government as explained below.

THE PRODUCTION SHARING AGREEMENTS

On the other hand, the Exploration and Production Sharing Agreements signed by the Kurdistan Regional Government relate mainly to the discovery and development of some of the promising oil and gas fields in addition to the development of a few small previously discovered but undeveloped fields.

These Agreements are based on giving the oil companies a share of the crude oil produced depending on the prospect of finding it as well as the oil reserves expected to be held in such structures.

Though the percentage of the shares given to the different oil companies have not been published and hence unknown, such percentages are usually high and could vary widely from 20% up to 35% of the oil produced, since they will have to cover the risk associated with the exploration of failing to find oil in commercial quantities, the costs of exploration, development and production and finally the corresponding higher than usual profit.

Hence these Agreements are much more attractive and advantageous for the oil companies as compared with the Production Service Contracts awarded by the Ministry of Oil in Baghdad. This is because the oil companies net profits are expected to be much higher than 2% of the oil produced and that they will grow even higher in dollar terms as a result of the anticipated rise in the international prices of the crude oil during the much longer terms associated with such agreements of up to 50 years. Such Agreements also tend to give the oil companies much more power over the control of the fields.

It must be highlighted that these Production Sharing Agreements are considered to be illegal by the Central Government in Baghdad and have been the subject of bitter disputes between the Central Government and the Kurdistan Regional Government. Countless claims, counter claims, accusations, counter accusations and endless conflicting statements have been made on this subject by both sides during the past few years and are still being made today.

The main factors which are causing this controversy are:

- The ambiguity of the new Constitution which was drafted after the invasion of the country in 2003 on the subject of oil and gas. The two main articles which are creating this confusion are no. 111 and 112.

  So, while article 111 states that "Oil and gas are the ownership of all the people of Iraq in all the regions and governorates", article 112 states that the Central Government has the right for "the management of oil and gas extracted from current fields".

  This language has led to the contention over what constitutes a "new" or a "current" field, a question that has profound ramification for the ultimate control of future oil and gas resources.

  The Kurdistan Regional Government (KRG) took the view that the statement in article 111 "the ownership of all the people of Iraq in all the regions and governorates" conveys ownership to each region and governorate and as such it has the right to sign exploration and production agreements without having to consult with the Central Government in Baghdad.

  Furthermore the Kurdistan Regional Government took the view that the wording "current fields" in article 112 to be limited to the previously producing fields and does not include the previously discovered but non-producing fields such as Taq Taq and Kor Mor or any of the newly discovered or to be discovered fields. These views by the Kurdistan Regional Government are completely rejected by the Central Government in Baghdad and as a result it has declared that all the Exploration and Production Sharing Agreements signed by the KRG to be illegal and as a result has blacklisted all the oil companies which have signed these contracts.

- The never-ending delays that have been experienced in finalising the country's proposed Hydrocarbons Law which had been first drafted in August 2006, redrafted, amended, refined and endlessly debated by all the political parties including Parliamentarian Committees for the past five years without any tangible result.

  This is mainly due the different interpretations of articles 111 and 112 of the Constitution as highlighted above and the short-sighted agendas that are being adopted by the numerous political parties which are promoting their own immediate political and financial gains instead of the adoption of the much broader national policy that would result in the welfare and prosperity of the people and the unity of the country.

Regretfully, it seems that the current confusion and indecision will continue to rumble on for some time to come before some sort of a final and comprehensive settlement could be reached to resolve all these very complex issues.

In the meantime, the main losers are the ordinary people of Iraq

Definitions and Abbreviations

It is though appropriate that before discussing the individual fields, it would be useful to explain the various terms used to characterize these fields for the benefit of those readers who are not familiar with the jargon of the oil and gas industry.

*   An oil and/or gas field is an area of land or sea under which a porous and permeable sedimentary rock structure bearing hydrocarbons (oil/gas/ condensate) is found. Often, the structure is an Anticline resulting from the folding of the rock structure due to compression forces resulting from collision of the earth's tectonic plates in geological times. This gives the anticline the shape of a dome and thus a good trap for hydrocarbons.

*   A 'Formation' is a rock structure with certain characteristics in common such as 'Lithology', composition, age and 'Stratigraphy'. Formations are usually named after the nearest town or village to an outcrop of that rock type is found, or named after similar formation in another field in the area. More than one reservoir can exist at different depths of the same field, separated by layers of tight rock. Generally the depth of a reservoir determines the pressure and temperature of the reservoir fluids.

INOC	Iraq National Oil Company
IPC	Iraq Petroleum Company.
BPC	Basra Petroleum Company .
MPC	Mosul Petroleum Company.
API	American Petroleum Institute
API Gravity	= (141.5/Specific Gravity at 60 Fahrenheit) - 131.5
Porosity	The ratio of the volume of void space to the total volume of a rock
Permeability	The ability of a rock with interconnected pores and/or fractures to transmit fluid through the pore spaces

mD	Milli Darcy is a unit of measurement of permeability (A porous medium has a permeability of 1 Darcy when differential pressure of atmosphere across a sample 1 cubic centimetre in volume will force a liquid of 1 centipoise of viscosity through the sample at the rate of 1 cubic centimetre per second).
GOC	Gas / Oil Contact.
OWC	Oil / Water Contact.
GOR	Gas / Oil Ratio (number of cubic feet of associated gas in one barrel of oil produced).
SCF/B	Standard Cubic Feet of Gas per Barrel (unit to measure the GOR).
Oil Column	The vertical thickness of oil bearing formation in an oil reservoir.
PPM	Parts per million (usually used for H2S content of gas).
MBO	Thousand Barrel Oil.
MMBO	Million Barrel Oil.
BBO	Billion Barrel Oil.
BOPD	Barrel Oil per Day.
MBOPD	Thousand Barrel Oil per Day.
MMBOPD	Million Barrel Oil per Day.
SCFG	Standard Cubic Foot Gas.
SCFGD	Standard Cubic Feet Gas per Day.
MSCFGD	Thousand Standard Cubic Feet Gas per Day.
MMSCFGD	Million Standard Cubic Gas Feet per Day.
TSCFG	Trillion Standard Cubic Feet Gas.

The Oil and Gas Fields

Many of the fields listed hereunder have been developed and many more are awaiting development.

A few small old and newly discovered fields have been developed during the first decade of the twenty first century by the Kurdistan Regional Government and dozens more promising fields are being explored and discovered in the Kurdistan region. The comprehensive list of such fields is shown at the end of this chapter.

1- ABU AMUD

This oilfield was discovered in 1982 and located about 250 km south of Baghdad. Its oil had 30° API gravity and its reservoir formation is Zubair sands. It was awaiting appraisal and not considered as a priority field for development until after the end of the Iraq/Iran war only to be delayed by the invasion of Kuwait and the subsequent events of the Gulf War and the prolonged and cruel sanctions against Iraq during the 1990s and beyond.

2 - ABU AMUD EAST

This field was discovered in 1982 soon after the discovery of the original Abu Amud field and is located some 50 km east of it. It had a similar reservoir with 30° API gravity oil. This field was overtaken by the same subsequent unfortunate events of the Abu Amud field.

3 - ABU GHRAB

This field was discovered in 1971 by the French company ERAP (later on ELF/ERAP) under its service agreement with Iraq National Oil Company (INOC). It is located in the south-eastern region of the country, north east of the city of Amara and close to the Iranian border and the Buzurgan field.

The reservoir is an anticline stretching in a northwest-southeast direction and measures roughly about 40 km in length by 8 km in width. It has two reservoirs; the upper reservoir is an Asmari Formation sandy limestone of Oligocene-Miocene age and is at a depth of 2,900 metres with an oil column ranging between 60 and 100 metres and has a tilted oil/water contact. It contains heavy oil with 23° API gravity and 3.7% sulphur. The lower reservoir is a Mishrif Formation limestone of Middle Cretaceous age and is at a depth of 3,650 metres having a lighter oil of 32° API gravity. The reserves were estimated at between 1 and 1.5 billion barrels.

The field was subsequently developed, after some delays due to certain contractual disputes between ERAP and INOC, and came on stream during 1977, with a design capacity of 160,000 barrels of oil per day.

The field, together with two other fields in Missan Province (Fakka and Buzergan) have been the subject of tenders and negotiations in recent years and a service contract was finally awarded in 2010 to the Chinese Hong Kong based company in partnership with the Turkish company TPAO for the further development of these three fields.

This is expected to raise the production capacity of the three fields from their combined current capacity of 115,000 to 1,450,000 barrel of oil per day.

4 - ABU KHAIMAH

This field was discovered in 1976 in the south of the country near the Kuwait and Saudi Arabian borders. The field is very small and was considered marginally economical at that time and was left pending future appraisal. The reservoir is in a Zubair Sands formation (Lower Cretaceous) about 3,000 metres deep and has a 33° API gravity oil.

5 - AFAQ

Discovered in 1961, this field is located about 100 km south of Baghdad. It has an anticlinal structure with reservoirs in the upper and lower cretaceous. It was not developed. No further information is available.

6 - AHDAB

This field was discovered in 1979 and situated about 100 km south of Baghdad along the eastern bank of the river Tigris close to the East Baghdad field. The oil bearing reservoir is the Zubair sands formation of the Lower Cretaceous.

Seven wells had been drilled in this field by 1988 for delineation purposes. The ultimate recoverable reserves were estimated at around one billion barrels of 30° API gravity oil.

The field was earmarked for development in the early 1990's. However the Gulf War and the subsequent sanctions disrupted its planned development.

It was not until recently when, after lengthy negotiation, an agreement was reached during August 2008 between the Ministry of Oil and the China National Oil Corporation (CNOC) to develop the field. The recoverable reserves of the field are estimated to be about 1.0 BBO and the plan is to attain a production rate of 110,000 BOPD.

7 - AIN ZALAH

This is one of the smaller oil fields in northern Iraq. It was discovered in 1939 by the Mosul Petroleum Company (MPC) which was taken over at a later stage by the Iraq Petroleum Company (IPC). It is located about 80 km northwest of the city of Mosul. .

The structure is an east-west trending steeply folded anticline about 16 km in length and 4 km in width and contains two reservoirs connected by fractures.

The upper (first pay) reservoir is limited both vertically and horizontally by the extent of fracturing. It consists of 75-90 metres of fractured marly limestone of the Upper Cretaceous Shiranish formation sealed by shale. It has an 11% porosity and negligible permeability. The pore space is water saturated and recoverable oil is mainly in the fractures. The second pay consist of 400 metres of Qamchuqa and Mushorah formations carbonates of the basal Upper and Middle Cretaceous and is separated from the first pay by 600 metres of poorly fractured Shiranish formation. This is illustrated by Fig. AZ-1 which shows a cross section through the field and Fig. AZ-2 showing a contour map on top of the Shiranish formation indicating the locations of the wells and the location of the fault in this structure.

Production started in 1951 and reached a maximum rate of 25,000 BOPD during 1961-62. The first pay, at a depth of about 1,615 metres, and the second pay at a depth of some 2,225 metres from the surface of the ground. The oils from the two zones are heavier than that of Kirkuk. The First Pay zone produced oil of 33.7° API gravity and 3% sulphur with a GOR of 290 cu. ft. / barrel containing 100 ppm H2S. The oil of the Second Pay zone had an API gravity of 31.4° degrees and a sulphur content of 2.6%. The gas of the second pay contains up to 400 ppm H2S. First pay gas was used to reduce the H2S content of the second pay gas through cold stripping The two reservoirs are in communication through an intervening finely fractured but otherwise tight interval. It was considered that the First Pay oil accumulation originated by the upward migration of Second Pay oil via this fracture system. The Second Pay has a fairly active water drive.

The Ultimate Recoverable Reserves were estimated at between 195 and 220 MM barrels for the two pay zones, with about 37 million barrels in the First Pay and about 158 million barrels in the Second Pay. The development of the field was delayed during the Second World War and did not come into production until 1953.

The early wells from the first pay were flowing naturally at about 5,000 barrels per day and those of the second pay flowed at about 4,000 barrels per day. However the reservoir pressures declined with time and a water injection scheme was implemented later on to maintain the pressure. This proved to be unsustainable and ultimately down-hole pumps had to be used. Except during their early years the combined production from this field and the nearby Butmah field was maintained between 21,000 and 25,000 barrels per day just above the minimum concession obligation of one million tons per year (20,000 BOPD.) Ain Zalah field production was maintained at an average rate of between 18,000 to 19,000 BOPD (the 1960 actual average output figure was 18,500 BOPD) and the remaining quantity was produced from the Butmah field.

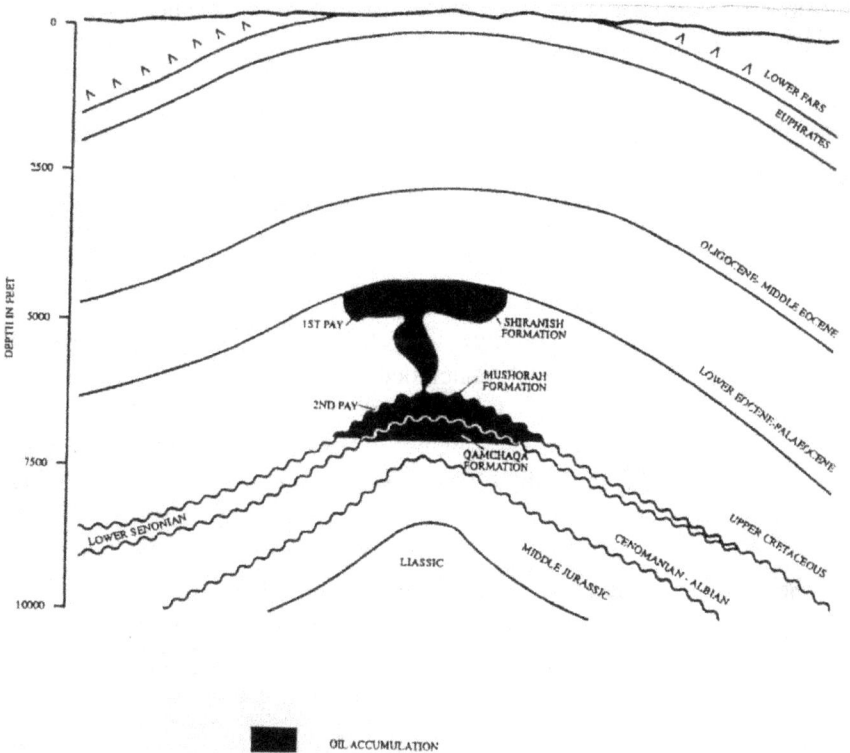

OIL ACCUMULATION

Fig. AZ-1

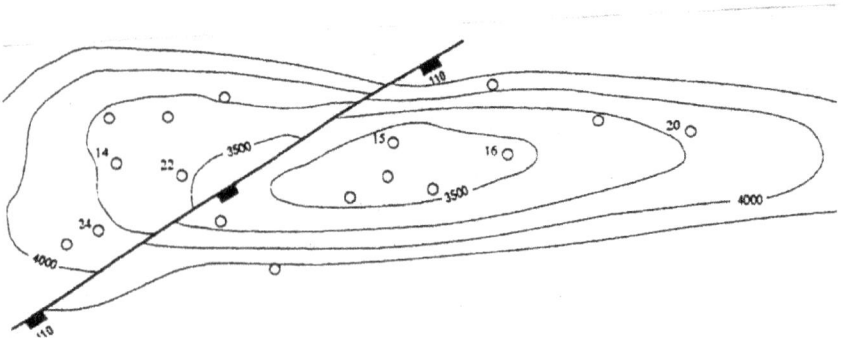

Fig. AZ-2

The Mosul Petroleum Company (MPC) continued to maintain the production of the Concession minimum obligation of one million tons per year until the nationalization of the Iraq Petroleum Company (IPC) in 1972. In the meantime the production from this field continued from there on to the end of the twentieth century albeit at reduced rates of production.

8 - AJIL

This field was discovered in 1983 and located some 120 km to the southeast of Kirkuk along the eastern bank of the river Tigris not too far from the Hamrin field.

The discovery well found gas only at a depth of about 1,500 metres. The drilling of a further three appraisal wells concluded that it was a gas field and plans were prepared to develop it as such. However on drilling the fifth well further to the southwest, some oil was noted being produced with the gas during testing. As a result a sixth well was drilled further down the structure which established the existence of an oil rim.

Further drilling and testing confirmed the existence of light oil of a 36° -37° API gravity with low sulphur and H2S contents and high GOR of 1,000 SCF/B. The large gas cap contained gas with low H2S of around 1.0%. Further reservoir studies indicated a large oil field with oil in place estimated at 3.0 billion barrels with ultimate recoverable reserves exceeding 1.0 billion barrels of oil. The main reservoir is the Komitan limestone formation of Upper Cretaceous age. The drive mechanism is gas cap expansion and solution gas drives with no significant water drive being detected.

A development plan was implemented to produce 45,000 barrels of oil per day and its associated gas as well as dome gas when required. The oil processing facilities were designed to handle 60,000 BOPD of wet crude from both Ajil and Hamrin fields. The gas gathering, dehydration and compression facilities were to handle up to 360 million standard cubic feet per day from all stages of separation and processing from both fields as well as dome gas when required.

The oil was to be transported, in a new pipeline, across the river Tigris for injection into the nearby Iraq-Turkey pipeline at IT-2 pumping station or to be delivered to the nearby Salahuddin refinery complex near Baiji. The associated gas and the dome gas, when required, were to be transported some 100 km in a newly constructed pipeline to the Liquid Petroleum Gas (LPG) plant near Kirkuk.

Although the implementation of the project was disrupted by the first Gulf war, it was completed and became operational towards the end of 1992. The total number of wells drilled to 1990 was close to hundred including five wells completed in the gas cap for dome gas production. Although studies indicated that the dome gas production has only minimum adverse effects on the ultimate oil recovery, dome gas production was to be only approved in cases of emergency. However, the expected increase in the gas/oil ratio with time will gradually reduce the need for dome gas production.

9 - AKKAS

Seismic surveys identified this huge structure about 35 km long and 7 km wide in 1983 but drilling was only contemplated in the late 1980s because the area was remote and far from any oil activity centre. The location is situated in the extreme west of the country close to the Syrian borders. The exploration well, Akkas 1, was spudded in August 1992 and early results were encouraging, even before reaching the target depth of 5,000 metres. The completion of the exploration well in April 1993, together with further drilling, established the field as a gas field.

Later appraisal wells confirmed that the field has an estimated gas in place of between 2.1 and 5.6 trillion standard cubic feet.

The field has been the subject of an auction and negotiations in recent years and a development and service contract was finally awarded by the Ministry of Oil in June 2011 to a consortium led by the Korean Gas Corporation (KOGAS) for its development. The field is expected to have a production capacity of 400 MMSCFGD.

10 - ALLAN

This field was discovered by the Mosul Petroleum Company (MPC) in 1954 south of Mosul in the vicinity of the Qaiyarah field. The structure is an anticline and oil of 13° API gravity was encountered in the Sargelu (Jurassic) limestone formation at a depth of 1,250 metres and 33° API gravity oil was encountered in the Qurra Chine (Triassic) limestone formation at a depth of 2,850 metres. The field was small and considered marginally economical at that time and was left undeveloped.

Drilling started again in 1987 and the well flowed at 3,000 BOPD with 33° API gravity and sulphur content of 2.8%. Further appraisal wells were planned and the development of the field was scheduled for the mid 1990s, but these were delayed by the invasion of Kuwait and the subsequent events of the Gulf War and the prolonged sanction against Iraq during the 1990s and beyond.

11 - ATRUSH

This field which is located in the northeast of Duhok, adjacent to the Tawke oil field became the subject of negotiations for exploration and development and as a result a Production Sharing Agreement was finally signed by the Kurdistan Regional Government with a consortium of Canadian ShaMaran, Turkish GEP, USA Aspect Energy and USA Manhathon Oil.

The Atrush block is located immediately north and adjacent to the recently discovered Shaikhan oilfield. The Atrush-1 exploration well was spudded during October 2010. It is planned to drill the well to a depth 3,100 metres to test the same reservoir sections as those of the Shaikhan field

During January 2011 the well reached a depth of 3,400 metres and encountered 726 metre potential gross oil column in the lower Cretaceous and Jurassic . Drilling continued and log results indicate additional net pay zones of up to 140 metres in the Upper Butmah and Cretaceous formations. Excellent flow rates were established totalling some 6,400 barrels per day from the three Jurassic horizons. The three tests in the Middle and Upper Jurassic reservoirs produced 26.5 API oil.

The appraisal programme is in hand and it is expected to start the installation of the production facilities during 2012.

12 - BADRA

Badra field is located about 90 km east of the city of Kut. The field was discovered by the IPC in the early 1960s but the full extent of the field was not realized and hence was left undeveloped at that time. Subsequent drilling after the nationalization of the IPC proved the field to be quite large.

However it was not until recently when the field became the subject of an auction and negotiations and a service contract for the development and production of the field was finally awarded by the Ministry of Oil in January 2010 to a consortium comprising the Russian Gazprom Naft, the South Korean KOGAZ, the Malaysian Petronas and the Turkish TPAO.

The field's recoverable reserves are estimated at about 3.0 billion barrels of 34°-35° API gravity oil and is expected to have an ultimate production capacity of 170,000 BOPD.

13 - BAI HASSAN

This field was discovered by the Iraq Petroleum Company in 1953. It is located in northeast Iraq in the vicinity of the Avanah dome of the Kirkuk field. The structure itself is an anticline about 28 km long and about 4 km wide trending in a northwest-southeast direction almost parallel to the Kirkuk field. It has two domes the Kithke and the Daoud which are separated by the Shahal saddle.

The principle producing horizon at Bai Hassan is the Eocene-Oligocene-Miocene Main Limestone (of Tertiary age) similar to the Kirkuk Main Limestone at the Baba Dome but has no surface seepages. Fig. BH-1 shows a structure contour map on top of the Tertiary reservoir. The reservoir is 300 metres thick and has an extensive high pressure gas cap in both domes. The predominant production mechanism is gas cap expansion assisted by solution - gas drive. The crude oil from the main limestone pay zone is slightly heavier than the Kirkuk crude but relatively less sulphurous with 33°-34° API gravity and a sulphur content of 2.3%.

The Cretaceous pay zones are similar to those in Kirkuk. The Maastrichtian - Campanian Shiranish formation is a fractured limestone reservoir containing slightly heavier and more sulphurous crude with a 28° API gravity and a sulphur content of about 3.9%. It is pressure- connected with the overlying Main Limestone accumulation.

A deeper fractured early Campanian carbonate reservoir with 27.8° API gravity oil is in communication with the underlying accumulation in the Upper Albian Qamchuqa limestone formation which is the largest and most important Cretaceous reservoir containing 26.8° API gravity oil. The Albian limestones contain deeper pools which may be connected to each other but are probably not connected with the Upper Qamchuqa.

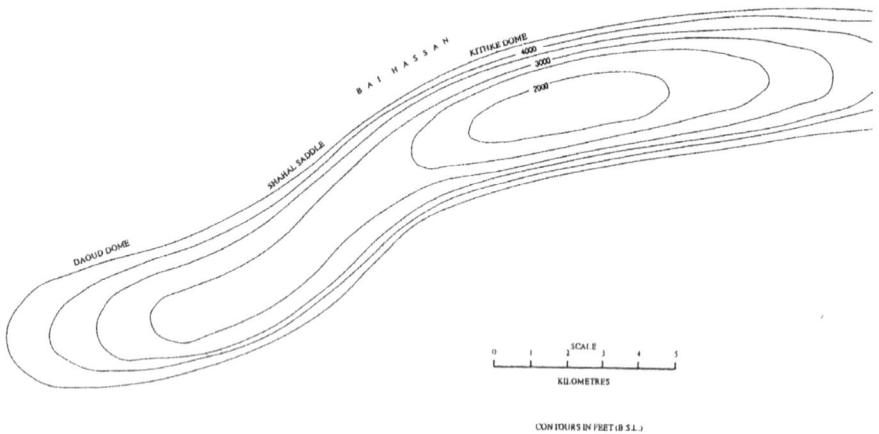

Bai Hassan Field-Fig. BH-1

The field started production of dome gas in 1957 from well BH-2 on the Kithke dome for injection into the Kirkuk Tertiary reservoir for pressure maintenance. This continued until 1961 when the water injection project for Kirkuk was completed. Oil production started in 1960 through two degassing stations, Bai Hassan North and South.

As a result of reservoir studies during the late 1970's and early 1980's, a decision was made to further develop the field and increase production to about 240,000 BOPD. For this purpose, a third degassing station was constructed in the mid 1970s in the Daoud dome by the same name. Further drilling was carried out and a peripheral water injection project was decided upon. Excess treated water from the existing Kirkuk water injection plant was utilized for this purpose and two parallel 20 inch lines were laid to the north and south flanks of the field with 8 and 10 inch diameter branches leading to individual injection wells.

The average rate of production was relatively stable over the years at about 240,000 BOPD. The Bai Hassan crude is processed separately and then mixed with that from the Jambur field before being exported separately in batches through the main Kirkuk-Mediterranean pipelines system. It is estimated that the accumulated production from this field by 1980 had reached some 320 MMBO and that the ultimate recoverable reserves are estimated at 1.0 to 1.5 billion barrels of oil which makes it one of the large fields.

14 - BALAD

This field was discovered in 1983 and located some 70 km north of Baghdad along the eastern bank of the river Tigris. The field was considered small with initial estimated recoverable reserves of some 200 to 300 million barrels of oil. By the late 1980's, however, the field was producing between 1,000 and 2,000 BOPD through four wells under pilot production scheme. The main reservoir is the Lower Senonian carbonates. The 18°-20° API gravity crude oil was being transported by road tankers to the not too far Salahuddin refinery complex near the town of Baiji to be blended with other lighter crudes before being refined.

Further plans for the development of this field were scheduled to take place in the mid 1990s, but these were disrupted by the invasion of Kuwait and the subsequent events of the Gulf War and the sanctions against Iraq during the 1990s and beyond.

15 - BAZIAN

This field which is located in the Sulaymaniyah area became the subject of negotiations for exploration and development and a production sharing agreement was finally signed by the Kurdistan Regional Government in November 2007 with a consortium led by the Korean National Oil Corporation.

Actual drilling in the field started later on and oil was discovered during August 2010 with the well flowing at a rate of just under 1,000 barrels per day.

The drilling programme is schedule to continue through 2011, 2012 and possibly 2013 before the full potential of the field could be established.

16 - BINA BAWI

This field which is located east of Erbil became the subject of negotiations for exploration and development and a production sharing agreement was finally signed by the Kurdistan Regional Government with the Australian company Oil Search.

The company has finally confirmed during June 2011, a drilling success in its Bina Bawi Block. It reported that the company was drilling exploration well Bina Bawi-3 and encountered hydrocarbons in one of the primary reservoir targets. A spokesman for the company stated " We are very pleased to announce this discovery of oil. It seems good quality oil and it was flowing to the surface following a drawdown test. We are now going to continue drilling but I am confident that the final results will be promising".

17 - BUTMAH

This field which was discovered in 1952 is located some ten kilometres southeast of the Ain Zalah field and parallel to it. It consists of two domes, east and west, which are not in pressure communication with each other. Development wells were drilled on the west dome which is some 12 km long and 6 km wide. The main oil reservoir is an anticline some 1,150 metres below the surface of the ground. It is a fractured Shiranish limestone formation of an Upper Cretaceous age.

Fig. Butmah-1 shows a structure contour map on top of the Shiranish formation in the west dome. The reservoir rock is oil stained and water logged and oil is produced from the fractures only and almost exclusively from the west dome. The oil has a gravity of 29.8° API. Heavier oil of 20.6° API gravity was encountered in well Butmah-7 which was the only well drilled in the east dome and was sometime produced to supply road asphalt.

However, small amount of highly sulphurous lighter oil of 34.5° API gravity was encountered in well Butmah-2 at a rate of 2,540 BOPD from a depth of 3,110 metres in the Kurra Chine formation of Triassic age. A second Triassic well, Butmah-15, was drilled in 1988 and tested 1,500 BOPD. The ultimate recoverable oil was, initially, estimated at 40 MMBO but this was probably an underestimate.

The field was first put in production in 1953. Fast pressure decline (800 psi during the first three years of production) necessitated the use of artificial lift. Electric submersible pumps were installed in three wells during 1960-61. Production rate peaked to over 5,000 BOPD during the early 1960's and then declined gradually to 3,000 BOPD. To maintain pressure above bubble point, a small scale water injection was started during 1963 through well Butmah-13 and continued intermittently as required. The field was often shut down during periods of low off take requirement.

The crude oil from this field is delivered to be mixed with the Ain Zalah crude for export through a 12 inch diameter pipeline which joins the Kirkuk –Mediterranean pipeline system at K-2 pump station.

BUTMAH WEST DOME

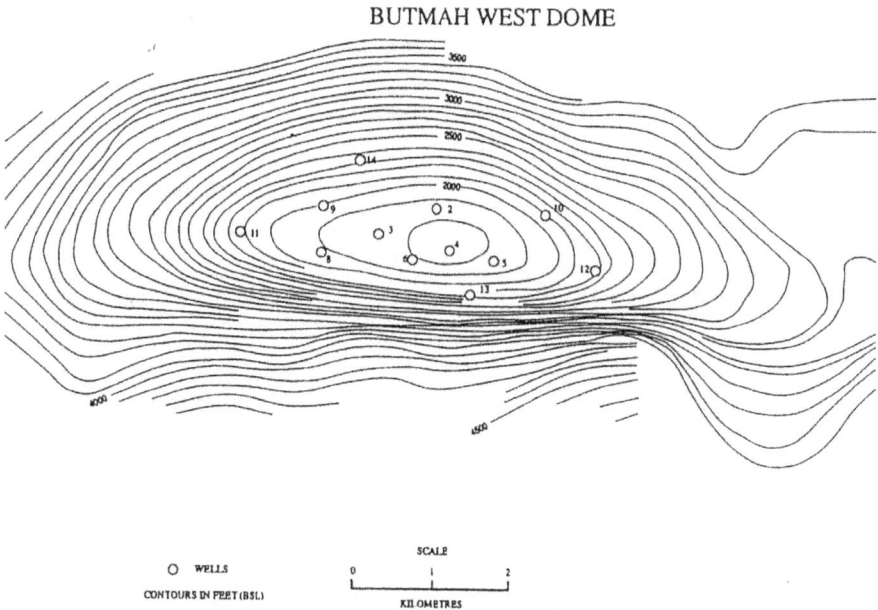

Butmah Field-Fig. Butmah-1

18 - BUZURGAN

This field was discovered in 1969 by the French company ERAP under a service contract with Iraq National Oil Company (INOC). The field is located along the Iranian borders about 300 km southeast of Baghdad and some 40 km northeast of the city of Amara. It is about 50 km in length and 8 km in width. The structure is a simple anticline trending northwest-southeast and has two domes with a central saddle and has an oil column of around 152 metres.

The main reservoir is the Cenomanian-Turonian Mishrif carbonate formation at an average depth below 3,200 metres and has an oil column of about 150 metres, was encountered in the discovery well, Bu-1 on the north dome and in Bu-3 and Bu-4 on the southern dome. Bu-1 yielded 3,000 BOPD of 23° API gravity with 3.7% sulphur on testing and also found non-commercial oil in the Lower Miocene, Euphrates-Jeribe and Oligocene intervals. The Lower Cretaceous Zubair sandstone reservoir produced 24°API gravity oil from a depth of approximately 3,960 metres. **Buzurgan** is considered as a large field with recoverable reserves estimated between 2.0 to 2.5 billion barrel of oil.

The field finally went on production in 1977 at a rate of between 30,000-40,000 barrels per day, after some delays due to certain contractual disputes between ERAP and INOC.

Further development of the field was disrupted by the invasion of Kuwait and the subsequent events of the Iraq/Iran War, the Gulf War and the prolonged sanctions against Iraq during the 1990s and beyond.

However the field, together with two other neighbouring fields in Missan Province (Fakka and Abu Ghrab) have been the subject of an auction and negotiations in recent years and a production service contract was finally awarded in 2010 to the Chinese Hong Kong based company in partnership with the Turkish company TPAO for the further development of the fields.

The plan is expected to raise the production capacity of these three fields from the current 115,000 to 1,450,000 barrels per day.

19 - CHEM CHEMAL

Discovered by the IPC in 1958, this gas field is situated to the east of the Kirkuk field in a highly folded zone. Gas was encountered in the discovery well Chem Chemal-1 in the Eocene. Chem Chemal-2 was drilled to test the Tertiary prospects at a structurally lower level. Gas was tested in the Eocene limestones implying a gas/water level at 576 metres.

Sweet gas and condensate of 64° API gravity were also produced from fractured Upper Cretaceous Shiranish limestone at a rate of 7.0 MMSCFGD. Albion Qamchuqa limestone contained only bitumen and gas. The field was not developed due to the lack of market for gas in those days.

However, in the 1980s, the field was considered for gas, LPG or petroleum products storage but the plan was rejected due to its small size and more importantly for being far from the existing oil/gas processing facilities of Kirkuk field.

The field became the subject of negotiations and a Production Sharing Agreement for its redevelopment was finally signed in recent years between the Kurdistan Regional Government and the two Sharjah, UAE, based companies, Dana Gas and Crescent Petroleum Company.

20 - CHIA SURKH

This is the oldest field to be discovered in the Middle East and located about 180 km northeast of Baghdad in the Khaniqin region close to the Iranian borders and measures about 6.4 km in length and 1.6 km in width with the main reservoir at a depth of about 500 metres. The field was discovered 1903 by D'Arcy who had acquired a concession from the Shah of Persia on 28 May 1901.

Drilling on the first well started in November 1902 (see Fig. Chia Surkh-1) and continued at a very slow rate due to the remoteness of the region and recurring labour problems. By April 1902, the well was about 300 metres deep and, although oil was found in small quantities, drilling continue to reach a depth of about 400 metres by 23 June 1902 after which drilling was suspended due to the poor show of oil.

Drilling was then resumed on well No.2 which, on the 4 January 1904, reached a depth of about 250 metres when oil flowed at a rate of some 600 BOPD accompanied by brine. Unfortunately the oil failed to flow regularly in sufficient quantities and, as a result, the drilling was continued until 23 June 1904 when a depth of 430 metres was reached without further encouraging signs. It was then decided to halt further drilling for the time being as the attention moved to drilling in the Majidi-Sulieman region south of Persia where oil was found in commercial quantities in 1908.

Drilling was not resumed at Chiah Surkh until 20 July 1912. This time the drilling operation suffered prolonged delays as a result of technical problems and was eventually suspended during April 1913 after a bit had dropped in the well and the casing was badly damaged in trying to retrieve it.

It is to be highlighted that the region of Chiah Surkh became part of Iraq as a result of the return of the Transferred Territories as show on the map below (Fig. Chia Surkh-2).

The field, subsequently became part of the concession of Khaniqin Oil Company (KOC) which was owned by the Anglo-Persian Oil Company after acquiring the D'Arcy concession.

Chiāh Surkh no. 1 well 1903

Fig. Chia Surkh-1

KOC signed a new agreement with the government of Iraq in 1951 to develop the fields in the Khaniqin region including the Chiah Surkh field to produce two million tons of oil per year (approximately 40,000 barrels per day)within seven years of the date of signing the agreement.

In 1951, 42° API gravity oil flowed from well Chiah Surkh well No. 7 at a rate of about 3,000 BOPD and the total number of wells drilled in the field at that time was nine. However KOC was unable to achieve the contractual production rate and the agreement came to an end by handing over this field as well as the nearby Naftkhanah field back to the government in 1959.The field was not developed any further at the time.

It was not until the late 1980s when appraisal drilling was planned for the early 1990s but this was disrupted by the invasion of Kuwait and the subsequent events of the Gulf War and the prolonged sanctions against Iraq during the 1990s and beyond.

However this field became the subject of negotiations and a Production Sharing Agreement for its redevelopment was finally signed in recent years between the Kurdistan Regional Government and a partnership from the Turkish Genel Enerji and the Canadian Longford.

21 - DEMIR DAGH

This is a small anticlinal structure discovered in 1960 by the IPC and is located some 20 km to the north of the Kirkuk field. It produced mainly gas with some 50° API gravity condensates from the Upper Cretaceous Shiranish limestone formation at a depth of about 1,570 metres and was considered uneconomical at that time.

Further drilling was planned for the early 1990s but this was disrupted by the start of the by the invasion of Kuwait and the subsequent events of the Gulf War and the prolonged sanctions.

22 - DHAFRIYAH

This field was discovered in 1988 and is located 150 km southeast of Baghdad on the river Tigris. The discovery well encountered 30° API gravity oil in the Lower Cretaceous Zubair sandstone and the appraisal of the field was deferred due to the invasion of Kuwait and the subsequent events of the Gulf War and the prolonged sanctions.

23 - DUJAILA

This field was discovered by the BPC in 1961and the discovery well tested at about 2,000

BOPD heavy 15° API gravity oil in the Mishrif limestone formation (of Cenomanian-Turonian age) at an average depth of about 2,825 metres. Oil shows were also present in Upper Cretaceous and Lower Cretaceous sands. However, the heavy nature of the oil rendered its development uneconomical at that time.

N

Transferred territories

— — — Old Turco-Persian frontier

— · — New Iraqi-Iranian frontier

Chiāh Surkh

Zuhāb

Qasr-i Shirin

Sar-i-Pul

To Kirmānshāh

Khanaqin

R. Alwand

R. Sirwan

Naft Khāna

Scale

5   0   5   10   15 Miles

5   0   5   10   15   20 Kilometres

To Baghdad

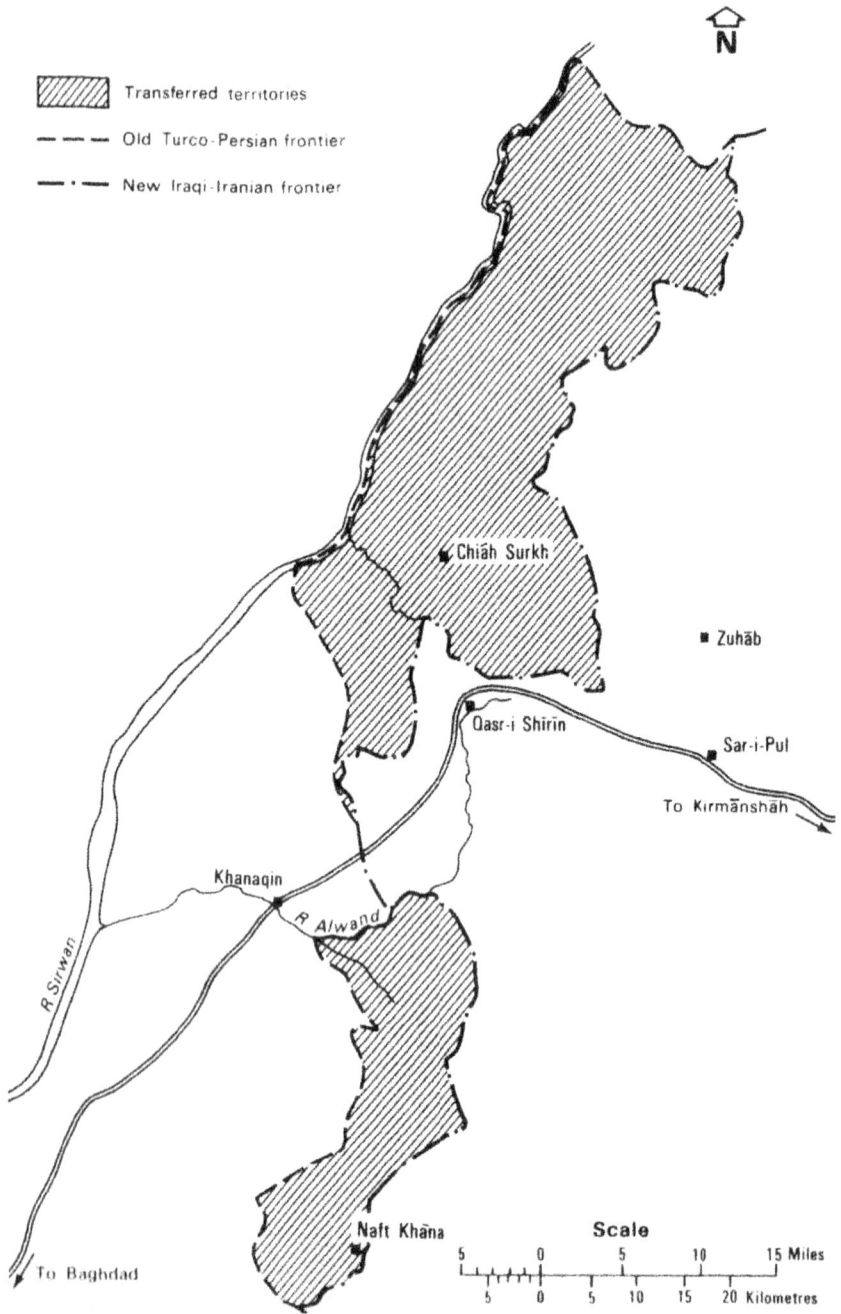

Fig. Chia Surkh-2 - Transferred Territories

24 - EAST BAGHDAD

This field was discovered by INOC in 1975. Subsequent appraisal drilling and reservoir studies indicated that this was a giant field. It is located to the east of Baghdad stretching along the river Tigris and measuring some 70 km in length by an average of 7 km in width.

The Structure is a northwest-southeast trending anticline. Strong northwest-southeast and northeast-southwest trending faults, at the Cretaceous and Jurassic horizons, were indicated by seismic data and may have influenced the formation of the structure.

The field contains oil in several reservoir horizons. The main reservoir is the Lower Cretaceous Nahr Umar sands formation at a depth of about 3,213 metres and has a porosity ranging between 18% and 31%. Another principal reservoir is the Upper Cretaceous Hartha/Taunuma/Khasib carbonate formations. The Lower Cretaceous Zubair sandstone formation produced 30° API gravity oil at a depth of about 3,200 metres. An Upper Cretaceous reservoir produced heavier oil of 23° API gravity oil at a depth of 2,100 metres.

A plan to develop the field in stages was adopted, the first stage of which was to implement a pilot scheme to produce 20,000 BOPD which was completed and commissioned in 1989. During this period the drilling activities were progressing well and by the end of 1988 some 80 wells had been completed including some for a water injection scheme which was planned to start early in the production life of the field..

The second stage was to increase the production to 140,000 BOPD by 1993 and the third and final stage was to raise it to 240,000 BOPD by 1996. However the implementation of the second and third stages was disrupted by the invasion of Kuwait and the subsequent events of the Gulf War and the prolonged sanctions that followed.

The early estimates of the proven recoverable reserves from this field were quoted at between 7 and 11 billion barrels of oil and the probable reserves were estimated at 18 BBO which ranks it as one of the giant fields in the country.

25 - FALLUJA (WEST BAGHDAD)

This field was discovered by the IPC in 1958. The discovery well, Falluja-1, produced heavy oil of 15° API gravity from the Upper Cretaceous Hartha limestone formation at a depth of about 800 metres and gas from the Jurassic Najmah limestone formation at a depth of about 2,880 metres. Oil shows were also encountered in the Cenomanian Rumaila limestone formation at a depth of about 1,160 metres. The discovery was thought uneconomical to develop at that time and no further drilling followed.

However during the middle of the 1980's, a new interest was shown in this location and the area just south of it, where seismic surveys indicated interesting anomalies. A major American oil companies showed interest but no agreement was reached on further exploration and possible development.

26 - GHARRAF

This field was discovered in 1984 and is located about 270 km southeast of Baghdad. Oil of 30° API gravity was produced from the Lower Cretaceous Zubair formation. The discovery was not classified as a priority field at the time and was left for future development.

However, the field has been the subject of an auction and negotiations in recent years and a Production Service Contract was finally awarded by the Ministry of Oil in December 2009 to the Malaysian state company Petronas and the Japanese Exploration Co. (JAPEX) for its development. The field is expected to have an ultimate production capacity of 230,000 BOPD.

27 - GILLABAT

This field was discovered by the IPC in 1959. It is located about 125 km south of Kirkuk. The discovery well Gillabat-1 was drilled to assess the prospects of the Tertiary limestone formations in a Kirkuk type anticline. Light crude of 41° API gravity was encountered in the Miocene sandstones of the Upper Fars and gas in the saliferous beds of the Miocene Lower Fars at a depth of about 1,900 metres.

A second well, Gillabat-2, was drilled to the Upper Cretaceous in the early 1960s but had to be abandoned due to the high pressure encountered which became close to the pressure rating of the Blow-out Preventer (BOP) and other wellhead equipment.

A third well was drilled during the 1970s which confirmed light oil, condensate and high gas/oil ratio of about 3,000 SCFPB and the field was considered as a low priority for development at that time.

However, further deep drilling, using 15,000 psi rating BOP was planned for the early 1990s and the development of the field. However, this was disrupted soon after by the invasion of Kuwait and the subsequent events of the Gulf War and the sanctions.

28 - HALFAYA

This field was discovered in 1977 in the southeast of the country some 40 km south of the Buzurgan field not too far from the Iranian borders. The studies for this field were delayed for several years until the late 1980s. It was anticipated to develop the field for production in the early 1990s; however this was delayed by the Gulf war and the subsequent sanctions.

This field was considered large with the initial estimate for the recoverable reserves being quoted at 4.1 billion barrels of oil of 28° API gravity oil reservoired in the Middle Cretaceous Mishrif carbonates formation. The field was expected at that time to have an ultimate production capacity of 100,000 BOPD.

The field has been the subject of an auction and negotiations in recent years and a Production Service Contract was finally awarded by the Ministry of Oil in January 2010 to a consortium from China National Petroleum Company (CNPC), the French company Total and the Malaysian state company Petronas for the development of the field. In the meantime the production capacity of the field has been revised sharply upwards of 535,000 BOPD.

29 - HAMRIN

Discovered in 1961, this field has a long structure of over 60 km in length and steeply dipping surface anticline trending northwest-southeast parallel to the axes of the Kirkuk and Bai Hassan-Jambur fields on the east bank of the river Tigris. The structure then extends across the river at Fatha into the Jabal Makhool area on the west bank. The structure on the eastern bank of the river comprises three domes; the Albu Fudhoul, Allas and N'khailah.

The discovery well, Hamrin-1, was drilled on the Allas dome by the IPC in 1961 and encountered sweet gas and some medium gravity of 31° API oil in the Lower Miocene interval. The IPC did not consider the development of the field at that time.

However the same well was re-entered after nationalisation in 1974 and re-tested producing 2,000 BOPD from the previous formation after stimulation. The well was then deepened to a lower formation which tested residual oil and brine. Fourteen wells were drilled during the 1970s and 1980s and oil was confirmed in the Tertiary reservoir on both the Allas and N'khailah domes. However only non commercial oil was found in the two wells drilled in the Abu Fudhoul dome to the northwest. Wells drilled to the Cretaceous reservoir found heavier oil of 23°-25° API gravity. Two wells drilled in the Makhoul structure across the Tigris, found little heavy oil.

Artificial lift was anticipated and pumping was considered necessary since most the wells in the N'khailah dome did not flow naturally. Water injection was also planned to maintain the pressure above the bubble point and to enhance the recovery.

Hamrin was originally scheduled for development concurrently with the Ajil field to be brought on stream during 1990. Crude from the two fields would be mixed and share one central oil and gas processing facility. However, though drilling continued, the completion of the development was deferred by the invasion of Kuwait and the subsequent events of the Gulf War and the sanctions.

30 - HAWLER

This field which is located in the Irbil area became the subject of negotiations for exploration and development and a Production Sharing Agreement was finally signed by the Kurdish Regional Government in 2007 and the Russian company Norbest.

The drilling of Hawler No.1 commenced in November 2007. It has been reported that an influx of oil was observed while drilling through the top of the Cretaceous reservoir horizon. Oil shows were also observed in several additional interval while drilling.

A 7 inch casing was installed before deepening the well to evaluate some additional potential reservoir horizons. In the Jurassic interval an open hole test was conducted delivering approximately 9,000 barrels of oil and 11 million standard cubic feet of gas per day through a one inch chock size.

A test towards the top of the Jurassic flowed 1,500-2,000 BOPD with heavier oil quality than the open hole test.

It was reported that Hawler No. 2 was drilled through the Jurassic interval and to a planned total depth in the Tiassic.

The Hawler structure is being studied to evaluate the potential of the reservoir

31 - INJANAH

This field was discovered by the IPC in 1958 and is located south of Kirkuk. The structure is a long, sinuous, sharply asymmetric anticline trending northwest-southeast with a total of four domes which are from the northwest: Injana, Khashm al Ahmer, Suhaniyan and Mansuryat al Jabal

The discovery well, Injanah-5, flowed 31.7° API gravity oil and gas from fractures in the upper part of the Campanian-Maastrichtian Shiranish limestone formation at a depth of 1980 mertes. Oil of 33° API gravity also flowed at a rate of 1,000 BOPD from the fractured limestones of the Turonian-Santonian Kometan/Balambo formation, below a large gas cap. The field was considered uneconomical for development at that time.

However, appraisal drilling was planned during the early 1990s but these were disrupted by the invasion of Kuwait and the subsequent events of the Gulf War and sanctions.

32 - JABAL FAKKA

Discovered in 1974, this field is situated east of the Buzurgan field in the southeast of the country and very close to the Iranian borders. The structure is an anticline about 30 km long by 8 km wide and is parallel with the Buzergan and Abu Ghrab fields. Commercial oil was encountered in both Tertiary and Middle Cretaceous reservoirs Oligocene-Miocene Asmari limestone and sandstone have 215 metres of closure and an oil column of about 90 metres. The Cenomanian-Turonian Mishrif formation again contains three reservoirs in porous reefal facies with an oil column of about 100 metres. The average depths to the Tertiary and the Cretaceous reservoirs are approximately 1900 metres and 3,900 metres with 18° and 28° API gravity respectively. Oil was also encountered in the Aptian Shuaiba

The field was developed during the following few years and it went on stream in 1979. However due to its close proximity of the Iranian borders its production was interrupted at the beginning of the Iraq/Iran war. Its ultimate recoverable reserves are estimated between one and one and a half billion barrels of oil.

The field, together with two other fields in Missan Province (Abu Ghrab and Buzergan) have been the subject of an auction and negotiations in recent years and a production service contract was finally awarded by the Ministry of Oil in 2010 to the Chinese Hong Kong based company in partnership with the Turkish company TPAO for the further development of these three fields.

This is expected to raise the production capacity of the three fields from their combined current capacity of 115,000 to 1,450,000 barrel of oil per day.

33 - JABAL KAND (QAND)

This is a huge structure about 35 km northeast of Mosul . An exploration well was drilled in 1980 and encountered 30 API gravity oil in the Campanian-Maastrichtian Shiranich limestone formation. Further drilling was planned during the 1990s but these were again disrupted by the invasion of Kuwait and the subsequent events of the Gulf War and sanctions.

34 - JABAL SINJAR

A very huge structure situated about 80 km to the northwest of Mosul. One well was drilled in the 1980s with the objective of investigating both the salt formations for possible cavity storage utilisation and the hydrocarbon potential of the various formations. Some hydrocarbon shows were encountered, but did not prove significant. Further drilling was planned for the early 1990s but this was disrupted by the invasion of Kuwait and the unfortunate subsequent events that followed.

35 - JAMBUR

Discovered by the IPC in 1954, this field lies about 14 km to the south of the southeast plunge of the Kirkuk field and runs parallel to it. It is a gently dipping asymmetric anticline about 40 km long and about 3 km wide.

Two main reservoirs intervals are present in this field, the Tertiary and the Cretaceous.

The Tertiary consists of three pay zones of Miocene age, the Jeribe, Euphrates and Jaddalah Limestone formations at an average depth of around 1740 metres. A large gas cap covers the tertiary reservoirs in the south-eastern section of the field. The oil column is relatively thin in this section and the Jaddalah was mostly water logged with oil only found in very few wells. In the north-western section of the field, which was discovered in the 1970s after the nationalisation of the IPC, the Jeribe and Euphrates have thicker oil columns and a smaller gas cap, but the Jaddalah was water logged. It is thought that the north-western section of the Tertiary reservoir is separated from the south- eastern section by a permeability barrier.

The oil in the Tertiary is saturated and is closely similar in the three pay zones with 1.3% sulphur content. Oil gravity initially averaged about 41°-43° API, decreasing with time to 37°-39° API due to gas production (rich in condensates) and gas coning. Oil production mechanism is mainly by gas cap. expansion and solution gas drive.

The Cretaceous reservoirs were discovered in 1962 when well Ja-13 was drilled to the Cretaceous and encountered 35° API gravity oil in the Albian Komitan Limestone and, more significantly, 39° API oil in the Albian Qamchuqa Limestone where 240 metre gas column and 305 metre oil column were found below 2,557 metres. Subsequent drilling indicated the Cretaceous reservoirs were mainly water logged in the south-eastern section of the field but oil bearing and well developed in the north-western section where a significant oil column was also encountered in the Tertiary.

The field went into production from the south-eastern section in 1959 and by 1980 it had produced a total of 71.5 million barrels of oil averaging 4,370 BOPD with a peak rate approaching 20,000 BOPD. During most of this period, the main emphasis was on producing gas with oil being a by product. Sweet dome gas was produced from the Tertiary gas cap at rates ranging between 20 and 100 million cubic feet per day throughout the 1960s, the 1970s and the early 1990s.

A 12 inch diameter pipeline transported the gas to the Kirkuk area for use as feed gas for the cold stripping units at the central process plant treating the sour crude of the Kirkuk reservoirs. Additional quantities of this gas were sent through one of the two old 16 inch diameter Mediterranean crude export pipelines which was converted to a gas pipeline to supply fuel for the newly installed gas turbines pumping sets, after the

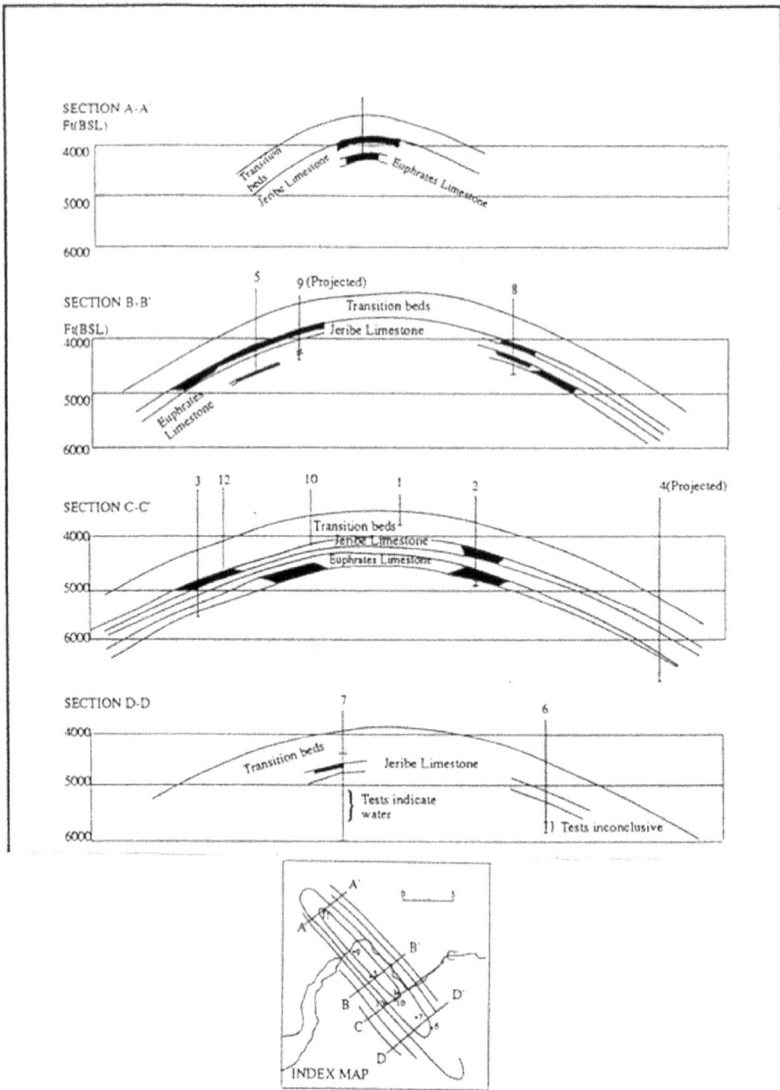

SECTION A-A'
Ft(BSL)
4000
5000
6000

Transition beds
Jeribe Limestone
Euphrates Limestone

SECTION B-B'
Ft(BSL)
4000
5000
6000

5 9 (Projected) 8
Transition beds
Jeribe Limestone
Euphrates Limestone

SECTION C-C'
4000
5000
6000

3 12 10 1 2 4(Projected)
Transition beds
Jeribe Limestone
Euphrates Limestone

SECTION D-D
4000
5000
6000

7 6
Transition beds Jeribe Limestone
Tests indicate water
Tests inconclusive

A'
A
B'
B
C
D'
D
INDEX MAP

Jambur Field

retirement of some of the diesel driven pumping sets, at the main pumping stations both in Iraq and Syria.

During the mid 1970s, and as a part of the expansion of the export capacity of the Kirkuk fields from 1.0 to 1.2 MMBOPD, a new plan for the development of the Jambur Tertiary and Cretaceous reservoirs in the north-western section of the field was implemented. This included the construction of a new degassing and dehydration station by the name of Jambur North.

In the meantime development drilling continued and by the end of the 1980s, the total number of wells had exceeded 52, of which 35 were producers bringing the total production capacity of the field to between 90,000 and 100,000 BOPD. By then dome gas production has all but stopped. Nevertheless, the gas production capacity of the field had been raised to 200 MMSCFD for possible use in extreme cases of emergency.

The field's ultimate recoverable reserves were estimated at between 1.5 to 2.0 billion barrels of condensates.

36 - JARYA PIKA

Identified, by seismic by the Soviet geologists during 1960 in the Khaniqin region. Two wells were subsequently drilled which tested gas. No market existed for the gas at that time and no further work was carried out.

37 - JAWAN

This field is one of four adjacent and connected oil-bearing structures: Jawan, Najmah, Qaiyarah and Qasab (see Fig. Qaiyarah-1). They will be described together with the Qaiyarah field.

38 - JERISHAN

This field was discovered in 1982 south of the Rumaila field near the Kuwaiti borders. Oil of 30° API gravity was found in the Lower Cretaceous Zubair sandstone formation. However no further work could be carried out at that time due to its proximity to the continuing Iraq/Iran war zone during the 1980s.

39 - KHABBAZ

Identified by seismic in 1976, the Khabbaz structure is situated about 15 km to the southeast of the Bai Hassan field on the same Bai Hassan-Jambur axis and within a few kilometres of the main Kirkuk oil and gas processing facilities. The discovery well was drilled in 1983 and found a 130 metres column of 36° API gravity oil in the Miocene Jeribe carbonate formation (of Tertiary age) at a depth of around 1,907 metres. It has a high Gas/Oil Ratio of around 1,000 standard cubic feet per barrel.

At a depth of around 2,687 metres, the well encountered a 120 metres column of 30° API gravity oil in the Cretaceous Albian Upper Qamchuqa limestone formation. Then a 170 metres column of 41° API gravity oil was encountered at a depth of around 2,900 metres in the Lower Qamchuqa. It also has a high average GOR of around 2,000 SCFPB.

Since it was very close to the main Kirkuk oil and gas processing facilities, its development and connecting to these facilities required modest investment and since it has a high GOR which would help in satisfying the ever increasing demand for gas, it was given high priority for development.

Appraisal and development drilling continued and construction work started in 1987 and although interrupted by the Gulf war and sanctions, the project was completed late in 1992 and became operational towards the end of the same year.

The project was designed for a maximum off take of 60,000 barrels of oil per day and the sustained production capacity of 45,000 barrels per day producing approximately 45,000 million standard cubic feet of associated gas per day.

The proven reserves of the field are estimated at between 1.5 to 2.5 billion barrels of oil which classifies it as a large field.

40 - KHASHAB

This small structure was located by seismic surveys in the 1970s and is situated about 150 km southwest of Kirkuk. One exploration well, Khashab-1 was drilled in the early 1980s and found some gas in the Tertiary reservoir and traces of oil in the Upper Cretaceous which tested one to two MMSCFD of sweet gas. The well was plugged since the find was not considered significant and no further drilling was contemplated for the foreseeable future.

41 - KHASHM AL-AHMAR

Situated, about 120 km to the northeast of Baghdad, this structure saw the drilling of several shallow wells during the period between 1927 and 1932. Most of the wells penetrated only the Lower Fars formation in the Upper Tertiary. One well penetrated the top of the Jeribe formation and tested good quality oil of 35° API gravity in the Lower Fars and in the Jeribe but drilling problems led to the abandonment of the well. Further attempts to drill a well deeper to the Euphrates formation met with new technical problems and were also abandoned. No further drilling operations were contemplated during the 1970s and the 1980s because of security problems.

New appraisal and exploration drilling to investigate the Tertiary reservoirs and to explore the deeper Cretaceous were planned for the early 1991. Geological and reservoir studies were planned to be completed before the end of 1992 and the field development soon after for completion during the end of 1993-1994. However these plans were disrupted by the invasion of Kuwait and the subsequent events of the Gulf War and sanctions.

42 - KHIDAR AL-MAA

This field was discovered in 1982 near the Kuwaiti borders. The well encountered oil of 30° API gravity in the Lower Cretaceous Zubair sandstone formation . The development of field was deferred due to its proximity to the Iraq-Iran war zone in the 1980s and later on by the invasion of Kuwait and the subsequent events of the Gulf War and sanctions.

43 - KIFL

This field was discovered in 1960 and is located about 125km southwest of Baghdad on the river Euphrates. The main production was a flow of 21.7° API gravity, slightly sulphurous oil from the top of the Lower Cretaceous Zubair sandstone formation at a depth of about 1,984 metres. Oil was also encountered in the Albian Nahr Umar sandstone below 1,800 metres.

Furthermore , there were several bitumen and oil shows encountered in limestone intervals within the Tertiary, Upper and Lower Cretaceous, and Jurassic Periods.

The discovery was not considered economical at that time, however , it was anticipated that further appraisal drilling may be carried out in the future.

44 - KIRKUK

The Iraq Petroleum Company which had obtained its oil concession from the Iraqi government in 1925 had started, soon after, drilling for oil at several locations in northern Iraq. One of these locations was in the vicinity of the famous Eternal Fires a few kilometres outside the city of Kirkuk. It was in the middle of October 1927 that oil was struck at this location with dramatic suddenness. A gusher had been found and oil was spouting in the air above the rig with many tons of the black gold spraying the surrounding area before the well was brought under control.

Well No. K-1 At Baba Gurgur-Kirkuk - 14 October 1927

This was the first sign of the discovery of a huge structure, which would reveal itself as one of the most remarkable in the world at that time. Thereafter, up to nine rigs were working for the next three years to establish the magnitude of this amazing field.

The Kirkuk structure itself is a sinuous surface anticline about 105 km long, and about two 3.2 km wide trending in a northwest-southeast direction. There are three relatively high areas known as the Baba, Avanah and Khurmalah domes connected through two saddles, the one between Baba and Avanah domes is called Amshe and the one between the Avanah and Khurmalah domes is called Dibega. The oil bearing reservoir lay some 700 metres below the surface of the ground.

The main reservoir in the Kirkuk field is the Main Limestone reservoir (MLS). It is of Tertiary age and it varies in thickness and age along the structure, from about 100 metres in the Khurmalah dome to over 350 metres at the crest of the Baba dome which quickly gets thinner towards the southeast forming the Tarjil plunge. In the Khurmalah dome, the reservoir rock is mainly of Paleocene and Lower Eocene age. In the Avanah dome, it is mainly of Eocene age. In the Baba dome it is mainly of Oligocene age which truncates gradually towards the Tarjil Plunge leaving thin beds of Lower Miocene age.

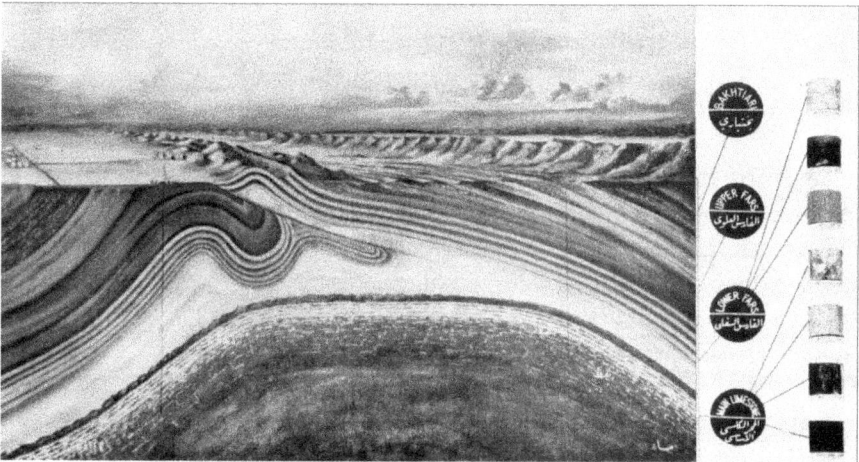

Kirkuk Field-Cross Section

The Main Limestone reservoir is capped by a few metres of Basal Fars Conglomerates (BFC). The BFC, especially in the Baba area , is overlain by a succession of thin layers of limestone of Miocene age (the Transition Beds) separated by alternating layers of anhydrite. The BFC is generally continuous throughout the field . However , in some areas of the Baba dome and the Amshe Saddle, communication is thought to exist with the MLS through some tortuous channels giving rise to the oil migration into the Transition Beds and similar channels to the surface appearing as seepages of oil and gas (the Eternal Fires) near the crest of the Baba dome. The transition Beds become insignificant in the Avanah dome area and nonexistent in the Khurmalah dome area.

The main Limestone reservoir is extensively fractured particularly in the crestal parts of the Baba and Avanah domes and in the Amshe Saddle. The fractures become less extensive and of smaller dimensions away from the crests, towards Khurmalah and in the deeper formations. This fracturing lead to very high productivities in some wells, for example well KK-164 tested on completion an amazing 104,000 barrels of oil per day.

Prior to production, the Avanah dome was full to the crest with slightly under saturated oil. The Baba dome had a small crestal secondary gas cap formed as a result of the pressure decline caused by the surface seepages but the underlying oil was still slightly under saturated. The Khurmalah dome had a large gas cap which grew larger as a result of pressure decline caused by oil migration into Avanah.

The main drive mechanism in the Tertiary Main Limestone was solution gas drive which in the Khurmalah dome, was supplemented by gas cap expansion. Only a weak and insignificant water drive was observed. The edge water salinity, even before the start of water injection was rather low. It varied between 50,000 and 100,000 ppm along the reservoir.

Because of the intensive fracturing, the three domes were initially in communication in oil and there was active migration of oil within the Baba and Avanah domes across the Amshe Saddle. The Khurmalah dome did not produce directly until 1992, but with the declining field pressure, its gas cap expanded and much of the oil had been driven across the Dibega saddle and produced at the Avanah or Baba domes.

Initially, production was through natural depletion and the pressure decline was moderate as long as the off take rates remained relatively small. However, in 1952 the production rate was more than doubled (after the construction of the 30/32 inch diameter pipeline to Banias to compensate for the loss of production from Iran during the Mossadeq regime) by increasing production from the Baba dome and starting production from the Avanah dome. Thus pressure decline became steeper and, by 1956, the reservoir pressure in Baba had dropped about 260 psi as shown in Fig KK-4. This resulted in the requirement of injecting gas in some of the wells to kick off the start of flow.

Therefore pressure maintenance became necessary and water injection was chosen which would, in addition improve recovery. Pending the completion of the water injection plant, gas injection was started in 1957 to avoid further decline. For this purpose Bai Hassan dome gas from well BH-2 was injected into well KK-101 in Avanah. This arrangement was continued until the end of 1961, at the time when the water injection plant was completed and the injection of water started into northeast and southwest flanks of the Amshe Saddle.

AGE		ROCK UNITS		LITHOLOGY
T E R T I A R Y	MIOCENE	Upper Fars Form		
		Lower Fars Form		
		Jeribe Form		
		Dhiban Form		
	OLIGOCENE	Euphrates Form		
		Kirkuk Group	Ibrahim Form	
			Torjil Form	
			Palani Form	
	EOCENE	Jaddala Form		
	PALEOCENE (Up)	Aaliji Form		
C R E T A C E O U S	CAMPANIAN	Shiranish Form		
	TURONIAN	Kometan Form		
	ALBIAN			
	APTIAN BARREMIAN HAUTERIVIAN	Qamchuqa Form		
	VALANGINIAN	Sarmord Form		
	BERRIASIAN	Garagu Form		
J U R A S S I C	UPPER	Karimia Form		
		Chia Gara Form		
		Barsarin Form		
	MIDDLE	Naokelekan Form		
		Sargelu Form		
	LOWER	Alan Form		
		Mus Form		
		Adaiyah Form		
		Butmah Form		
T R I A S S I C	UPPER	Baluti Form		
		Kurra Chine Form		
	MIDDLE AND LOWER	Geli Khana Form		
		Beduh Form		
		Mirga Mir Form		

Fig. KK-1 - Stratigraphic Sequence of Well KK-109

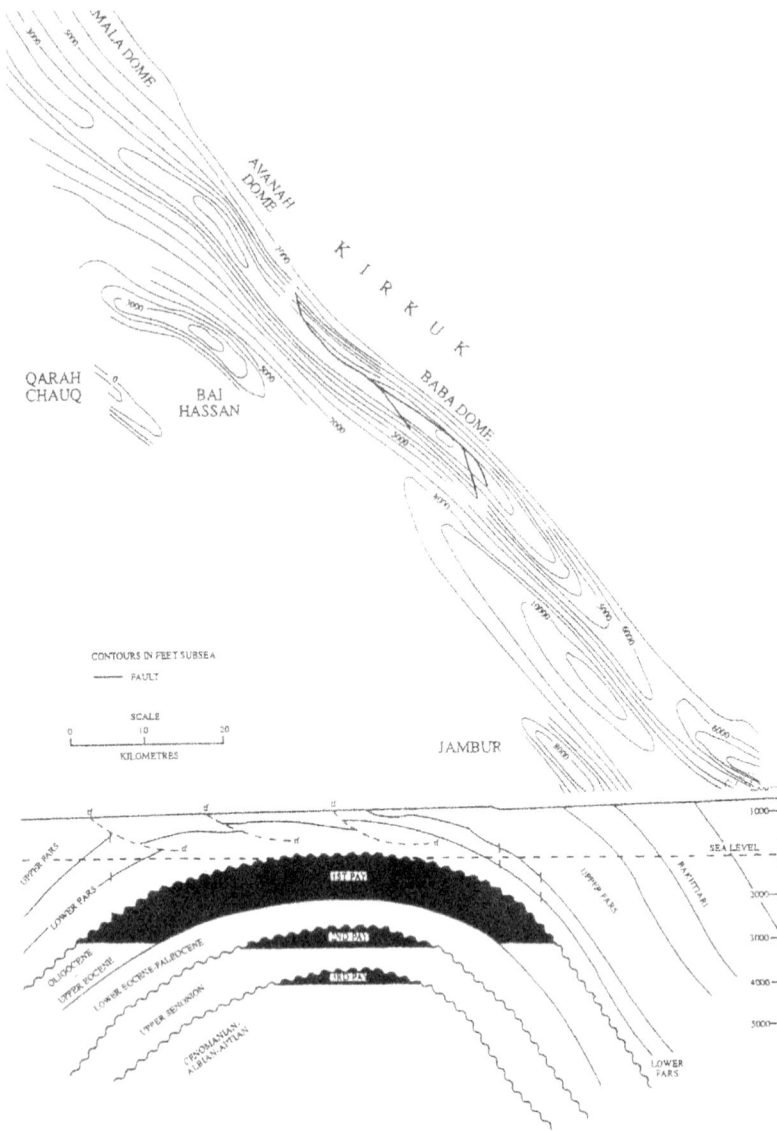

Kirkuk Field

To avoid humping of the Oil/Water Contact (OWC) level, injection was extended in 1972 to the Tarjil area and in 1978 to the northwest Avanah area to avoid trapping oil in these areas. By the middle of the 1970s, the pressure decline in Baba dome had been reduced to between 180 and 185 psi and was kept at that level. By the end of the 1970s, the Amshe Saddle had already been flooded and the Baba and Avanah domes were no longer connected in oil and thus began to be treated as separate reservoirs.

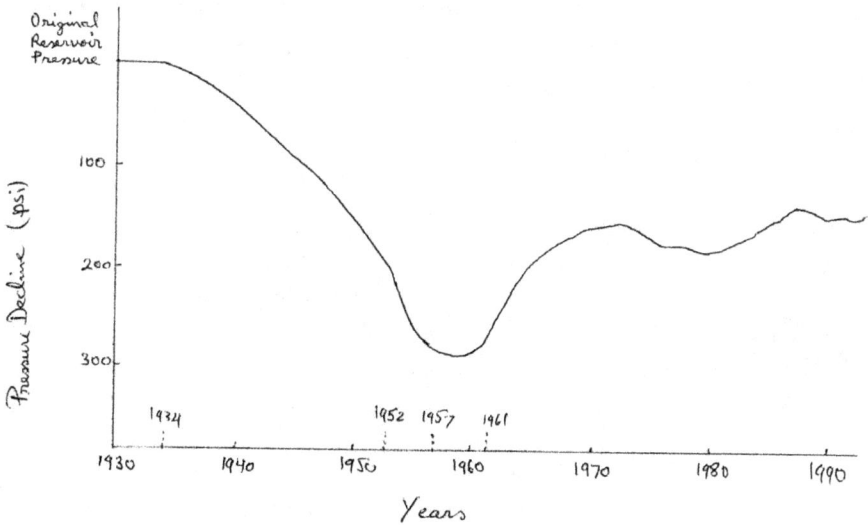

Kirkuk Main LimestoneResevoir - Baba Dome-Pressure History

Oil produced from the Main limestone is of uniform quality throughout this reservoir with an API gravity of 36.7° and sulphur content of 1.8%. The H_2S content in the associated gas is about 0.7%. The Gas/Oil Ratio (GOR) however was different in the three domes. In Baba it was about 140 standard cubic feet per barrel (SCF/B), in the Avanah dome 170 SCF/B and in the Khurmalah dome around 220 SCF/B.

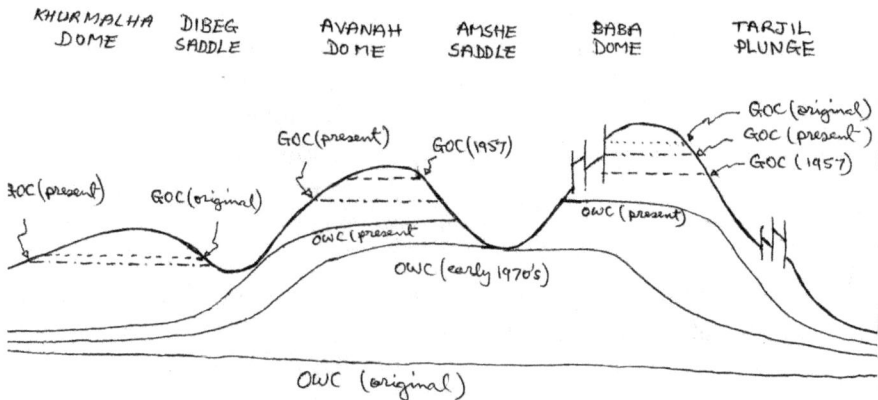

Kirkuk Main LimestoneRerervior - Fluid Contacts History (1990)

Although the Main Limestone is prominent source of oil in the Kirkuk field, oil was also discovered in the deeper reservoirs of Cretaceous age. These are oil bearing mainly in the Baba dome area except for the Qamchuqa reservoirs in

Khurmalah dome and in the Tarjil Plunge. Fractured Campanian-Maasstrichtian Shiranish Limestone contain oil of 33.6° API gravity only in fractures. Oil of 34° API gravity was encountered in the lower Senonian-Mushorah Komitan formation. The Khurmalah dome houses a small pool of 32.6° API gravity oil in the Lower Qamchuqa reservoir.

The first field's production facilities together with the two 12 inch diameter export pipelines were completed and oil production started soon after and by 1935 the first quantity of the Kirkuk oil reached the Mediterranean ports for export. The combined capacity of these two pipelines, one ending in Haifa in Palestine and the other in Tripoli in Lebanon, was approximately 80,000 barrels per day.

The rising water level in the reservoir began to affect some of the oil producing wells which were low on the structure and as a result some of them were lost. Plugging them back to delay water coning was considered costly and ineffective due to the extensive fracturing of the reservoir since once a well is watered out, the water cut rise very steeply and the well ceases to flow naturally. Hence flooded wells were abandoned or converted into oil/water contact observation wells and new wells were drilled further up the structure. This method was considered more economical due to the relatively low drilling cost in the shallow Kirkuk field. As a result the number of wells drilled by the middle of the 1990s had reached more than 250,though the number of producing wells was around sixty.

The associated gases from the field were continued to be flared for about 35 years until the late 1960s when some were gathered and delivered to feed the newly constructed Sulphur Plant. The remaining gases were ultimately gathered and utilised in the mid 1980s to feed the North Gas Project for the production of Liquid Petroleum Gas (LPG) for the local markets and fuel gas for the power stations and the larger industrial plants.

The average well productivity in the Baba and Avanah domes from the Tertiary wells is about 30,000 barrels per day and about 10,000 barrels per day from the Cretaceous. However the productivity of the Khurmalah wells is lower averaging between 3,000 and 5,000 barrels per day.

The off take capability from the Baba and Avanah domes was increased gradually over the first three decades to about one million barrels per day by the late 1960s and to 1.2 million barrels per day in the early 1970s. The off take then reached a peak rate close to 1.4 million barrels per day and from there on the actual off take rate was reduced from the Baba dome but increased from the Avanah dome. This was achieved through increasing the capacities of the two existing Saralu and Sarbashakh degassing stations and the construction of a third one in the far northwest region in the 1980s.

Except for the migration of oil from the Khurmalah dome to the Avanah dome across the Debiga Saddle, no direct production from the Khurmalah dome had ever taken place up to 1992. The development of the Khurmalah dome became necessary to compensate for the planned reduction of production from the Baba and Avanah domes which have been the main producing domes in the past.

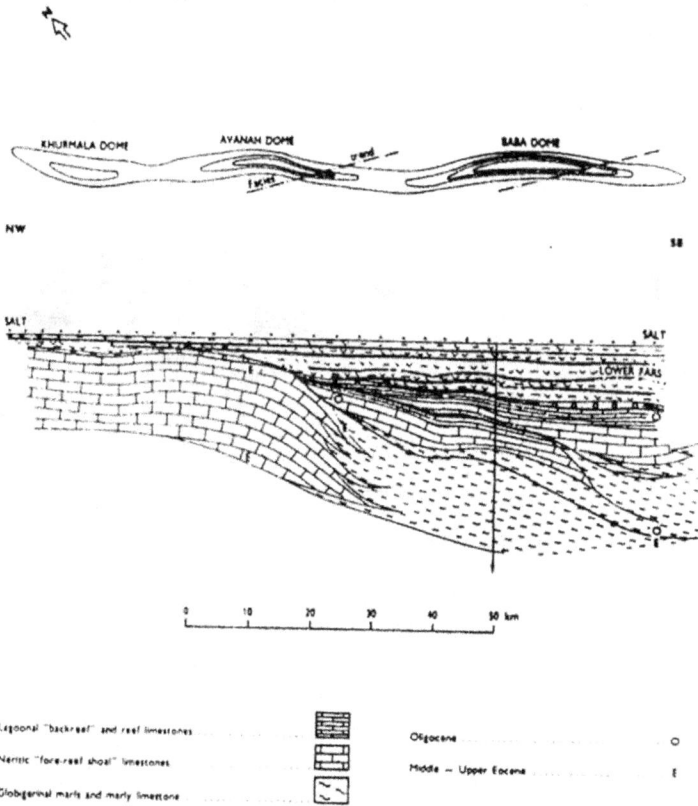

Kirkuk Field

The Khurmalah development plan involved the construction of three new degassing stations, two remotely controlled and the third as a centre of operations containing the necessary crude processing, pumping and gas gathering facilities. The design capacity of this development was 100,000 barrels per day from 30 wells. Water injection would be facilitated through more than 20 peripheral wells. The necessary water would be supplied through the extension of the existing water injection pipeline feeding the northwest of the Avanah dome.

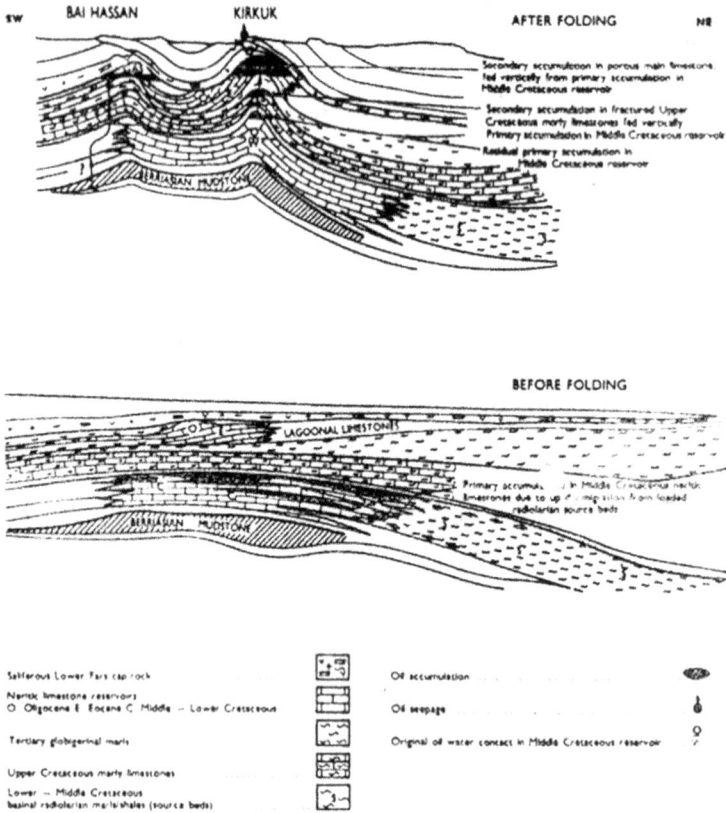

Kirkuk and Bai Hassan Fields

The drilling work was started during the second half of the 1980s and the construction work was initiated in1989. The project was however disrupted during the Gulf war and was finally completed and put in operation in 1992.

It is important to highlight that by 1975, the cumulative production from this giant Kirkuk field had exceeded seven billion barrels of oil and by the end of 1989 its cumulative production had topped the massive figure of fourteen billion barrels of oil and that this marvellous field is still going as strong as ever today in producing more of its precious oil.

It is also of interest to record that the original oil in place was estimated at 36 billion barrels and the recoverable reserves were estimated in the early 1970s at 16 billion barrels. However, a comprehensive study in the early 1980s, employing a 3-D fractured simulation model, put the ultimate recoverable reserves close to 22 billion barrels.

Finally, this remarkable giant field which has been in production for three quarters of a century since 1935, is considered to be the eldest currently producing field in the world and is expected to continue to hold this record for approximately another half a century to around 2060 and possibly beyond, depending on its future rates of production and further appraisals of its performance employing more sophisticated techniques.

45 - KOR MOR (ANFAL)

This field was discovered by the Iraq Petroleum Company (IPC) in 1953 and formed a southern extension to the Kirkuk field. The discovery well Kor Mor-1 encountered gas/condensate in the Eocene-Lower Miocene Main Limestone. A second well, Kor Mor-2, penetrated the main reservoir below 1,420 metres which was wholly gas bearing and severely fractured. Gas and condensate were produced on test at the rate of 27,000 SCFD. The field was considered as a gas field which had no market at that time.

Further drilling in 1988 confirmed the existence of gas, rich in condensates, in commercial quantities. Because of the shortage of gas, a high priority was given to the development of this field. As a result an accelerated pilot development project was started in 1989. Four new wells were drilled and completed as gas producers and a full development plan was scheduled for completion in 1991 after the completion of the geological and reservoir studies to determine the reserves and the depletion rates.

In the meantime the laying of a pipeline to bring the gas and condensates to the Kirkuk oilfield area was started. Unfortunately, these plans seem to have been disrupted by the invasion of Kuwait and the subsequent events of the Gulf War and the prolonged sanctions.

However this field became the subject of negotiations in recent years and a production sharing agreement for its redevelopment and operation was finally signed by the Kurdistan Regional Government and the two Sharjah, UAE, based companies Dana Gas and Crescent Petroleum.

It has also been reported recently that the field's gas reserves are estimated to be about 3.0 trillion standard cubic feet and the current gas processing plant has a design capacity of some 300 million standard cubic feet per day. The Liquid Petroleum Gas (LPG) from the plant is bottled and marketed locally, the condensates are delivered to the central crude oil facilities at Kirkuk and the remaining gas is sent by two pipelines as fuel for the power stations at Erbil and Sulaimaneyah cities.

46 - KURDAMIR

This field which lies to the southeast of the Pulkhana field became the subject of negotiations for exploration and development and a production sharing agreement was finally signed between the Kurdish Regional Government in 2005 and the Canadian Western Zagros Resources company.

The company made a discovery of 327 metres combined gas and hydrocarbon column in the Oligocene formation in its Kurdamir-1 exploratory well. The well flowed after acidization at a maximum rate of 18.3 million cubic feet per day of gas with a yield of 86 barrels of high quality, 62° API condensate per million cubic feet of gas.

The company's best estimate of gross contingent gas and condensate is 850 billion cubic feet and 33 million barrels respectively as of December 2010.

The Kurdamir structure is being processed to evaluate the full potential of the reservoir.

47 - LUHAIS

This field was discovered by the BPC in 1961 and is located west of the Rumaila field in the south of the country. The depth of the oil bearing layer was about 2,800 metres and had a thickness of some 30 metres. The discovery well, Luhais-1, encountered weak to moderate oil staining in the Albian Nahr Omar formation. Additional wells drilled by the Iraq National Oil Company

(INOC) produced 32.5° API gravity oil, which flowed at a rate of about 5,000 barrels per day from the upper part of the Zubair formation.

The field was developed in the mid 1970s and came on stream in 1977at an initial rate of 50,000 barrel per day. The ultimate recoverable reserves are estimated at more than 500 million barrels of oil.

48 - MAJNOON

This field was discovered in 1977 by the Brazilian Oil Company Petrobras which was working under a service contract with the Iraq National Oil Company (INOC). The field is located 60 km north of Basra in the southeast of the country and close to the Iranian border. The discovery was the result of the appraisal drilling to delineate the Nahr Omar field which was discovered in 1948. The field produces from multiple reservoirs. In the Cretaceous section, seven zones tested some hydrocarbon but few only contained producible oil. The Upper Cretaceous Hartha limestone tested 4,000 BOPD, the Barremian Zubair limestone produced 45° API gravity oil and the Lower Cretaceous Rattawi limestone formation produced 41° API gravity oil. Other reservoirs include the Turonian-Cenomanian Mishrif formation, the Albian Nahr Omar sandstone formation and the Aptian Shuaiba formation.

The early development of the field was halted during 1980s as a result of the Iraq/Iran war due to its close proximity to the war zone. It was scheduled for development in the early 1990s but the plan was delayed again by the invasion of Kuwait and the subsequent tragic events of the Gulf War and the prolonged and inhumane sanctions.

The field was put in production on a small scale later on by the South Oil Company. However the production rate was reduced further to 45,000 barrels per day after the 2003 invasion of Iraq.

The field became the subject of an auction and negotiations in recent years and a production service contract was finally signed by the Ministry of Oil and a consortium of the Royal Dutch Shell (45%), Petronas of Malaysia (30%) with the remaining 25% held by the Iraqi government. In the meantime the Royal Dutch Shell was appointed as the operator.

The consortium took over the operation and development of the field in January 2010 with the aim of quadrupling the production rate by drilling over

40 production wells, the construction of three degassing stations and two crude oil processing plants, to increase the production capacity after the completion of the initial phase from 45,000 barrels per day to 175,000 BOPD. It has been reported that subsequent phases could increase the field's production up to the massive rate of 1.8 million barrels per day.

This field is classified as real giant with an estimated ultimate recoverable reserves of 12.0 billion barrels.

Finally one can only pose to reflect on past events which have enabled the return of the Royal Dutch Shell to Iraq after an absence of almost 35 years since it was forced to leave the country as one of the main shareholders of the Iraq Petroleum Company (IPC) and the Basra Petroleum Company (BPC) after their nationalisation in 1972 and 1975 respectively.

49 - MANSURIYAH

This structure is located about 80 km to the northeast of Baghdad close to the main Baghdad-Khaniqin road. It was identified by seismic in the early 1970s. An exploration well was drilled during the mid 1970s and found gas but an oil rim was suspected. Appraisal drilling started after the end of the Iraq/Iran war in 1989 and confirmed gas and condensates although the possibility of finding oil was not completely ruled out until further drilling far enough from the crest is completed. Later appraisals confirmed the field as a gas field with an estimated gas in place between 3.3 and 4.5 trillion standard cubic feet.

Early development of this field was planned whether an oil rim is found or not as the existing pipeline between the Naftkhanah field and the Daura refinery passes close by and has an excess capacity which could be used and thus result in reducing the cost of the development work. Again these plans were disrupted by the invasion of Kuwait and the subsequent events of the Gulf War and the sanctions.

In recent years, the field has been the subject of an auction and negotiations and as a result a production service contract was finally awarded by the Ministry of Oil in June 2011 to a consortium from the Korean Gas

Corporation (KOGAS), the Turkish State Company TPAO and Kuwait Energy for its development.

The field is expected to have a production capacity of 320 million standard cubic feet of gas per day.

50 - MIRAN

This field which is located in the Sulaymaniyah area became the subject in recent years of negotiations for exploration and development and a production sharing agreement was finally signed by the Kurdish Regional Government to the Canadian company Heritage Oil.

Condensate and gas were subsequently discovered in 2009 and a test well flowed at a rate of about 75 million standard cubic feet per day.

The field has two structures and it has been reported that Miran West is estimated to have reserves of between 7.0 to 9.0 trillion standard cubic feet of gas while Miran East's reserves are estimated at about one trillion standard cubic feet of gas.

51 - NAFT KHANAH

This field was discovered in May 1923 by the Anglo-Persian Oil Company (present day British Petroleum, BP). The drilling began in February 1919 and it was not until the first week of May 1923 that oil was discovered. The well caught fire and burnt for a week before it was brought under control. The initial pressure of the well was considered very high at that time, measuring some 2,500 psi.

The structure is a relatively small surface anticline12 km long and 1.5 km wide. It extends across the border into Iran where it is named Naft-i-Shah field. Production is from the Miocene Kalhur limestone (a member of the Asmari limestone). The reservoir is 76 metres thick and at an average depth of 650 metres.

This field became the first oilfield to be discovered in modern Iraq, after the discovery of the Chiah Surkh field in 1903, and set the scene for the oil industry in the country. An agreement was signed between the government and the Anglo-Persian Oil Company to develop the field and to construct a small refinery at the nearby town of Khaniqin. The refinery was called Al-Wand, which came on stream in February 1927, taking its crude oil feed from the NaftKhana field. The products were marketed in north Iraq but after the construction of the Daurah refinery in Baghdad in the mid 1950's, a 12 inch diameter pipeline was constructed to transport some of this crude to it as explained further under the heading Refineries.

The production of this 42° API gravity crude oil continued at rates ranging from 12,000 to 30,000 barrels per day with several periods of shutdown. Both gas and water coning became a problem during the 1970s which affected the production rate. However, further drilling indicated a larger oil area than was thought previously and oil was found at deeper depths. Hence it was decided to rejuvenate the field by installing new pumps and upgrading the pipeline to Daurah to withstand higher pressure to bring its capacity to some 25,000 barrels per day.

The cumulative production from this field to the end of 1980 was estimated at 120 million barrels at an average rate of 3,000 barrels per day and the estimated ultimate recoverable reserves are quoted at about 300 million barrels.

52 - NAHR OMER

Discovered by the BPC in 1948, the Nahr Omer field is located 20 km northeast of Basra close to the Iranian border . Nahr Omer-1, the discovery well encountered oil bearing sands between 2,450 and 2,590 metres. A second well found the same sands water bearing. This discouraged further drilling. Thus, the field was not explored further at that time because it was thought to be too small and hence uneconomical to develop.

It was Petrobras the Brazilian oil company which had signed a service agreement in 1972 with INOC that began its appraisal work on this field and found it to be much larger than it was originally thought and pleasantly discovered during its appraisal work the adjacent giant Majnoon field as well.

The structure is a northwest-southeast tending anticline about 20 km long. The Albian Nahr Omer formation (of Lower Cretaceous age) forms the main pay zone at a depth of about 2,450 metres. Other producible intervals were also reported in the Lower Cretaceous Zubair formation.

The field was developed and went on steam in the late 1970s producing 43° -45° API gravity oil from an average depth of about 2,590 metres. The production was, however halted soon after the start of the Iraq/Iran war in 1980 due to the proximity of the field to the war zone.

The ultimate recoverable reserves of this field were estimated at 1.1 billion barrels of oil.

53 - NAJMAH

This field was discovered by the MPC in 1933 and is one of the four adjacent and connected fields of the Qaiyarah area namely : Jawan, Najmah, Qaiyarah and Qasab.

Two appraisal wells were drilled during the late 1980s, one penetrated the Cretaceous Hartha formation on the northeast flank of the structure and found, contrary to expectation, oil of lighter gravity than the Tertiary.

The field has been the subject of an auction and negotiations in recent years and a production service contract was finally awarded by the Ministry of Oil in January 2009 to the Angolan company Sonagol for the further development of the field. Sonagol is expected to bring the field's production to 110,000 barrels per day.

The field ultimate recoverable reserves are estimated at about 850 million barrels of oil. Other details are to found under the Qaiyarah field.

54 - NASIRIYA

This field was discovered in 1979 and is located some 150 km northwest of Basra. The discovery well produced oil from the Lower Cretaceous Zubair sand and Rattawi limestone.

The appraisal and development of the field was deferred during the Iraq/Iran war and later on due to the Gulf war and the subsequent sanctions.

The field has been the subject of an auction and negotiations in recent years and as a result a production service contract was finally awarded by the Ministry of Oil in January 2009 to the Japanese companies Nippon Oil, Inpex, and Japan Gas Co. (JGC) to develop the field with the aim of achieving a production rate of 200,000 barrels per day.

The recoverable reserves of the field were initially estimated at about 4.4 billion barrels of oil.

55 - NOWDOUMAN

This field is located about 30 km to the south of the Naftkhanah field and some 90 km northeast of Baghdad. The discovery well tested high pressure light oil and high gas/oil ratio. Two appraisal wells were scheduled to be drilled during 1992-1993 and the development of the field for production was planned for completion in the mid 1990s. The plan was disrupted by the invasion of Kuwait and the subsequent events of the Gulf War and the prolonged and sustained sanctions.

56 - NUR

This field was discovered in 1978 and located north of Basra near the Iranian border. The field is not too far from the Buzurgan and Halfaya fields. It produces oil from reservoirs similar to those producing from the nearby fields of Buzurgan and Halfaya. The main Production comes from the Turonian-Cenomanian Mishrif limestone formation and the oil produced has 28° API gravity.

Appraisal work could not begin due the invasion of Kuwait and the subsequent events of the Gulf War and sanctions.

57 - PULKHANAH

This field was discovered by the IPC in 1959 and is located to the southeast of the Jambur field and not too far from it. The structure is that of a long sinuous asymmetric anticline. Surface seepages of viscous oil at the town of Tuz Khermato, which sits on the top of the Pulkhanah structure, were exploited by shallow digging as far back as 1870 and continued through the First World War. Deep drilling began in 1927. The first two wells were abandoned, due to mechanical difficulties, before reaching target.

The discovery well, Pulkhana-5, encountered oil of 35° API gravity and a sulphur content of 2.7 % from fractures in the Lower Miocene Euphrates limestone formation from a depth below 1,220 metres. The second reservoir is the upper part of the Maastrichtian-Campanian Shiranish limestone (of Upper Cretaceous age). It produced 500 Barrels of oil per day of 27°-31° API gravity from a depth of 1, 650 metres. The field was considered too small and uneconomical for development at that time.

This field became the subject of negotiations for exploration and development and a production sharing agreement was finally signed between the Kurdish Regional Government and the Canadian company ShaMaran Petroleum.

Crude Oil Seepage at Pulkhanah

58 - QAIYARAH

The Qaiyarah area is situated on the west bank of the river Tigris some 50 kilometres south of the city of Mosul. It contains four adjacent and connected structures by the names of Qaiyarah, Najmah, Jawan and Qasab as shown in Fig. Qaiyarah-1. The first three are successive individual culminations on a sinuous fold axis 45 km long and 5 km wide, which trends towards the northwest from the western bank of the river Tigris at the town of Qaiyarah. The fourth, Qasab, is a parallel anticline 25 km long and 5 km wide, with two domes, which is offset to the northeast and separated from Jawan by a broad shallow syncline.

Heavy oil with asphalt has been seeping to the surface of the ground in that region from time immemorial. The Sumerians, in the south of Iraq, seem to have utilized the asphalt for waterproofing some of their fishing boats over five thousand years ago and the Babylonian are known to have employed it as a water proofing material in the construction of their Ziggurats and the walls of their fabulous city of Babylon with its hanging gardens over three thousand years ago.

Oil is present continuously in the four domes except for small crestal gas caps. It is reservoired in porous and permeable Euphrates-Jeribe limestones of early Middle Eocene age. The seal for these accumulations is provided by marls and anhydrites of the Lower Fars. A similar distribution of oil is found in the relatively less porous limestones of the Hartha formation of Late Cretaceous age. Between the two accumulations are Upper Cretaceous Eocene and Oligocene marls.

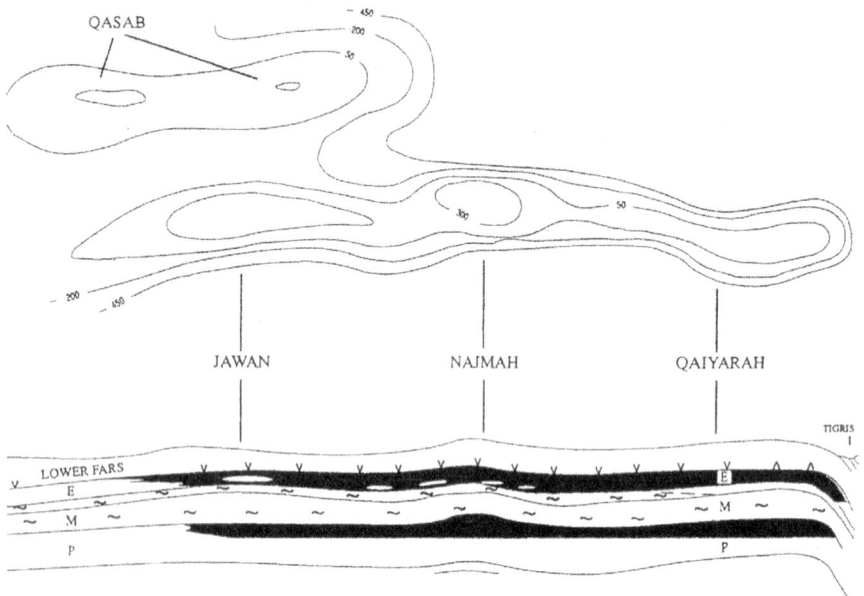

Fig. Qaiyarah-1. Qaiyarah, Najmah, Jawan & Qasab Fields

Oil is present continuously in the four domes except for small crestal gas caps. It is reservoired in porous and permeable Euphrates-Jeribe limestones of early Middle Eocene age. The seal for these accumulations is provided by marls and anhydrites of the Lower Fars. A similar distribution of oil is found in the relatively less porous limestones of the Hartha formation of Late Cretaceous age. Between the two accumulations are Upper Cretaceous Eocene and Oligocene marls.

The oil from Qaiyarah was first produced on a large scale in 1908. The oil is very heavy with an API gravity ranging from 11°-19° in the Tertiary reservoirs and from 11.5°-18.0° in the Cretaceous reservoirs. It is very viscous with an asphaltene content of some 60% by weight and highly sulphurous with a sulphur content of 6.5-8.0% by weight and H2S as high 2,000 parts per million. The Gas Oil Ratio (GOR) is 100 standard cubic feet per barrel with the associated gas containing some 25%-30% of H2S by volume. The oil is density stratified, the heavier occupying the deepest parts of the structure.

The early production from these fields had been intermittent depending on demand at a rate fluctuating between 2,000-5,000 barrels per day which was delivered to a small local refinery specifically designed for the production of asphalt. However due to the greater demand for asphalt during the 1970s a new degassing station was constructed and the production rate was increased to 15,000 barrels per day.

In the late 1980s, drilling was resumed and by 1990 the total number of wells had reached ninety. The aim was to raise the production to 100,000 barrels per day to use some of the crude as fuel to a large thermal power station south of Mosul. However this plan was disrupted by the invasion of Kuwait and the subsequent events of the Gulf War and the prolonged sanctions.

The cumulative production from these fields to the early 1980s was estimated at ten million barrels of oil and the estimated ultimate recoverable reserves of these four fields are quoted at about two billion barrels.

These fields have been the subject of an auction and negotiations in recent years and a production service contract was finally awarded by the Ministry of Oil in January 2009 to the Angolan company Sonagol for the further development of the field.

59 - QARACHAUQ

This is a big structure situated about 60 km to the northwest of Kirkuk running parallel to the Khurmalah dome of Kirkuk field and to the southwest of it. Two wells had been drilled and tested about 2,000 barrels of oil per day each. Further appraisal and development drilling were planned for the early 1990s and development work to start soon after. These plans were disrupted by the invasion of Kuwait and the subsequent events of the Gulf War and sanctions.

60 - QASAB

This field is one of the four fields in the Qaiyarah area. The field had been inactive for a long time but two wells were drilled recently, one on each dome of the structure and confirmed previous results. Other details are mentioned under the Qaiyarah field. The ultimate recoverable reserves of this field are estimated between 300 to 500 million barrels of oil.

61 - QUMAR

This structure was identified by seismic and is located about 90km to the south of Kirkuk. The first well, Qumar-1, was drilled in 1980 and tested about 1,500 BOPD of medium gravity crude. Further drilling of two appraisal wells was planned for the early 1990s and if the result were more positive the development work would follow soon after. The plans were disrupted by the invasion of Kuwait and the subsequent events of the Gulf War and the sustained sanctions that followed.

The ultimate recoverable reserves of this field are estimated at about 70 million barrels of oil.

62 - QUWAIR

This is a small structure located about 30 km to the southeast of Mosul on the main Mosul-Kirkuk road. The exploration well was drilled in the 1950s by the IPC and found no significant hydrocarbons and no further drilling was attempted. It was not until the early 1980s when a second well was drilled to the Cretaceous formations and again found only traces of oil. No further drilling was planned on this structure.

63- RACHI

This small anticlinal structure was discovered by the BPC in 1956 and is located to the west of the Rumaila field. The discovery well, Rachi-1, produced 31° API gravity oil from the Albian Nahr Umer sands at a depth of about 2,735 metres. The Upper Cretaceous Hartha limestone, Lower Cretaceous Zubair sands, Ratawi limestone and Yamama limestone gave slight oil shows. The Ratawi gave some gas as well as the oil. The main producing reservoir is the Nahr Umer sands. No further drilling was carried out as the field was considered too small and hence uneconomical for development at that time.

64 - RATAWI

This field was discovered by the BPC in 1950 and is located to the north of the Rumaila field about 70 km west of Basra. The Structure is a north-south trending surface anticline located by seismic surveys. The discovery well, Ratawi-1, encountered oil indications in several reservoirs: The Upper Cretaceous Mishrif formation carbonates, the Albian Mauddud limestone formation and the Lower Cretaceous Nahr Umer sandstone and the Zubair sands formations.

The main reservoirs are in the Lower Cretaceous Nahr Umer (at an average depth of 2,590 metres) and Zubair formations which contained oil of 21° API gravity oil. The Mishrif formation produced heavier 17° API gravity oil containing 5% sulphur. At the time, the field was considered as too small to develop and was abandoned.

Later drilling, however, discovered a third reservoir in the Lower Cretaceous Ratawi limestone formation which produced 28° API gravity oil. This latter reservoir was anticipated to be the main producer.

The ultimate recoverable reserves are estimated at about 1 billion barrel of oil.

65 - RUMAILA

This field was discovered by the BPC in 1948 and is located near the Zubair field in the Basra area, about 54 km to the west of Basra city. The structure is slightly asymmetrical trending nearly north-south and measures about 70 km in length and 10 km in width. It is divided into two parts, Rumaila and Rumaila North, with the northern Rumaila dome being much larger and structurally lower than the southern one.

The whole field produces oil from the Lower Cretaceous Zubair formation sandstones and the Middle Cretaceous Mishrif formation sandstones. The oil produced from the Zubair formation reservoir has 35° API gravity with 2.0% sulphur. The depth to the top of this main reservoir is about 3,050 metres and the net pay thickness ranges from 200-230 metres. The porosity averages 25% and the permeability ranges from 1,000 to 5,000 mD (Milli Darcy). The gas/oil ratio (GOR) is about 700 SCF/B (standard cubic feet per barrel). A horizontal OWC (oil/water contact) exist throughout the reservoir at about 3,270 metres. The production mechanism is oil expansion supplemented by a strong water drive.

The Lower Cretaceous Zubair Upper Shale Member is a significant reservoir consisting of 19 units of interbedded sandstones and shales, three of which are oil-bearing sandstones with an average porosity of 25% and permeability of 1,000 mD. It produced heavier oil of 32.2° API gravity oil and 2.75 sulphur but no H2S. The production mechanism is solution gas drive.

The Middle Cretaceous Mishrif reservoir is a huge not fully exploited reservoir. Its top is about 2,300 metres with a gross thickness of about 150 metres. Oil produced has 27 API° gravity with 3.7% and 3% by weight of sulphur and asphaltene respectively. The production mechanism is strong water drive.

In 1989, a new deeper discovery was made where 3,500 barrel of oil per day of 49.5 API° was tested in the Middle Jurassic Najma limestone reservoir.

The BPC started its production from the southern part in 1954 and INOC started its production from the northern part in 1972. The cumulative production reached 4.6 billion barrels of oil in 1984. The ultimate recoverable reserves were originally estimated at 20 billion barrels of oil for the whole field, but as a result of the deeper pay discovery this figure has been revised to 30 BBO which makes Rumaila a real giant of a field.

These fields have been the subject of an auction and negotiations in recent years and as a result a production service contract was finally awarded by the Ministry of Oil in 2009 to British Petroleum and China National Petroleum Company (CNPC) for further development of the field. The Agreement is expected to raise field's current production of about one million to a massive 2.85 million barrels per day.

This marks the return of BP, one of the four main shareholders of the Basra Petroleum Company (BPC) to its much disputed and sought after precious giant oilfield some 35 years after it was initially deprive from the North Rumaila by the famous Law number 80 in 1961 and ultimately from the Rumaila after nationalization of the BPC in 1975.

Hence one can only pose to reflect on past events that have affected the life of this giant field and on how they have enabled BP to regain back its lost treasure with such ease after being unable to do so by all other means.

66 - SAFWAN

This field was discovered in 1983 and located a few kilometres south of the Zubair field near the Kuwaiti borders. A 36° API gravity oil was produced from the Lower Cretaceous Zubair sands. The discovery was awaiting appraisal.

67 - SAMAWA

This field was discovered by the BPC in 1959 and located some 250 km south of Baghdad west of the river Euphrates. The structure is anticlinal and the discovery well, Samawa-1, encountered 26° API gravity oil in the Middle-Upper Jurassic Najma limestone formation at a depth of 2,750 metres. Lighter oil, of 40° API gravity, was also found from the deeper Ratawi limestone and an even deeper horizon in the Lower Jurassic Alan limestone was also reported to contain oil. The field was considered too small for development at that time and is still awaiting further appraisal.

68 - SANGAW

This field is located about 50 km southeast of Kirkuk oil field and on trend with the Taq Taq and Chem Chemal fields. It became the subject of negotiations for exploration and development and a production sharing agreement was finally signed by the Kurdistan Regional Government and the USA company Sterling Energy.

The company announce in July 2011 that Sangaw North-1 exploration well was drilled to a total depth of 4,190 metres into the Triassic Kurra Chine formation and that three flow tests were conducted across intervals between the Triassic Kurra Chine and the Cretaceous Kometan formations.

Gas was produced , along with formation water, at rates that are not commercial and that the well has been plugged and abandoned.

69 - SARQALA

This field which lies to the southeast of the Pulkhana field became the subject of negotiations for exploration and development and a production sharing agreement was finally signed in 2005 between the Kurdistan Regional Government and the Canadian company Western Zagros Resources.

The company made an oil discovery in the Miocene Jeribe formation at the Sarqala-1 exploratory well. The Jeribe formation flowed light oil of 40° API gravity at rate of some 6,000 barrels per day.

The Sarqala structure is being processed to evaluate the full potential of the reservoir.

70 - SASSAN

This field was discovered by the MPC in 1956 and located in the northwest of the country about 50 km west of the city of Mosul. The discovery well tested about 2,000 barrels per day of 40° API gravity oil from the fractured Upper Cretaceous Shiranish limestone and Albian fractured carbonates. However the field was not developed since it was considered too small and non-commercial at that time.

71 - SHAIKHAN

This field which is located in the Duhok area became the subject of negotiations for exploration and development and a production sharing agreement was finally signed between the Kurdistan Regional Government and the British company Gulf Keystone.

The drilling of Shaikhan-1 made a major discovery soon after in mid 2009. The well tested five levels from 1,450 metres through to 2,850 metres, with a combined rate of flow of more than 20,000 barrels per day.

This was followed by appraisal well Shaikhan-2 which had a flow test from the lower section of the Kurre Chine B zone in the upper Triassic zone of 2,600 barrels of 40° API gravity oil per day with associated gas of 5.4 million standard cubic feet of gas per day.

Shaikhan-3 was completed soon after as a production well from the Jurassic reservoir in the Sargelu formation.

Shaikhan-4 appraisal well was being drilled at the time of writing at a depth of some 2,500 metres.

The latest independently audited report estimated the oil in place at around 7.5 billion barrel of oil which ranks it as a giant field.

72 - SHAKAL

This field which lies immediately southeast and on a trend with the Pulkhana field became the subject of negotiations for exploration and development and a production sharing agreement was finally signed in 2008 between the Kurdistan Regional Government and the Australian company Oil Search and the Turkish company PetOil.

The drilling of the discovery well Shakal-1, which was completed in 2009 flowed at a rate of 2,450 barrels per day.

The Shakal structure is being processed to evaluate the full potential of the reservoir.

73 - SHEIKH ADI

This field which is located in the northeast of Duhok, and lies to the west and on trend with Sheikan field became the subject of negotiations for exploration and development and a production sharing agreement was finally signed between the Kurdistan Regional Government and the British company Gulf Keystone.

Drilling of the Sheikh Adi -1 well started in August 2010 to reach a depth of 3,780 metres in the Triassic Zone.

Gulf Keystone has recently revealed the results of an independent preliminary evaluation of the field by the Houston based exploration consultants, Dynamic Global Advisers based on Sheikh Adi-1 wireline logging data, core samples, 2D and 3D seismic and regional data, which indicated a significant range of between one billion and three billion barrels of gross oil-in-place calculated on a P90 to P10 bases, with a P50 estimate of 1.9 billion barrels.

74 - SIBA

This field was discovered in 1969 and is located near the mouth of Shat al-Arab, about 30 km southeast of Basra. It is an anticlinal structure delineated by seismic. The discovery well, drilled by Elf-Iraq in 1968/69, tested 6,000 barrels per day of 24° API gravity oil in the rather shaly Lower Cretaceous Zubair formation sandstone at a depth of about 3,425 metres. The gross thickness of the Upper Sandstone Member is about 50 metres with a net pay of 15 metres. The field was left awaiting appraisal before development.

Later appraisals confirmed the field as mainly a gas field with an estimated gas in place between 1.5 and 3.0 trillion standard cubic feet of gas (TSCFG).

The field has been the subject of an auction and negotiations in recent years and as a result a production service contract was finally awarded in June 2011 by the Ministry of Oil to a consortium of the Turkish company TPAO and Kuwait Energy for its development. The field is expected to have a production capacity of 100 million standard cubic feet of gas per day.

75 - SUBA

This field was discovered in 1974 and is located about 130 km northwest of Basra close the river Euphrates. The discovery well tested 30° API gravity oil from the Lower Cretaceous Zubair sands and the Ratawi limestone reservoirs. The field was developed in the late 1980s and came on stream in early 1990 at a rate of 60,000 BOPD.

76 - SUFAYA

Situated west of the Ain Zalah field about 120 km to the northwest of Mosul, the structure straddles the Iraq-Syrian border and is known as Suwaidiya on the Syrian side. Suwaidiyah went on production as far back as 1965 but the first well in Sufaya was drilled in 1974 after seismic surveys showed the extension of the structure inside Iraq. The well found 25° API gravity crude in the Upper Cretaceous Shiranish and Kometan limestone formations at a depth of about 1,400 metres

Lighter oil of 32°-36° API gravity was also indicated in the Triassic Butmah and Qurra Chine carbonate formations and clastic reservoirs but was not significant. Only traces of oil were detected in the Tertiary formations.

Several appraisal wells were drilled during the second half of the 1970s. Those wells that encountered fractures, produced oil through natural flow, other which were drilled in the tight matrix rock required artificial lift.

As a result a pilot scheme was implemented quickly and the field started producing in mid 1980 from those wells on natural flow. The off take rate fluctuates between 4,000 and 8,000 barrels of oil per day which was transported by road tankers.

A full scale development plan which involved the construction of a degassing station, oil dehydration facilities and a pump station was implemented including the installation of sucker rod pumps on wells that did not flow naturally. Well productivities were around 2,000 to 3,000 BOPD for wells on natural flow and around 200 to 1, 200 BOPD for wells on pumps. It was anticipated however that all the wells will eventually be on pumps particularly after water coning sets in.

Further development work was completed and commissioned in 1986 which raised the off take from the field to around 15,000 BOPD. In the meantime drilling continued and by 1990 the number of wells had exceeded forty with cumulative production reaching some 30 million barrels of oil (MMBO). The ultimate recoverable reserves of the field are estimated at around 300 MMBO.

77 - SWARA TIKA

This field which is located in the northeast of Duhok, adjacent to the Tawke oil field became the subject of negotiations for exploration and development and a production sharing agreement was finally signed between the Kurdistan Regional Government and the USA company Hillwood International Energy.

The Swara Tika-1 discovery went to a total depth of 12,500 feet and encountered 1,500 feet of gross oil column. During July 2011, the flow rates established from three zones totalled 7,000 barrels per day.

78 - TAQ TAQ

This field was discovered in 1960 by the IPC and located about 60 km to the northwest of Kirkuk and was not considered significant at that time. A second well, Taq Taq-2, was drilled in the 1970s to deeper horizons penetrating the Tertiary Pilaspie limestone and the Cretaceous formations and found oil in both. One of these was considered a significant find where the well tested 2,000 to 3,000 barrels of oil per day of 48° API gravity with very low GOR (gas/oil ratio) of about 50 standard cubic feet per barrel and low sulphur content.

The field was scheduled for further drilling and development since the early 1980s through a single stage degassing station as no further processing was required. The gravitation of the oil all the way to Kirkuk was considered feasible due to the great diffidence in elevation between the field and the central oil area in Kirkuk. This plan was disrupted by the invasion of Kuwait and the subsequent events of the Gulf War and the prolonged sanctions.

The field became the subject of negotiations for development and a production sharing agreement was signed in January 2004, between the Kurdistan Regional Government and Turkey's Genel Enerji, later joined by Switzerland's Addax Petroleum, a subsidiary of China's Sinopec.

During 2011, through a selective completion programme, three reservoir intervals were tested separately and flowed at a maximum aggregate rate of 29,790 barrels per day of light, 47 degrees API oil.

The ultimate recoverable reserves were estimated at 350 million barrels of oil.

79 - TAWKE

This field which is located in the Duhok area became the subject of negotiations for exploration and development and a production sharing agreement was signed between the Kurdistan Regional Government and the Norwegian company DNO International which discovered oil in 2006.

The field's reserves were originally estimated at about 100 million barrels, but have been revised later on to 300 million and finally to over 600 million barrels of oil.

The field is currently producing at a rate of 50,000 barrels per day.

Originally the oil which was produced at much lower rates was transported by road tankers but it has been reported recently (2011) that an agreement had been reached between the central government in Baghdad and the Kurdistan Regional Government to allow the Tawke crude oil to be delivered by a pipeline to the pump station near the Iraqi-Turkish border where it would be exported through the Iraq-Turkey pipelines to the port of Ceyhan on the Mediterranean.

80 - TEL GHAZAL

This field was discovered in the late 1970s and is located about 15 km south of Naft Khanah field in the Khaniqin area. The discovery well, Tel Ghazal-1, tested about 3,000 BOPD of light, low sulphur oil with high gas/oil ratio. Appraisal drilling was planned during 1993-1994 and a development work was to start soon after.

The oil was to be delivered to Daura refinery in Baghdad by utilizing the excess capacity of the existing Naft Khanah-Daura pipeline. The plan was disrupted by the invasion of Kuwait and the subsequent events of the Gulf War and the sustained sanctions.

81 - TIKRIT (WEST TIKRIT)

This structure which is fragmented into four separate blocks was identified by seismic and located in central Iraq in the region of the city of Tikrit. Four wells were drilled but only two on one of the blocks found oil in 1986. A pilot production scheme for the long term evaluation of the field came on stream in 1989 with two wells, each producing, wet crude of 200 to 300 BOPD of 27° API gravity oil from a depth of 2,500 metres. The oil was transported by road tankers to the not too far away Salahuddin refinery complex at Baiji. No further plans were earmarked for this field.

82 - TUBA

This field was discovered by the BPC in 1959 and is located between the famous fields of Zubair and Rumaila. The structure is an anticline trending almost north-south. The main reservoir is the Turonian-Cenomanian Mishrif limestone formation encountered at a depth of 2,132 metres and has a gross pay thickness of 327 metres. It tested 25°-28° API gravity oil at a rate of 1,470 BOPD. The other reservoir is the Lower Cretaceous Zubair sandstone (interbedded with shale) encountered at a depth of 3,507 metres with a gross thickness of 6 metres. It produced heavy oil and gas at a rate of 1,000 BOPD

The field was developed by Iraq National Oil Company and the Indian ONGC. The ultimate recoverable reserves were estimated to be about 800 million barrels of oil.

83 - WEST QURNA

This field was discovered in 1973 and located close to the northern tip of the Rumaila field and appears to be a structural extension of North Rumaila.

Subsequent appraisal and development drilling in the late 1980s established the presence of a major oil field. West Qurna is believed to hold 43 billion barrels[△] of recoverable reserves, making it the second largest field in the world after Saudi Arabia's Ghawar oil field.

Oil bearing reservoirs were encountered in the Middle Cretaceous Turonian-Cenomanian Mishrif limestone formation and the Lower Cretaceous Ratawi and Zubair formations.

The Mishrif limestone reservoir produced 27° API gravity oil from an average depth of about 2,350 metres. The Zubair sands reservoir produced 33° API gravity oil from an average depth of about 3,050 metres.

The field was being developed during the period 1989-1990 with an initial production capacity of 200,000 barrels per day. Further development was interrupted by the wars and the painful and relentless sanctions that followed.

The field has been the subject of an auction and negotiations in recent years and as a result two production service contracts were finally awarded in June 2011 by the Ministry of Oil as follows:

The first contract for Phase I development of the field was awarded in November 2009 to a joint venture of ExxonMobil and Royal Dutch Shell. The estimated astronomical cost of $50 billion of this contract requires the two companies to raise the current production capacity of 244,000 barrels per day to a massive 2.25 million barrels per day within 7 years. The Iraqi government, in turn, will pay the joint venture $1.90 per each extra barrel produced by them. The contract is expected to create about 100,000 new jobs in the region.

ExxonMobil announced recently in March 2011 that it has managed to raise the initial production capacity of the field from 244,000 barrels per day to 285,000 barrels per day, which exceeds the 10% improved production target established under its production service contract.

The second Phase II contract for, the further development of West Qurna oil field was awarded in December 2009 to Russia's Lukoil and Norway's Statoil companies. The two companies are required to produce a further 1.8 million barrels per day over a period of 13 years. The two companies, in turn, will receive $1.15 per barrel they produce.

A new multi-billion dollar water-injection project is expected to be awarded to operator ExxonMobil. The project includes the construction of a water plant which will help the development of six major oil fields in the area amongst which are West, Qurna, Rumaila, Majnoon and Zubair. The water injection plant will have a capacity of 10-12 million barrel of highly purified water per day and will involve oil companies such as Shell, Eni SpA, Lukoil, China's National Petroleum Corporation and Petronas.

Again, this marks the return of ExxonMobil, one of the four main shareholders of the Basra Petroleum Company (BPC) to one of Iraq's giant oil field after some 35 years when it was initially deprive from the North Rumaila by the famous Law number 80 in 1961 and ultimately from the Rumaila after nationalization of the BPC in 1975.

84 - ZUBAIR

This field was discovered in 1948 by the BPC, located some 25 km west of Basra, it is an anticlinal structure trending north-south. It measures some 24 km in length and 8 km in width. It has three domes, the north, Hamar dome is the smallest, the middle, Shuaiba dome is the highest structurally and the southern, Rafidain dome is the largest and structurally lowest, the lithology of which is shown in Fig. Zubair-2.

The sandstone /shale complex of the Lower Cretaceous Zubair Formation constitutes the major reservoir. Its average thickness is 390 metres and the top is at a depth of about 3,200 metres. This formation is divided into five members: Upper, Middle, and Lower Shales, Upper and Lower Sandstones, which are subdivided into units. Fig. Zubair-1 is a contour map showing the structure on top of the Upper Sandstone Member Zubair Formation in both the Zubair and the Rumaila fields.

Production has been mainly from the Upper Sandstone Member, the (Third Pay), which is about 100 metres thick, with a net pay zone of about 60 metres. The oil quality varies with structural position with the crestal wells having a gas/oil ratio (GOR) of approximately 800 standard cubic feet per day while the flank wells having 600 SCF/B. The oil gravities show similar segregation within the reservoir, the average being 36° API with 1.9% sulphur. The porosity averages 20% and the permeability ranges from 250-400 mD. The reservoir mechanism is mainly gas expansion with a week water drive.

The second significant productive horizon is the (Fourth Pay) or the Lower Sandstone Member. Its average net pay thickness is 47 metres with its top being at a depth of about 3,400 metres. A large gas cap is present at this reservoir which contains better quality oil of 42° API gravity; but it has lower porosity (10-20%) and lower permeability (80-400 mD) than the (Third Pay).

The Middle Cretaceous Mishrif reservoir constitute the (Second Pay). The top of this reservoir is at a depth of 2,150 metres and its thickness is about 160 metres. The oil is found only in the Shuaiba dome. It has an API gravity of 28.1°, with 3.5% and 2.8% by weight, of sulphur and asphaltene respectively.

Oil of 20° API gravity is also found in the Tertiary Miocene Lower Fars limestone and Ghar sandstone. It is a shallow reservoir (First Pay) which is encountered at 300 metres and has a thickness of 220 metres.

The field came on stream in 1951 and the cumulative production by 1990 was estimated at about 1.5 billion barrels of oil.

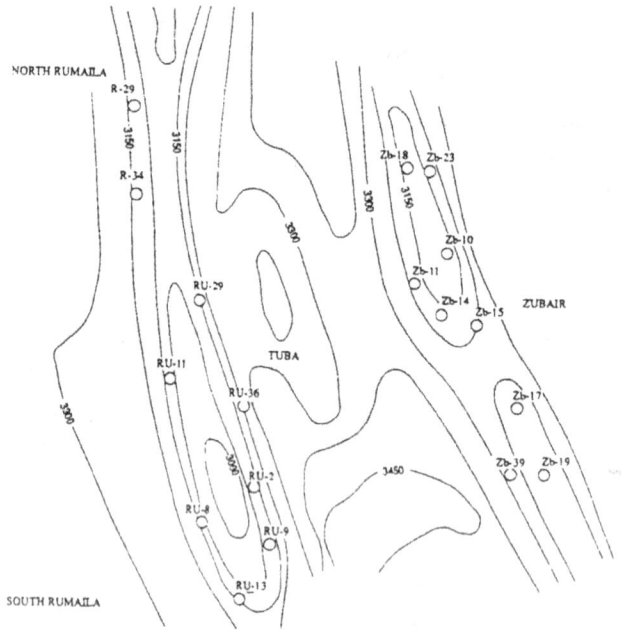

Fig. Zubair-1. Rumaila, Zubair & Tuba Fields

Again this field has been the subject of an auction and negotiations in recent years and as a result a production service contract was finally awarded in January 2010 by the Ministry of Oil to the Italian company ENI in partnership with the US Occidental and the South Korean KOGAS for the further development of the field. The consortium is to raise the current production capacity of 195,000 per day to 1.25 million barrels per day

The field came on stream in 1951 and the cumulative production by 1990 was estimated at about 1.5 billion barrels of oil.

The ultimate recoverable reserves which have been revised towards the end of the twentieth century are estimates at 7.7 billion barrels of oil which classifies the field a real giant.

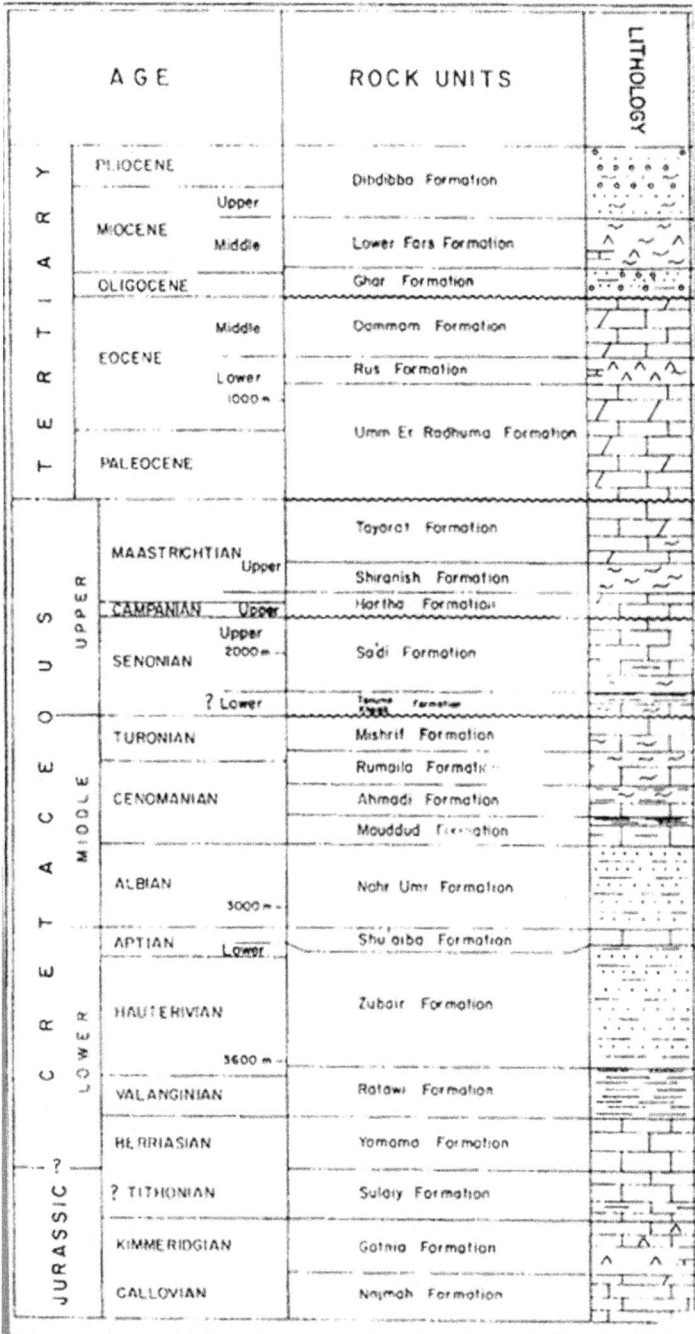

AGE				ROCK UNITS	LITHOLOGY
TERTIARY		PLIOCENE		Dibdibba Formation	
		MIOCENE	Upper		
			Middle	Lower Fars Formation	
		OLIGOCENE		Ghar Formation	
		EOCENE	Middle	Dammam Formation	
			Lower 1000 m	Rus Formation	
				Umm Er Radhuma Formation	
		PALEOCENE			
CRETACEOUS	UPPER	MAASTRICHTIAN	Upper	Tayarat Formation	
				Shiranish Formation	
		CAMPANIAN	Upper	Hartha Formation	
		SENONIAN	Upper 2000 m	Sa'di Formation	
			? Lower	Tanuma Formation	
	MIDDLE	TURONIAN		Mishrif Formation	
		CENOMANIAN		Rumaila Formation	
				Ahmadi Formation	
				Mauddud Formation	
		ALBIAN	3000 m	Nahr Umr Formation	
		APTIAN	Lower	Shu aiba Formation	
	LOWER	HAUTERIVIAN		Zubair Formation	
		VALANGINIAN	3600 m	Ratawi Formation	
		HERRIASIAN		Yamama Formation	
JURASSIC	?	? TITHONIAN		Sulaiy Formation	
		KIMMERIDGIAN		Gotnia Formation	
		CALLOVIAN		Najmah Formation	

Fig. Zubair-2. Stratigraphic Sequence of Zubair Field

Oil and Gas Fields

	Field	Discovery Year	Status	Reserves (Billion Barrels)
1	Abu Amud	1982	Undeveloped	Unknown
2	Abu Amud East	1982	Undeveloped	Unknown
3	Abu Ghurab	1971	Producing	1.00
4	Abu Khaimah	1976	Undeveloped	Unknown
5	Afaq	1961	Undeveloped	Unknown
6	Ahdab	1979	Undeveloped	1.00
7	Ain Zalah	1939	Producing	0.20
8	Ajil (Saddam)	1983	Undeveloped	1.00
9	Akkas	1993	Undeveloped	Gas
10	Allan	1954	Undeveloped	Unknown
11	Atrush	2011	Being appraisal	Unknown
12	Badra	1960	Being Developed	3.00
13	Bai Hassan	1953	Producing	1.00
14	Balad	1983	Producing	0.20
15	Bazian	2010	Being developed	Unknown
16	Bina Bawi	2011	Being Appraised	Unknown
17	Butmah	1952	Producing	0.040
18	Buzurgan	1969	Producing	2.00
19	Chem Chemal	1958	Being developed	Gas
20	Chia Surkh	1903	Being developed	Unknown
21	Demir Dagh	1960	Undeveloped	Unknown
22	Dhafriyah	1988	Undeveloped	Unknown
23	Dujaila	1961	Undeveloped	Unknown
24	East Baghdad	Mid 1970s	Producing	7.00
25	Falluja	1958	Awaiting Drilling	Unknown

	Field	Discovery Year	Status	Reserves (Billion Barrels)
26	Gharraf	1984	Undeveloped	Unknown
26	Gillabat	1959	Awaiting Drilling	Unknown
28	Halfaya	1977	Undeveloped	4.10
29	Hamrin	1961	Awaiting Drilling	Unknown
30	Hawler	2008	Being developed	Unknown
31	Injanah	1958	Awaiting Drilling	Unknown
32	Jabal Fakka	1974	Producing	Unknown
33	Jabal Kand	1980	Awaiting Drilling	Unknown
34	Jabal Sinjar	1980	Awaiting Drilling	Unknown
35	Jambur	1954	Producing	1.50
36	Jarya Pika	1960	Undeveloped	Unknown
37	Jawan	1908	Undeveloped	Unknown
38	Jerishan	1982	Undeveloped	Unknown
39	Khabbaz	1976	Producing	1.50
40	Khashab	Early 1980s	Uneconomical	Unknown
41	Khashm Ahmar	1932	Awaiting Drilling	Unknown
42	Khidar Al-Maa	1982	Undeveloped	Unknown
43	Kifl	1960	Awaiting Drilling	Unknown
44	Kirkuk	1927	Producing	16.00
45	Kor Mor	1953	Producing	Gas
46	Kurdamir	2010	Being developed	Unknown
47	Luhais	1961	Producing	0.50
48	Majnoon	1977	Being developed	12.00
49	Mansuriyah	Mid 1970s	Being developed	Gas
50	Miran	2009	Being developed	Unknown
51	Naftkhana	1923	Producing	0.30

	Field	Discovery Year	Status	Reserves (Billion Barrels)
52	Nahr Omer	1948	Producing	1.10
53	Najmah	1933	Producing	0.85
54	Nasiriya	1979	Being developed	4.40
55	Nowdouman	1980s	Awaiting Drilling	Unknown
56	Nur	1978	Undeveloped	Unknown
57	Pulkhana	1958	Being developed	Unknown
58	Qaiyarah	1908	Producing	1.30
59	Qarachauq	1980s	Being appraisal	Unknown
60	Qasab	1908	Undeveloped	0.30
61	Qumar	1980	Undeveloped	0.07
62	Quwair	1950s	Abandoned	Unknown
63	Rachi	1956	Undeveloped	Unknown
64	Ratawi	1950	Undeveloped	1.00
65	Rumaila	1948	Producing	30.00
66	Safwan	1983	Undeveloped	Unknown
67	Samawa	1959	Undeveloped	Unknown
68	Sangaw	2011	Abandoned	Unknown
69	Sarqala	2010	Being appraised	Unknown
70	Sassan	1956	Undeveloped	Unknown
71	Shaikhan	2009	Being appraised	Unknown
72	Shakal	2009	Being appraised	Unknown
73	Sheikh Adi	2010	Being appraised	Unknown
74	Siba	1969	Undeveloped	Gas
75	Suba	1974	Producing	Unknown
76	Sufaiya	1974	Producing	0.30
77	Swara Tika	2011	Being appraised	Unknown

	Field	Discovery Year	Status	Reserves (Billion Barrels)
78	Taq Taq	1960	Undeveloped	0.35
79	Tawke	2006	Producing	Unknown
80	Tel Ghazal	Late 1970s	Undeveloped	Unknown
81	Tikrit	1986	Producing	Unknown
82	Tuba	1959	Undeveloped	0.80
83	West Qurna	1973	Producing	43.0
84	Zubair	1948	Producing	7.7
	TOTAL			**143.51**

Production Service Contracts
For the Development of Oil and Gas Fields
Awarded by the Ministry of Oil During 2008-2011

Field	Company
1 - Abu Ghurab	Chinese Hong Kong Co. and Turkish State Co TPAO.
2 - Ahdab	Chinese National Petroleum Corp (CNPC).
3 - Akkas	Korean Gas Corp (KOGAS)
4 - Badra	Russian Gasprom, Korean KOGAS, Malaysian Petronas and Turkish TPAO.
5 - Buzurgan	Chinese Hong Kong Co. and Turkish State Co TPAO.
6 - Gharraf	Malaysian Petronas and Japanese Exploration (JAPEX).
7 - Halfaya	Chinese National Oil Co. and Malaysian Petronas.
8 - Jabal Fakka	Chinese Hong Kong Co., Turkish State Co TPAO and French Total.
9 - Majnoon	Royal Dutch Shell and Malaysian Petronas.
10 - Mansuriyah	Korean KOGAS, Turkish TPAO and Kuwait Energy.
11 - Najmah	Angolan Company Sonagol.
12 - Rumaila	British Petroleum and Chinese National Petroleum Corp.
13 - West Qurna	
Phase 1	USA Exxon Mobil and Royal Dutch Shell.
Phase 2	Rusian Lukoil and Norwegian Statoil Hydro.
14 - Zubair	Italian Eni, US Occidental and Korean Gas Corp (KOGAS).

Exploration and Production Sharing Agreements
Awarded by the Kurdistan Regional Government
During 2003-2011

Field	Status	Company
1- Aqri Bijeel	Awaiting Drilling	British Gulf Keystone and & Hungarian Mol.
2- Atrush	Being Appraised	Canadian ShaMaran, Turkish GEP, USA Aspect Energy & USA Marathon Oil.
3- Bar Bahar		Turkish Genel Enerji & British Gulf Keystone.
4- Bazian	Producing	Korean National Oil Company.
5- Bina Bawi	Being Appraised	Turkish A&T Petroleum & USA Prime & Murphy Oil & Australian Oil Search.
6- Chem Chemal	Producing	UAE Dana Gas and Crescent Petroleum.
7- Chia Surkh	Producing	Turkish Genel Enerji and Canadian Longford.
8- Chinguetti		USA Sterling Energy.
9- Dinarta	Awaiting Drilling	USA Hess Corp.
10- Dohuk	Awaiting Drilling	USA Hunt Oil.
11- Hawler	Producing	Rusian company Norbest
12- Kalar Bawanoor		Canadian Western Zagros Resources & Taliman.
13-Khalakan	Awaiting Drilling	Turkish Dog
14- Kiwa Chirmila		Topco.
15- Kor Mor	Producing	UAE Dana Gas and Crescent Petroleum.
16- Kurdamir	Being Appraised	Canadian Western Zagros Resources.
17- Mala Omar	Awaiting Drilling	Austrian OMV Petroleum Exploration.
18- Miran	Producing	Canadian Heritage Oil.
19- Pulkhana	Producing	Canadian ShaMaran Petroleum.
20- Qara Dagh	Being Drilled	Canadian companies Groundstar Resources, Forbs, Manhattan, Niko Resources & Vast Exploration.

Field	Status	Company
21- Rovi	Awaiting Drilling	Indian Reliance Industries.
22- Sarqala	Producing	Canadian Western Zagros Resources.
23- Sangaw	Abandoned	USA Sterling Energy
24- Sarsang	Being Appraised	HKN Energy – USA
25- Sarta	Awaiting Drilling	Indian Reliance Industries.
26- Shakal	Awaiting Drilling	Australian Oil Search and Turkish PetOil.
27- Shakrok	Awaiting Drilling	USA Hess Corp.
28- Shaikhan	Being Appraised	British Gulf Keystone, Hungarian Kalegran, Hungary & USA Keystone.
29- Sheikh Adi	Being Appraised	British Gulf Keystone.
30- Shorish	Awaiting Drilling	Austrian OMV Petroleum Exploration.
31- Sindi-Amedia	Awaiting Drilling	French Perenco.
32- Swara Tika	Being Appraised	USA Marathon Oil Corp.
33- Taq Taq	Producing	Turkish Genel Enirji, Swiss Addax.
34- Tawwke	Producing	Danish DNO.

Food For Thought

Our discussions so far of Iraq's oil and gas fields have been concerned mainly with their discovery, description, development, production and other historical and technical aspects.

Hence it is time to pause and reflect on other various events that have affected the long and colourful lives of the most famous of these fields.

It is to be highlighted that though the country's total reserves of 143 billion barrels of oil (BBO) are held in 84 fields, most of these reserves are in actual fact held in a small number of fields as follows:-

1. WEST QURNA

    This super giant oil field alone holds 43.0 BBO representing 30% of the total reserves. Though the field was discovered in 1973, its full extent had not been realised until many years later and hence its previous meagre production rate of some 240,000 barrels per day could have barely scratched the surface of its vast and lucrative reserves.

    It has however succumbed recently to being awarded through two of the recent Production Service Contracts which are expected to double its current production rate by seventeen fold to the massive and unbelievable figure of 4.15 million barrels per day.

2. RUMAILA

    This famous super giant field with its current remaining reserves of 30.0 BBO representing over 10% of the total reserves, had one of the most colourful lives of most of the other fields. It has been in production for the past 56 years since it came on stream in 1954 and is still going strong.

    North Rumaila, its northern and larger part was taken over by the Government through the legislation of the renowned law No. 80 in 1961 and as a result the field became the subject of a bitter and lengthy dispute between the Government and the Iraq Petroleum Company Group (IPC) for many years.

    The North Rumaila field then became the centre stage of a joint venture negotiations between Iraq National Oil Company (INOC) and the IPC

Group during 1964/1965 for the creation of the Baghdad Oil Company (BOCO). This failed to materialise and as a result the IPC Group's desperate efforts to regain the control of this field were finally dashed. The field was subsequently developed by INOC with the help of the Soviet Union and came on stream in 1971, albeit at a very low rate of production.

In the meantime the southern part of the field remained under the control of the IPC Group until its final nationalisation in 1975.

3.   KIRKUK

This legendary field with its remaining reserves of 16.0 BBO, which represents more than 11% of the country's current total reserves, is believed to be the oldest super giant producing field in the world.

It was discovered in 1927 and has been in continuous production for the past 75, since 1935, and is expected to remain in production for the next 50 years.

The field was the crown jewel of the IPC Group and remained under their control for 45 years from it discovery to its nationalisation in 1972.

Kirkuk at the moment is one of two giant fields that remain under the full and direct control of the Ministry of Oil, since it failed to attract any bid during the recent auctions. The other such giant field is the East Baghdad field.

4.   MAJNOON (THE CRAZY)

This giant field with its reserves of over 12.0 BBO that represents more than 8% of the country's current total reserves, has remained imprisoned like a crazy Jennie for the past 33 years since its discovery in 1977, but not for much longer since it has finally been awoken recently through its award for development through one of the recent Production Service Contract to the international oil companies.

It is expected that the field's current meagre production capacity of 45,000 barrels per day will ultimately be doubled by an amazing forty fold to the impressive figure of 1.8 million barrels per day.

5.   ZUBAIR

This famous giant field was the third precious field of the IPC Group. It has been in production for the past 60 years since it first came on stream in 1951, and its current remaining reserves are estimated at 7.7 BBO, representing over 5% of the total reserves.

The field remained under the control of the IPC Group for 27 years between its discovery in 1948 and its final nationalisation in 1975.

The total reserves of the above five fields is the astronomical figure of 108.7 billion barrels of oil representing 76% of the total current reserves of Iraq.

Current status of these fields

So what is the current status of each of these five giant fields which together hold more than three quarters of the country's oil reserves?

Regretfully, only Kirkuk field remains today under the full and direct control of the Ministry of Oil while the other four precious giant fields have been auctioned like a heap of scrap metal and awarded to the international oil companies through the controversial and much debated Production Service Contracts.

Mercifully, the terms of these contracts are much better for Iraq than those of the Production Sharing Agreements which were preferred and fiercely lobbied for by the oil companies and which as a result were originally adopted by the Ministry of Oil.

It must however be highlighted that the failure of the oil companies to achieve their aim of obtaining Production Sharing Agreements was mainly due to the staunch, courageous and continuous opposition they faced from Iraq's oil experts, independent politicians, oil workers union, intellectuals and the public at large which finally persuaded the Ministry of Oil to adopt the Service Contract alternative.

As a result both the Rumaila and the North Rumaila fields were awarded in June 2009 through a Production Service Contract to the British Petroleum Company in partnership with China's National Petroleum Corporation. Hence this marks the historic return of BP, one of the main shareholders of the IPC Group, to its long lost precious and much sought after field after 35 years of absence.

Two Production Service Contracts were awarded for the development of West Qurna field.

Phase-I was awarded in October 2009 to a joint venture from the USA company ExxonMobil and the Anglo-Dutch company, Royal Dutch Shell. It is to be recalled that each of these two companies was a main shareholder of the IPC Group.

Zubair field met the same fate when a Production Service Contract was awarded in October 2009 for its further development to a consortium from Italy's Eni, the USA Occidental Petroleum and Korea Gas Corporation.

While phase-II of the West Qurna field was awarded soon after in December 2009 to the Russian company Lukoil in partnership with the Norwegian company Statoil Hydro.

Majnoon, on the other hand, succumbed to the same fate when a Production Service Contract was awarded in December 2009 for its development to the Anglo-Dutch company, Royal Dutch Shell, one of the main shareholders of the IPC Group, in partnership with the Malaysian company, Petronas.

Hence, after an absence of 35 years, we see four of the original main shareholders of the IPC Group, the American Exxon and Mobil, the British BP and the Anglo-Dutch Royal Dutch Shell, returning, albeit with others to control one of their nationalised fields, Rumaila in addition to the super giant West Qurna and the giant Majnoon fields. The total reserves of these three fields is a staggering figure of 85 billion barrels of oil representing some 60% of the total current oil reserves of the country.

This reminds us of the controversial and repeatedly asked question,
WAS THE INVASION OF IRAQ IN 2003 ABOUT OIL?????

9

THE DEVELOPMENT OF IRAQ'S OILFIELDS

Introduction

THE BARREL OF OIL

Crude oil, since its early discovery, in commercial quantities in the United States, was sold by the barrel, which was made of wood and based on the old standard 40 US gallon whiskey barrel which was modified to 42 gallon for measuring oil.

The British however adopted the ton in their measurement in the early days of the oil industry. This is evident from the terms of their early crude oil concessions in Persia and Iraq where the tons, Pounds and Shillings were used.

Since the United State was the dominant producer as well as the exporter of crude oil and petroleum products in the world in the early years of the oil industry, its Barrel and Dollar also became dominant in the international market. With time these two units became the accepted international standard units for the measurement and pricing of the crude oil.

So what is a barrel of oil?

1 Barrel = 42 US gallons.
= 35 Imperial gallons.
= 159 Litres.

Degree API (American Petroleum Institute) = (141.5/S.G. at 60 Fahrenheit) − 131.5

1 Metric Ton = approximately 7.578 barrels of Kirkuk crude oil with a specific gravity of 0.8445 or 36.054 degrees API. However this figure

could be lower or higher depending on the specific gravity of each of the hundreds of crude oils in the world.

The Formation of Crude Oil

SO WHAT IS OIL MADE OF AND HOW AND WHEN WAS IT FORMED?

Crude oil is composed mainly of carbon and hydrogen, which is generally known as hydrocarbons. However, in its natural reservoir it usually contains other elements such as sulphur in the form of hydrogen sulphide, oxygen in the form of carbon dioxide and nitrogen in the form of nitrogen oxide in addition to other less common elements.

It is formed from the remains of tiny marine organisms and fossil from plants that lived millions of years ago. It is commonly thought that such period could stretch anywhere from one hundred to two hundred million years ago.

When these marine organisms died they were mixed with other material such as silt, sand and other mineral deposits. The accumulation and compaction of such layers of deposits resulted in the formation of a layer of sedimentary rock.

These sedimentary rock layers trap inside them the marine organisms, which usually constitute about 1% of the mass of the rock.

Over a period of millions of years more layers of such sediments are deposited on top of each other until they are finally covered with further layers of silt and sand which would later on turn into limestone and sandstone rocks. These sedimentary layers gradually sink deeper and deeper under the ever-increasing weight of the layers of rock above them, which result in raising their temperature and pressure. Eventually the temperature and pressure become high enough to transform the organic material trapped in the sediment into a dark waxy substance called Kerogen.

As the temperature and pressure increase further the Kerogen molecules eventually undergo decomposition, which produce hydrocarbon, (oil and gas) in addition to carbon dioxide, nitrogen oxide and water.

As the temperature and pressure increase even further, they become high enough to release and expel the hydrocarbon and other material gradually from the sedimentary rock, the Mother Rock or source rock.

After their expulsion the hydrocarbons migrate through the permeable (porous) rocks adjacent to them and eventually move upwards towards the surface of the earth. Then two main things may have happened to them. They may have continued their upwards journey to escape eventually at the surface, showing themselves as gas, oil or bitumen seepages and ultimately lost. Alternatively they may have been trapped in a suitable structure.

A suitable structure must satisfy three conditions which are:-

a.   It must contain formations which have a porous or sponge like texture for the oil to occupy the spaces between the grains of the rock. Oil can also be found in crevices, cracks and fissures in the rock. Any rock capable of holding oil in this manner is known as a Reservoir Rock and is usually limestone or sandstone.

b.   Above the reservoir there must be a suitable Cap Rock or seal to prevent the escape of the oil into higher layers. These are usually shale, sandstone, salt, limestone or clay.

c.   There must be a fold or bending in the reservoir rock which effectively traps the oil and prevents it from further external movement within the layer.

Water and free gas are also trapped in the reservoir rocks together with the oil, but in the course of time, they will separate out into three layers with the gas at the top, the oil in the middle and the water at the bottom.

Due to the various factors that enter or affect the formation of the crude oils, such as the constituents of the organic materials, pressure, temperature etc, each crude oil has been found, so far, has its own characteristics. Hence there are no two identical oil reservoirs in the world nor two identical crude oils that have ever been produced.

Therefore, and due to the existence of hundreds of types of crude oils being produced all over the world, some benchmark crudes have been adopted commercially to indicate their general specifications. The most commonly used benchmark crude oils today are the American West Texas, the North Sea

Brent, the Saudi Arabian light and heavy, the Iraqi Kirkuk and Basra and the united Arab Emirates Dubai.

As we have seen it takes some 200 million years to form the crude oil in the ground and hence there is no doubt that it will be exhausted if we keep on producing it at the rates we are doing now of some 85 million barrels per day, that is, unless we want to wait another 200 million years for it to be reformed!

The Finding of Crude Oil

We have seen how oil was formed millions of years ago and how it accumulated in a layer of permeable (porous) rock called the reservoir. We have also learnt how the oil was trapped and prevented from escaping to the surface of the earth by another layer of impervious rock called the cap.

Hence to find oil the geologists must find these two layers of rock first. Therefore, and apart from where there are visual signs of seepage of gas or oil, the geologists would initially go around the world with their usual simple tools of hammers and magnifying lenses looking at rocks and collecting samples for further inspection in their laboratories. They would also observe the terrains and the rock outcrops and study their formations, thickness and inclinations. From such observations and studies they will be able to form a preliminary idea as to whether these indicate the possibility of the existence of a Reservoir and a Cap type of rocks below the surface.

When such preliminary investigation appears to be promising, it is usually followed by the more advanced techniques such as the seismic, magnetic, gravity and radioactivity exploration methods.

Seismology is a fairly reliable method for the location of rocks beneath the surface of the earth. It employs the technique of aiming a shock wave at the surface of the ground and measuring the length of time it takes for the waves to reflect back to the surface by picking and recording them by Sensors. The speed of the shock wave depends on the type of rock it travels through, and by comparing the travel times to known densities of rock the geologist can then predict the type of rock existing beneath the surface of the earth. From this information the geologists will be able to tell if these rocks are of the types that are known to contain and retain oil.

If the initial indications are positive this will be followed by a comprehensive seismic survey of a large area of that region which will be conducted to establish the extent of the existence of such rocks.

If the results of such detailed seismic survey are encouraging then the only way to make sure whether hydrocarbons exist in these rocks or not is by adopting the final and more costly method of drilling exploration wells.

Early Oil Exploration in Iraq

Various geologists from different counties had been making preliminary oil explorations all over Iraq at the end of the nineteenth and the early twentieth century amid reports of oil and gas seepages which indicate the presence of oil.

However intensive geological exploration activities were put in hand by the Turkish Petroleum Company before and after its signing of the Concession Agreement with the Iraqi government on 14th March 1925. These covered several promising geological structures in the regions of Kirkuk, Jabal Hamrain, Qaiyarah, Jambur, Injanah, Pulkanah, Chemchamal and Bai Hassan.

The reports and recommendations submitted by the various highly qualified geologists regarding the existence of oil in some of these structures, though deferred, they all pointed in one direction that the prospect of finding oil was good.

An example of such recommendations concerning three of the main principal structures of Iraq at that time were listed in the book (A History of the Exploration for Petroleum by E.W. Owen) as follows:-

Geologist	Kirkuk	Qayarah	Pullkanah
E. H. Pascoe 1919	Scarcely promising enough to warrant deep boring	First class: probably a large field	A speculation
H. Noble and R. du Evans 1920	If it is decided to make a test in the Kirkuk-Kifri area, Kirkuk anticline would be the most promising.	Prospect favourable for good production	Very speculative
A. H. Noble	Of outstanding merit	Of outstanding merit	Of outstanding merit

Geologist	Kirkuk	Qayarah	Pullkanah
E. w. Shaw 1926	First class	First class	First class
A. C. Trowbridge 1926	Not so good as others	Khanuqah preferred	Favourable, in front rank
10 Field Geologists 1926	Primary consideration	Primary consideration	Recommended
H. E. Bockh 1926	Do not recommend	Eighth choice	Third choice

Actual drilling started by the spudding of Pulkanah No. 1 on 5 April 1927 which was followed soon after by the spudding of other wells in several other locations including some of the regions mentioned above. This intensive drilling programme resulted in the discovery of oil in Kirkuk on 14 October 1927 as has already been mentioned before.

As a result of this pleasant discovery, the IPC's attention was diverted to the development of the Kirkuk field and the drilling activities in some of the other locations were curtailed or suspended and several of their drilling rigs were moved to Kirkuk to establish the extent and magnitude of the field.

Baba Gurgur, Kirkuk, Well K-1- 14 October 1927

Courtesy of IPC Society Newsletters

The Development of the Northern Fields

KIRKUK FIELD-SUMMARY OF THE DEVELOPMENT

The development of Iraq's Northern Oilfields production facilities and export pipelines during the last seventy five years of the twentieth century was gradual and made in phases. Initially this was carried out by the Iraq Petroleum Company, IPC, and later on after nationalisation, first by the Iraqi Company for Oil Operations, ICOO, the name of which was changed a few years later to the North Petroleum Organisation, NPO to finally become known by its present day name the North Oil Company, NOC.

There were five distinct phases over that period which could be summarised as follows:

Phase I - 1927 / 1934

Objective - To produce and export 4.0 million tons of crude oil per year equivalent some to 80,000 barrels of crude oil per day by the end of 1934.

This phase began with the discovery of the Kirkuk Oilfield in October 1927 and the subsequent acceptance of the terms of the revised concession Agreement in March 1931 by the government of Iraq and the Iraq Petroleum Company, the IPC.

To meet the objective of this phase the following facilities needed to be completed:-

- Drilling and completion of sufficient production and observation wells.

- Construction of three degassing stations by the names of Hanjira, Baba and Shurau together with their necessary transfer pipelines to the Process Plant.

- Construction of a new crude oil Process Plant consisting of four crude oil Process Units being Nos. 1, 2, 3 and 4 together with a small Distillation Plant.

- Construction of a crude oil storage tank farm immediately upstream of the first export pumping station at K-1.

- Construction of twin 12 inch diameter pipelines to the Mediterranean, the first to Haifa in Palestine and the other to Tripoli in the Lebanon.

- Construction of twelve pipeline pump stations each with its own pumping plant, electricity, storage tanks and water supply, stores, offices and housing.

- Construction of the necessary infrastructures including a power plant and distribution network, a communication system potable and industrial water supplies.

- Provision of all the industrial, administrative and accommodation facilities.

- Construction of two crude oil terminals at Haifa and Tripoli.

The objective of this phase was met with the exception of the completion of the Process Plant with the first Process Unit being completed in 1936.

Phase II - 1945 / 1948

Objective – To increase the production and export capacity from 4.0 million tons per year to 13.0 million tons of crude oil per year equivalent to some 260,000 barrels per day by the end of 1948.

This phase was planned as early as 1940 but could not be started due to the prolonged years of the Second World War, which delayed it till 1946.

Main IPC Offices-Arrapha – Kirkuk

Late 1940s

Courtesy of IPC Society Newsletters

To meet the objective of this phase the following facilities needed to be completed:-

- An accelerated drilling programme after the end of the War for the completion of sufficient production and observation wells.

- Construction of four new degassing stations in Qutan, Sarbashakh, Saralu and Malhawali together with their necessary transfer pipelines to the Process Plant.

- Expansion of the Process Plant by constructing four additional crude oil Process Units being Nos. 5, 6, 7 and 8.

- Construction of additional crude oil export tanks at K-1 Tank Farm.

- Construction of new twin 16 inch diameter pipelines to the Mediterranean, the first to Haifa in Palestine and the other to Tripoli in the Lebanon.

- Modifications to some of the existing pumping equipment and the installation of new pumping equipment at the main export pipelines pump stations.

- Construction of a new industrial area comprising an enlarged workshops, stores, and offices.

- Construction of a new steam turbines Power Station.

- Construction of new offices at Arrapha.

The phase was scheduled to be completed by the end of 1948, but was delayed until 1949 due to the shortage of equipment and materials especially line pipe during the period immediately after the end of the Second World War.

Though the actual construction works for this phase were finally completed albeit behind schedule, it was unfortunate that its objective of increasing the export capacity to 13.0 million tons, of crude oil per year, could not be met. This was solely due to the shutdown of the 12 inch and the abandonment of the nearly completed 16-inch pipelines to Haifa during the 1948 hostilities in Palestine. As a result of this catastrophic loss of the two pipelines to Haifa, the export capacity of the remaining two pipelines to Tripoli could only achieve a modest increase in the export capacity of 2.5 million tons per year from 4.0 million tons to 6.5 million tons per year.

This loss of about 50% of the planned export capacity for this phase was to lead to the acceleration of Phase III.

Phase III - 1950 / 1953

<u>Objective</u> - To increase the production and export capacity from 6.5 million tons per year to 27.5 million tons of crude oil per year equivalent to some 570,000 barrels per day by 1953.

This Phase together with Phase IV represented the most ambitious expansion programme ever embarked upon by the IPC before its nationalisation in 1972. It was driven by four main factors:

- The persistent demand by the governments of Iraq to increase the crude oil export to satisfy their ever-increasing needs for additional revenues for the development of the country after the stagnation period of the Second World War.

- The loss of half of the IPC's export capacity as a result of the loss of 12 and 16-inch diameter pipelines to Haifa which resulted in the loss of the anticipated revenue for the Government.

- The anticipated worldwide increase in the consumption of crude oil after the end of the Second World War and the fast spread of the use of motor car.

- The result of the settlement between the IPC shareholders to end the Red Line agreement to satisfy the CFP's and Gulbenkian's demand to increase production as described separately under the heading "The End Of The Red Line Agreement".

To meet the objective of this phase the following facilities needed to be completed:-

- A further acceleration of the drilling programme for the completion of the necessary production and observation wells.

- Construction of a new degassing station for the Tarjil dome in the southern region of the Kirkuk field at Jabalbur together with the implementation of the necessary modification and the installation of new separators to increase the capacity of some of the existing degassing stations to meet the new production and export objective.

- Expansion of the Process Plant by constructing three additional crude oil Process Units being Nos. 9, 10A and 10B.

- Construction of additional crude oil export tanks at K-1 Tank Farm.

- Construction of new 30/32 inch pipeline to the Syrian port of Banias on the Mediterranean.

- Modifications to some of the old pumping equipment and the installation new gas turbine pumping sets at some of the main pipelines pump stations.

- Construction of a road bridge on the Lesser Zab River.

The objective of this phase was met

Phase IV - 1953 / 1964

Objective - To increase the production and export capacity from 27.5 million tons per year to 50.0 million tons of crude oil per year equivalent some one million barrels per day by the end of 1963.

This phase could be considered as an extension to Phase III since it was executed gradually over a period of several years soon after the completion of that Phase.

To meet the objective of this phase the following facilities needed to be completed:-

- The drilling programme during this phase was extended to the newly discovered fields of Bai Hassan and Jambur as well as the Ain Zalah and Butmah fields.

- Construction of two new degassing stations for the new Bai Hassan field by the names of Bai Hassan North and Bai Hassan South together with a pump station and a transfer line to deliver their oil to the Process Plant.

- Construction of one degassing station for the new Jambur field by the name Jambur degassing station together with a pump station and a transfer line to deliver its oil to the Process Plant. This degassing station was renamed Jambur South after the construction of a new station by the name of Jambur north in later years.

- Construction of a gas line from Jambur degassing station to the Process Plant for the delivery sweet gas.

- Construction of one degassing station for the Ain Zalah field by the name of Ain Zalah and another for the Butmah field by the name of Butmah degassing station.

- Construction of a new pump station together with a new pipeline to deliver the combined crudes of Ain Zalah and Butmah to K-2 pump station.

- Expansion of the Process Plant by constructing two additional crude oil Process Units being Nos. 11 and 12.

- Construction of new water Injection Plant on the south bank of the Lesser Zab River.

- Construction of additional crude oil export tanks at K-1 Tank Farm to bring the total number to 28 tanks together with the necessary modification for changing the operation of the large tank farm valves from manual to electrical actuation.

- The Construction of new 30/32 inch pipeline to the Lebanese port of Tripoli on the Mediterranean.

- Installation of new gas turbine driven pumps at some of the main pipeline pump stations together with some modification in other stations

- Expansion of the Industrial Area with additional workshops, stores, etc.

This phase represented the last expansion of the oilfields in north Iraq by the IPC before its nationalisation in June 1972.

Phase V - 1973 / 1979

Objective - To increase the production and export capacity from 50.0 million tons per year to 70.0 million tons of crude oil per year equivalent some 1.4 million barrels per day by the end of 1979.

The expansion during this phase was made in two stages, first by raising the export capacity to 1.2 million and immediately afterwards to the 1.4 million barrels per day.

To meet the objective of this phase the following facilities needed to be completed:-

- The drilling programme during this phase was significantly extended to cover all the oilfields in north Iraq.

- Construction of a third degassing station for the Bai Hassan field by the name of Bai Hassan Dawood together with its transfer line for the delivery of its oil to the Bai Hassan pump station to join the Bai Hassan north and south crudes to the Process Plant.

- Construction of a second degassing station for the Jambur field by the name Jambur North together with its transfer line to join the existing transfer line of the first degassing station.

- Construction of a new crude oil Process Unit No.13 at the old Process Plant.

- Construction of a new one million barrels per day Process Plant consisting of four Desorber Units of 250,000 barrels per day each, complete with all the necessary spherical tanks, furnaces, boilers, flares system, and pipe networks for fuel gas, steam, water etc.

- Construction of a new crude oil Tank Farm for the Iraq-Turkey Pipeline.

- The construction of a new mainline pump station by the name of K-2 West complete with all the necessary pumping equipment, power generation and all the other facilities. It is of interest that this station was completed by the IPC just before its nationalisation in June 1972 as part of its 1.2 million barrel per day expansion programme and hence remained uncommissioned.

- Expansion of the main export pipelines by replacing some of the existing pump sets by new gas turbine driven sets at some of the mainline stations as well as the addition of new sets at other stations.

- Construction of a new gas compression station to deliver the required fuel gas to the ever increasing number of gas turbines in operation in the main pipeline pump stations.

This phase was completed on time.

During this phase, two new export pipelines were also constructed as follows:

- The Strategic pipeline between K-3 pump station and the Southern Iraqi oilfields with the capability of pumping in either direction.

- The first Iraq-Turkey pipeline from Kirkuk to the Mediterranean terminal at the port of Ceyhan in Turkey.

Phase VI - 1980 / 1999

Objectives-This phase had two objectives the first was to construct alternative crude oil export facilities after the destruction of the two deep water terminals of Khor al-Amayah and Mina al-Bakr in the Gulf at the beginning of the Iraq/Iran war in 1980, and the subsequent closure of all the Mediterranean pipelines through Syria. The second objective was to develop the Khormala dome which had been separated from the rest of the Kirkuk oilfield and the utilisation of the associated gas.

To achieve these objectives the following facilities needed to be completed:-

• Construction of three degassing stations for the Khormala dome of the Kirkuk field complete with a pump station and a transfer pipeline as well as the necessary water injection facilities.

• Construction of the North Gas project for the gathering of the associated gases from the fields of Kirkuk, Bai Hassan and Jambur. The project involved the building of a Liquid Petroleum Gas (LPG) plant; five underground salt caverns storage facilities, and an LPG bottling plant in addition to various pipelines for the distribution of natural gas.

• Construction of the second Iraq-Turkey pipeline from Kirkuk to the Mediterranean terminal at the port of Ceyhan in Turkey.

• Construction of the Iraq Tran-Saudi Arabia Pipeline from Zubair in southern Iraq to the Red Sea terminal at the port of Yanbu.

DETAILS OF THE DEVELOPMENT OF KIRKUK FIELD

Drilling

In the former days, during the search for oil, a hole was made by pummelling it with a heavy instrument. This was the method used by the Chinese 2,000 years ago to drill water wells and with refinements it was still in use during the first half of the twentieth century in some parts of the world.

However, where shallow wells through hard rocks are required to be drilled for low pressure reservoirs; the system called cable-tool drilling was used.

As a matter of interest, early wells in the Kirkuk Field were drilled with "California Type" rigs, which were equipped to drill by both percussion and rotary systems and in fact both systems were used during the course of drilling a well.

However, by the early 1920s, the most commonly used system; the "rotary" system of drilling was developed. In this system the hole is drilled by boring in much the same way as a carpenter bores a hole into a piece of wood by means of a Brace and Bit. The Bit used in oil well drilling is a tool with hardened steel cutters or in some cases commercial diamonds set in matrix.

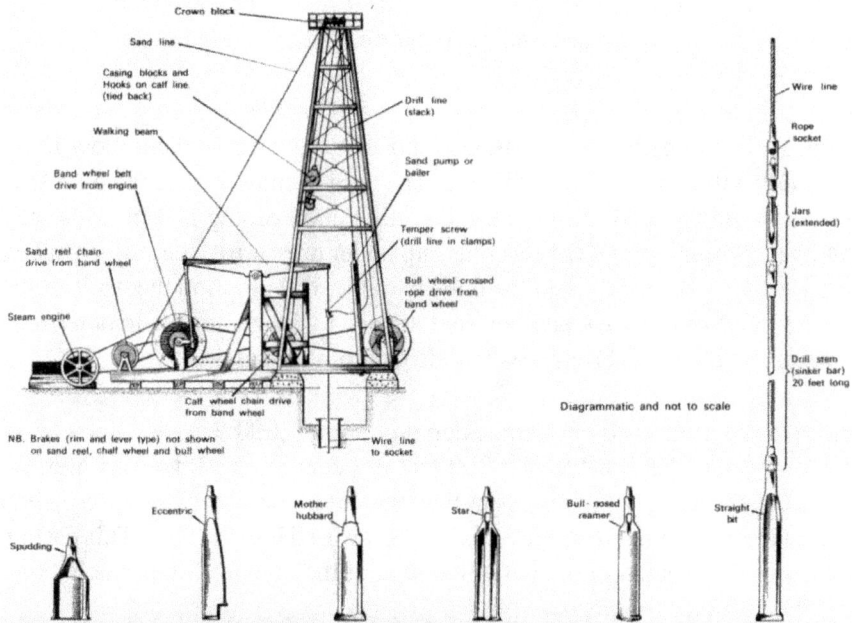

Cable Tool Type Percussion Rig-Circa 1910

However, certain steps must be taken before any drilling can begin. First specialists, including a geologist, petroleum, civil and mechanical engineers must select a suitable site for the well. Next, a road must be constructed to the site capable of supporting the rig and the required heavy machinery. A water supply line must then be laid and a strong concrete foundation built capable of supporting the drilling rig and the long and very heavy drill pipe. It is also necessary to construct a concrete "cellar" to provide space for the wellhead equipment below the drilling rig floor.

In the early days of the oil industry, a derrick was constructed of either timber or steel, to permit the drilling tools to be lowered in or hoisted out of the hole.

These derricks are a thing of the past as they have been replaced by masts, often mounted on a trailer or a truck together with the necessary drilling machinery.

When drilling starts, the Bit which is fixed to the lower end of the drill pipe begins to grind its way into the rock, driven by the weight and rotation of the drill pipe.

The rotation of the drill pipe is controlled by a steel turntable, called the "Rotary Table" in which a square, or hexagonal-section pipe, known as the "Kelly" fits. The Kelly is the uppermost section of the drill pipe. The rotary table may be driven by an electric motor or an internal combustion engine.

As the grinding process begins, a special "Mud" made with clay and certain chemicals is pumped through a flexible hose into the top of the hollow Kelly and so down the inside of the drill pipe. The mud eventually is jetted out of the holes between the teeth of the bit, lubricating and keeping it cool. This mud with its rock-cuttings and debris comes up under pressure to the surface again, but this time it comes between the outside of the drill pipe and the walls of the hole. Samples of this rock are then sent at once to the geologists to determine the nature of the rock through which the drill pipe is passing.

In a typical Kirkuk well of average depth of some 2,000 feet, the diameter of the hole is 20 inches for the first 200 feet of penetration. When this depth is reached, the drilling equipment is pulled out and a heavy steel pipe, 16 inch in external diameter, known as the "Casing" is lowered into the hole. This casing, is of course has a smaller diameter than that of the hole itself but much larger than that of the drill pipe.

Once the casing is centred into position, cement slurry is then pumped inside the casing and forced up between the outside surface of the casing and the rough side of the surrounding rock surface of the hole and left to set and thereby fix the casing securely in the hole.

The drilling is then resumed by lowering the drill pipe with a smaller bit inside the casing. The drilling goes on and when a depth of about 1,500 feet is reached, a second casing, smaller in diameter than the first one is lowered inside the entire 1,200 feet of the new hole and cemented securely in position.

With even a smaller bit, the drilling is resumed to a depth of about 2,000 feet, which is the average depth at which the top of the oil-bearing limestone in the

Kirkuk Field is reached. Drilling is then suspended again and a final smaller casing is fitted to this section of the hole.

Drilling Bits Used in Kirkuk Field. Courtesy of IPC

Further drilling is made and when sufficient penetration of the reservoir limestone rock has been made, to ensure that a satisfactory productive capacity has been obtained, drilling is completed and permanently stopped. The tools are pulled out of the well and the valve which had been fitted to the wellhead inside the concrete cellar, known as the "Master Gate Valve" is closed and the drilling rig and equipments move on to another well site.

An arrangement of valves and pipes known as the "Christmas Tree" is then finally fitted to the wellhead with a flowline connected to one of them for transporting the oil to a degassing station.

It is of interest to record that the average time taken to drill production wells in the Kikuk Field in the early years was 68 days. This time was reduced to about 15 days in the early 1960s and well K-167 was drilled and completed to a depth of 2,700 in12 days only.

As it has been already mentioned, the drilling activities were accelerated in the Kirkuk Field after its discovery and by the end of 1930 some twenty producing wells with others for oil/water and gas/oil observation had been completed.

Modern Rotary Drilling Rig-Kirkuk-Circa 1965

Courtesy of IPC

However with the lapse of the 1925 concession agreement and the signing of the new concession agreement in 1931, came the firm commitment by the IPC to begin the export of crude oil through a pipeline from Kirkuk to the Mediterranean by the end of 1934.

As a result of this tight schedule, the drilling programme was modified to ensure that enough production and observation wells are ready to meet this target date, which was finally achieved.

During this period, the necessary Flowlines were laid from the production wells and made ready for connection to one of the three planned degassing stations by the names of Shurau, Baba and Hanjira.

Christmas Tree - Typical Wellhead Valves Arrangement

Courtesy of IPC Society Newsletters

The drilling activities continued unabated during the 1930s but were suspended in 1941 during the political unrest that took place in Iraq during the government of Rashid Ali Al Gailani. As a result of these events, ten of the production wells and many of the observation wells were plugged as precautionary measure.

Typical Oil Well
Courtesy of IPC Society Newsletters

This suspension of drilling activities was to last for approximately two years, when it was finally resumed in 1943 in the Baba dome as well as the Avanah and Khormalah domes in the northern part of the reservoir. Good progress was made with the completion of fifteen production and nine observation wells by the end of 1947. With the delays in the completion of this project there was no shortage of wells for phase II.

During Phases III and IV in the 1950s and 1960s the drilling programme continues unabated in all the three main domes of Baba, Avanah, and Khormalah of the kirkuk field providing enough production, observation and water injection wells to satisfy the needs of these two phases It is worth highlighting that a milestone was reached in March 1965 with the drilling of well number K-164 for the Qutan degassing station which flowed, through a twin 10 inch diameter flow line, at 100,000 barrels per day and proved to be one of the world most productive wells at that time.

DEGASSING STATIONS

Crude oil, as it is found in the rock formation under the earth, contains a considerable quantity of gas dissolved in it and this gas must be removed before the crude can be sold and loaded on the oil tankers for export to countries hundreds of miles away.

When the crude oil is allowed to flow to the surface from the oil bearing rock formation, the pressure to which it has been subjected under the earth is reduced, and the gas which has been dissolved in it comes out of solution. This type of reaction is similar to the bubbling and frothing which occur when the sealing cap is removed from a bottle of soda water.

If we allow the pressure exerted on the crude oil to drop suddenly to atmospheric pressure there will be a loss in quantity and quality of the oil as some of the very light liquid fractionations would be flashed off with the gas as it emerges from the oil.

Hence the crude oil/gas mixture is transported from each well along a pipeline referred to in the oil industry as a "flowline", to the degassing station where the required quantity of oil from the well is controlled by opening selected valves on the production control "Harp".

In the case of the Kirkuk Field, the crude oil coming from the wellhead to the degassing station is fed into the large vertical gas/oil separators. The incoming oil/gas mixture is then partially degassed by permitting its pressure to drop inside the separator to 60 pounds per square inch, "p.s.i.". By keeping the pressure steady inside the separator, the oil and gas are partially separated by the effects of gravity and centrifugal force, whereby sufficient gas is removed before transferring the remaining partially degassed crude oil to the Process Plant for further treatment.

During the period 1928 to 1930, geologists, surveyors, engineers and other technicians were sent to Kirkuk to gather the necessary field's information in preparation for the design work for the development of the oil field.

Serious planning and design works were initiated by the end of 1931. Project teams were organised, lists of major equipment and essential long term delivery materials were completed and the relevant purchase orders were placed as a matter of urgency to meet the tight schedule.

During Phase I of development of the Kirkuk field, three degassing stations, each with an initial capacity of 60,000 barrels per day were initially planned by the names of Shurau, Baba, and Hanjira. The capacity of each of these degassing stations was expanded over the coming years to some 200,000 barrels per day.

These degassing stations were located close to the planned central crude oil Process Plant, which is situated in the vicinity of the Eternal Fires and very close to the discovery well K-1, with Baba degassing station sitting next door to the process plant.

The main production and test gas/oil separators together with the other necessary equipment for the construction of these three degassing stations were procured in good time.

In the meantime, preparatory construction work of pipe fabrication, foundations, roads, fencing etc, was started early and the erection of equipment followed soon after and by the middle of 1934 these three degassing stations were completed and made ready for operation.

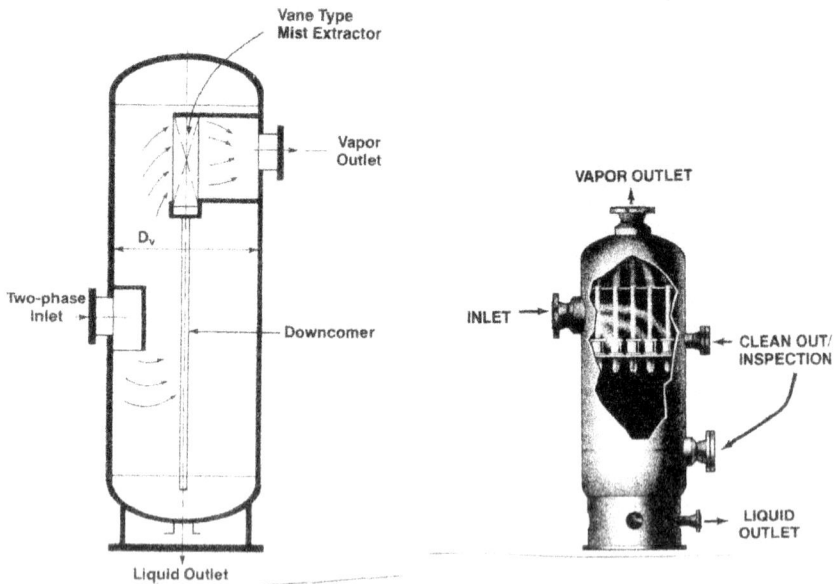

Typical Gas/Oil Separators

The transfer pipelines, which deliver the partially degassed crude oil from these degassing stations to the process plant, were also laid and made ready for operation during this period and were all 16 inch in diameter. The length of the Shurau transfer pipeline was approximately five kilometres, that of Baba was only a few hundred metres, and the third of Hanjira was approximately 12 kilometres in length.

No pumping facilities were required at these three degassing stations since their partially degassed crude was capable of being delivered to the process plant under gravity.

Four more degassing stations were constructed for Phase II of the development of the Kirkuk field during the period of 1948 and 1953, being Qutan, Sarbashakh, Salalu and Malhawali, with varying capacities of up to 200,000 barrel per day each.

The partially degassed crude oil from Qutan station was gravitated to the Process Plant through a pipeline 16 inch in diameter and about 22 kilometres in length.

The Malhawali, Saralu and Sarbashakh, stations are constructed across the River Zab on the Avanah dome of the Field which had not been produced thus far.

Separators - Baba Degassing Station

Courtesy of IPC

The degassed crude from the Malhawali degassing station is gravitated separately to the spherical tanks at Avanah pump station through a short transfer line.

The partially degassed crude oil from Sarbashakh degassing station is also gravitated to the spherical tanks at Avanah pump station through a pipeline 18 inch in diameter and approximately 25 kilometres in length, picking up on its way the Saralu degassed crude oil, which is delivered to it through a 16 inch diameter spur pipeline.

Separators & flow lines at Qutan Degassing Station.

Courtesy of IPC

Finally the combined partially degassed oil from the three degassing stations is then pumped from there to the Process Plant by six electric motor driven pump sets through a pipeline 24 inch in diameter and approximately 35 kilometres in length.

During Phases III and IV a new degassing station was constructed on the Tarjil dome in the southern region of the Kirkuk field by the name of Jabalbur together with pumping equipment for the delivery of its partially degassed crude to the process plant through some 20 kilometres of 16 inch diameter pipeline.

It is to be recorded that during the very late 1950/early 1960s the Malhawali degassing was watered out and its separators and other equipment were cannibalised for use in other stations.

Similarly the Qutan degassing station watered out in 1975 with some its equipment being cannibalise for use in other stations.

No new degassing stations were required until the 1990s when it was decided to develop the Khormala dome which had become an independent field after its separation from the Avanah dome.

As a result, three new degassing stations were constructed, two remotely controlled and the third as a centre of operations containing the necessary degassing and pumping facilities. Other degassing stations in the fields of Bai Hassan, Jambur and Ain Zalal are described under the development of these fields.

THE CENTRAL CRUDE OIL PROCESS PLANTS

Kirkuk crude oil is "sour" that is it contains significant proportion of hydrogen sulphide dissolved in the crude.

Though large fraction of this gas is evolved with the other hydrocarbon gases at the degassing stations, yet enough remains in the partially degassed crude to make it corrosive and difficult to handle in pipelines and refineries.

Hence the main function of the Process Plant is to remove this hydrogen sulphide from the Kirkuk crude, thus changing it from "sour" to "sweet" crude. This is achieved, without losing much of the valuable light ends,(the volatile hydrocarbons) like butane and results in the production of a stabilised crude oil of export quality.

Oil from the degassing station is first received in the Process Plant by the several large spherical tanks designed to hold crude oil under pressure known as the Horton Spheres. They are normally kept about half full, so that in the event of any trouble at a degassing station the plant operators have enough time to take whatever action is necessary. Similarly, if trouble occurs in the Process Plant, the degassing station operators have time to reduce or stop production.

From the Horton Spheres the oil flows to one of the twelve Process Units which had been constructed in stages over the years, of which there are three types.

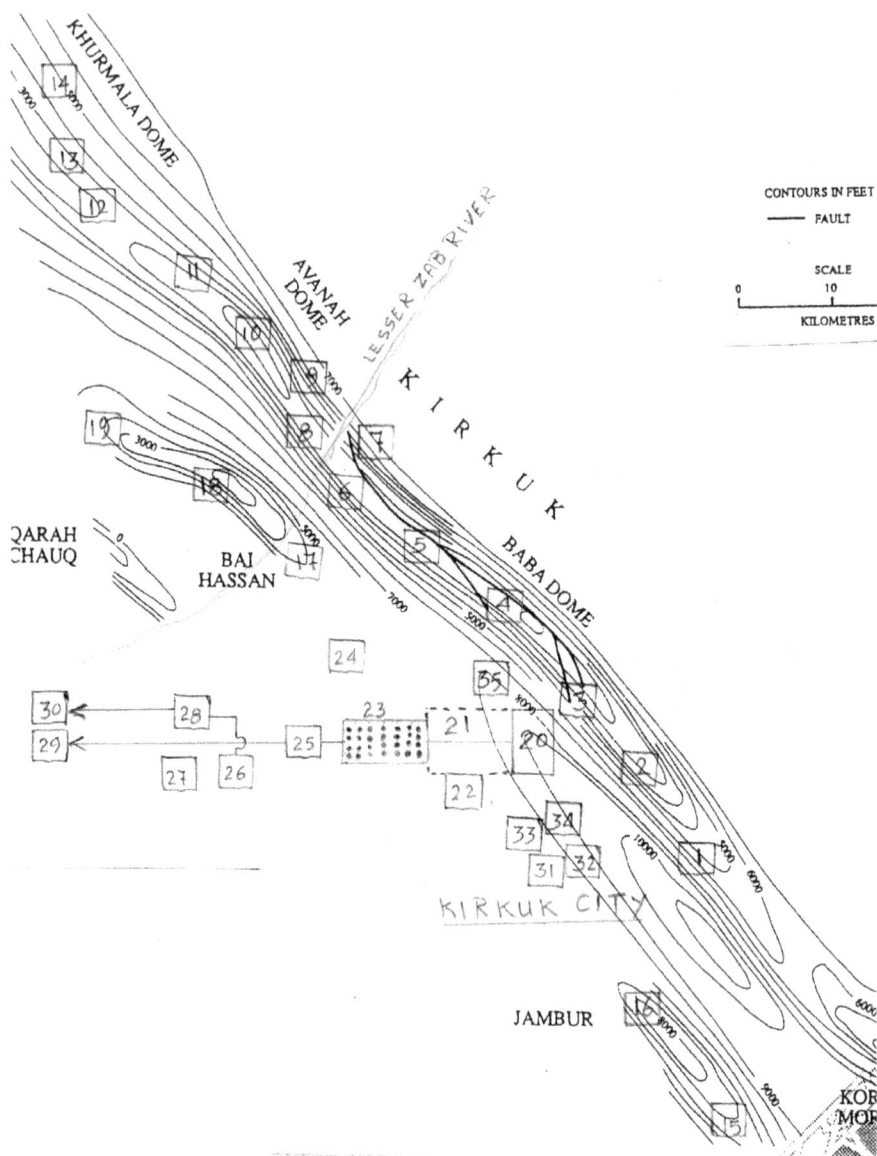

Kirkuk OilFields

Production & Pumping Facilities

1. Jabalbur Degassing Station.
2. Shurau- D/S
3. Baba-D/S
4. Hanjera D/S
5. Qutan D/S
6. Water injection plant
7. Zab water Pump station
8. Avanah crude oil pump station
9. Malhawali D/S
10. Saralu D/S
11. Sarbashakh D/S
12. Khurmalah 1 D/S
13. Khurmalah 2 D/S
14. Khurmalah 3 D/S
15. Jambur South D/S
16. Jambur North D/S
17. Bai Hassan South D/S
18. Bai Hassan North D/S
19. Bai Hassan Dawood D/S

20. Process Plant
21. Industrial Area
22. Fields Power Station
23. K-1 Tank Farm
24. Sulphur Plant
25. K-1 Pump Station
26. New Process Plant
27. North Gas Plant
28. First Iraq-Turkey Pump Station (IT1)
29. To Mediterranean Through Syria
30. To Mediterranean Through Turkey
31. IPC Offices-Arrapha
32. Arrapha Staff Residential Area
33. Arrapha Employees Residential Area
34. ICOO 2,000 Houses Residential Area
35. Baba Staff Residential Area

a. Two Stage Thermal Stabilisers

There are eight such units using two stage fractionation columns at the Old Process Plant namely unit number 1,2,3,4,5,6,7 and 8.

The purpose of a fractionating column is to separate the constituent parts of the oil, light from heavy. The partially degassed oil from the Horton Spheres is fed continually to the first column of such unit and is heated to boiling in the bottom. The rising vapour passes through a number of trays where it is mixed with the descending oil. The vapour from the top of the column passes through water cooled condensers, and some of the condensate is pumped back to the top of the column as reflux to control the temperature. This first larger column removes all the light gases, mixed with some of the lighter constituent of the oil.

This mixture is then fed to the second column, where it is again distilled, the light oil being returned to the main oil stream, while the gas including most of the harmful hydrogen sulphide is passed to the plant fuel gas main.

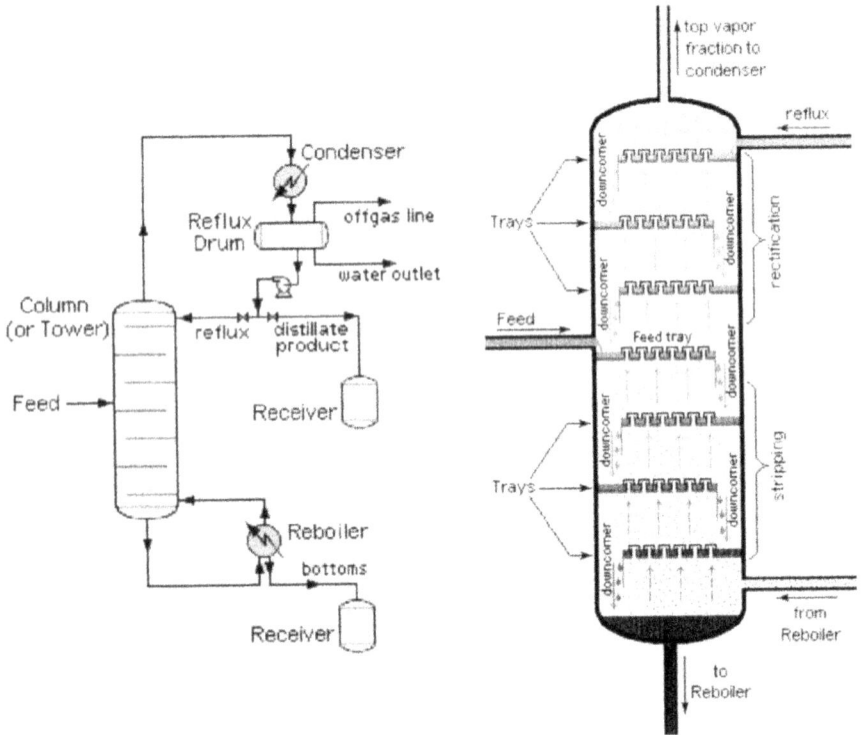

Typical Fractionation Column

These two-stage process units give very good results, but are expensive to build and to operate. Process unit No 8 is normally used for processing Bai Hassan crude oil, which is exported as a Jambur/Bai Hassan blend separately from the Kirkuk oil as it is different in quality.

b. Desorbers Units

Units Nos. 9, 10A, 10B and 12 are "Desorber" Units. In this process oil is continually fed to the top of a single column, passes down over the trays, and boiled at the bottom. The rising vapours mix with the crude oil on the trays, where valuable light oils in the vapour dissolve back into the crude oil, while the remaining unwanted gases pass on via the column top to the fuel gas system. The main difference between this process and the fractionating columns of the two-stage stabilisers is that the latter use specially condensed "reflux" to control their columns top temperatures, while the desorber column tops are governed by the temperature of the crude feed.

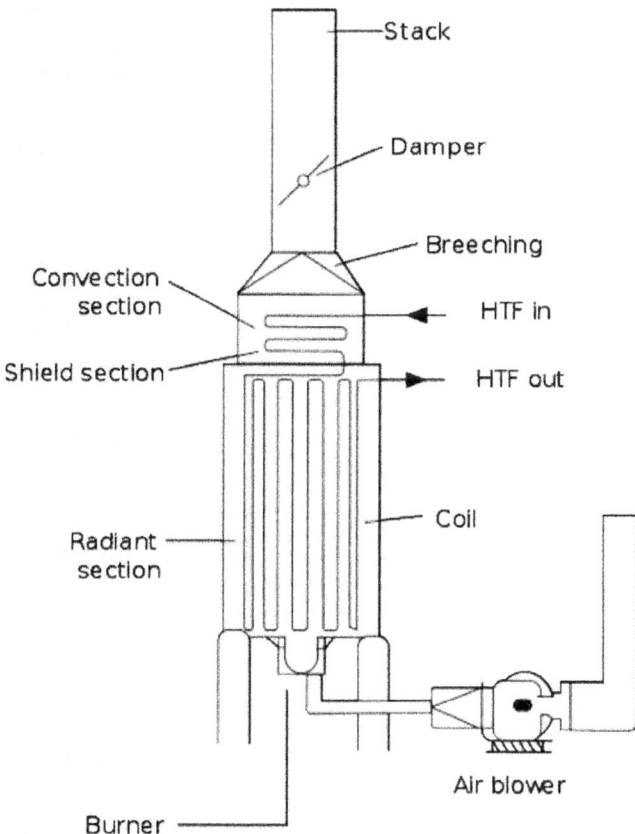

Typical gas furnace

The desorbers give results which are almost the same as the two-stage units, and are considerably cheaper to build and operate. They can also process considerably more oil.

PROCESS FURNACES

Heat for both the fractionating and desorbing processes is obtained in a furnaces or heaters called "tube stills". Some or all of oil is pumped through long steel tubes suspended in the furnce and heated by the gas fire. Both the process units and the Fields power station use, as fuel, waste gases from the stabilisation and desorbing operations. Fuel oil lines are also connected to all furnaces in case any trouble should arise in the fuel gas system.

c. Cold Stripper

The remaining Unit, No. 11, is "Cold Stripper", and uses "sweet gas" from the Jambur oilfield. Crude oil is fed to the top of a column, and passes down over trays, where it is mixed with the sweet gas fed from the bottom. Unwanted gases evaporate from the crude oil into the sweet gas stream. This process does not give much good results as the other types, but the unit is cheap to build and operate, and can be started or shutdown very quickly, giving flexibility to the Process Plant as a whole.

THE OLD PROCESS PLANT

The first four stabilisation process units No. 1, 2, 3 and 4 were planned for Phase-I, each with a capacity of 50,000 barrels of crude oil per day. Unit No. 4 capacity was upgraded later on to 64,000 barrels per day.

The main equipment such as the process stabilisation columns, heaters, Horton spherical tanks, pumps, motors, heat exchangers, flare stacks, fire fighting and other equipment were put on order early. In the meantime the site preparatory works such as pipe fabrication, foundations, roads, fencing etc were started in earnest.

Unfortunately progress of the construction work faced serious problems mainly due to prolonged delays in the delivery of some of the major equipments and hence these Process Units could not be completed as required by the end of 1934.

PLATE XVII.   KIRKUK FIELDS.
Extension to Stabilisation Plant under construction, 1947.

Stabilisation units under construction-Process Plant, 1946/7

Courtesy of IPC

This meant that the crude oil from the degassing stations could not be stabilised and stripped of some of its hydrogen sulphide, which is poisonous as well as corrosive. Though this is a prohibited dangerous practice by today's standards, nevertheless it was accepted at that time despite being a health hazard and corrosive agent to all the steel storage tanks, pumps, pipelines and ship tanks which come in contact with it. However the concession deadline for the export of crude oil by the end of 1934 could not be delayed and the export of the somewhat unsterilized and slightly corrosive crude oil had to be accepted.

It was not until the end of 1936 that the erection of the first of the four stabilisation units was completed and brought into operation early in 1937. While the other three units suffered further delays due to the start of the Second World War with the last unit finally coming on stream in mid 1939.

Four more crude oil process units were constructed for Phase II being No. 5, 6, 7 and 8 each having an initial capacity of 50,000 barrels per day. Each of these four units was expanded later on to a capacity of 70,000 barrels per day.

These units were designed to be capable of producing tailored crude for the planned government Daura refinery in Baghdad. They continued to do so until this practice was ultimately discontinued in 1972.

Process unit No.8 is normally allocated for processing Bai Hassan oil, which is exported separately from the Kirkuk oil as it is different in quality.

Process Units Nos. 9, 10A and 10B were constructed during Phase IV with Unit No. 9 being a Desorber with a capacity of 90,000 barrels per day and Units 10A and 10B being cold strippers with a capacity of 70,000 barrels per day each.. However both Units 10A and 10B were redesigned and later converted to Desorbers.

During Phase V Process Units Nos.11 and 12 were constructed with Unit No. 11 being a Cold Stripper while Unit no. 12 being a Desorber. Each of these two units has a capacity of 250,000 barrels per day. It is to be recorded that Unit No. 12 was destroyed by shelling in 1969 but repaired and returned to service.

The last Desorber Unit to be constructed at the old Process Plant was Process Unit No.13. This unit was built after the nationalisation of the IPC as part of the 1.2 million per day expansion project in 1975 and has a capacity of 250,000 barrels per day.

Units 12, 10A &10B –Process Plant (Unit 12 Heater in front)

Circa 1965-Courtesy of IPC

General View of the Old Process Plant-Kirkuk-Circa 1965

Courtesy of IPC

DISTILLATION UNIT

In addition to the main units for processing export oil, the Process Plant has a small Distillation Plant which has two units the first with a capacity of 24,000 gallons per day and the second with a capacity of 70,000 gallons per day. The products from these, which are for the Company's sole use, are petrol for transport, kerosene for domestic use, and gas oil which is used as fuel for diesel engines. Gas oil is also used in the Process Plant itself mainly as a sealing medium for pump glands.

Distillation Plant-Process Plant

Courtesy of IPC

However the completion of this refinery was also delayed beyond phase I target date of end of 1934 and as result all the main diesel engines driving the main pumps in all the main pumping stations on the 12-inch pipelines to Haifa and Tripoli were made to run on sour crude oil. This is unimaginable today since the bellowing black exhaust fumes would contain the poisonous sulphur gases; this is apart from the damage that it would cause to the diesel engines themselves.

The practice was finally discontinued after the completion of the first distillation unit, when gas oil was started to be delivered in batches to the main pumping stations through one of the twin 12 inch diameter Mediterranean pipelines.

AUXILIARIES

The oil refinery industry has always been one of the pioneers of automation, and in the Process Plant nearly all temperatures, pressures, flows and levels are automatically controlled. The average process unit has a dozen or more control instruments together with two or three hundred gauges, meters and indicators for measuring plant conditions. Some of the larger valves are motorised, the motors being driven by compressed air.

The process units also require other vital services. Some 25,000 gallons of cooling water is pumped through the plant every minute, the water being cooled in turn by forced draught cooling towers.

A large unit uses 1,000 kilowatts or more of electricity, mainly for driving motors driving pumps, while its furnace burns over 100,000 cubic feet of fuel gas hourly.

Boilers supply steam for various small heating jobs, and steam is also available at various key points such as furnaces, for fire fighting if necessary.

A network of fire hydrant water lines also covers the whole plant. A flare system is also available for burning the unwanted surplus, and sour gases.

THE NEW PROCESS PLANT

A new process plant was constructed during the 1.4 million barrels per day expansion project and was commissioned in 1978. It is located a few kilometres west of K-1 pump station and has a total capacity of one million barrels of crude oil per day.

The Plant is truly gigantic and included the following main equipment:-

- Seven 38 feet diameter spherical tanks each with of and a maximum storage capacity of 5,000 barrels of crude oil.
- Four Desorber Process units each with a capacity of 250,000 barrels of crude oil per day.
- Four heaters, one for each Desorber unit, each of which having 70 huge gas burners and 244 crude oil stainless tubes where the temperature of the crude oil is raised to some 130 degrees Celsius.
- Two enormous chimneys each serving two of the heaters.
- Three boilers each capable of generating twenty tons of steam per hour.
- Three powerful electric fin-fan coolers.

- Several crude oil and water circulation pumps.

- Fire fighting water ring main.

- Flares system.

- Crude oil transfer pumps to the Iraq Turkish pump station with all the necessary manifolds, valves, piping network etc.

SUMMARY OF THE OLD AND NEW PROCESS PLANT UNITS

Process Units No.	Type	Barrels per Day	Barrels per Day
Phase I : 1934 - 1939		Initial Capacity	Final Capacity
1, 2, and 3	Fractionation stabilisers	50,000 Each	50,000 *
4	Fractionation stabiliser	50,000	64,000
Distillation Plant			
Unit 1		700	700
Unit 2		2,000	2,000
Phase II : 1945 -1950			
5,6,7 and8	Desorbers	50,000 Each	70,000 **
Phases III and IV – 1952/1972			
9	Desorber	90,000	90,000
10A & 10B	Stabiliser/ Desorber	70,000 Each	105,000 Each***
11	Cold Stripper	210,000	250,000
12	Desorber	250,000	250,000 ****
Phase V – 1972/1999			
13	Desorber	250,000	250,000
New Process Plant			
1, 2,3 &4	Desorbers	250,000 Each	250,000

* These four units were retired in 1963.

** These units were capable of producing tailored crude for Dora refinery. This practice was discontinued in 1972.

*** Both Units 10A and 10B were originally stabilisers but were later redesigned and converted to Desorbers with their capacities increased to 105,000 barrel per day.

**** The original Unit 12 was destroyed by shelling in 1969 but repaired and returned to service.

The K-1 Crude Oil Exort Tank Farm

After the crude oil has been sweetened and stabilised in the Process Plant, the oil flows under gravity into the export storage tanks at K-1 Tank Farm where it is held in readiness for the start of its long journey through the main pipelines to the Mediterranean terminals of Tripoli and Banias.

Several of these crude oil tanks were constructed during each of Phase I, II, III and IV of the development of the Fields over a period which stretched over some 30 years.

The final number of these tanks was 28 of various sizes, comprising five small, six medium and seventeen large with 140 feet in diameter and 30 feet in height giving a storage capacity of 200,000 barrels.

The total maximum storage capacity of these 28 tanks is in the order of 152 million gallons with an average of 5.43 million gallon each equivalent to 155,100 barrels per tank. One of the tanks is filled with water for fire fighting purposes.

K-1 Tank Farm

Courtesy of IPC

Each of these huge tanks has a floating roof whereby the tank roof floats upon the crude oil stored in it. The roof is designed to move vertically up and down within the shell of the tank in order to provide a constant minimum void between the surface of the crude oil and the underside of the roof. In the meantime the floating roof is designed to provide constant seal between it periphery and the tank shell which prevent the lighter constituents of the oil from evaporating. The seal is usually made from a tough resilient rubber martial which would stand the harsh summer and winter weather conditions.

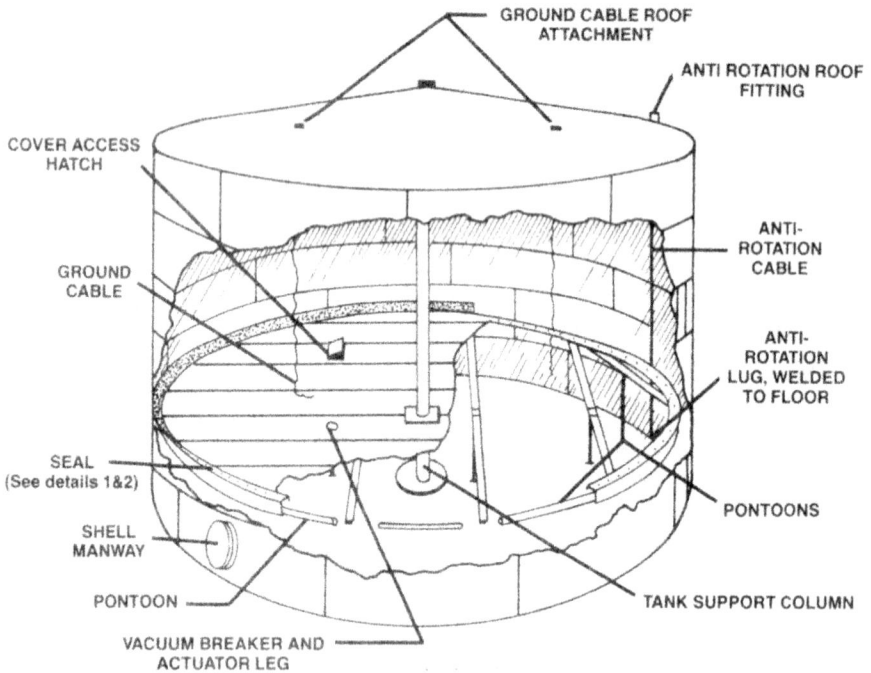

Typical Floating Roof Tank

The tanks are spaced at a safe distance from each other and each one is surrounded by an earth bund large enough to contain any spillage of oil. They are also connected to each through a piping network and then through a common manifold to a number of booster export pumps at K-1 pump station. All of these tanks and their auxiliary pipe work are fitted with large diameter motorized valves for ease of operation.

CUSTODY MEASUREMENT OF THE EXPORTED KIRKUK CRUDE OIL

The original method used during the early days of exporting the Kirkuk oil in the 1930s was based on the height or weight of the oil in the tank. Each of the tanks was strapped and calibrated by an independent third party inspection agency so that by measuring the difference in height of the oil in the tank before and after its emptying, the volume or weight of the oil drained could be calculated.

Although many different methods of measurement were developed over the years such as the orifice plates, the positive displacement and the turbine meters, the old method of basing the measurement on the calibrated tanks continued to be used for the export of the Kirkuk crude oil until the nationalisation of the IPC in 1972.

Oil Export Tank No. 327 – K-1 Tank Farm

Courtesy of IPC

In using this old method, before a tank is "Opened" for pumping for the custody transfer to the main export pipelines, an agreed measurement of the weight of the oil in the tank is obtained on an instrument called the "Mercury Column" gauge. This reading is carried out by the IPC representative, the "Gauger" and witnessed by the representative of the Iraqi government. Once the tank has been emptied and pumping had been stopped and the tank is "Closed", the same procedure of taking measurement of the weight of the remaining oil in the tank is repeated by reading the Mercury Column gauge of the tank. The difference between these two readings represents the weight of the oil despatched from the tank.

The calculations of the government revenues from the sale of its crude oil are then based on these quantities.

In emptying a tank, booster pumps are used to pump the oil from the tank through an arrangement of pipes, valves and filters to the suction side of the main pipeline pumping system at K-1 pump station. These powerful main line pumps then deliver the oil to the main export pipelines and send it on its journey to the Mediterranean terminals.

Electric Power Generation

FIRST POWER STATION

During the early days of the IPC operations, portable diesel driven generator sets were used to provide electric power supply for the drilling rigs, construction sites, office and residential compounds since the local Kirkuk city power supply was either inadequate or too distant.

The first IPC power station was built as part of the Process Plant complex in the early 1930s and was referred to as the (A Power Station). It comprised 3No.s 2.5 mega watt generators driven by 3Nos. steam turbines with 3Nos. steam boilers and 2 Nos. huge concrete natural draught cooling towers.. The generation voltage being 3.3 k.v. The main 3.3 k.v. high voltage switch board was of the oil filled type. It supplied the crude oil stabilisation units and their ancillaries in the process plant, Baba degassing station and adjacent area as well as the main water pump station on the Lesser Zab river via 2Nos. 2.2 k.v. overhead power lines. There was no other distribution network outside the process plant.

In the meantime K-1 pump station had its own power generation through two Sulzer diesel engine driven d.c. generators.

FIELDS POWER STATION

With the increasing power demand and future power requirement, it became clear that a much larger power station was needed. Hence a new 56.25 mega watts power station was constructed in the Baba industrial area close to the Process Plant. It was named Fields Power Station.

Fields Power Station-Kirkuk

Courtesy of IPC

This station comprised 3No. steam turbine driven generators each with a site rating of 18.75 mega watts, 6No. boilers providing super heated steam, 4No. forced draught cooling towers and all the necessary station auxiliaries.

The station control room was equipped with all the required monitoring and control instrumentation not only for the station itself but also for all the external outgoing cables.

The station had a duel fuel system of either associated gas from the Process Plant or crude oil.

It was also provided with a 500 kw diesel driven generator for the start-up of the main steam turbine generators..

The station was completed and commissioned in 1948 which rendered the old (A power station) redundant. As a result the old three steam turbines and their generators were removed from the (A power station) and transferred the Barsra Petroleum Company.

ELECTRIC POWER DISTRIBUTION

Electric power generation and supply from the Fields Power Station was at 11kv. The main electrical load centres were at the Process Plant with two substations each with two 11 kv feeder cables, K-1 Oil Pump Station had one substation with four 11 kv feeder cables, the industrial area in the vicinity of the Process Plant and the residential complex in Baba had five substations on a ring fed by 11 kv cables with one at either end.

The Arapha area which comprised the main IPC offices, Training Centre, the staff residential area and the large employees estate, had four substations on a ring fed by two 11 kv overhead lines from either end. It also included two connections to Kirkuk city's overhead 11 kv power network. It is of interest to record that the electric power requirement of the city of Kirkuk was supplied from the Fields Power Station up to 1961, the time of the commissioning of the national power station in Dibbis on the Lesser Zab River.

The IPC facilities at the Lesser Zab area was supplied through a high voltage outdoors step-up switch yard with two transformer banks each with one 5 MVA transformer plus one 2.5 MVA transformer. The transmission voltage was 66 kv. The main step-down outdoors switch yard for the same area was initially adjacent to the water pumping station.

Avanah had its own step-down switch yard connected to the main yard by 66 kv overhead power lines across the Lesser Zab River.

The main yard was transferred in the late 1950s to the site of the Water Injection Plant. Provision was made in the new yard to feed not only the existing load and that of the new Water Injection Plant but also that of the new Bai Hasssan South oil pumping station by means of two 66 kv overhead lines, as well as the new water pumping station for Kirkuk City by a single 66 kv overhead line.

After the handover of the Kirkuk City water pumping station in 1962 to Kirkuk Municipality, the 66 kv link was retained for electric power exchange with Dibbis power station or the Iraqi National Grid which was being built at about that time.

All circuits had either a spare built-in capacity for load growth or provision for future expansion without the need for undue shutdown.

MULLAH ABDULLAH POWER STATION

A new Mullah Abdullah power station was constructed by the State Organisation of Electricity in late 1970s at a location west of K-1 pump station close to the New Process Plant.

This station, though connected to the National Grid, it fed an outdoor 132 kv switch yard which was dedicated for the sole requirement of the North Petroleum Organisation. This was mainly to satisfy the huge new additional electric power demand of the New Process Plant and the nearby first pumping station of the Iraq-Turkish pipeline which were under construction at that time.

Provisions were also made to supply the planned North Gas complex which was constructed in the same area at a later date.

FIELD SERVICES

During Phase I in the 1930s, the necessary services such as water supply, power generation and distribution network, telecommunications, roads, workshops, stores, offices, canteens and dwellings etc, went hand in hand with the fields drilling and construction work. The famous K1 hospital and some of the early office accommodation were also completed in 1936.

During the period 1945 to 1949 a permanent water pump station was built on the south bank of the Lesser Zab River and a pipeline 16 inch in diameter and 35 kilometres long was laid to the numerous oil installations and residential areas to satisfy their increasing industrial and domestic water demand.

The industrial area was expanded considerably during the period 1945 to 1949 with additional offices, workshops, stores, petroleum and geological laboratories together with that time state of the art telephone exchange.

A railway line was laid between Arrapha and the Baba main industrial area. This line was then extended to the Fields Power Station, mechanical workshops, main stores, tank farm and the pump station at K1 area to facilitate the movement of materials and equipment as well the daily transport of the ever-increasing labour force.

Over thirty houses were constructed and an ambitious housing and town-planning scheme was already in hand. The subject of the town planning and housing estates will be described in more details separately.

The Development of Bai Hassan Field

Bai Hassan was the newly discovered crude oil field in 1953, is located about 40 kilometres north of the central Process Plant, and stretching across the Lesser Zab River as described in details in Chapter 8 " The IPC Crude Oil Fields". The objective of the development of this field is the production of some 12.0 million tons of crude oil per year equivalent to 240,000 barrels per day.

This called for the following:

• Drilling of the necessity production and observation wells.

• Construction of two new degassing stations being Bai Hassan North which is located north of the Lesser Zab River and Bai Hassan South which is located south of the River. Each of these two degassing stations having a capacity of some 150,000 barrels of crude oil per day.

• Construction of a pipeline 16 inch in diameter and some 25 kilometres long to deliver the Bai Hassan North crude to Bai Hassan South degassing station. This crude is delivered by gravity.

• Construction of spherical tanks at Bai Hassan South degassing station for receiving the combined crude oil from both Bai Hassan North and South degassing stations.

• Construction of a pump house inside Bai Hassan South degassing station for pumping the combined crude oils of both Bai Hassan North and South to the central Process Plant.

• Construction of a pipeline 24 inch in diameter and some 35 kilometres in length to deliver the combined crude to the Process Plant.

It was discovered in the early 1970s, after nationalisation that the Bai Hassan Field actually extended much further to the north than originally thought. As a result the Field was developed further during the subsequent years of the 1970s, as part of the 1.4 million barrels per day, by the construction of the following facilities:-

- Construction of a new degassing station by the name of Dawood which was located further north of the old Bai Hassan North degassing station.

- Laying of a new 12 inch transfer line from Dawood degassing station to Bai Hassan South degassing station, where the oil from Dawood joins that from the other two degassing stations before being pumped to the Process Plant.

The Development of Jambur Field

The Jambur field which was discovered in 1954, is a condensate/gas field located some 80 kilometres south of the central process plant as described in Chapter 8 "The IPC Crude Oil Fields". Its gas is sweet and was intended for use as fuel for the proposed gas turbines that were to replace the old diesel engines driving the pumps at some of the main pipelines pump stations.

The development of the field was implemented during the 1950s and involved the following major works:-

- Drilling of the necessary production and observation wells.

- Construction of 10,000 barrels per day degassing station together with the necessary gas dehydration equipment.

- Laying of a transfer pipeline 8 inch in diameter and some 80 kilometres in length to deliver the condensates from this station direct to the central Process Plant at Kirkuk.

- Laying of a pipeline, 20 inch in diameter and some 80 kilometres in length to deliver sweet gas to the Process Plant and the K-1area to feed one of the old 16 inch diameter a pipeline, which was converted to a gas pipeline, to deliver the necessary fuel gas to the newly installed gas turbines at some of the main pumping stations.

The expansion of the production facilities of Jambur field was included in the 1.4 million barrels per day expansion project during the 1970s as follows:-

- Construction of a new degassing station by the name of Jambur North with the old degassing station being renamed Jumbur south.

- Installation of additional gas dehydration units at both Jambur North and South stations to supply the additional quantities of sweet gas for the additional number of higher horse power Sulzer gas turbines pumping and gas compression sets at K-1 and the other similar gas turbine pump sets at the remaining Kirkuk-Mediterranean pump stations.

• Construction of a new gas compression station in the K1 area consisting of two Sulzer gas turbine compressor sets complete with a modern control room and all the piping and manifolds arrangement to enhance the pressure of the gas in the old 16 inch gas pipeline to ensure that enough fuel gas supply is made available for the additional number of gas turbines at the main Mediterranean pipeline pump stations.

Jambur Well Fire

During the drilling of one of the wells in the Jambur field in the late 1970s, the well went out of control and caught fire. The fire was a real furnace and in no time the rig and the all other equipment melted and prevented any access to the wellhead.

Despite the mobilisation of the Company's enormous resources, all efforts to clear the wreckage and extinguish the fire and bring the well under control failed to do so.

It was finally decided to seek the services of the famous American Red Adair the "Red Devil", who specialises in bringing such oil well fires under control. On his arrival he took control of the operations.

It took a few weeks before the wellhead was finally freed from the entangled mass of metal and finally brought under control thankfully without any injury.

The Construction of the Water Injection Plant

It was anticipated that the ambitious expansion in the production of crude oil from the Kirkuk field after the completion of the 30/32 inch diameter pipeline to Banias in 1952, would result in an accelerated drop in the reservoir pressure.

It had been calculated that the rate of drop in the reservoir pressure in the early years had been approximately one pound per square inch for every one million tons of crude oil produced and that this rate was gradually increasing with time. It has been shown later on that the total drop in pressure during the years had been calculated at 270 pounds per square inch against a corresponding total production of 260 million tons of oil. Such drop in pressure if allowed to continue would ultimately reduce the reservoir pressure to a point that such pressure will not be enough to lift the crude oil to the surface and that pumps will have to be used to produce it.

One of the methods used to maintain the pressure in the reservoir is to inject water into the reservoir which will result in raising the level of its water and thereby pushing the oil above it upwards, which will result in maintaining the pressure. This, and the injection of gas, is usually the preferred method of maintaining reservoir pressure and the availability of plenty of water from the nearby Lesser Zab River made water the obvious choice.

Hence it was decided to build a water injection plant on the River Zab for this purpose. The plant was designed to treat about one and quarter million barrels of raw river water per day to a high degree of purification to ensure that it contains no particles, even of minute sizes, which are if left may result in impairing the permeability of the reservoir rock.

The Water Injection-Tanks and Filters

Courtesy of IPC

The completion of the plant involved the following works:-

- Drilling of five carefully selected injection wells in an area between the main two domes of the Kirkuk field namely Baba and Avanah, an area referred to as the Amsha saddle. This central location was chosen to facilitate the spread of the injected water into both domes at the same time.

- Installation of an elevated pump house at the bank of the river to enable the off take of water by seven powerful vertical shaft electrically driven pumps.

- Laying of seven 20-inch diameter water lines from the river pumps to the water treatment tanks.

- Installation of six water treatment and purification tanks each measuring a 100-foot in diameter and 26 foot in height and having a treatment capacity of over 200,000 barrels of water per day. The tanks were catholically protected against corrosion.

- Installation of sixty horizontal sand filters each ten are designed to filter the treated water from one of the treatment tanks.

- Construction of a main pump house for the injection of the purified water into the injection wells. Three pumping sets are installed, each set consisting of a 6,000 horsepower General Electric Company EM85 gas turbine driving a Mather and Platt pump each having a capacity of some 10,000 gallons of water per minute. The generated pressure from these pumps is 600 pound per square inch which is enough to overcome the reservoir pressure.

- Laying of five-water injection pipelines from the pump house to the injection wells.

- Laying of a pipeline from the nearby Bai Hassan oil field to the water injection main pump house for the supply of the necessary fuel gas to the gas turbines

- Construction of a central control room.

The project was successfully completed and the first quantity of water was injected into the reservoir on 27 January 1961.

Three Gas Turbine Pumping Sets-Water Injection Plant

Courtesy of IPC

The Development of Ain Zalah and Butmah Fields

Exploration works in the Mosul Petroleum Company concession area to the west of the River Tigris were carried out during the 1930s resulting in the identification of many promising structures.

Drilling work was carried out in many such structures along the western bank of the River Tigris as well as in the Heet and al- Qaim area along the banks of the River Euphrates. These included Qaiyarah, , Jarwan, Najmah, Ain Zalah and Butmal.

Considerable deposits of heavy crude oil were discovered at Qaiyarah, which proved later on to be of limited commercial value at that time.

However the drilling in the Ain Zalah area struck crude oil in 1939 which proved to be of commercial value resulting in the discovery of the modest Ain Zalah field.

Further drilling activities were suspended in the MPC areas during the Second World War only to be resumed in 1946.

As a result a second crude oil field was discovered in 1952 in the Batmah area, not too far away from the Ain Zalah field.

Though these two Fields proved to be rather modest, nonetheless they managed to continue to produce the Concession's minimum requirement, of one million tons of oil per year, equivalent to some 20,000 barrels per day, up to the nationalisation of the IPC in 1972, albeit with some difficulty at times.

The development of these two fields in the late 1940/1950s included the following:-

- Drilling of the necessary production and observation wells.

- Construction of two degassing stations, one for the Ain Zahah field and the other for the Butmah field.

- Laying a transfer pipeline 8 inch in diameter and some 15 kilometres in length from Butmah field to the main crude oil tanks in the Ain Zalah field with. the Butmah crude oil being gravitated without the need for pumping.

- Constructions of a diesel pump house comprising three diesel-driven Slush pumps for pumping the combined crudes oils of Ain Zalah and Butmah to K-2 pumping station.

- Laying an export pipeline 12 inch in diameter and some 216 kilometres in length from Ain Zalah to K-2 pumping station where the Ain Zalah/ Butmah crude oil is pumped again by the old Sulzer diesel pump sets through the old IPC 12 inch Tripoli pipeline.

- Construction of a power house consisting of four 1,250 horse power Ruston gas turbines for the supply of the necessary electric power to all the oil installation as well as the other numerous industrial and domestic needs.

- Construction of all the necessary industrial and supporting facilities of offices, workshops, stores, etc.

- Construction of a water pump station on the bank of the River Tigris near the village of Zammar together with the laying of a water pipeline 8 inch in diameter and some ten kilometres in length.

- Construction of a beautiful staff residential area and employees bachelor quarters.

The Development of the Southern Oil Fields

RUMAILA FIELD

This giant field was discovered in the Basra region by the Basra Petroleum Company, BPC, in 1948. It tends nearly north-south and stretches about 70 km length and about 10 km in width.

It consisted of two parts, Rumaila and North Rumaila

The BPC started the development of the Rumaila part of the field in the early 1950s with the actual production and export commencing in 1954.

ZUBAIR FIELD

This field was discovered in 1948 by the BPC and located some 25km west of Basra. The field tends north-south and measures some 24km in length and 8km in width.

The development of the field started in 1951 and was completed with the actual production and export commencing in 1954.

PHASE I-(1954-1972)

The objective of this phase was to develop the production and export facilities of both the Rumaila and the Zubair fields to attain a capacity of 650,000 barrel of crude oil per day.

The development of these two fields started in 1951 and continued until 1972 and involved the construction of the following major facilities:-

- Drilling of the necessary production and observation wells.
- Construction of four degassing and pumping stations for the Rumaila field by the names of Gurainat, Shammiyah, Central and Janubiyah.
- Laying four 16 inch diameter transfer lines from each of the degassing stations to Zubair crude oil tank farm.
- Construction of two degassing stations for the Zubair field by the names of Hammar and Zubair.

- Laying a transfer pipe line from each of these degassing stations to Zubair crude oil tank farm.

- Construction of a crude oil tank farm at Zubair

- Construction of a pumping station at Zubair.

- Laying a 12inch diameter and 108 km long pipeline which was followed by another 30/32 inch diameter pipeline from the pumping station at Zubair to the tank farm at Fao.

- Construction of a tank farm at Fao.

- Construction of four jetties and loading facilities at Fao which were limited to handling up to 30,000 tons tankers. Due to their limited capacities these facilities were retired and handed over to the Iraqi Ports Authority after the completion of the Khore al-Amayah deep water terminal in 1964.

- Expanding Fao tank farm during the construction of Khore al-Amayah deep water terminal.

- Laying a second 30/32 inch diameter loading pipeline from the pumping station at Zubair to the tank farm at Fao.

- Construction of a new gas turbine driven pump house at Fao.

- Laying two 30/32 inch diameter loading pipelines from the new gas turbine driven pump house to the new Khore al-Amayah deep water terminal.

- Construction of Khore al-Amayah deep water terminal with a loading capacity of 32 million tons per year equivalent to an average of 650,000 barrels of crude oil per day. The terminal was designed to be capable of handling simultaneously two 100,000 ton tankers.

PHASE II- (1972-1975)

The objective of this phase was to expand the production and export capacity of the Basra Petroleum Company from the Rumaila and the Zubair fields from 650,000 barrels per day to 1.6 million barrels per day.

The construction work of this ambitious expansion project was started in 1972 and completed in 1975. The project involved the construction of the following major facilities:-

- Drilling of the necessary additional production and observation wells.

- Expanding the capacity of the degassing stations of the Rumaila and Zubair fields.

- Laying a third 32 inch diameter export pipelines from the Zubair pumping station to the Fao tank farm.

- Expanding the storage capacity of the tank farm at Fao.

- Laying a new 42 inch diameter onshore/submarine pipeline between Fao tank farm and Khore al-Amayah deep water terminal.

- Expanding the loading capacity of the Khore al-Amayah terminal from 32 million to 80 million tons of crude oil per year, equivalent to an average rate of 1.6 million barrel of oil per day by adding more berths to bring the total to eight berths.

- The terminal was expanded to be capable of handling tankers of up to 250,000 tons.

Khore al-Amayah Deep Water Terminal

Courtesy of IPC

PHASE III- (1976-1999)

The objectives of this phase was to develop the North Rumaila field and the other newly discovered fields in the south of the country.

North Rramaila Field

The development of this field started in the late 1960s/early 1970s by Iraq National Oil Company, INOC with the assistance of the Soviet Union. Actual production started in 1972. The initial production and export capacity at that time was a meagre 50,000 barrels of crude oil per day.

This capacity was expanded during the 1970s and 1980s to reach a staggering 1.6 million barrel of crude oil per day.

The development work involved the completion of the following facilities:-

•   Drilling of the necessary production and observation wells.

•   Construction of five degassing stations.

•   Laying the necessary transfer lines from each of the degassing stations to a central crude oil tank farm.

•   Construction of the central crude oil tank farm consisting of a number large floating roof tanks.

•   Construction of a new large capacity export pumping facilities.

•   Laying two parallel pipelines between the central tank farm and the new Mina al-Bakr deep water terminal including two submarine pipelines the first is 48 inch in diameter and the second is 41 inch in diameter.

•   Construction of a deep water terminal by the name of Khor al-Khafja which was renamed later on as Mina al-Bakr. It has four berths each having a loading capacity of 400,000 barrels per day. The terminal is capable of handling very large crude carriers (VLCCs) of up to 350,000 tons of oil.

Buzurgan Field

This field was discovered in 1969 by the French company ERAP under a contract with Iraq National Oil Company (INOC). The field is located along the Iranian borders about 300 km southeast of Baghdad and some 40 km northeast of the city of Amara. It is about 50 km in length and 8 km in width.

The field finally went on production in 1977 at a rate of between 30,000-40,000 barrels per day, after some delays due to certain contractual disputes between ERAP and INOC.

The oil was pump to the oil terminal at Fao for export through the retired old loading facilities of the BPC.

Further development of the field was disrupted by the Iraq-Iran war, the invasion of Kuwait and the subsequent events of the Gulf War and the prolonged and cruel sanction against Iraq during the 1990s and beyond.

Abu Ghrab Field

This field was discovered in 1971 by the French company ERAP under its service agreement with Iraq National Oil Company (INOC). It is located in the south-eastern region of the country, north east of the city of Amara and close to the Iranian borders.

The field was subsequently developed, after some delays due to certain contractual disputes between ERAP and INOC, and came on stream during the third quarter of 1977, with a design capacity of 160,000 barrels of oil per day.

The oil was pumped to the oil terminal at Fao for export through the retired old loading facilities of the BPC.

West Qurnah Field

This field was discovered in 1973 and located close to the northern tip of the Rumaila field.

The field was developed during the period 1989-1990 with an initial production capacity of 200,000 barrels per day.

Jabal Fakka Field

This field was discovered in 1974, and is located east of the Buzurgan field in the southeast of the country and very close to the Iranian borders.

The field was developed during the following few years and it went on stream in 1979. However due to its close proximity of the Iranian borders its production was interrupted at the beginning of the Iraq/Iran war.

Nahr Omar Field

This field was discovered by the BPC in 1948 and is located north of Basra close to the Iranian border. It was not developed at that time because it was thought to be too small and hence uneconomical. It was Petrobras the Brazilian oil company which had signed a service agreement in 1972 with INOC that began its appraisal work on this field and found it to be much larger than it was originally though and pleasantly discovered during its appraisal work the adjacent giant Majnoon field as well.

The field was developed and went on steam in the late 1970s, however the production was halted soon after the start of the Iraq/Iran war in 1980 due to the proximity of the field to the war zone.

Suba Field

This field was discovered in 1974 and is located about 130km northwest of Basra close the river Euphrates. The field was developed in the late 1980s and came on stream in 1990.

10

IRAQ'S CRUDE OIL EXPORT PIPELINES

The Ancient Pipelines

Pipelines of one sort or another are known to have been used to transport water for drinking and irrigation for thousands of years. Short lengths of earthenware pipes cemented together to form pipelines for carrying water are known to have been use by many ancient civilisations in the Middle East some two to three thousand years ago. There are references to the Egyptians using small diameter copper pipes to transport water some 3,000 years ago. The Greeks are known to have used stone, lead and bronze pipes from as early as 1,600 BC.

The Romans are also well known for their use of lead pipelines as far back as 500 BC to transport and distribute water.

It has also been reported that the Chinese had built pipelines around 500 BC to transport natural gas from brine/gas wells to heat brine in order to recover salt. Lengths of bamboo were split lengthwise and their internal nodes were cleaned and smoothed before the two halves were then glued back together and bound with twine. These could be considered as representing the first known hydrocarbon pipelines on earth. Other records indicate that the Chinese used similar bamboo pipes wrapped in wax to transport gas to light part of their capital city Peking as early as 400 BC.

Modern Oil Pipelines

While iron pipes were used in the United States as far back as the 1830s, the use of iron pipes for oil transportation did not start until after the discovery of the first commercial oil well which was drilled by the American Colonel Edwin Drake in 1859 in Tutisvillle, Pennsylvania.

In the early days of the oil industry, the difficult work of finding, drilling and producing the crude did not end once the well was drilled and the oil brought to the surface. In fact it could be argued that the transportation of that oil over long distances to the refinery could be equally as challenging, especially as these distances increased from a few kilometres to hundreds and more recently to thousands of kilometres both onshore and offshore.

The very first commercial quantities of oil were transported to the nearby river barges and rail stations by teamsters using converted whiskey barrels on horse drawn wagons. As a result the whiskey barrel came to be recognised as the standard unit for measuring oil after it had been sold in a variety of different containers which had caused confusion and distrust by the buyers. Consequently sellers and buyers decided they needed a standard unit of measure to convince buyers that they were getting a fair volume for their money. Hence they agreed to base this measure on the standard 40 US gallon whiskey barrel, but added an additional two gallons to ensure that any measurement errors would always be in the buyer's favour. This is how the 42 US gallon barrel came to be known today as the international standard unit of measurement of crude oil, bearing in mind that this barrel is equivalent to 35 Imperial gallons only. These wooden oil barrels were often leaky and at times broken which made this method of transportation very difficult and expensive especially as the teamsters became organised to monopolise this business.

Teamsters Wagon with wooden oil Barrels-USA

The railway then came to be used for the transport of these barrels of oil to faraway places and this made the oil captive to the rail bosses and their workers the Teamsters.

Pipelines were the cheapest obvious solution to this problem. The early gas pipelines were reported to be wooden, constructed of hollow logs to transport natural gas over short distances.

In 1865 the American Samuel Van Syckel built the first successful oil pipeline, a 2 inch wrought iron pipeline covering a distance of five miles with a capacity of approximately 2,000 barrels per day. The most difficult problem for this pipeline was the tumultuous teamsters who felt their livelihood being threatened and repeatedly tried to sabotage the pipeline. This problem was solved by hiring and posting guards along its entire length and thereby proved that the transportation of oil by pipelines was a more cost effective method.

The oil industry's pipeline ventures continued to cover relatively short distances until the late 1870s.

The Nobel brothers built, in 1878, their 10 kilometres pipeline, of 3 inch diameter in Baku, Azerbaijan. The pipeline reduced their transport costs by about 95% and paid for itself in one year.

Oilfield - Baku-Azerbaijan- Circa 1900

In 1878 the American Benson proposed to build a 6 inch diameter pipeline covering a distance of 109 miles over high elevations by the use of two steam pumps. The pipeline was completed in May 1879 and both pipeline and pumps proved to be reliable. The success of this pipeline revolutionised the transportation of crude oil for ever.

Early Construction of Pipelines-USA, late 19th Century

Long pipelines started to be built at the turn of the twentieth century and in 1906 a 472 mile, 8 inch diameter pipeline was built from Oklahoma to Texas.

The first crude oil pipeline built in the Middle East was constructed between the Persian oilfield of Masjidi Salaiman and the port of Abadan. The length of the pipeline was 138 miles, some 221 kilometres. The pipeline was constructed from the combination of some 59 miles of 5 inch diameter pipes and 79 miles of 8 inch diameter pipes. They were of the screw type which required intensive manpower. Some 37 Europeans and one thousand local labourers were employed on the undertaking which was completed in eighteen months in late July 1911. Gangs of fifty men under an overseer carried out the work on various sections, cleaning and greasing the pipes before screwing them together using six pairs of giant tongs with six men on each.

Transportation of pipe - Persia 1910

Laying a pipeline - Persia 1910 (Courtesy of BP)

Kirkuk's Crude Oil Pipeline Routes

Kirkuk crude had only two practical outlets to the sea. The first was through Iraqi territory to reach the Gulf in the south and the second was to reach the Mediterranean through a combination of possible routes through Syria, Jordan Lebanon and Palestine.

The pipeline to the Gulf had the following advantages:

1. The total length of the pipeline is shorter than that to the Mediterranean.

2. The entire length of the pipeline would traverse through Iraqi territory and hence be under the sole control of the Iraqi government.

3. No transit dues would be paid to other countries.

The main disadvantage of this option is that the oil will have to travel a much longer distance by sea to reach the main consumers of that time in Europe.

The main Advantages of the Mediterranean option are:

1. That the crude could be delivered to the European market very quickly.

2. It could supply the IPC refinery at Haifa and the proposed refinery in Lebanon with readily available cheap crude.

3. A big saving could be made in the freight costs around the Arabian Peninsula and in the avoidance of the Suez Canal dues.

The main disadvantages of this option are:-

1. That the pipeline would pass through neighbouring counties that may hold it to ransom by demanding unreasonably high transit fees or imposing political pressures as actually happened with the successive Syrian governments in years to come.

2. The length of the pipeline is longer and hence more costly as compared with that to the Gulf

However the risks associated with traversing through other countries were considered small at that time since all the counties through which the pipeline would pass were mandated territories and hence practically under the full control of Britain and France, the governments of the main shareholders of Iraq Petroleum Company..

Based on this, the decision at that time was obvious in pumping the oil to the Mediterranean coast.

Construction of the Twin 12 Inch Pipelines to Haifa and Tripoli

We have seen before how the interests of the French and the other shareholders differed on the timing of the development of the Kirkuk field, which was resolved finally by the terms of the 1931 Concession, which made the completion of the pipeline by the end of 1934 a definite obligation.

A similar disagreement arose between the British and the French regarding the diameter, route and final destination of the pipeline at the Mediterranean.

The British wanted the pipeline to terminate in Haifa in Palestine, which was under their mandate, while the French preferred it to terminate in Tripoli in Lebanon, which was under their mandate.

This difference in opinion arose from conflicting national interests was finally resolved by a compromise, which satisfied both parties by building two pipelines instead of one, the first terminating at Tripoli in Lebanon and the other at Haifa in Palestine Though this was a much more costly alternative than constructing a single pipeline with a larger diameter, the other shareholders reluctantly agreed to accept it.

However, in order for these two pipelines to reach the Mediterranean, they needed to traverse through the territories of Syria, Lebanon, Jordan and Palestine. The transit conventions from these governments were secured during 1931 on favourable terms and with little difficulties since all of these territories were under the British and French mandates.

Interesting IPC Document

It is of interest to reproduce the following paper which was presented to the IPC Board of Directors in June 1932.

"MEMORANDUM ON THE COUNTRY TRAVERSED BY THE PIPELINE ROUTE

The following short account has been prepared for the purpose of giving the members of the Board a general impression of the country between Kirkuk and the Mediterranean, through which the pipeline will pass, and of the varying conditions which will be encountered in its construction.

DUPLICATE LINE (150 MILES)-HASSAR TO HADITHA (K3)

The line will run in duplicate from the Field at Kirkuk to the west of the Euphrates River, where it bifurcates. It begins at Hassar, approximately 1,000 feet above sea level, where the first pumping station is situated. The route passes through the cultivated land of the Kirkuk plane in a south-westerly direction to Fatha gorge, where it crosses the River Tigris, about 400 feet above sea level. Since the river bed consists of rocky ridges, running diagonally, it is intended to lay the pipe in a trench, for which blasting will be necessary. The approaches to the River Tigris which are rough on both sides, introduce the first difficulty which the pipeline will meet.

The transport of supplies and stores materials across the Tigris will be facilitated by the construction of a "Blondin" ferry, capable of carrying a three and a half ton load. This type of ferry consists of a conveyer running on a wire rope suspended across the river by means of a tower on each bank. It will be in commission in the earlier half of 1933.

As a point of interest, it may be remarked that at Fatha during low water a small rival industry flourishes in the form of a native still, operated by a few Arabs, using oil obtained from seepages in the river bed. Fatha itself consists merely of a few ruins on the left bank of the river. Baiji, situated approximately four miles from the pipeline route, will be the most important railhead used by the company during the constructional period, and it is estimated that nearly half of the total tonnage involved in the pipeline construction will be handled there.

From the Tigris the line continues in a south-westerly direction, crossing two or three sand hills of loose, blown sand, and passing the site of the second pumping station (No. K-2) at mile 66. At mile 95 the line crosses the Wadi Tharthar, a depression about 200 feet above sea level.

The Wadi Tharthar presents some difficulty, especially in winter, on account of seven or eight miles of salt marsh alternates with gypsum. There after the route continues on flat gypsum out crops until within a few miles of the Euphrates River the approaches to which are steep and rocky.

The Euphrates will be crossed south of Haditha at a point where the river bed, which is rocky and overlaying with gravel, is most level. This is longer than the alternative island crossing which has been considered, but it is justified by the more level condition of the river bed.

As in the case of the Tigris crossing, the pipe will be trenched in the river bed, necessitating considerable blasting. A "Blondin", capable of taking a maximum load of ten tons, will be erected across the Euphrates for the transport of pipe and miscellaneous stores.

The third pumping station (K-3)- the last on the double line-is situated a little over a mile from the west bank of the Euphrates. Approximately six miles beyond this point the line bifurcates.

SOUTHERN ROUTE (467 miles)- Haditha-RUTBA- HAIFA

For the first 20 miles this route, which continues in a south-westerly direction, is somewhat rough, but thereafter to Rutba, where it rises to 2,000 feet above sea level, it is extremely good.

Before reaching Rutba the line crosses the former main caravan route between Damascus and Hit, the track of which crosses the Wadi Hauran near Muhaiwir where there is a Police Station and two small water wells.

Rutba consists of a fort built by the Iraq government about 5 years ago, a landing ground, wireless station, and rest house. It is the half way point between Damascus and Baghdad and a place of call for motor and air transport on that journey.

Leaving Rutba, the line takes a more westerly direction and passes over a flat desert, varied at times with rather rolling stony country and a few small wadis. About 80 miles west of Rutba is the Tran- Jordan border, which has not yet been definitely delimited.

The summit of the southern line is reached about 35 miles west of station H-4 where it crosses the slope of an extinct volcano at 3,150 feet. The lava country extends from Burqa, where there are the remains of large masonry reservoirs used to conserve water in former times, to Umm el Jimal, and a distance of over 100 miles. Operation over this country presents one of the greatest difficulties in the construction of the pipeline. The lava is basalt rock, appearing in some places as a solid sheet and in others as loose boulders, varying in size up to a cubic yard, with loose and abrasive soil beneath. Transport of pipe and essential supplies in this section will be a difficult problem.

Over this stretch there are no signs of any former occupation along the route of the pipeline, with the exception of two groups of stone buildings, apparently ancient shrines or monuments of some description.

Before reaching Umm el Jimal the pipeline route crosses the southern slopes of the Jebel Druse. Umm el Jimal is a ruined town built entirely of lava blocks, and was at one time occupied by the Romans. Here again there are the remains of masonry reservoirs used to conserve the rain water; the nearest wells are5/6 miles to the north in the foothills.

From Umm el Jimal to Mafrak the country is flat, rising as Mafrak is approached. Mafrak, on the Hidjaz railway, consists of a railway siding and a few Arab dwellings. It is the railhead for the southern route and as such will have stores, workshops, sidings, etc. Unfortunately, there is no water at Mafrak, and it is proposed to pump supplies through a 3 or 4 inch line from a point on the Zerka river, near the village of zerka, which is about 15 miles south of Mafrak.

After Mafrak the route passes through limestone hills rising to 2,600 feet above sea level after Irbid , 18 miles east of the Jordan, and then falling very rapidly to the Jordan valley crossing, at which point it is 850 feet below sea level. From Irbid it passes through populated districts with numerous villages and much cultivation. It again rises rapidly, so that 10 miles west of Jordan it is 750 feet bove sea level. Thereafter it falls steadily through the valley of Esdradon to the terminal site on the Bay of Acre. The site is located in the sand dunes approximately 2 miles to the north-east of the town of Haifa.

Haifa is a town of some 40,000 inhabitants and has cement, soap, and tobacco industries. The construction of a harbour, started in 1929, is likely to increase its importance. The main breakwater is practically completed, with the exception of the depositing of the large blocks for the protection of the side exposed to the sea. Dredging is well in hand and it is anticipated that the ships will be able to make limited use of the harbour in the spring of 1933.

At present, buildings in Haifa are being used as offices, but later workshops, stores, and a certain amount of office accommodation will be built on the terminal site. The railways will put in the necessary sidings, both at Mafrak and Haifa, to take care of construction needs. The Company intends to drill for water in the sand dunes, where it is expected an adequate and suitable supply will be found.

NORTHERN ROUTE (381 miles) - HADITHA - PALMYRA – TRIPOLI

From Haditha this route proceeds in a westerly direction more or less parallel with the River Euphrates. Up to the point where it crosses the deep depression of the Wadi Rutka, which approximately marks the Syrian/Iraqi frontiers; the ground is generally rocky, with numerous ridges. There is a gradual rise from the Euphrates, and the general desert level 1,800/2,000 feet is reached about 20 miles west of station T-2. The line passes close to and south of Palmyra, the ancient Tadmur, where it is at an elevation of 1,250 feet above sea level. Although there is a large water supply from the underground stream in this area, it is generally sulphurous and it is doubtful whether a sufficient quantity of suitable quality will be available from this source.

From Palmyra the line climbs steeply to 2,000 feet above sea level and eventually reaches 2,600 feet, the summit of this route, a few miles west of Furklus; thence the line is in stony limestone, dropping into the valley of the Orontes, south of Homs.

Homs is an important town, having several small industries as well as a considerable amount of agriculture. The railway passing through here links Damascus and Tripoli by rail with Constantinople and Europe. Homs is the railhead for the Northern route and will be provided with the necessary workshops, sidings, etc; the latter being now under construction.

Leaving the Homs area, the line passes near the village of Tel Kelah, a few miles south of the largest Crusaders castles built in Palestine or Syria. The line crosses about 15 miles of lava country west of the Orontes valley and rises to 1,750 feet above sea level before dropping more or less steadily to the terminal site, some four and a half miles from the town of Tripoli and from its port, the small harbour of El Mina. Tripoli itself is about one and a half miles island. The terminal site is on fairly steeply sloping ground with a rocky outcropping over most of the area. Submarine loading lines will be used for loading tankers which will lie offshore. Construction materials will be brought into port of El Mina, where additional loading facilities are being built for the purpose.

PUMPING STATIONS

The location of the pumping stations will be noted from the attached plan showing the route on pages 30 and 31. Every effort is being made to place them in the most suitable positions, having special regard to water supply, aeroplane landing facilities etc; they are being spaced at such distances apart and so located as to ensure the maximum mechanical efficiency in their operation".

Each of these two identical pipelines was of a 12-inch diameter and had a design capacity of some 2,000,000 tons of oil per year.

The construction work on these two pipelines together with their 12 pump stations, each complete with all the necessary amenities was considered as an enormous feat of logistic, engineering and construction at that time. The work was carried out simultaneously on both pipeline systems which were both completed in November 1934 in accordance the terms of the Concession.

The total length of the northern pipeline to Tripoli in the Lebanon is 580 miles (928 kilometres) and that of the southern pipeline to Palestine is 620 miles (992 kilometres).

Construction work on the two pipelines began in early 1931 and during the period 1931 to 1932 the following activities were carried out:

- Detailed planning and design work.
- Necessary land acquisitions for the right of way.
- Demarcation of the pipelines route on the ground.
- Drilling for water wells for the supply of industrial and domestic uses required during the construction period and the subsequent permanent water supply for the mainline pumping stations.

The main tasks of construction for which full and specialised organisation were called for, were as follows:

- Establishment of railheads, main depots and lay down areas.
- Delivery and stringing of pipes along the length of the pipelines.

Delivery and Stringing 12 inch diameter pipes-Early 1930s

Courtesy of IPC Society Newsletters

- Ditching work.

- Fabrication and welding work for pipes, fittings, valves, manifolds, launching and receiving scraper traps etc.

- Doping, wrapping, laying and back filling work of the lines.

Ditching Machine-Early 1930s

Courtesy of IPC Society Newsletters

Lowering 12 inch diameter Tripoli Pipeline-Early 1930s

Courtesy of IPC Society Newsletters

- Construction of tracks and oil stabilised roads along the entire lengths of the two pipelines.

- Provision of telephone and telegraph land lines running parallel with the pipelines.

- Crossing of four major rivers, the Tigris, Euphrates Jordan and Orontes.

- Construction of 12 main pump stations each resembling a small town, complete with its oil installations such as the pump house with its engines, pumps and the necessary connecting piping arrangement, fire fighting equipment as well as a number of large oil storage and relief oil tanks. They also included offices, stores, dwelling houses, guesthouses, clubs, messes, canteens, cinemas, tennis courts and the inevitable golf courses together with the necessary services such as roads, water and power supplies, telephone networks and landing strips.

The number of the work force during the peak period of the construction reached some 25,000 people which was administered and provided with a comprehensive range of essential services such as accommodation, catering, commissariat, social, medical, transport, and many others.

The two pipelines run together from the first Kirkuk Pump Station, K-1 in the Kirkuk field area through K-2 station on the western bank of the river Tigris to reach K-3 station on the western bank of river Euphrates. Soon after that, they bifurcate, the Northern Pipeline continues its journey through the first Tripoli Pump Station, T-1 near the Syrian border, before crossing into Syria passing through three more pump stations T-2, T-3 and T-4 before entering the Lebanese borders to terminate at the Mediterranean port of Tripoli.

The southern pipeline changes course and diverts to the southwest passing through three pump stations H-1, H-2 and H-3 inside Iraq before crossing the Jordanian borders. It then continues its journey to pass through H-4 and H-5 pumping stations before crossing the Palestinian border to terminate at the port of Haifa.

The crude oil and power generation at K-1 pump station was provided by six 1,800 horse power Sulzer diesel engines, each of which driving a Worthington Simpson reciprocating pump as well as a generator. The generators were driven through a gear arrangement on the main shafts between the diesel engines and the pumps.

The crude oil pumping requirement at K-2 pump stations was provided by six 1,800 horse power Sulzer diesel engines, each of which driving a Worthington Simpson reciprocating pump.

The power generation requirement of K-2 pumping station as well as the Takartah water pumping station on the nearby river Tigris was provided by two Harlandic diesel engines driving electric generators.

The crude oil pumping and power generation arrangements at K-3 pump station were similar to those of K-1 pump station.

The crude oil pumping requirement at T-1 pumping station was provided by four 500 h.p. Harland and Wolff diesel engines each driving a Worthington Simpson reciprocating pump.

The power generation requirement for this station was provided by three Harlandic diesel engines driving electric generators.

The tank pumping arrangement was used in these early days where the pumps at each station take suction from the station tanks and pump into the tanks of the succeeding station

The completion of these two pipelines was considered, at that time when the pipeline technology was still in its early stages, as a great achievement.

With a combined throughput of slightly exceeding 4,000,000 tons of crude oil per year, the Tripoli pipeline was commissioned on 14 July 1934 and the Haifa pipeline on 14 October 1934, carrying their first batch of Iraqi crude oil which reached the Mediterranean coast at Tripoli in late July 1934 whereby the Iraqi crude oil was made available to the outside world for the first time in history. This occasion was celebrated as a national triumph and marked by ceremonies at Kirkuk and the capitals of Iraq, Syria, Lebanon, Jordan and Palestine.

The first shipment of oil was made from Tripoli terminal on 3 August 1934, when a quantity 14,500 tons of oil made its way for La Harve in France while the shipment from Haifa took place on 27 October 1934 with 13,000 tons heading for the same port.

Upon the completion of these two pipelines, the IPC itself marked the occasion by proudly publishing the *"The story of the Iraq - Mediterranean Pipeline"*.

The following is an extract from that story:-

"Materials from overseas exceeded 200,000 tons, and building materials obtained locally at least equalled that figure.

More than 37,000,000 ton-miles of these materials were carried by the railways by the countries traversed and in the desert beyond rail heads a haulage of over

23,000,000 ton-miles was achieved by the Company's own main motor transport fleets, this figure excluding more than 13,000,000 miles run of passenger and light service vehicles.

These figures are eloquent of the scale of the enterprise which involved, beside the construction of main 12 inch lines, trunk lines of 1,159 miles in length, a host of connected operations, some temporary for construction purposes and some as integral part of the final system.

Twelve powerful major pumping stations, each a veritable township, were erected, three on the fringes of civilisation and nine in pure desert, with a relief station in the Jordan depression.

A dozen small pumping installations were called for to supply drinkable water to these and to the construction depots.

Behind these in turn lay the drilling in the desert, by a special organisation of more than a 100 wells for the location and exploitation of water, which was carried out by over 200 miles of water pipelines.

Main oil tankage, provided at stations and terminals, exceed half a million tons.

Terminal works included eight submarine lines, two mooring berths a mile from the shore.

A communication system, telegraph, telephone, wireless was installed to deal with construction and operation needs, with an air service for rapid passenger traffic.

The work of construction called for four main rail heads or transhipment depots, each containing essential stores, workshops and offices on a scale proportionate to the task and employing a labour force numbering hundreds."

It is sad to record that after all his personal involvement in the negotiations of the concession agreement, King Faisal The First never saw the completion of these two pipelines which were subsequently inaugurated by his son King Ghazi.

The Southern Haifa pipeline was kept in continuous service from 1934 until 1948. However when Italy entered the Second World War in the middle of 1940, the Mediterranean became closed to the Allied shipping and the export of crude oil was suspended and as a result the whole throughput of this pipeline was diverted to the oil refinery at Haifa. The pipeline was initially shutdown in 1948 during the Palestine conflict only to be permanently abandoned later on.

However the Northern pipeline to Tripoli also had to be shut down for three years during the closure of the Mediterranean to the Allied shipping from the middle of 1940. As a result of this shutdown, Iraq's crude oil export fell from 3.9 million tons per year in 1939 to 1.4 million tons in 1941.

The Construction of the Twin 16-Inch Pipelines to Haifa and Tripoli

A similar compromise to that of the 12-inch pipelines system was adopted by the IPC shareholders and a decision was made to build a parallel 16-inch pipeline system side by side with that of the existing 12 inch with a southern pipeline terminating at Haifa and a Northern pipeline terminating at Tripoli at the Mediterranean.

The total design capacity of this twin pipeline system was nine million tons of crude oil per year equivalent to some 180,000 barrels per day.

The work was put in hand in May 1946. However progress was very slow due to the difficult circumstances after the Second World War. Some of the main factors that hindered the smooth progress of the construction work included the worldwide shortage of certain materials, especially steel, the currency restriction that was in place at that time, the uncertain delivery dates, and the inevitable subsequent delays in the delivery of major materials and equipment.

Nevertheless, progress up to the first four months of 1948 was satisfactory, with the laying of the southern Haifa pipeline itself complete except for the Palestine sector and a short length in Jordan. In addition to that some important works had been completed, or were in hand, for the provision of new pumping installations, storage tanks and industrial areas. With such progress in hand it was hoped to begin partial operation of this pipeline before the end of 1948. However the conflict in Palestine at that time put a temporary stop to any further progress of the construction work of the Southern Line and with the worsening of the hostilities no further work could be carried out and ultimately this part of the project had to be completely abandoned. Unfortunately this also meant the loss of the old 12-inch Haifa pipeline. This resulted in the reduction of Iraq's crude oil export capacity through the 12 inch pipeline system by fifty per cent to two million tons per year at the time when the country was in a desperate need for additional revenues.

In the meantime the construction work on the 16-inch Northern Pipeline to Tripoli continued uninterrupted and was finally completed and commissioned in July 1949.

During the construction period of these two 16 inch pipeline systems, some of their completed sectors were looped to the existing 12 inch pipeline systems which raised Iraq's export capacity by 10% in 1947 from the previous 4.0 million ton per year to 4.4 million tons per year.

It is worth highlighting that the sectors inside Iraq of the abandoned 12 and 16 inch Haifa pipelines between K-1 pump station and the point at which they bifurcate towards Jordan were looped to the 12 and 16 inch Tripoli pipelines. While certain parts of the remaining sectors inside Iraq between the bifurcation point and the Jordanian borders were salvaged and utilised elsewhere by the IPC in the 1950s.

Doping & Wrapping 12 inch pipeline-Early 1930s

Courtesy of IPC Society Newsletters

Doping & Wrapping 16 inch pipeline-Late 1940s

Courtesy of IPC Society Newsletters

Modifications to the Pipelines Pumping Facilities

New pumping and power generation equipment were added to enhance the export capacity of the 12 and 16 inch pipeline system as follows: -

K-1 PUMP STATION

With the anticipated completion of the new Fields Power Station, new electric motor driven pumps were installed at K-1 pumping station with the old Sulzer pump sets being kept as standby.

This resulted in the deployment of following pumping arrangement: -

- Six 1,500-horse power Mather and Platt electric motors driving six low-pressure Mather and Platt centrifugal pumps.

- Five 2,000-horse power Mather and Platt electric motors driving five high-pressure Mather and Platt centrifugal pumps.

- One 1,800-horse power Mather and Platt electric motor driving one high-pressure Mather and Platt centrifugal pump.

Each of the low-pressure pumping units is connected in series to act as booster to one of the high-pressure pumping unit.

The electric power for these motors was supplied from the newly constructed main Fields Central Power Station.

K-3 PUMP STATION

A new pumping arrangement was also deployed at this station consisting of six 2,000-horse power Crossly Premier diesel engines each driving a Mather and Platt 1850 KW power generator. The electric power generated from each of these generators is used to drive a corresponding 1800-horse power electric motor, which in turn drives a Mather and Platt centrifugal pump.

 The other station electric power requirement is supplied by four new additional Crossly Premier diesel engines/Mather and Platt generators sets, three of which with a rating of 800 kilowatts and the fourth with a rating of 1,500 kilowatts.

With the completion of the Tripoli 16 inch pipeline, which had an export capacity of approximately 4.5 million tons per year the total IPC export capacity of these two pipelines to Tripoli was raised to 6.5 million tons per year equivalent to some 130,000 barrels per day.

It is also worth recording that Iraq's total cumulative crude oil export up to the end of 1947 was approximately 47.27 million tons.

It is ironic to see how the original dispute between the British, who wanted all the pipelines to terminate in the territory under their mandate at Haifa, and the French who wanted them to be terminated in the territory under their mandate in Tripoli, which resulted in the compromise of constructing two separate pipelines, the first ending in Haifa and the second ending in Tripoli, has saved the Iraqi government and the IPC from complete loss of export and consequently financial ruin had all the pipelines been terminated in Haifa.

T-1 PUMP STATION

A new pumping arrangement was deployed at this station consisting of five new pumping sets each comprising one 1,180 horse power Harland and Wolff diesel engine driving a reciprocating pump.

Another three pumping sets, each comprising Werkspoor diesel engine driving a reciprocating pump, were allocated for pumping Ain Zalah crude oil.

The power generation requirement for this station was provided by three Harlandic diesel engines driving electric generators.

The Rehabilitation of the Abandoned 12 and 16 inch Haifa Pipelines

It was in 1979 that the Iraqi government appointed a committee to study the possibility of utilising the abandoned sections of the 12 and the 16 inch Haifa pipelines between the bifurcation point and the Jordanian borders for irrigation purposes. The committee examined the remaining parts of these pipelines and found that the 12 inch pipeline was corroded. However the 16 inch pipeline was in a fairly good condition but some five kilometres of it had been cannibalised by the IPC. As a result a recommendation was put forward for the rehabilitation of the 16 inch pipeline between K-3 pump station and H-2 for water supply.

The pipeline needed to be cleaned from oil and the missing five kilometres section to be relayed. A new water pumping station would need to be installed on the river Euphrates near the town of Hahitha. The purpose was to deliver the much needed water to the farmers and nomadic communities in that region.

However it is not known to the author whether the project was implemented or not.

The Construction of the First 30/32 Inch Pipeline to Banias

The loss of the Haifa 12 and 16 inch pipelines and the rapid post war development made it necessary to provide greater pipeline capacity than that afforded by the 12 and 16 inch Tripoli pipelines. It was therefore decided to increase the pipelines system capacity drastically by constructing a new 30/32 inch pipeline from Kirkuk to a new terminal at Banias on the Syrian coast. The total length of this pipeline is 555 miles or 888 kilometres.

The construction work, which lasted approximately two years, was started in November 1950 and was completed in April1952 to be finally commissioned on the 18th November the same year.

This pipeline raised the total capacity of the new pipeline system from the previous 130,000 barrels per day to approximately 500,000 barrel per day equivalent to some 25.0 million ton per year.

It was the completion of this new pipeline, which brought Kirkuk field into the forefront of the world's producing oilfields.

It is of interest to record that the combination of the 30 and 32inch pipe diameters were chosen mainly to save on the transportation costs by fitting a joint of 30 inch pipe inside that of a 32 inch pipe. It is estimates that the actual steel volume of a 30/32-inch pipe amounts to some 10% of its total volume with the remaining 90% being air. Hence by adopting this method of "nestling" by inserting a 30 inch joint into the 32 inch joint, a great saving was achieved in the transportation cost.

The pipeline was inaugurated on 18 November 1952 by the late King Faisal the second in the company of his uncle Prince Abdul Illah at a big ceremony in Kirkuk. During their tour of the IPC installations they visited the new Fields Power Station and signed the visitors register as shown hereunder.

Visitors Book dated 19 November 1952 at Fields Power Station showing signatures of
King Faisal 2nd and his uncle Price Abdul Illah

King Faisal II of Iraq & King Hussain of Jordan

Meeting Prince Abdul Illah

It was during his visit to the United Kingdom in 1955 that I met prince Abdul Illah. I was at Brooklands Technical College in Weybridge, Surrey at that time preparing for my first year GCE Advance Level when we were invited by the Iraqi Embassy to a reception in London to meet the Prince. It was a remarkable occasion where we, the young students from such very diversified backgrounds found ourselves meeting the Prince and other high ranking diplomats, Embassy staff, and other dignitaries. The atmosphere was amazingly relaxed as the Prince circulated between us listening to what we had to say about our studies, living conditions and general welfare. Looking back now, I am amazed at the fatherly caring attitude of the Prince as compared with the uncaring behaviours of the leaders who came to rule Iraq after the abolition of the monarchy.

The Construction of the Second 30/32 Inch Pipeline to Tripoli

In view of the persistent demand by the government of Iraq to increase the crude oil export to satisfy its ever-increasing needs for additional revenues and the anticipated worldwide increase in the consumption of crude oil as a result of the fast spread of the use of the motor car, it was decided to construct a second 30/32 inch diameter pipeline to Tripoli. This pipeline was completed in phases by adopting the looping method.

However, while the work on the sectors of this pipeline (loops) and the construction of the new pumping equipment was in progress, the Suez invasion took place in October 1956. As a result the main pump sets and other main equipment at the T-2, T-3 and T-4 pumping stations were blown up on 2 November by detachments from the Syrian army. This set the stations on fire and brought the pumping of oil to a complete halt. Most of the pumping equipment were destroyed beyond repairs and had to be replaced. Luckily for the IPC the new pumping installations which were being constructed at that time for the new 30/32 inch diameter pipeline at T-3 pumping station were spared.

The interruption to the export of the entire Iraqi crude oil lasted for 128 days.

Luckily again since the by-passes at these crippled stations were not damaged, it was possible to restart pumping on the 30/32 inch diameter Banias pipeline using the maximum power available from the pumping sets at T-1 pumping station in Iraq. Hence it was possible to resume pumping on 11 March 1957 at the modest rate of 5.0 million tons per year equivalent to 100,000 barrels per day.

Soon after the 12 and 16 inch diameter pipelines were brought into operation and a throughput of slightly over 10.0 million tons per year equivalent to over 200,000 barrels per day was achieved on 25 March.

Meanwhile the laying of the 30/32 inch diameter loops and the reconstruction work at the three damaged pumping stations continued unabated. By 1958 the new pumping equipment at T-3 station were completed and commissioned which restored the pumping rate back to the previous 25 million tons per year.

During this period the method of solid pumping was adopted on the 30/32 inch diameter Banias pipeline through which a pumping rate of 24.5 million tons per year was achieved. Solid pumping had the advantage of requiring no booster pumps at the suction side, no receiving tanks at the receiving station and as a result the residual pressure which is usually lost in the receiving tanks, is utilised at the next station.

Meanwhile the tank pumping continued on the 16 diameter pipeline to Tripoli to carry the Jambur/Bai Hassan blend at a rate of 2.9 million tons per year and the 12 inch diameter pipeline to carry the Ain Zalah crude oil at a rate of up to 1.3 million tons per year.

The laying of the loops continued and by August 1961 the second 30/32 inch diameter pipeline to Tripoli was completed. The new pumping equipment at T-2, T-3 and T-4 pumping stations as well as the additional pumping equipment at the pumping stations inside Iraq were also completed by this time.

It was decided then to operate each of the 30/32 inch Banias and Tripoli pipeline independently which required providing each of them with separate pumping equipment. As a result the Tripoli pipeline was equipped entirely with new gas turbine driven pump sets.

With the completion of this expansion work, an export capacity of 48.0 million tons of crude oil was achieved through the pipeline system in the early 1960s.

In the late 1960s it was possible to raise the discharge pressure of some of the pumping stations gradually from 900 up to 1080 psi which increased the throughput capacity of the entire pipeline system to about 50.0 million tons per year equivalent to one million barrels per day

NEW PUMPING AND POWER GENERATION EQUIPMENT

New additional pumping and power generation equipment was added during the years of the second half of the 1950s and early 1960s as follows: -

K1 STATION

Two new 6,800 horsepower Clark gas turbines were installed in the early 1960s each driving a Mather and Platt centrifugal pump with the old electric pump sets being kept as standby. .

An additional General Electric Company (GEC) EM85 gas turbine was installed in the late 1960s.

K3 STATION

Two 6,800 horse power Clark gas turbines were installed in the early 1960s each driving a Mather and Platt centrifugal pump with the old Crossly Premier pump sets being kept as standby.

These two Clark gas turbine were replaced in the late 1960s by one 8,400-horse power GEC EM85 gas turbine supported by a number of the old Crossly Premier pump sets with the remaining sets being kept as standby

K-2 WEST STATION

In order to ease the rather high discharge pressures of the pumping sets especially in the rather long sector between K-1 and K-3 nd equalise the pressures in both 30/32 inch pipelines, it was decided to construct an intermediate new pumping station west of the old K-2 station, by the name of K-2 West. The construction work commenced in early 1970s.

The station has three 8,400-horse power General Electric Company (GEC) EM85 gas turbines each driving a centrifugal pump.

Two 1750 Ruston gas turbines each having a rating 1,500 horsepower were also installed at this station for power generation.

The station was just about being made ready for commissioning when the IPC was nationalised on 1 June 1972 and hence it was never used by the IPC.

T1 STATION

Four 1,180 horse power Harland and Wolff diesel engines were installed at this station in the mid 1950s each driving five cylinders opposed pistons Mather and Platt reciprocating pumps.

Three English Electric diesel engines for the generation of electric power were also installed in the mid 1950s.

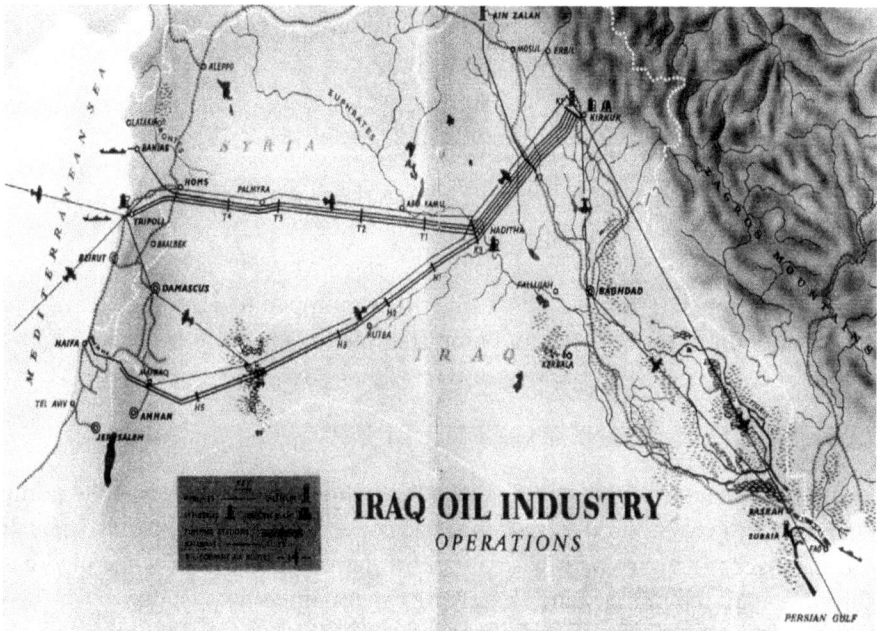

The IPC Crude Oil Export Pipelines

Courtesy of IPC

PIPELINES' PRESSURE

It is of interest to record that the maximum initial pumping pressure used on the two 30/32 inch diameter pipelines was 900 psi. However following cautious testing it was possible to raise the pressure gradually up to 1080 psi which was close to 80% of the steel yield stresses which is nearly 20% higher than the that stipulated by the pipeline code. It was argued that this higher figure was acceptable since the pipelines mostly traverse though remote unpopulated areas. Luckily there were no major incidents of leak or rupture in the pipelines until their final closure by the Syrian government in April1984.

Ain Zalah-Tripoli Pipeline

We have seen that the Ain Zalah and Butmah oilfields were developed in the early 1950s. The crude oil blend of these two fields was of different quality to these of the Kirkuk fields and had to be marketed separately.

As a result it was decided to pump this crude oil to Tripoli terminal through an independent 12 inch diameter pipeline consisting of the following two sectors:-

• A new 12 inch diameter pipeline, of some 216 kilometres in length between Ain Zalah and K-2 pump station.

• The existing sector of the old 12 inch diameter northern pipeline between K-2 pump station and Tripoli terminal.

The crude oil is pumped from Ain Zalah to the tanks at K-2 pump station by two of three diesel-driven Slush pumps.

From K-2 pump station the crude oil is then pumped to Tripoli utilising the old diesel pump sets at the main pump stations.

FUEL GAS FOR THE NEW GAS TURBINES

In 1961, the sector of the Tripoli 16-inch pipeline between K-1 and T-4 pump station in Syria was thoroughly cleaned and converted to a gas pipeline to deliver the necessary Jumbur sweet gas as fuel for the numerous newly installed gas turbines at all the pump stations along the main pipelines system.

BANIAS TERMINAL

A new crude oil terminal was built and commissioned in 1952 at Banias in Syria which comprised 24 crude oil tanks each 140 feet in diameter and 30 feet in height giving a storage capacity of 200,000 barrels, six loading pump sets, six 24 inch diameter sea lines and six buoyed berths.

Banias Tank Farm
Courtesy of IPC Society Newsletters

Banias Harbour
Courtesy of IPC Society Newsletters

MAJOR PIPELINE RIVER CROSSINGS

1. Tigris and Euphrates pipeline crossings

The main crude oil export pipelines cross the river Tigris at Fahta, the opening in the Jabal Humrain Mountain near the town of Baiji just before K-2 pumping station. They then cross the Euphrates near the town of Haditha just before reaching K-3 pumping station.

The original two 12 inch diameter pipelines to Haifa and Tripoli crossed both rivers via two 12-inch diameter pipelines each, one being spare.

The subsequent two 16 inch diameter pipelines to Haifa and Tripoli crossed each river via two 16-inch diameter pipelines each, one being spare.

16 inch diameter Pipeline Crossing - Tigris River at Fatha-Late 1940s

Courtesy of IPC Society Newsletters

The final two 30/32 inch diameter pipelines to Banias and Tripoli crossed both rivers via three 16 inch diameter pipelines each, one being spare.

These 12 and 16 inch diameter pipeline crossings had much thicker walls than normal to allow for corrosion, erosion and other possible physical damage. They were weighed down by heavy concrete blocks along their lengths, in order to anchor them to the riverbed and prevent them from possible movement or floating.

A manifold was installed on either bank of the rivers with suitable valves arrangement to enable the isolation of any of these pipe crossings during emergency, inspection, repairs or replacements.

An inspection party is usually sent at regular intervals along the entire length of the main export pipelines between Kirkuk and the Mediterranean including the river crossings to check for any signs of leaks.

2. River Jordan pipeline crossing

The 12 inch diameter pipeline to Haifa crossed River Jordan via two 12-inch diameter pipelines.

12 inch diameter Haifa Pipeline - Jordan River Crossing 1933

Courtesy of IPC Society Newsletters

3. The Lesser Zab River crossing

There was a ferry arrangement on the Lesser Zab River to facilitate the movement of equipment, materials and personnel as shown in the photograph.

Ferry on the Lesser Zab River-Kirkuk - Early 1940s

The frequent daily crossing of the river by personnel and equipment to the two degassing stations and the drilling location made the ferry cumbersome and obsolete and as a result a concrete bridge was constructed by the IPC in 1948 at a convenient location which resulted in the retirement of the ferry.

The bridge was also used to carry the 24 inch diameter crude oil pipeline from Avanah pump station to the process plant which used to cross via smaller diameter pipes laid on the river bed.

4. Ferry and Blondin Crossings for the Tigris and Euphrates Rivers

An ordinary floating cable ferry service was provided along each of the pipeline crossings on the Tigris and Euphrates Rivers to facilitate the movement of vehicles carrying pipes, equipment, material and personnel between Kirkuk and the pipeline pumping stations.

Since these floating ferries were liable to become unusable during the flood season in spring, the provision of an alternative means of crossing was necessary.

Hence it was decided to install an aerial ferry crossing "Blondin" on each of these two rivers. This type of ferry consists of a conveyor running on a wire rope suspended in mid air across the river by means of a tower on each bank.

The Blondin at the Tigris River had a loading capacity of three and a half tons while that on the River Euphrates had a loading capacity of ten tons.

It was during the late 1960s that I had planned to spend a few days with my family in Mosul. We set off early in the morning by car via the usual Kirkuk, Arbil Mosul road. The distance between Kirkuk and Mosul is about 180 kilometres (some 110 miles). The road in these days was the narrow two lane graded type that hugs the natural terrains which included countless steep hills and wadis. There were no signs to warn drivers at such blind hills and accidents, some fatal, were a common occurrence. The journey usually takes between three and four hours but that was the shortest road between Kirkuk and Mosul.

Our journey that morning was uneventful until we reached the first of the numerous large wadis on our way. There had been heavy rain recently and we found the wadi flooded and dangerous to cross. Bearing in mind, that two tragic accidents had occurred in recent years, the first which resulted in the drowning of the wife of one of the IPC's expatriate staff and the second in the drowning of the entire shift team of the Bai Hassan field of several people, we decided to go back.

The other alternative road is from Kirkuk to Fatha which was the IPC oil stabilised road that could be dangerously slippery during the rainy season. The crossing of the Tigris is facilitated by the IPC ferry before one can join the main Baghdad-Mosul road. As a result this route was much longer and time consuming.

We had planned our journey for some time and hence we decided to travel via Fatha. However when we reached the Tigris we found it flooded and the floating rather fast ferry service is suspended. Hence the only way across was by the aerial ferry the "Blondin".

We got onto the platform and were lifted high into the mid air before the load of cars and people started to move towards the other bank of the river. There was a swift breeze and the platform began to sway in mid air over the roaring river below us which was quite a nerve-racking experience for many especially the few women on board.

Thankfully this whole complicated arrangement at the Tigris crossing was finally replaced by the construction of a government concrete road bridge in the early 1970s. The bridge was designed to have enough space to carry the crude oil pipelines across it with spare spaces for future pipelines. This at last made the crossing safe and the inspection of the pipelines crossing much easier as well as eliminating the risks of corrosion and erosion at the riverbed and the resultant laborious and very expensive repairs or replacement work.

CATHODIC PROTECTION

Whenever metallic structures such as large pipelines are laid in the ground, they are subject to corrosion. To mitigate such corrosion, the pipelines should first have a good coating and wrapping which not only provides physical protection but helps to reduce, but not eliminate, the small Direct Currents, (DC) associated with the chemical process of corrosion. These currents circulate from one part of the metallic structure to another part or to an adjacent metallic structure through the surrounding ground acting as an electrolyte. When a cathodic protection system is used, these currents are diverted to a specially installed heap of scrap metal termed ground beds or anodes or sacrificial anodes.

This technique was applied to the IPC export pipelines in 1953 after the 12 inch pipelines have been in service without such protection for nearly twenty years. As a result these two pipelines began to develop leaks and many hundreds of patch or half sole repairs had to be made with many other joints having to be replaced. It is of interest to record that the leaks in the old 12 inch pipelines increased after the cathodic protection was first applied as the rust deposits got loose and removed by the flow.

To determine optimum sizes & number of main components needed, it was necessary to undertake extensive studies to determine the soil resistivity along the entire length of the pipelines. The findings of this study would determine the magnitude of the expected corrosion currents. Such currents are variable & depend on soil temperature, which was found to change almost sinusoidally in the course of the year. Thus an optimum size of a transformer/rectifier unit was arrived at and a supplier selected to specially make the number of units required to be installed along the pipelines. To provide power supply to these units a special non standard single phase cable was also ordered, that would hang on a catenary slung below the existing telecommunication overhead lines. Several improvements to the telephone network such as installing stronger cross arms and heavier stay wires were also needed. This cable was looped from one transformer/rectifier unit to the next. There were 54 initial locations along the Iraqi part of the pipelines. With the addition of the 30/32 diameter pipelines the number was increased to 90. Power was provided by means of two 11 kv feeder cables, one to the west and one to the east of each pipeline station with the system being commissioned in steps. Following its installation significant maintenance, follow up, measurements, modifications and upgrades to ground beds and other components were necessary.

The system proved to be a success and the two 16 as well as the two 30/32 inch diameter pipelines were virtually leak free up to their closure by the Syrian government in 1984.

PIPELINE PIGGING

Crude oils normally contain certain amount of wax and some other impurities, which over the months and years deposit themselves on the inner walls of the pipelines and hence reduce their diameter and subsequently their capacity.

Hence it is important to clean such deposits periodically. Nearly all crude oil pipelines of reasonable lengths have such a cleaning facility called Pigging equipment. These are permanent fixtures of the pipeline and consist of launching and receiving traps fitted with different arrangement of valves. A cleaning Pig, which is normally made of tough neoprene or similar material of slightly smaller diameter than the inner diameter of the pipeline and varies in length to suit the different pipeline sizes, is launched through the launching trap. This pig is then pushed by the pressure of the travelling crude oil along the length of the pipeline until it is received at the other end by the receiving trap. During its journey the pig would scrape and clean the inner walls of the pipeline pushing in front of it all the impurities which are then received and disposed of at the receiving trap.

A pig can sometimes get stuck inside the pipeline and different methods are normally used to dislodge it without having to resort to the drastic method of cutting through the pipeline.

THE BATCHING OF DIFFERENT CRUDE OILS

It is worth mentioning that two types of crude oils are exported from the Kirkuk region namely the neat Kirkuk field crude and the Jambur/Bai Hassan fields crude oil blend. These two crude oils have different specifications and hence are exported and marketed separately. They are therefore produced and stored in separate export tanks. Since the quantity of the Jambur/Bai Hassan blend is much smaller than that of the Kirkuk, it is despatched through the export pipelines in batches. This operation is usually carried out through the switching between the different export tanks containing the two separate crude oils. The arrival of the different crude oils is detected at the oil terminals and directed to the appropriate storage tanks. Each crude is then shipped on a separate oil tanker for its final destination.

CONTROL OF THE PIPELINES

Each of the main crude oil pumping stations along the Mediterranean pipelines has its own control room which is equipped with the necessary instruments to monitor the oil movement, pressures, temperatures, level of oil in various storage tanks, remote opening and closing of various valves, batch detection, emergency shutdown, etc.

THE VIP VISITOR AND THE EMERGENCY SHUTDOWN BUTTON

As we have already seen, crude oil pipelines normally stretch along many hundreds and in some cases thousands of kilometres. They pass through many pumping stations to boost their pressure to keep the oil moving. They often travel under seas and oceans, cross rivers and ravines, traverse over mountains, swamps and corrosive terrains. They are subject to earthquakes, mechanical damage and human error. All such risks could rupture the pipelines and result in costly shutdowns and pollution.

To monitor the smooth operation of the pipeline and detect any abnormal operation condition, a control room is placed in each pumping station. As we have seen, the control room usually contains all the necessary monitoring and control equipment.

One of the most important gadgets in any control room is a simple emergency shutdown push button. This usually has a bright red colour and positioned on the control desk in front of the control room attendant. Its main purpose is if pressed it would shutdown the whole pipeline including all the pumping equipment at all the pumping stations, close the necessary isolating valves and bring the movement of the crude oil to a standstill.

It was said that one of the VIP visitors of the IPC was on a tour of the main Kirkuk Mediterranean pipeline pumping stations. He was visiting one of the control rooms when he noticed this bright red button. He asked the operator what it was for and was told that it was the emergency shutdown pushbutton, which if pushed will shutdown the whole of the pipeline from Kirkuk to the Mediterranean. The VIP was surprised that such a small pushbutton could result in the shutdown of such an enormous and complex pipeline system. On the spur of the moment he apparently said "really?" and pushed it. As expected and to his surprise and the amazement of everybody around him all the machinery came to a halt and the whole pipeline was shutdown.

It was said that after the VIP regained his composure, he quickly turned to the poor operator giving him a verbal warning for leaving such an important pushbutton so exposed that anybody could so easily push it intentionally or otherwise.

It is a common practice is these days to find such push buttons protected with a small bright red coloured steel ferrule.

The Expansion of the Export Capacity of the Tran-Syrian Pipelines from One Million to 1.4 Million Barrels Per Day

Soon after the nationalisation of the IPC in 1972, its successor the Iraq Company for Oil Operations, ICOO, embarked on expanding the capacities of its fields and export pipelines from one million to 1.4 million barrels per day. The expansion was made in two phases, phase one expanded the capacities to 1.2 million and the second phase raised them to the 1.4 million barrels per day. The expansion work was carried during the 1970s.

This expansion of the export pipelines involved the following works:

1. PIPELINES

No additional Pipelines were added to the existing IPC pipeline system apart from piping modification at the various pump stations in connection with the tie-ins of the new pumping equipment and that associated with the commissioning of the new K-2 west pump station.

2. K1 PUMP STATION

Two 10,000 horse power S7 Sulzer gas turbines were installed in 1976, each driving a centrifugal pump, with the old electric pump sets being kept as standby.

3. K2 WEST PUMP STATION

This brand new pump station was completed by the IPC in March 1972 but was never put in operation by the IPC. It was however finally utilised after nationalisation for the 1.4 million barrels per day expansion project.

4. K3 PUMP STATION

Two 10,000 horse power S7 Sulzer gas turbines were installed in 1976 each driving a centrifugal pump, with the old GEC Em85 gas turbine pump set being kept as standby.

5. T1 PUMP STATION

Three 10,000 horse power S7 Sulzer gas turbines were installed in 1976 each driving a centrifugal pump, with the old Harland and Wolff diesel pump sets being kept as standby. Sadly these brand new pumping sets were never used since they were completed during the prolonged shutdown periods of the pipelines at the time of the strained relations between Iraq and Syria between 1976 and April 1982 when the pipelines were permanently closed by the Syrians as will be described later.

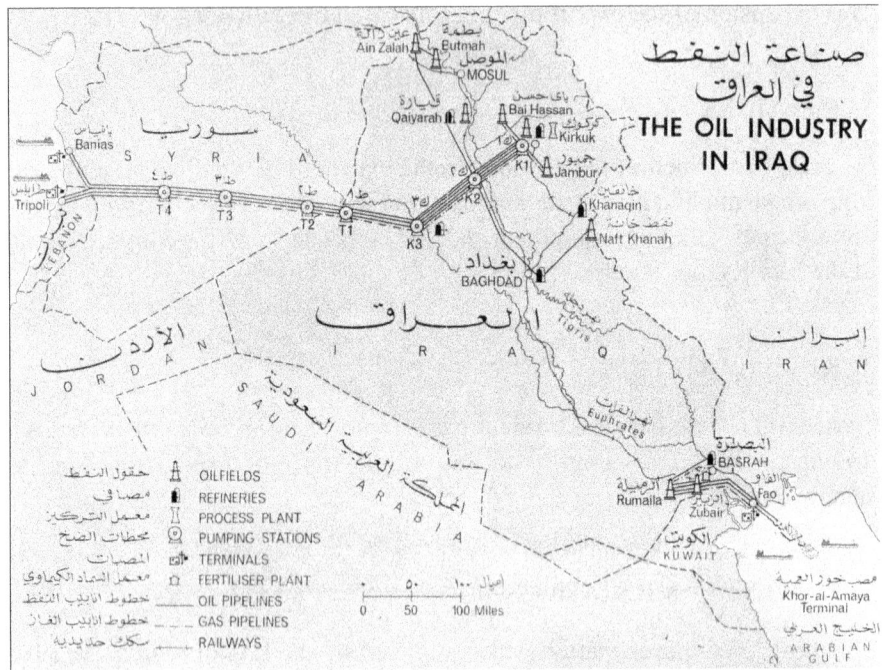

Mediterranean Pipelines-1960s

Courtesy of IPC

The Strategic Pipeline

It was in September 1971 that the influential Follow-up Committee of Oil Affairs and Implementation of Agreements was established under the chairmanship of the newly appointed Vice President of Iraq the young Saddam Hussain.

Soon after the humiliating signature of the exacting Syrian transit agreement in January 1973 which was dictated on Iraq under the Syrian threat of unilateral action, a technical committee was formed in March 1973 to study the alternative routes for a strategic pipeline which would lift the strangle hold of the Syrian government on the Kirkuk crude oil. The committee was under the chairmanship of the veteran Dr Fakhri Qadduri, a former minister of economy and a current member of the Economic Affair Bureau of the Revolutionary Command Council. Its members were Majid Hamdani and the author from the Iraq Company for Oil Operations in Kirkuk, Rajeh Muhialdeen and Issam Al-Chalabi, who became Minister of Oil in the Mid 1980s from the State Company for Oil Projects and Othman Al-Rawi from INOC.

The committee met for several days in Baghdad to discuss the subject in detail before arriving at its final recommendation to construct a pipeline that will run from the oil fields in the Basra area to connect into the Kirkuk-Mediterranean pipelines at K-3 pump Station on the western bank of the river Euphrates. This represented the most convenient junction between the Kirkuk oil fields and the southern fields, which will result in connecting the Iraqi Khor al-Amayah and Fao terminals in the Gulf and Banias and Tripoli terminals on the Mediterranean as well as a future Turkish terminal for the much talked about Iraq-Turkey pipeline.

By running along the western bank of the Euphrates the pipeline would be able to supply crude oil to the proposed refineries for the supply of petroleum products to the many cities and towns along its route. Furthermore the accompanying gas line would be able to supply fuel gas to the proposed power plants to satisfy the growing electricity requirement for these fast expanding cities and towns.

Meeting Saddam Hussain

The committee was then called upon to present its recommendations at a special meeting chaired by Vice President Suddam Hussain. Dr Qadduri explained the committee's findings and the case for recommending the proposed route and K-3 pumping station as the best central location, which would give the best flexibility for the export of the country's different crude oils to any of the available terminals. The Vice President, who was only 36 years old at that time listened attentively and then after querying a few details thanked the committee and the meeting which lasted about half an hour came to a close.

This pipeline, which was to become known as the Strategic pipeline was 42-inch in diameter and some 730 kilometres in length and had the flexibility of pumping in both directions. Thus depending on the political circumstances, transit fees and prevailing freight rates, both Kirkuk and Rumaila crudes could be lifted either from the Mediterranean or the Gulf terminals.

The pipeline's north-south ultimate design capacity was projected at approximately one million barrels of crude oil per day while its corresponding south-north ultimate capacity would be some 880,000 barrels per day. It has four gas-turbine driven pumping stations, with the fuel gas supplied from the Rumaila field through a parallel 18-inch diameter gas line.

The detailed design was rushed through quickly and a contract for the construction of the pipeline was awarded to the Italian company Saipem under the supervision of the Snam progetti with a contract price of $237 million.

The construction of the pipeline was then carried out in haste, since it was strategically important to commission it before the end of the 1973 Syria transit agreement, which expires at the end of 1975. This target was met and the pipeline was, subsequently officially and proudly inaugurated in December 1975 by Vice President Saddam, who had become to be known as Al-Naib (the Vice or Deputy) by then.

It must be highlighted that the construction of the Strategic pipeline proved to be one of the wisest decision made after nationalisation and was well worth its cost for breaking the stranglehold of Syria over the export of the Kirkuk crude which had been held captive to the whims of the different Syrian regimes and the inter party politics and rivalry between the two ruling factions of the Baath party in Syria and Iraq as we shall see later on.

Mina al-Bakr

If the Kirkuk crude was to be diverted to be lifted from the Gulf, Khor al-Amayah, the deep water terminal which was constructed by the BPC in 1964 was not capable of handling both crudes from the northern and the southern fields. As a result a new deep water terminal by the name of Khor al-Khafja which was renamed later as Mina al-Bakr was constructed. The contract was given to the American company Brown and Root at a cost of $341 million. It has four loading platforms with an initial loading capacity of 40 million tons per year (800,000 barrels per day) from two berths and capable of expansion to 80 million tons per year (1.6 million barrels per day) with the completion of the other two berths. The berths were designed to be capable of loading tankers with capacities of up to 350,000 tons of oil.

The project also involved the construction of two parallel offshore pipelines the first having a 41 inch diameter and the second having a 48 inch diameter each measuring some 40 kilometres in length.

The terminal was expanded later on to its final capacity of 80 million tons per year equivalent to 1.6 million barrels per day.

The Twin Iraq – Turkey Pipelines

The history behind the construction of this twin pipeline system through Turkey will be described in detail later on under the heading Cross-Borders Pipelines-Disputes and Shutdowns._

First Iraq-Turkey Pipeline

The contract for the construction of the first Iraq-Turkey pipeline was awarded to the Italian company Snam Progetti. The pipeline would run in parallel with the IPC pipelines from Kirkuk to cross the river Tigris before diverting north towards the Turkish borders to end at the Mediterranean port of Ceyhan.

The Pipeline is 40 inch in diameter and has a total length of 1005 kilometres, of which 345 kilometres inside Iraq and the rest in Turkey and has a design capacity of 750,000 barrels of crude oil per day. It has five pump stations, two of which, ITP-1 and ITP-2 are inside Iraq and the another three PS-1, PS 2 and PS-3 in Turkey. Each of the pump stations has a number of electric motor driven centrifugal pumps.

A metering station was installed at the Iraqi/Turkish borders consisting of three turbine meters for custody transfer together with all the associated pipe work and tanks.

The stations are remotely controlled though they are regularly visited by various engineers and maintenance technicians and hence they only have limited accommodation facilities.

The construction work started in November 1975 and was rushed through for early completion. The construction work was completed as planned and the pipeline was inaugurated in January 1977.

However the commissioning of the pipeline was delayed due to some financial disagreement between Iraq and Turkey. This was soon sorted out and the commissioning work went ahead in earnest when the Kirkuk crude oil finally reached Ceyhan with the first shipment being loaded on 25 May 1977.

Second Iraq-Turkey Pipeline

The destruction of Iraq's two deep water terminals in the Gulf, Khor al-Amayah and Mina al-Bakr immediately after the start of the Iraq-Iran war in September 1980 and the subsequent closure of the entire export pipeline system through Syria in April 1982 left Iraq's crude oil export dependent on the Iraq-Turkey pipeline with its limited capacity of 750,000 barrels per day. This happened when Iraq was in a desperate need of oil revenue to finance her war efforts and satisfy the country's needs.

One of the options available to alleviate this desperate situation was the construction of a second pipeline through Turkey.

However since the construction of a second pipeline would take a long time and involves large capital expenditure which was not readily available to both the Iraqi and Turkish governments , it was decided to implement the project in two phases.

PHASE 1

The objective of this phase was to expand the existing capacity of the pipeline from 750,000 to one million barrels per day by implementing the following measures which were estimated to be completed within 12 months plus a further 2 months for commissioning.

1. The injection of chemicals into the pipeline which would reduce the friction and streamline the flow of oil in the pipeline. The chemical used was Arcoflo which was injected initially at each of the existing five pump stations and later on at all ten stations at an average rate of approximately 2,500 US gallons per day.

2. The laying of 75 km of 46 inch diameter pipeline which would be looped with the existing pipeline immediately upstream of the terminal at Ceyhan.

3. The replacement of all the existing electric pumping sets at all the pumping stations both in Iraq and Turkey with higher capacity pumping sets.

4. The installation of booster pumping sets at the first pump station ITP-1 near Kirkuk.

5. The construction of five new intermediate pumping stations, one between each of the existing pump stations by the name of ITP-1a and ITP-2a inside Iraq and PS-3a, PS-4a and PS-5a inside Turkey.

6. The construction of relief valves and tanks at PS-3 pump station inside Turkey.

7. The installation of a fourth turbine meter at the borders metering station.

8. The replacement of the computer and telecontrol system with new higher capacity equipment which would enable the control of the entire pipeline from both the first pump station at Kirkuk and the terminal at Ceyhan.

9. The installation of an extra high voltage (400kv) electric power link between the national grids of the two countries. The purpose of this link was either to provide power across the border to the Turkish pump station at PS-3 from the Iraq national grid or the Iraqi pump station of IT-2a from the Turkish national grid.

The contract for the entire project was awarded in March 1983 to the Turkish company ENKA in conjunction with the Japanese company Toyo.

The project was completed in mid 1984 and as a result the export capacity was increased to more than one million barrels per day.

PHASE 2

The objective of this phase was to construct the second pipeline in parallel with the first Iraq/Turkey pipeline and expand the combined capacity of the two to 1.5 million barrels per day.

The first pipeline had been working steadily without any serious problem and the engineering and design works were readily available for the second pipeline. Furthermore the infrastructure of roads pumps stations and communication etc were all in place which would hasten the construction and completion of this desperately needed second pipeline.

The Pipeline is 46 inch in diameter and has a total length of 930 kilometres since 75 km of which was constructed as part of phase-I. It would run in parallel with the first pipeline and has a similar design capacity of 750,000 barrels of crude oil per day.

No new pumping equipment were required for this phase since this was well taken care of in phase-I by the construction of the additional five new intermediate pump stations and the replacement of the old pumping sets by higher capacity ones.

A protocol between Iraq and Turkey for the construction of the new pipeline was signed in August 1984 with the signature of the final agreement taking place in April 1985.

The contract for the project was awarded in December 1985 and the construction work started soon after and the work proceeded at full speed.

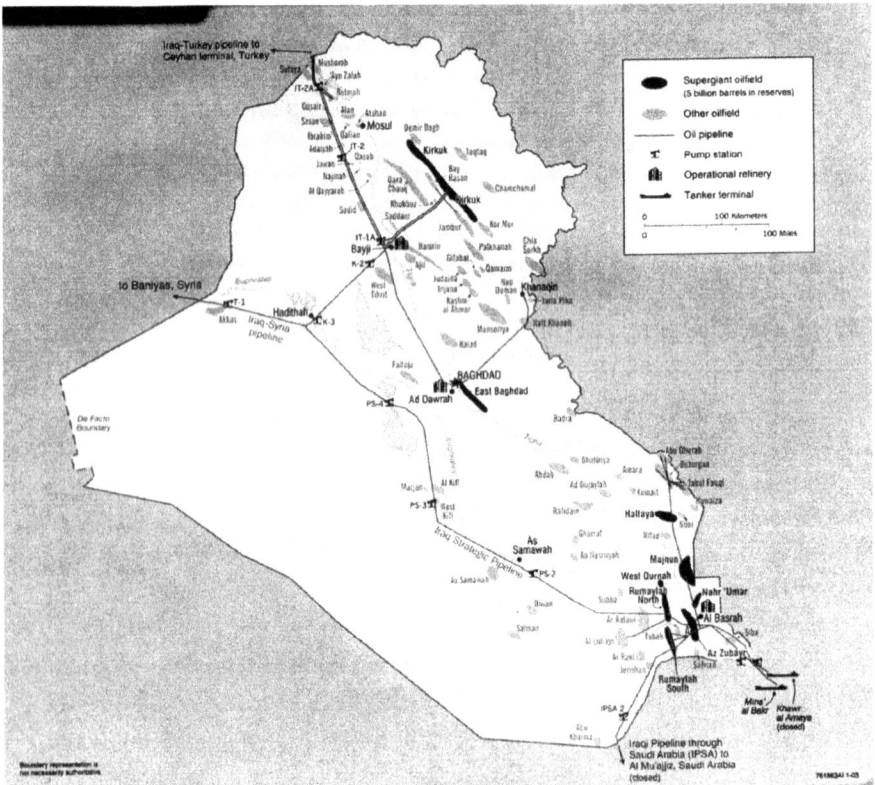

Iraq's Crude oil Export Pipelines-1999

The project was finally completed by the end of June and the pipeline was inaugurated on 27 July 1987.

It is to be noted that though the commissioning of this second pipeline doubled Iraq's crude oil export capacity to 1.5 million barrels per day, this was still very low compared with the maximum production rate of **3,480.**million barrels per day achieved during 1979, just prior to the start of the Iraq-Iran war in 1980.

Iraq Pipeline Trans-Saudi Arabia (IPTSA)

Though Iraq's crude oil export through Turkey had been smooth, a monopoly situation has been created a similar to that of the pipelines through Syria which had been subject to the threats of closure and unreasonable transit fees.

To avoid the creation of similar monopoly situation a second outlet for the Iraqi crude oil had to be found and two options were considered one through Jordan to the port of Aqaba on the Red sea and the other through Saudi Arabia to the port of Yanbu on the Red sea.

After some consideration it was decided to go ahead with the Saudi option and in 1985 plans were announced for the construction of a pipeline from Zubair in south Iraq through Saudi Arabia to the port of Yanbu..

PHASE 1

The Construction of the first phase of the Iraq Pipeline Trans-Saudi Arabia started in early 1984 and the project was completed in mid 1986, the details of which are as follows:-

1.   The design capacity of this phase is 500,000 barrels per day.

2.   The construction of 615km of 48 inch diameter pipeline, 150km of which is inside Iraq and the remaining 465km inside Saudi Arabia. The pipeline started at Zubair in Iraq and ended by joining the existing Saudi Arabian's (ARAMCO's) east –west or Abqueeq-Yanbu, 48 inch diameter pipeline (Petroline) at IPS-5 Pump station near the town of Khurais.

3.   The construction of three Pump stations, two of which are inside Iraq being IPS-1 at Zubair and IPS-2 near the Iraq/Saudi border. The third pump station, IPS- 4 is inside Saudi Arabia.

4. Each of the three pump stations has three turbine- driven pumping sets. The turbines at the two pump stations inside Iraq, IPS-1 and IPS-2 use natural gas supplied from Zubair as a fuel. However the turbines at IPS-4 inside Saudi Arabia use liquid fuel which is produced locally inside the pump station by 30,000 barrels per day topping plant especially constructed for that purpose.

5. Pump station IPS- 4, inside Saudi Arabia is self sufficient by having its own electric power generation plant, water wells with filtration plant, housing facilities, a recreation centre, a swimming pool and a standard runway for a 737 Boeing plane.

6. During this phase, the Iraqi oil is received and stored at a newly constructed tank farm near Khurais, close to the point at which the Iraqi pipeline merges with the Saudi Abqueeq-Yanbu, Petroline. This tank farm was to be expanded later on in Phase-2, to become pumping station IPS-5.

7. During this Phase the Iraqi oil accumulated in this tank farm, is pumped in batches through the Saudi Petroline using an existing nearby Saudi Arabian pump station.

8. The Iraqi oil received at the Saudi oil terminal at the port of Yambu on the Red Sea is stored in allocated Saudi tanks from which it is exported through the Saudi deep water terminal.

9. This arrangement of shared pipeline system was successfully utilised up to the commissioning of phase-2 in January 1990.

PHASE 2

The construction of the second phase of the Iraq Pipeline Trans-Saudi Arabia started in March 1987 and was completed and commissioned in January 1990. The details of which are as follows:-

1. The completion of this phase raised the design capacity of the entire independent pipeline line between Zubair and Yanbu from 500,000 barrels per day to a massive 1,600,000 barrels per day.

2. The construction of 953km pipeline between Khrais and Yanbu, the first 863km of which having a 56 inch diameter with the final 90 km before Yanbu having a diameter of 42 inches. This brought the total length of the entire pipeline between Zubair and Yanbu to 1,568 km and created an entirely independent pipeline for the sole export of the Iraqi crude.

3. Very high tensile steel line pipe, API X-70, with fully automatic welding process was used for this pipeline.

4. The pipeline was externally coated with epoxy.

5. The pipeline is catholically protected using solar energy power.

6. The construction of four new Pump stations inside Saudi Arabia, namely IPS-3, IPS-5,IPS -6 and IPS-7 each having the usual three liquid fuel turbine pumping sets, the 30,000 barrels per day topping plant and all the necessary facilities as those installed at IPS- 4.

7. The pipeline is provided with Fibre Optic Telecommunication/Telemetry system with 30 repeater stations.

8. The construction of a new ten million barrels capacity tank farm at Yanbu consisting of ten floating roof tanks each with a useful storage capacity of one million barrels.

9. An independent deep sea water terminal was constructed at Yambu for the export of the Iraqi crude oil.

The total cost of both phase-1 and phase-2 was approximately 2.6 billion US dollars.

The Engineering and design work for the project was carried out by the US Company Brown & Root. The main contractor for the Iraqi portion of the project was the French company Spie Capaq. The main contractor for the pipeline and the five pump stations inside Saudi Arabia was the Italian company Saipem. Meanwhile Mitsubishi Heavy Industries of Japan was responsible for the construction of the onshore work at the Terminal while Huyndai of South Korea was responsible for the construction of the sea lines and deep sea terminal while Ericson of Sweden was responsible for the Fibre Optic System.

It is to be recorded with regret that such a vital and very costly pipeline system was operated during phase-1 at a capacity of 500,000 barrels per day for about two years and at full capacity of 1.6 million barrels per day after the completion of Phase-2 for about eight months only, when it was shut down for the Iraqi crude oil in August 1990 after the invasion of Kuwait.

Meanwhile, the sector of the pipeline between IPS-4 pump station and the terminal at Yanbu was taken over by the Saudis to be looped to their Petroline to enhance its throughput capacity.

Cross-Borders Pipelines - Disputes and Shutdowns

We have seen that the risks associated with the pipelines traversing through Syria, Jordan and Palestine were considered minimal in the 1920s and 1930s since these countries were, at that time under the mandate of the British and the French governments. However Syria, Lebanon and Jordan were soon to attain their independence and Palestine to be swarmed by the militant Jewish immigrants changed all that soon after.

Though the export of the crude oil from Kirkuk to Haifa and Tripoli through the twin 12 inch diameter pipelines went smoothly during the 1930s and most of the 1940s, this did not last for long and difficulties started to appear.

THE PIPELINES THROUGH SYRIA

1. Independent Syria

The original agreements made between the IPC and the four countries through which its oil transit was signed in 1931 at the time of the concession agreement between Iraq and the IPC. The agreements which were for 70 years did not provide for transit payments to the governments but instead granted a loading fee of two pence for every metric ton loaded at the terminals. The Pound Sterling at that time had twenty Shillings and each Shilling had twelve pence. Hence the loading fee of two pence per ton of crude oil represented just over four per cent of the four Shillings that Iraq received for every ton of its crude.

Up to 1946 there were no disputes over economic issues between the IPC and the Syrian government. This reflected the control exercised by France over the Syrian government during its mandate period with the French company CFP having 23.75 per cent equity interest in the IPC.

However soon after the independence of Syria in 1946, additional payments were made by the IPC during the period 1947 to 1950 and a transit agreement was negotiated and signed. The agreement provided for a transit fee and the provision of crude oil to Syria for domestic use at world prices. The transit fees were based on the quantity of oil transported. In the meantime the IPC was exempt from all other taxes, fees and customs duties.

This was not to last for long as in 1952 after the introduction of the fifty-fifty profit sharing agreement between the oil companies and the producing countries, both Syria and Lebanon tried to get a similar formula applied to pipeline profits. The profits attributable to the pipeline operations were to be equivalent to the difference between the posted price of the crude oil at the Mediterranean ports and the posted price of equivalent crude oil at the Gulf. This principle was accepted by the IPC which resulted in the signing of an agreement with Syria in November 1955 and another one with Lebanon in 1959.

The transit fees per mile were calculated by the IPC on the basis of the difference in value of the oil at the Syrian terminal of Banias and its value at Basra, the alternative Gulf loading port for the IPC oil, less the actual operation costs of the pipelines. Fifty per cent of the profit attributed to the pipelines was then allocated to the transit countries of Syria and Lebanon, which implied the adoption of the fifty per cent profit-sharing principle. This 50% of the profit would then be divided between Syria and Lebanon on the basis of the pipeline mileage within each and reduced to shillings per ton mile. Similarly profits which were attributed to the terminal operations and loading fees at Banias and Tripoli were to be shared on a 50/50 basis between the IPC and Syria and Lebanon was agreed. Both the IPC and the governments agreed that the intent of the agreement was to share pipeline and terminal profits equally between them.

The result of the actual calculation transpired into a transit fee of one shilling and four pence for every hundred metric ton-mile, and a loading fee of one shilling per metric ton.

Syria was also given an annual payment of £250,000 for the protection of the pipelines and other services.

This translated in quadrupling Syria's transit and loading revenues in addition to a lump-sum payment of £8.5 million made in settlement of past claims. By the mid 1960s Syria's revenue from the transit and loading fees had reached £10 million per annum.

2. The Suez Crisis

In July 1956, Egypt nationalised the Suez Canal after it was refused loans to finance the High Dam on the river Nile. As a result Britain, France and Israel attacked and occupied the Canal Zone in October of that year.

The author was at Sheffield University at that time and remembers the demonstration against the invasion that took place then in London and other major cities in the United Kingdom.

The invasion inflamed the Arab public opinions as well as most of the Arab governments and as a result a detachment of Syrian troops arrived in the late evening of 6 November 1956 at T-4 pumping station. The first thing they did was to destroy the communication equipment and isolate the station. They then rounded up all the operators and the other staff and took them far away from the station, leaving the pumping sets and other equipment still running. They also evacuated all the local employees from the station before setting to carry out their orders.

The troops then set to blow up the pump house which resulted in a series of explosions that set most of the area around the pump house ablaze with the fire being fed continuously by the incoming oil from T-3 pumping station.

Damage was also sustained by T-2 and T-3 stations though to a lesser extent than that of T-4 station.

This, of course, was carried out as a retaliation act against Britain and France whose nationals were the main shareholders of the IPC.

The destruction resulted in the shutdown of the entire pipeline system to the Mediterranean with loss of crude oil export for the IPC and a loss of revenue for Iraq. New pumping equipment were installed and the damage to the piping was repaired and though there were protests and claims for compensation by the IPC, nothing was forthcoming from the Syrian government for this deliberate act of its army detachment. This is in spite the fact that the Syrian government was receiving an annual special payment of £250,000 for the protection of the pipelines.

3. New Syrian Baath Party led government

A new government led by the Baath party had come to power in Syria in February 1966 and by August of that year it demanded that the IPC enter into negotiations with a view to increasing the oil transit payments. The Syrian government did not contest the existing agreement as such but contended that the IPC calculations of profit and its accounting methods had been incorrect. In particular, it argued that the operating cost per ton used in the calculation of profits had become too high because of the large increase in the pipelines throughput which has risen from the some 26 million tons in 1955 to over 40 million in 1965, which must have reduced the average per ton cost of pipelines and terminal operations. The IPC accepted that some increase was in order;

although it pointed out that it had incurred heavy expenditures in repairing the severe damage to its oil installations as a result of their destruction by the Syrian army in 1956 at the time of the Suez crisis despite the fact that Syria was receiving pipeline protection payment. No compensation had been made by the Syrian government for these repairs and loss of production which had raised its costs of operations at the time enormously. It also pointed out that its labour cost in Syria were excessive because it was forced by the government to keep on full pay some 3,500 workers who had been temporarily hired for construction when the pipelines were built, but for whom the company had had no work for several years.

Negotiations continued with the IPC making an offer to increase current payment which did not fall very short of the demands of the Syrian government. The government, sensing weakness from the IPC, started to insist on retroactive payments for alleged deficiencies in accounting which amounted to some £40 million.

The dispute continued with the refusal of the government to accept arbitration as provided by the agreement and a deadlock was reached.

It was on 23 November 1966 that the government officially broke off the negotiations and soon after that on first December issued a decree raising its transit fee by 46 per cent and the loading fee by 92 per cent. In addition it imposed an extra three shillings a ton for the company's alleged underpayment for the past ten years to continue until all the accounts are settled. The government then issued a writ of attachment on all IPC properties in Syria and informed the company to stop sending oil to Banias until it paid the amounts claimed and as a result pumping to Banias stopped completely in the middle of December 1966. Shortly afterwards, Syria alleged pumping problems in the pipelines which resulted in stopping pumping to Tripoli as well. The IPC was not allowed to investigate the problem and carry out the necessary repairs and as a result the entire pipeline system was shutdown with Iraq being the main loser.

Meanwhile the IPC shareholders with the exception the French shareholder CFP had, as we have seen, adequate alternative sources of oil at that time, and in view of the growing amounts of oil seeking markets throughout the world at that time, the loss of the Iraqi oil was not entirely unwelcome from a marketing point of view, although it did bring an unwelcome exacerbation of relations with the Iraqi government. The IPC was willing to increase the transit and loading fees, but it was adamantly unwilling to make the retroactive payments demanded since this would have set a dangerous precedent for other producing countries to follow. The IPC's bargaining position was strong in view of its ability to do without Iraqi oil for the time being. Furthermore the owners of the IPC were under pressure from other regional producing countries to expand their own production and hence by claiming the stoppage of the export of the Iraqi oil was due to Syria's unreasonable demands gave the IPC a welcome relief and isolated Syria. In these circumstances and faced with growing pressure from Iraq and its unwillingness to nationalise its oil industry as Syria had hoped, the Syrian government began to modify its position and in March 1967 a new agreement was reached. The Syrian government cancelled its decrees imposing a new schedule of fees and impounding the IPC properties. The IPC thus won acceptance of the principle of agreement as contrasted with unilateral legislation. The company agreed then to pay the fees which had been offered previously. The fees imposed by the government on account of retroactive charges were rescinded, but the company agreed to review its past accounts with the government. Thus all of the important matters of principle from the IPC point of view were also protected; including refusal to accept unilaterally imposed retroactive charges. On the other hand, the Syrian government could claim a victory because the company accepted the higher fees it had earlier decreed and thus recognised its sovereignty. The prestige of the Iraqi government suffered, and the prospect for the IPC shareholders of expanding their activities as provided for by the settlement of the conflict with Syria and the resumption of oil shipments immediately after that brought to a head the question of the Iraqi government's claim from the IPC for payment of revenues lost as a result of the stoppage of her export. During the dispute and the three months shutdown period of the pipelines, Iraq had remained neutral since she could not support the IPC which is considered as representing the unpopular western powers yet at the same time it was suffering great loss of revenues as a result of the Syrian action of unilaterally stopping the export of her oil.

The Iraqi government continued to press for full payment from the IPC equal to that of the revenues of the first three months of the previous year, arguing that the loss was due to a commercial dispute between the IPC and Syria which had nothing to do with her. In reply the IPC continued to plead force majeure. Finally the dispute was settled by a compromise in which the IPC made an advance payment of £14 million to the government which would be repaid out of future revenues. Although this dispute was amicably settled, relations between the IPC and both the Iraqi and Syrian governments remained uneasy.

4. The Nationalisation of the Syrian Pipelines and their Final Closure

The owner of Trans-Arabian Pipeline (Tapline) which carries Aramco's oil from eastern Saudi Arabia across Jordan and Syria to Zahrani in Lebanon had signed a new transit agreement in February 1971 with Syria agreeing higher transit charges than those paid by the IPC. As a result Syria approached the IPC for a revision to its 1966 agreement for the Iraqi crude oil transit and in July 1971 a revised agreement was signed which raised the fees substantially.

Less than a year later, on the first of June 1972 Iraq nationalised the IPC and immediately after Syria followed suit by nationalising the IPC's pipeline and terminal facilities there and this called for a new transit agreement between the two governments.

Subsequent discussions showed that the Syrians were asking for much higher frees than those paid by the IPC. The transit fees that were being paid by the IPC amounted to 22 cent per barrel and the Syrians wanted to double that to 44 cents per barrel. Iraq offered to guarantee the same fees paid by the IPC plus a fixed percentage of the profits made from the sale of its nationalised oil. Syria rejected this offer and Iraq invited two well-known Arab consultants, Nicolas Sarkis and Abdulllah al-Turiki to give their views. They reported that the only practical basis for calculating transit fees was with reference to the profits of pipelines, which should be calculated as the difference between the realised prices less costs at the Mediterranean, and realised prices less costs at the Gulf for the same crude. The difference between the two should be shared equally between the two countries. This resulted in giving Syria 2 cents per barrel more than she was receiving from the IPC just before nationalisation. Although Syria accepted the consultant's formula in principle she disagreed with the Iraqis on the level of realised prices.

Discussions continued but Iraq was in a very weak bargaining position and Syria was determined to exact as much as possible. The negotiations faltered and as a result Syria threatened unilateral action. The strengthening of the crude oil prices at that time undermined Iraq's weak position further and forced Iraq to accept an unfair compromise. The compromise was reached in January 1973 by giving Syria 41 cents a barrel for oil going to Banias and 30 cents a barrel for oil going to Tripoli. The agreement was to continue to 31 December 1975, although the obligation to use the pipeline and port facilities was for 15 years. Furthermore Iraq was to supply Lebanon and Homs refinery in Syria with their requirements of crude oil at a price of $2.45 in 1973 rising to $ 2.75 per barrel by the end of 1975 which were less than those paid to the IPC.

The extreme extent that Syria had taken advantage of Iraq's weak bargaining position by dictating its own terms left Iraq bitter and prompted her to seek other outlets for its crude oil and thereby short-circuited Syria's command over her crude oil exports. As a result she embarked on the construction of the north-south Strategic pipeline which was commissioned in December 1975 and soon after on the first Iraq-Turkey pipeline which was commissioned in July 1977 as has already been described.

During the subsequent negotiation in 1975 for the renewal of the 1973 agreement which was due to expire at the end of December 1975, Syria demanded higher fees again insisting that these should reflect the dramatic increase in the crude oil prices after the Arab-Israeli war in October 1973. However Iraq was in a better bargaining position this time after the commissioning of her Strategic pipeline and wanted either a reduction in Syria's domestic crude oil off take or the payment of higher prices for her oil. It pointed out that by 1975 Lebanon and Syria were lifting Iraq crude oil at $3.05 per barrel compared with its market price of $11.85 per barrel. Lebanon was allowed to lift up to 1.5 million tons equivalent to more than eleven million barrels of oil per year, while Syria could lift as much as it needed for her domestic consumption.

The talks between the countries failed to bring an agreement and in March 1976 Iraq stopped pumping through the Syrian pipelines and began diverting her Kirkuk crude to the south through the newly commissioned Strategic pipeline and advising her customers to make plans to lift their crude from her deep water terminals in the Gulf instead of from the East Mediterranean terminals. This was made possible by the very low level of freight rates which were prevailing at that time in the Gulf since the new higher transit fees demanded by Syria would have made the lifting of the Iraqi crude from the Mediterranean terminals uneconomical.

The commissioning of the first Iraq-Turkey pipeline in early 1977 together with the Strategic pipeline afforded an alternative outlet for the full expanded production capacity of 1.4 million barrel per day from Kirkuk and afforded the required flexibility to export the Iraqi crude through the Mediterranean or the Gulf terminals depending on the prevailing freight rates.

Syria was feeling the pinch this time and as a result pumping through her pipelines was resumed in February 1979 at the meagre rate of 80,000 barrels per day. The new arrangement involved transit fees that were a little bit less than the dues paid to Turkey as well as the various crude off take arrangement for her domestic consumption.

Exports ceased again in September 1980 at the start of the Iraq-Iran war for fear of damage to the Kirkuk oil installations. Pumping was resumed at much reduced rate in February 1981 through the Syrian pipelines to Banias and to Tripoli in December 1981. By mid 1981 Iraq was exporting 650 barrels per day through Turkey and 300,000 barrels per day through Syria. It is alleged that the Syrian throughput was held down by a combination of technical problems, demands for higher transit fees and above all political rivalries between the two wings of the ruling Baath party.

However with the loss of Iraq's deep water terminals in the Gulf during the early days of the Iraq-Iran war, the only outlets for her crude oil were through the pipelines through Syria and the single Iraq-Turkey pipeline.

Relations between Iraq and Syria deteriorated further as the war went on and Syria retaliated by closing all the pipelines passing through her land in April 1982, and thereby leaving Iraq to rely in her oil export on the limited export capacity of the single Iraq-Turkey pipeline of 750,000 barrels per day.

Initially Syria claimed that the closure of her pipelines was due to disputes with Iraq over transit fees but later admitted that it was due to a political as well as economic decision. It turned out that the closure was the result of a barter deal made with Iran to export agricultural products and phosphate in exchange for nine million tons of Iranian oil to be delivered over a period three years, of which one million tons were provided for free. This deal was clearly aimed at weakening Iraq's war capabilities. Hence as soon as the first shipment of the Iranian crude reached Syria the pipelines were closed and one and a half million barrels of Iraqi crude in Banias were confiscated by Syria. These pipelines remained closed throughout the remaining years of the twentieth century and beyond until now.

The Iraq-Turkey Pipelines

As we have already seen, the extreme extent that Syria had taken advantage of Iraq's weak bargaining position in the early 1970s had prompted her to seek other outlets for it crude oil in order to break the strangle hold that Syria had over her crude oil exports.

Turkey was the obvious alternative and had been considered by the IPC as early as 1956 after the destruction of its pumping equipment during the Suez crisis.

A gas pipeline from Kirkuk to Turkey had been under discussion since 1967 and as a result a protocol was drafted for the export of 600 million cubic feet of gas to Turkey. The protocol was finally signed by representatives from the Iraqi and Turkish governments in March 1967 and was ratified later on by both governments. A feasibility study was conducted and it was decided not to go ahead with the project.

In 1971 negotiations between Iraq and Turkey were resumed in earnest this time for the construction of a crude oil pipeline through Turkey. In October 1972, Iraq announced negotiations with the Italian company Snam Progetti for the construction of a Pipeline from Kirkuk to the Mediterranean in Turkey. In May 1973 a protocol was signed by the Iraqi and the Turkish governments for the construction of a 40 inch diameter pipeline between Kirkuk and Ceyhan. The pipeline, which has a design capacity of 750,000 barrels per day was a joint project with Iraq paying $203 million and Turkey $354 million. The relevant 20 year agreement was signed on 27 August 1973 stipulating a transit fee of 35 cent per barrel.

There was an initial eight month delay in implementation since Turkey had problems in arranging the finance for her part of the project. However this was sorted out and once the agreement was ratified by the Turkish parliament, the construction work went ahead with some haste and the pipeline was completed and inaugurated in January 1977.

The 1973 agreement allowed Turkey to lift ten million tons of the Iraqi crude per year for domestic consumption, to be increased to 14 million tons per year after 1983. Disputes over the price of this crude led to delays in the actual start of the pumping operations through the pipeline and it was not until 25 May 1977 that the first Kirkuk crude oil was loaded, after the original transit fee of 35 cents per barrel was raised to 38 cents.

While the Turkish and Strategic pipelines meant that Iraq was no longer dependent on Syria for her crude oil reaching the Mediterranean, Iraq's problems were far from over. The problems with the Syrian pipelines between 1976 and 1979 had left Turkey as the sole reliable transit country for the Iraqi oil to the Mediterranean. However it was the Strategic pipeline which had come to the rescue for preventing Turkey from securing a monopoly position and a stranglehold on the export of the Kirkuk crude oil similar to that taken previously by Syria.

In the meantime the pipeline problems were far from over. In November 1977 Iraq suspended deliveries for Turkey's domestic needs pending payment of $150 million for oil already drawn. Supplies were resumed in December 1977 following payment arrangement but were suspended again in January 1978 as the payment failed to materialise. Surprisingly the suspension of the domestic supplies did not interfere with the pumping of the Iraqi crude exports to the terminal at Ceyhan. These domestic supplies were eventually resumed in September 1978 following a barter agreement between the two countries.

The destruction of Iraq's two deep water terminals in the Gulf, Khor al-Amayah and Mina al-Bakr immediately after the start of the Iraq-Iran war in September 1980 left Iraq's crude oil export dependant on the Strategic, the Syrian and the Turkish pipelines. This situation was made far worse by the closure of the Syrian pipelines in April 1982 when Iraq was in a desperate need of oil revenue to finance her war efforts and satisfy the country's needs.

As a result three options were considered for expanding Iraq's crude oil capabilities. The first was by expanding the capacity of the existing pipeline through Turkey, the second was by building a new pipeline through Jordan to the port of Aqaba on the Red sea and the third was through constructing a spur line or an independent pipeline through Saudi Arabia to the port of Yanbu on the Red sea.

In July 1984 plans were reported for building a second parallel pipeline through Turkey which would double the current export capacity to 1.5 million barrels per day. A protocol for the construction of the new pipeline which had a design capacity of 750,000 barrels per day was signed in August 1984 with the signature of the final agreement taking place in April 1985.

The contract for the project was awarded in December 1985 and the construction work started soon after. The construction work was completed by the end of June and the pipeline was inaugurated on 27 July 1985. The cost of the pipeline was $485 million and the transit fee was 65 cent per barrel.

It is of interest to record that Turkey's revenues from her pipelines at that time had reached approximately $350 million per year.

Soon after the commissioning of the second Turkish pipeline it was reported that Turkey was interested in expanding the capacity of her second pipeline to one million barrels per day. At the same time it was reported that Iraq was considering constructing a second Strategic pipeline to run in parallel with the first one.

These plans were soon to be shelved after Iraq's invasion of Kuwait in August 1990 and the subsequent sanctions that were imposed on Iraq which resulted in closure of the Iraq-Turkey pipelines.

Discussions began in the mid 1990s for the resumption Iraq's oil export through Turkey under the United Nations humanitarian banner. Turkey demanded a substantial increase in her transit fees including a one-off payment of $264 million regardless of throughput. The disputes over the fees were compounded by a debate over whether or not to flush the pipelines and what should happen to the flushed crude. These issues were finally settled and an agreement was signed between Iraq and Turkey in September 1996 and as a result a restricted export of the Iraqi crude oil was finally resumed under the notorious UN Oil for Food Programme.

Iraq Pipeline Trans-Saudi Arabia (IPSA)

The particulars of this gigantic pipeline have already been detailed previously.

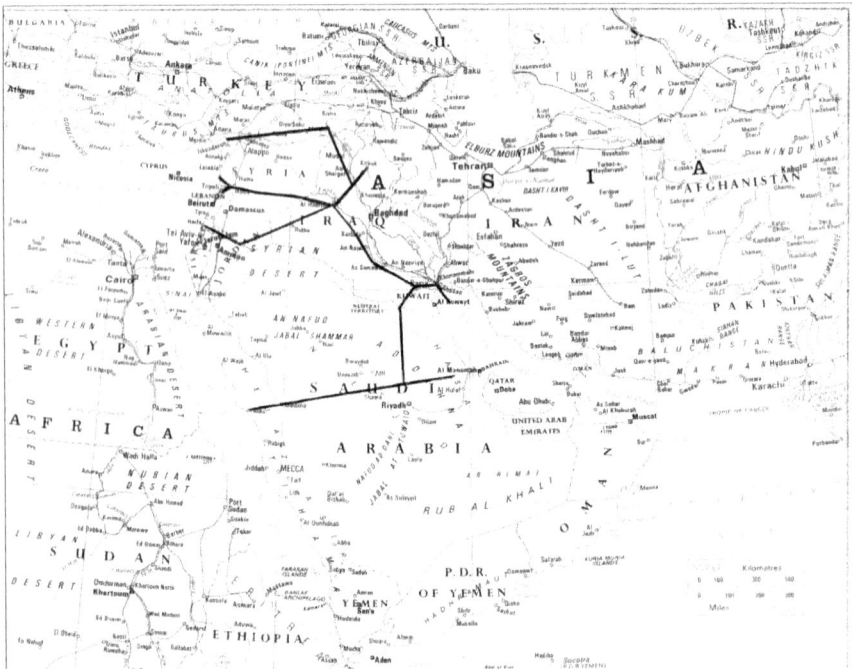

Iraq's Crude Oil Export Pipelines

All this brings back to light the high risks associated with cross-border pipelines which have been experienced by many other countries as well.

Iraq's Crude Oil Export Pipelines

Pipeline	From	To	Dia. Inches	Length Km	Capacity 1,000 B/Day	Year Completion
Kirkuk-Haifa	Kirkuk	Haifa	12	992	40,000	1934
Kirkuk-Tripoli	Kirkuk	Tripoli	12	928	40	1934
Kirkuk-Haifa	Kirkuk	Haifa	16	992	90	1948
Kirkuk-Tripoli	Kirkuk	Tripoli	16	928	90	1949
Kirku-Banias	Kirkuk	Banias	30/32	888	650	1952
Kirkuk-Tripoli	Kirkuk	Tripoli	30/32	928	650	1965
Ain Zalah-K-2	Ain Z	K-2	12	216	40	1953
Strategic	K-3	Zubair	42	730	1,000	1975
Iraq-Turkey 1	Kirkuk	Ceyhan	40	1,005	750	1977
Iraq-Turkey 2	Kirkuk	Ceyhan	46	1,005	750	1987
Iraq-Saudi/1	Zubair	Khrais	48	615	500	1986
Iraq-Saudi/2	Khrais	Yanbu	56/42	953	1,600	1990

11

IRAQ'S GAS INDUSTRY

Natural Gas

Gaseous forms of petroleum commonly called Natural Gas, consists predominantly of mixtures of hydrocarbon gases, the more common of which is methane.

Natural gas has been seeping through cracks in the rocks for thousands of years. Before there was any understanding of what natural gas was, it posed somewhat a mystery to man. Sometimes, such things as lightning strikes would ignite natural gas that was escaping from under the earth crust. This would create what looked like a fire coming out of the earth. Such fires puzzled most early civilisations and became the root of much myth and superstition. One of the more famous of these types of flames was found in ancient Greece, on Mount Pamassus around 1,000 B.C. A goat herdsman came across what looked like a Burning Spring, a flame rising from the fissure in the rock. The Greeks believing it to be of divine origin built a temple on the flame. This temple housed a priestess who was known as the Oracle of Delphi, giving out prophecies she claimed were inspired by the flame.

These types of Fire Springs became prominent in the religions of India, Greece and Persia. Unable to explain where these fires came from, they were often regarded as divine or supernatural.

Examples of such existing Fire Spring is the Eternal Fires in the area called Baba Gurgur, which is located a few kilometres north of the city of Kirkuk in Iraq. These continuous blazing flames are still burning vigorously as they had done so since time immemorial.

Many believed the Eternal Fires to be the same as the Fiery Furnace in the Book of Daniel, in the Old Testament, into which the King of Babylon Nebuchadnezzar (630-562 BC), threw some of the enslaved Jews that he brought back with him from Jerusalem, for refusing to worship his God.

They were also of a significant symbolic value, in the past, to the residents of Kirkuk and the surrounding areas as some women used to visit the Fires asking to have a baby boy. This is an ancient practice, probably linked to the Persian Zarathustrian (Zaradesht in Arabic) religion commonly known as fire worshipping. This religion was widespread in Persia and the surrounding areas and it portrayed a conflict between a spirit of light and good and a spirit of darkness and evil. It started in the middle of the 7th century BC and was eroded very quickly after the spread of Islam in the middle of the 7th century AD. It has almost disappeared by now except for small communities especially in India. It is worth mentioning that fires are lit on roadsides and rooftops even today in some parts of the Kurdish and Iranian regions to celebrate Nawrooz, the Zarathustrian New Year which begins on 21st March, despite the fact that the populations who light these fires are dominantly Muslims!

The actual cause of the Eternal Fires is gas seepage through cracks in the rock formation of the Kirkuk oil field. Since that burning gas is sour (containing high percentage of the poisonous hydrogen sulphide) the resulting flue gases are also poisonous with the smell of rotten eggs and people are advised to stand well away from them and on the side from which the wind is blowing.

The author, during the Iraq-Iran war, was coordinating the works for the protection of the oil installations of the North Petroleum Organisation, NPO, between, the Army, Air Force, Police, and the fire brigades when the Eternal Fires became a sticky issue. They thought that it would attract the attention of enemy warplanes and wanted it extinguished. But this, which is practically difficult and would have created a real poison hazard to anybody in the vicinity that, may not be aware of the existence of the gas or the wind direction. A compromise was finally but reluctantly agreed to camouflage the Fires as much as possible. It is worth mentioning that the Eternal Fires have been sitting in the middle of the oil installations and the industrial area of the Iraq Petroleum Company since the early days of their construction in the early 1930s and all public access to them and hence to the Eternal Fires has been restricted for decades.

However it is believed that the Chinese as early as the third century B.C. discovered the potential to use these gases to their advantage. Finding places where natural gas was seeping to the surface, they formed a crude pipeline out of bamboo shoots to transport the gas, where it was used to boil sea water to produce the precious salt.

Natural gas was known to have been ignited, with awe, by the natives Americans well before the discovery of the American continents. It was first recorded by a French explorer in 1626 that such gases were being ignited by the natives in and around Lake Erie.

It is worth highlighting that Natural Gas from gas fields was not utilised commercially until the second half of the nineteenth century.

Gas from Coal

In the 17th and 18th century Britain, several people demonstrated that coal, when heated, gave off a gas which burned with a bright flame but it was the Scottish engineer William Murdoch who first put this to practical use in lighting his house in 1792.

The first Gas Works for large users like factories was installed in a cotton mill in Manchester in 1806. Between 1806 and 1814, Gas Works were built to light over 30 industrial premises in Britain.

However it was the German Frederick Winsor who began in 1804 to give public demonstrations of gas lighting in London, in a bid to attract supporters for a rival strategy of making gas in centralised Gas Works and distributing it through pipes in the streets.

In 1807, he was able to demonstrate the use of gas to light streets in London's Pall Mall and in 1812 he obtained a Royal Charter to build the world's first Gas Works, which opened in Westminster in 1813. Gas lighting proved so popular that, within 15 years, almost every large town in Britain, as well as major cities in Europe, North America and beyond, had a Gas Works. The company which Winsor founded, the Gas Light and Coke Company, continued to supply most of London's gas until the industry was nationalised in 1949.

The basic process of making gas from coal used in the 19th century remained essentially unchanged right through until the last Coal Gas Works closed in the 1970s. Coal in a closed tube called a retort was heated in a furnace. The gases given off-mainly hydrogen and carbon monoxide passed through a water trap and were then cooled in a condenser where tar and some other liquids were removed. The gas then passed through a purifier to remove sulphur compounds and other impurities before being used or stored in a gas holder. Later in the

19th century steam driven exhausters were introduced to pump the gas through the gas works and into the mains system (History of Gas).

Making gas from coal

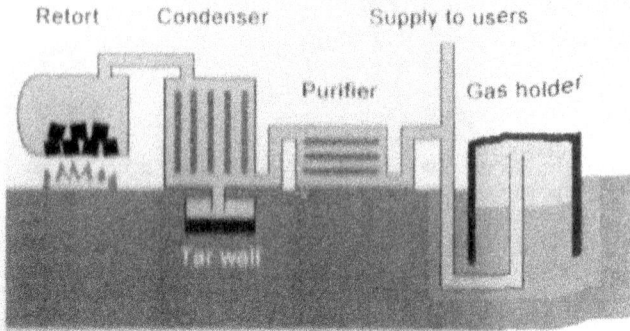

Courtesy of History of Gas

The retort had to be filled with coal (charged) and emptied by hand, but later in the 19th century, mechanical charging and vertical or inclined retorts were introduced in the larger gas works but hand-charging of horizontal retorts continued at small towns Gas Works until they closed in the 1960s.

Originally, gas was only used for lighting for a few hours at the start and end of each day so it was soon realised that it would be more efficient to make gas over a longer a period and store it. The first gas holders just consisted of a "bell" floating in a tank of water. Calibration marks on the floating bell showed how much gas was being made or used. Later on in the 19th century, gas holders became large and more sophisticated with many gas holders remaining in use today in Britain, being filled at night and emptied during the day in winter.

Simple Gas Holder - Courtesy of History of Gas

Early gas pipes were generally made of cast iron with socket and spigot joints which were packed with hemp and sealed with molten lead.

Early in the 19th century, gas was used almost exclusively for lighting mills and factories but by 1826 nearly every city and large town in Britain had its Gas Works, primarily for lighting the streets. Gas lighting was soon to spread to Public buildings, shops and by the last quarter of the 19th century most houses were also lit by gas. However gas lighting was gradually replaced by electric lighting which started to spread from about 1880 onwards and to finally replace gas lighting completely during the first half of the twentieth century (History of Gas).

Sources of Natural Gas

As we have seen, Natural Gas consists predominantly of mixtures of hydrocarbon gases, the more common of which is methane.

There are three sources of natural gas in the world:-

1. Gas Fields-These fields contain mainly natural gas with varying percentages of propane, butane in addition to very little other light petroleum liquids.

2. Condensate Fields- These contain more light petroleum liquids with a high percentage of natural gas.

3. Crude Oil Fields- These contain mainly light and heavy mixtures of petroleum liquids with natural gas dissolved in them. Such gas is produced with the crude oil and is normally referred to as the Associated Gas.

The Utilisation of Natural Gas

Natural gas was considered as a troublesome by-product of crude oil and was usually flared.

It is considered that the American gas industry got its beginning in 1859 when Colonel Edwin Drake dug his first well and hit oil and natural gas at a depth of 69 feet below the surface of the earth. A gas pipeline, two inch in diameter and five and a half miles in length, was built from the well to the nearby Village of Titusville, Pennsylvania. The construction of this pipeline proved that natural gas could be brought safely and relatively easily from its underground source and transported over certain distances to be used for practical purposes.

During most of the 19th century, natural gas was used almost exclusively as a source of lighting together with the gas produced from coal.

In 1885 Robert Bunsen invented what is now known as the Bunsen burner. He managed to create a device that mixes natural gas with air in the right proportions, creating a flame that could be safely used for cooking and heating. The invention of the Bunsen burner opened up new opportunities for the use of natural gas. The invention of the temperature-regulating thermostatic devices allowed for better use of the heating potential of natural gas, allowing the temperature of the flame to be adjusted and monitored.

Without any way to transport it effectively, natural gas discovered in remote places before the First World War was usually just allowed to vent into the atmosphere, or burnt, when found alongside the crude oil, or simply left in the ground.

One of the first lengthy pipelines was constructed in 1891. This pipeline was about 192 kilometres long, and carried natural gas to the city of Chicago. However this early pipeline was very rudimentary. and was not efficient at transporting natural gas. Hence it was not until the 1920s that any significant effort was put into building a proper pipeline infrastructure. Further welding techniques, pipe rolling and metallurgical advances after the Second World War allowed for the construction of more reliable crude oil as well as gas pipelines, and the subsequent pipeline construction boom.

Once the safe transportation and distribution of natural gas was possible, new uses for the natural gas began to be discovered. These included using natural gas to heat homes and operate appliances such as water heaters as well as cookers and many more. It was also begun to be used for electric power generation and in the huge chemical industry including the production of plastics and fertilisers.

As we have seen the obvious method of transporting natural gas is by pipelines. However it has become more common in recent years to transport natural gas after liquefaction.

Cooling natural gas to about minus 260 degrees Fahrenheit at normal pressure results in the condensation of the gas into liquid form, known as Liquefied Natural Gas (LNG).

LNG is typically transported by specialised tankers with insulated walls and is kept in the liquid form by refrigeration. This has made it possible to transport natural gas from its stranded far away sources to the industrialised countries over thousands of kilometres efficiently and cheaply.

The Associated Gas

Large quantities of associated gas had been produced in Iraq since crude oil was produced from the Naftkhanah field in 1927 then from the Kirkuk field in 1934 and the other numerous fields that were discovered over the following decades. These associated gases normally contain Methane, Ethane, Propane, Butane and Pentane and sometimes low percentages of heavier liquids.

Usually they also contain varying percentages of other gases such as carbon dioxide, CO_2 and hydrogen sulphide, H_2S which are referred to as Sour or Acid Gases and sometimes nitrogen and helium. Water vapour is also normally found in these associated gases.

Up to the 1950s there were very limited local or international markets for Iraq's valuable associated gases and as a result they were flared except for a small percentage which was used for the oil companies' own operational requirements as fuel for heaters, boilers, power generation plants and later on in gas turbines.

It is of interest to record that the lighting of these large flares at the various degassing stations and process plant was carried out in the early days manually. When a new flare is required to be lit a man would be sent to the flare area armed with a piece of wood with kerosene soaked rags wrapped at its end. He would stand a safe distance from the flare pipe on the side from where the wind is blowing and await a signal from the operator that gas was being sent to be flared. He would then light his torch and throw it at the gas coming out of the flare pipe much in the same way as some of the old gas cookers are lit by a match stick unlit now.

This practice was in use in the Kirkuk fields as late as the 1950s before it was replaced by the Zinc igniting system in much the same was as we light our modern gas cookers.

The Flaring of Iraq's Associated Gases

It is worth remembering that the continual flaring of these associated gases became one of the major disputes between the Iraqi government and the IPC

Group, in the late 1950s in the 1960s with the government pressing the IPC Group to utilise them commercially without much success..

The following table shows the quantities of the associated gases produced annually in Iraq during the period 1951-1979. It also shows the quantities of associated gases utilised and those flared which represented very high percentages of the total.

Iraq's Associated Gases

Year	Total Gas Billion Standard cubic foot	Utilised Gas Billion Standard cubic foot	Flared Gas Billion Standard cubic foot	% Flared Gas
1951	12.8	2.0	10.6	84.4
1952	38.9	8.0	30.9	79.4
1953	58.8	11.4	47.5	80.8
1954	70.4	12.0	58.4	83.0
1955	85.7	11.7	74.0	86.3
1956	87.3	12.7	74.6	85.4
1957	73.6	9.5	64.2	87.1
1958	99.8	7.6	92.2	92.3
1959	117.1	11.8	105.3	89.9
1960	127.5	21.3	107.2	83.4
1961	126.7	17.5	109.2	86.0
1962	126.8	13.7	113.1	88.0
1963	156.6	17.9	138.7	88.0
1964	186.8	18.3	169.5	89.0
1965	194.7	17.5	177.2	90.0
1966	218.6	19.2	199.5	91.0
1967	200.1	14.4	183.7	91.0
1968	177.4	17.1	160.3	91.0
1969	217.6	26.9	190.6	87.0
1970	216.4	27.6	188.8	87.0
1971	283.5	32.8	250.6	88.4
1972	261.5	32.5	228.9	87.5
1973	309.5	43.1	266.3	86.1

Year	Total Gas Billion Standard cubic foot	Utilised Gas Billion Standard cubic foot	Flared Gas Billion Standard cubic foot	% Flared Gas
1974	324.2	42.6	281.6	86.8
1975	372.3	57.3	316.0	84.6
1976	467.3	68.8	398.5	85.2
1977	480.8	86.9	393.9	81.9
1978	572.4	117.5	454.9	79.5
1979	711.7	151.5	560.2	78.7
Total	**6,377**	**931**	**5,446**	

In the meantime, it is worth remembering the value of these gases and the enormous waste and financial losses suffered as a result of their flaring.

Based on the current annual consumption of the United Kingdom of around 3,350 billion standard cubic feet of gas, the total quantity of gases flared over these years would have been enough to satisfy the U.K.'s gas needs for more than one year and seven months.

However based on the assumption that the calorific value of an average barrel of crude oil is estimated at some 6,000,000 British Thermal Unit, BTU, and that of a standard cubic foot of natural gas is estimated at 1000 BTU, then the calorific value of one barrel of crude oil is equivalent to the calorific value of 6,000 standard cubic feet of natural gas. This means that the total calorific value of all the associated gas flared in Iraq during the 29 years period between 1951 and 1979 is equivalent to the calorific value of some 908 million barrels of crude oil, the value of which would be worth billions of dollars.

The Typical Gas Gathering and Gas Processing Plant

It would be advantageous to describe a typical gas gathering system and gas processing plant which would save repeating such descriptions when we discuss the various Gas Gathering and Gas Processing Plants in Iraq.

Raw_gases whether associated or non-associated are usually sent to a Gas Processing plant to produce:-

1. Natural gas of mainly methane and ethane.

2. Propane

3. Butane

4. Condensate mainly of Pentane plus small quantities of heavier hydrocarbons.

5. Sulphur

The typical process used to extract the above products from the raw gases usually involves the following stages as shown in the diagram:-

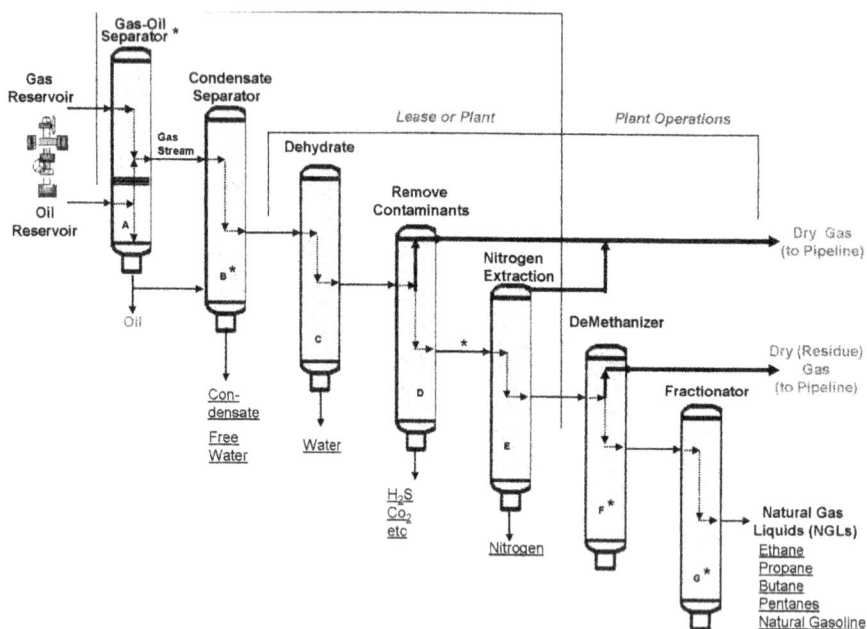

Typical Gas Process

1. GAS OIL SEPARATION

Crude oil with its associated gas leaves the wellhead under pressure via a flow line which delivers it to a degassing station. This stream of oil and gas is then fed into a single stage separator as in the case of Kirkuk field or into a multistage separation system of two or more separators in series as is the case in other high pressure fields. In these vessels the gas is separated from the crude and is collected from the top and sent to the gas compressors, while the crude is collected from the bottom of the separator.

This crude oil that is collected from the bottom of the separator is sent to the Central Process Plant, as in the case of Kirkuk field. Here the final separation of the remaining gas from the crude is completed and this gas too is sent for compression, while the stabilised crude oil is sent to the export tanks.

2. GAS GATHERING

A typical gas gathering system consists of collecting gases from various sources such as one or more gas fields or associated gases from the various degassing stations. Though Iraq has a few gas or condensate fields most of the gases used in its industry in the twentieth century were associated gases from its oil fields. These gases usually come from several degassing stations and oil stabilisation plants which could be scattered over an area stretching over hundreds of Kilometres.

Such associated gases could be of low pressure as in the case of the Kirkuk field or of higher pressures as it is the case of some of the southern fields. They are normally compressed after being gathered to a common pressure and sent through a single or several pipelines of various lengths and diameters to the main Gas Processing Plant.

3. SLUG CATCHERS

These gases are received at the Central Gas Processing Plant and after being combined and mixed together are then fed through Slug Catchers.

These are special separators designed either as single large vessels or as manifold systems of pipes which are capable of catching any residual liquids which have been separated in the pipelines during the transmission of the associated gases from the degassing stations to the gas processing plant. These liquids are then collected and sent back to join the main crude oil system.

The remaining gas is then diverted to the main high pressure compressors.

4. GAS COMPRESSION

The entire quantity of the gas received from all the slug catchers is usually compressed to a much higher pressures of 1,000 pound per square inch or more before being delivered to the dehydration unit.

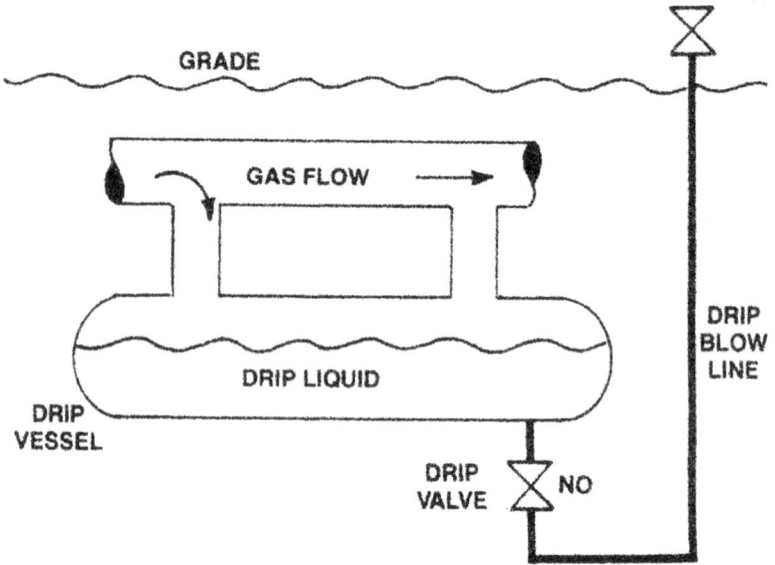

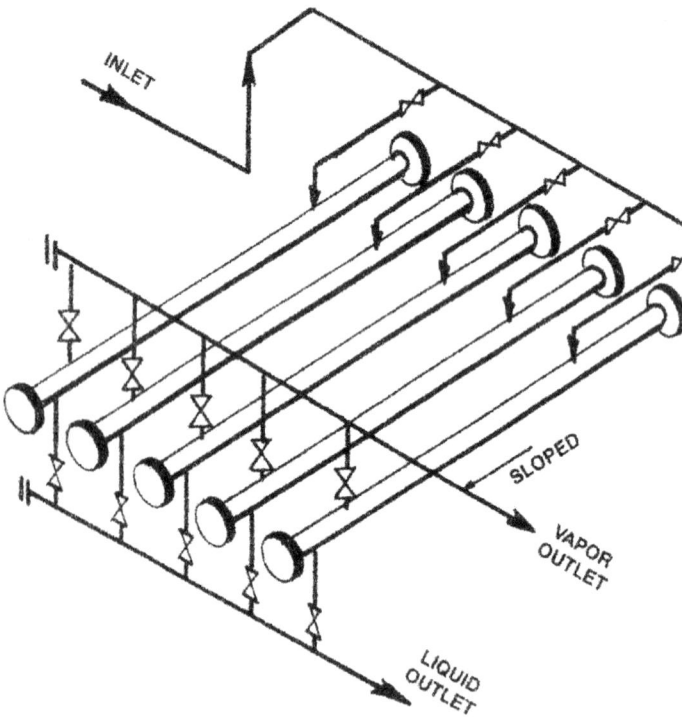

Typical Line Drip and Multiple Pipe Slug Catchers

5. GAS DEHYDRATION

Nearly all the associated gases contain some water and this must be removed to prevent corrosion and the formation of hydrates.

The gas is thus sent to one or more dehydration units which normally use glycol as an absorption agent. In this process the regenerated, water free Glycol, is pumped to the top of the contactor tower to flow down over trays to meet the rising wet gas from the bottom. The glycol absorbs the water from the gas and collects at the bottom of the tower while the dry gas comes out from the top. The water rich glycol is then pumped from the bottom of the contactor tower to the regeneration unit. Here the absorbed water is removed from the glycol at atmospheric pressure by heating the rich glycol. The regenerated glycol is then circulated back to the contactor tower and the cycle is repeated.

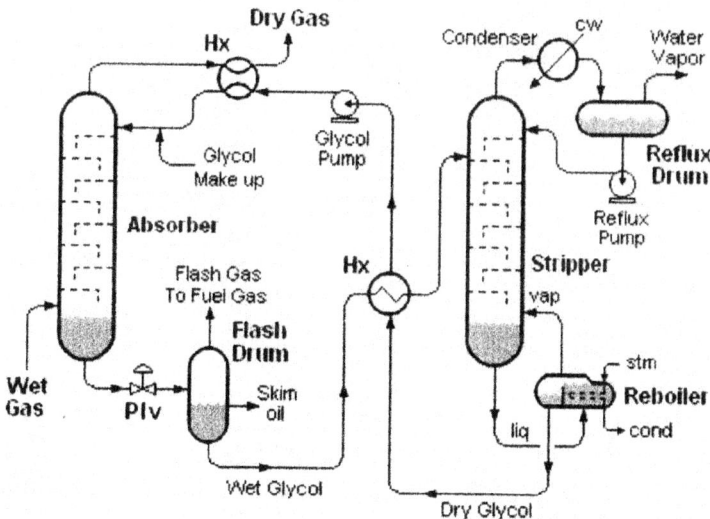

Typical Glycol Dehydration Unit

Other dehydration systems use solid desiccants that process the physical characteristics to absorb water from natural gas. This system consists of one or more dehydration units. Each unit consists of two towers containing the desiccant. The wet gas is fed through the top of the regenerated tower where the water is absorbed by the desiccant and the dry gas is led out from the bottom. When the desiccant is saturated with water the tower is then isolated for regeneration by passing hot stripping gas through it. The main stream of the wet gas is subsequently directed to the second tower which has already been regenerated and the cycle goes on.

One of the common desiccants used in this process is the Molecular Sieves which are manufactured or naturally found aluminosilicates in the form of granules or beads as shown in the diagram.

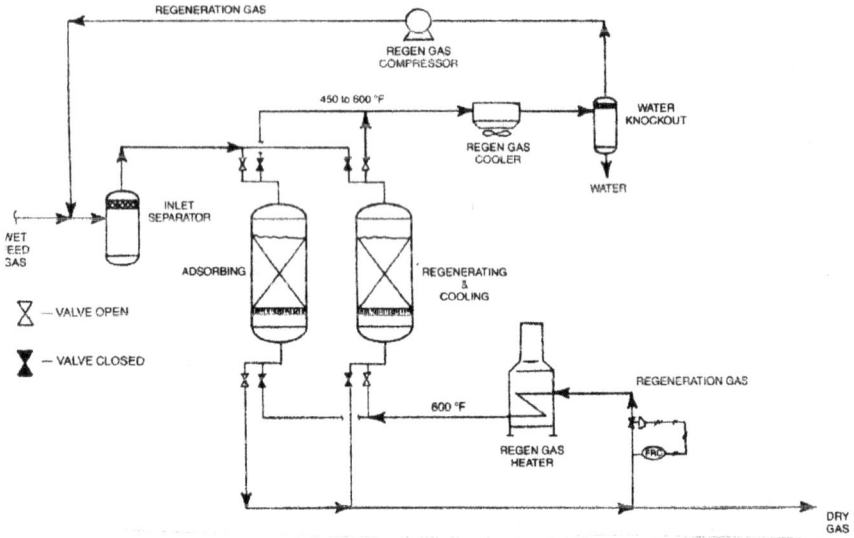

Typical Solid Desiccant Dehydration Unit

6. GAS SWEETENING

Some of the associated gases are sweet while others such as that of the Kirkuk field is considered sour for containing hydrogen sulphide and carbon dioxide. These two gases with the presence of water will practically ensure that corrosion conditions will exist. They will become acids which will attack the plant's steel equipment such as vessels, pipe work, valves etc. Hence they must be removed before they cause any damage to the plant, pipelines and consumer's equipment..

The processes used in removing these sour gases are similar to those used in the dehydration process.

The absorption process uses liquids, the most common of which is the Amine solution. The sour gas enters at the bottom of the Contactor Tower and flows upwards through trays contacting the counter current regenerated Amine stream. The lean Amine absorbs the acid gases and flows to the bottom of the tower to be pumped back to the Regeneration or Stripper Tower while the sweet gas flows out from the top. The rich Amine is then stripped of its acid gases in the Regeneration or Stripper Tower by heating and the lean Amine is then recycled back to the contactor tower while the acid gases are sent to the Sulphur plant other wise to the flares, and the cycle is repeated.

Molecular Sieves with affinity to absorb sour gases are used in a similar process as that used in the dehydration.

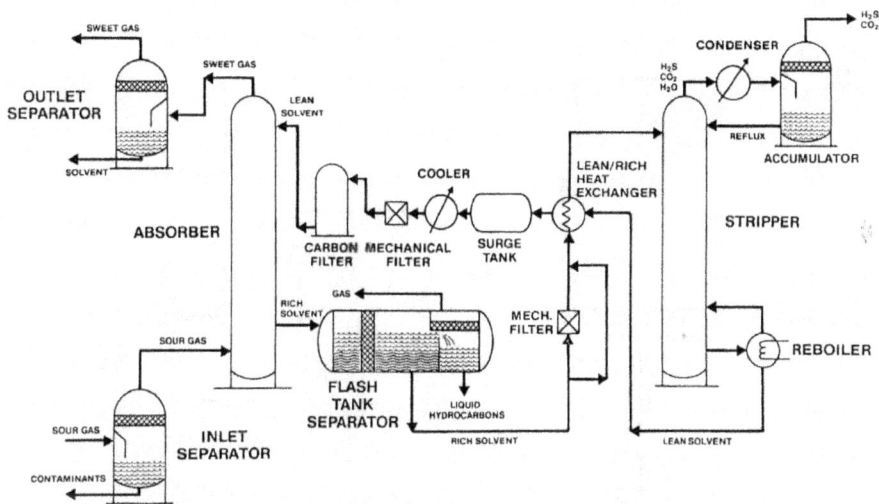

Natural Gas Sweetening Plant

7. TURBOEXPANDERS

The turboexpanders are very high speed machines of some 14,000 revolutions per minute, RPM, through which the high pressure gas is expanded to a much lower pressure which results in dropping the temperature of the gas to very low levels. They were first used in the gas processing plants in the early nineteen sixties and gained popularity in the nineteen seventies. This method has become the preferred means of achieving such low temperatures and has been replacing the old traditional method of refrigeration.

This, sudden drop in the gas stream temperature to around minus 120 degrees Fahrenheit , is enough to condense all the hydrocarbon components of the gas, except the methane which remains in the gaseous form.

One of the advantages of the turboexpander is that it also drives another gas turbine driving a compressor which is normally used to compress the methane and ethane gases which are recovered after their extraction as shown in the diagram.

It is also a normal practice to install the much less efficient Joule Thompson valve in parallel with the turboexpander which is used as a standby during the periods of the non availability of the turboexpander.

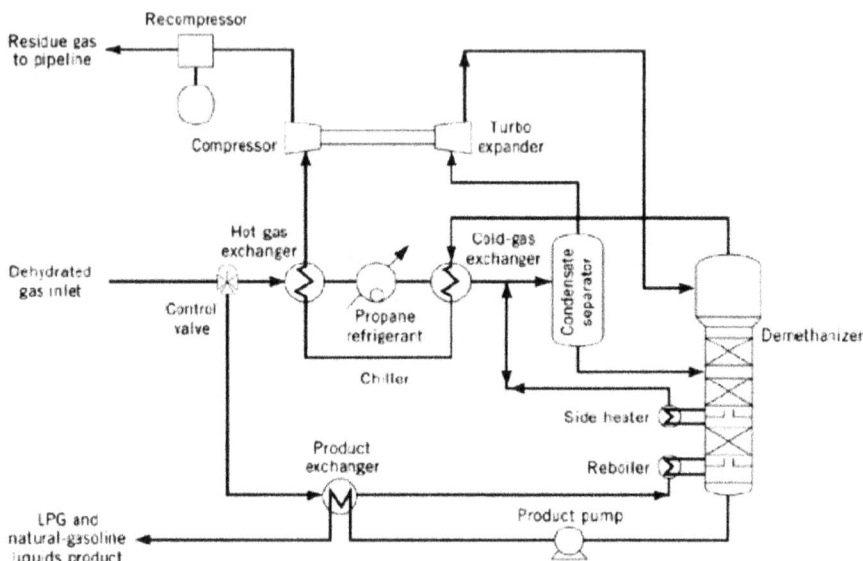

Typical Turboexpander Process

8. NITROGEN EXTRACTION

This process is used only in gas processing plants where the gas contains an appreciable percentage of nitrogen. The low temperature gas from the turboexpander is fed to a special column where the nitrogen is cryogenically separated and subsequently vented to the atmosphere.

9. DEMETHANIZATION

The low temperature mixture of methane gas and the condensed hydrocarbon liquids leaving the tudboexpander are fed into the methane separator where the methane gas is separated leaving through the top of the tower while the remaining liquids are directed to the deethanizer tower.

10. FRACTIONATION

The liquids leaving the demethanizer separator then pass through a series of fractionation towers called the, Deethanizer, Depropanizer, and Debutanizer.

Fractionation is the process of the separation of propane, butane and condensates by using the varying boiling points of these individual hydrocarbons.

In a typical fractionation tower the liquid at the bottom of the tower is heated to produce stripping vapour. The vapour rises through the tower contacting the descending feed liquid. The vapour leaving the top of the tower enters a condenser where it is cooled with some of the condensed liquid returning to the tower as reflux to limit the loss of heavy components. At the same time the remaining liquid at the bottom of the tower is then pumped as a feed for the next fractionation tower.

These fractionation towers are usually fitted with internals such as trays with valves or other types of packing to promote maximum contact between the rising vapour and the descending liquid in them.

11. DEETHANIZATION

The first of these fractionation towers is the deethanizer where the ethane gas is separated from the liquids arriving from the methane separator by using the fractionation process described above. The ethane gas leaving the top of the tower is then mixed with the previously separated methane to form the natural gas. This natural gas is then sent to be compressed by the compressor that is driven by the turboexpander before being sent to custumers through the sales pipeline. Meanwhile the remaining liquids from the bottom of this tower are directed to the depropanizer tower.

12. DEPROPONIZATION

In this tower the propane is separated and collected from the top of the tower, condensed and sent to be stored in large pressurised spherical tanks. From these it could either be sent to the LPG bottling plant where it is mixed in certain proportions of butane for the local market or to be refrigerated at around minus 42 degrees centigrade and stored in large insulated tanks ready for export by special refrigerated LPG carriers.

The remaining liquids are then directed to the debutanizer tower.

13. DEBUTINIZATION

This is the final tower in this series where the butane is separated and collected from the top of the tower, condensed and sent to be stored in large pressurised spherical tanks. It is then either mixed with the propane and bottled for the local market or refrigerated at around minus five degrees centigrade and stored in large tanks for export by refrigerated LPG carriers.

The remaining liquid, which is condensate, is normally returned to the main stream to be mixed with the crude oil.

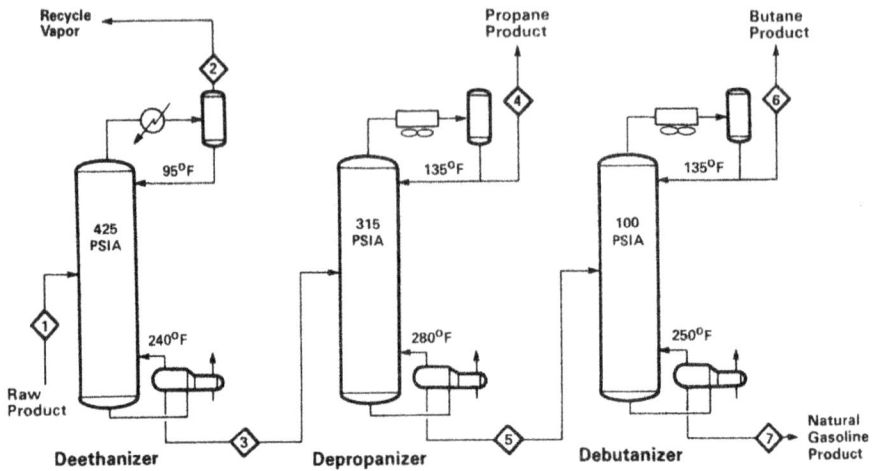

Typical Fractionation Process

14. SULPHUR RECOVERY

The acid gases collected from the sweetening towers, are mainly hydrogen sulphide (H_2S) with little carbon dioxide (CO_2). These gases are then either flared if their volume is small or sent to a sulphur plant which normally uses the Claus Process. The original Claus Process which was first used in 1883, in which the hydrogen sulphide was reacted over a catalyst with air (oxygen) to form elemental sulphur and water.

$$H_2S + 1/2O_2 = S + H_2O$$

The sulphur recovery efficiencies from this early primitive process were low.

In order to improve the efficiency a modification to the original process was developed in 1936 which basically involves the partial burning of about 30% of the hydrogen sulphide to produce sulphur dioxide (SO_2). This sulphur dioxide then reacts with the remaining unburned hydrogen sulphide (H_2S) to form elemental sulphur. This is an over simplification of the reactions actually taking place in the Claus Unit. The other by- product from this process is water.

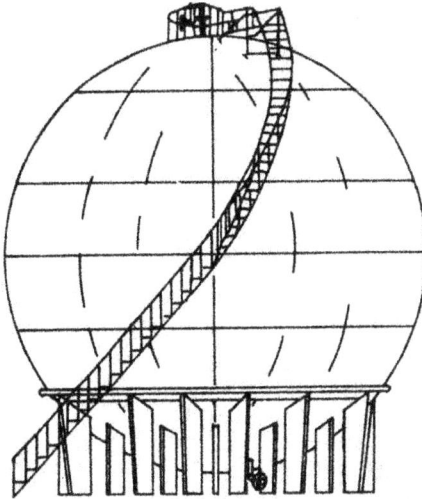

Courtesy of C-E Natco

Typical Pressurised Spherical Talk

Iraq's First Liquid Petroleum Gas (LPG)

Kerosene was the dominant cooking and heating fuel in Iraq during the 1940s and 1950s. The kerosene cooking and heating appliances during these years were very simple and usually did not achieve complete combustion of the kerosene and as a result they were smoky, dirty and very unhealthy.

The alternative cleaner fuel of Liquid Petroleum Gas (LPG) was first produced in Iraq in 1958 as a by-product in the Daura Refinery. The term (LPG) refers to propane and butane gases separately or in mixture which are maintained in a liquid state under pressure within a confining vessel or under very low temperatures.

The quantities produced in these early days were modest and the propane and butane were produced separately and stored in spherical tanks. A small cylinder bottling plant was constructed at Daura refinery and a mixture of the propane and butane was bottled in the usual 12.5 kilogram domestic size cylinders for the local Baghdad market. The proportion of propane/butane in the mixture varied from summer to winter.

As little as 250 tons of LPG was initially produced in 1959 only to rise gradually and steeply to as high as about 20,000 tons by 1969. As a result of the increasing popularity of the use of LPG which replaces and saves the kerosene, it was decided to produce LPG on a much larger scale by utilising the flared associated gases from the Kirkuk field through the construction of a Sulphur Recovery Plant at Kirkuk and an LPG Processing Plant at Taji north of Baghdad.

Kirkuk Sulphur Recovery Plant

We have seen that one of the main disputes between the Iraqi government and the Iraq Petroleum Company, IPC, was the flaring of the associated gases. Due to the continual refusal of the IPC to utilise these gases commercially, the Government decided to utilise them directly as early as 1964. Contracts were subsequently awarded for the construction of a sulphur recovery plant at Kirkuk, and a Liquid Petroleum Gas plant and an (LPG) bottling facility at Taji north of Baghdad.

Two parallel pipelines each measuring 305 kilometres in length were also constructed between the Kirkuk and the Taji faclities. The first pipeline having a 16 inch diameter was for the transfer of the natural gas and the second with an 8 inch diameter was for the transfer of Natural Gas Liquids (NGL) from the sulphur plant to the LPG Taji complex.

The site of the Sulphur plant was ideally located near the main sources of the associated gases namely the Central Crude Oil Process Plant and the nearby Kirkuk field degassing stations.

The Sulphur plant was completed in 1968 though continued to suffer from teething problems until 1972. It involved the construction of a gas processing plant and a sulphur recovery unit mainly as described previously, with the exception that the liquid leaving the Demethanizer tower is not processed further.

This liquid which is called Natural Gas Liquid, NGL, and which is a mixture of propane, butane and condensate is pumped to the Taji LPG Plant through the 8 inch diameter pipeline for further processing.

The natural gas of Ethane and Methane is also delivered to the Taji facilities through the 16 inch diameter pipeline for distribution to large consumers.

The design capacity of the plant was 100 million standard cubic feet of gas per day with the design capacity of the recoverable sulphur being estimated at some 60.000 tons per year which was mainly for export. However it was reported that the actual production of sulphur was in the range of 45,000-50,000 tons per year.

It is worth mentioning that Iraq also produces about one million tons of sulphur per year from the Mishraq mine near the town of Shirqat south of Mosul. The Frasch process of injecting hot water into the underground sulphur rich rock is used that melts the sulphur in the rock which is then forced up to the surface, usually by compressed air.

This Sulphur Plant had a very short life and was retired in the early 1980s after the construction and commissioning of the North Gas Project which was located in its vicinity. The Plant was later cannibalised for spare parts.

Taji LPG Processing and Bottling Plant

As we have seen, the natural gas and the Natural Gas Liquids (NGL) from the sulphur plant were delivered to the Taji LPG complex north of Baghdad which consisted of an LPG processing plant and LPG cylinders bottling facilities.

The LPG process is similar to the Typical LPG Fractionation Process described previously. The propane and butane produced are stored in separate spherical tanks. Domestic and industrial cylinders of different sizes are then filled with a mixture of certain proportions of propane and butane depending on the season and distributed to the local consumers.

The remaining condensate is then pumped through a pipeline to the Daura refinery to be blended with the crude oil feed of the refinery.

The natural gas received at the Taji complex from the sulphur plant is distributed by pipelines for power generation and to industrial consumers in and around Baghdad.

Large Scale Utilisation of the Associated Gases

During the 1970s, the use of LPG for cooking and heating became very popular throughout the country and the supplies became very limited. It was then envisaged in the mid 1970s to embark on expanding the county's LPG production on a grand scale. As a result it was decided to construct two Gas Processing Complexes at the main sources of the associated gases in the country one near the Kirkuk oil fields by the name the North Gas Complex and the other near the southern oil fields by the name the South Gas Complex.

The main objective was to utilise all the associated gases available from these oil fields to produce the following products:

1. Dry natural gas for use as fuel for power generation and other industrial plants and factories as well as raw material for petrochemical and fertilizers industries.

2. LPG for the domestic market as well as for export.

3. Natural gasoline as fuel and for blending with crude oil.

4. Sulphur for local industries and export purposes.

The North Gas Complex

To utilise the associated gases from the northern oil fields namely Kirkuk, Bai Hassan and Jambur for the production of dry natural gas, LPG, condensates and sulphur, it was decided to construct the North Gas Complex which has a design capacity of 520 million standard cubic feet per day, MMSCF/D.

The construction work started in 1979 and the project was scheduled for completion in 1983. Though the work was interrupted by the start of the Iraq/ Iran war in September 1980, nonetheless the construction work continued albeit at a slightly slower pace and the project was finally completed and commissioned in September 1983, only a few months behind schedule.

The site for this complex was chosen at a central location amongst the three major oil fields, west of K-1 crude oil pumping station. The project involved the construction of the following major facilities:-

1. Gas gathering system

2. Gas Compression system

3. Gas Processing Plant

4. Sulphur recovery units

5. LPG Underground cavern storage facility.

6. Supply of LPG to the old Kirkuk Bottling Plant.

7. LPG Pumping to Baghdad.

8. Natural gas pipeline distribution system.

1. GAS GATHERING SYSTEM

This involved the gathering of all the associated gases from the following sources:-

- The Baba, Jabal Bur, Shurau, Hanjira, Sarsalu and Sarbashash degassing stations of the Kirkuk field.

- The Bai Hassan South, North and Dawood degassing stations of the Bai Hassan field

- The Jambur North and South degassing stations of the Jambur field

- The two Central Crude Oil Processing Plants.

2. GAS COMPRESSION SYSTEM

The pressures of the gathered associated gases vary from one field to another. Those from the Kirkuk degassing stations and the two Central Process Plants have a pressure of about 60 psi; those from the Bai Hassan degassing stations come from two gas/oil separation stages at two different pressures, while those of Jambur degassing stations come from three gas/oil separation stages at three different pressures.

The gases from all these sources are then compressed to a common higher pressure before being delivered to the Gas Processing Plant.

3. GAS PROCESSING PLANT

The new Gas Process Plant had two separate trains each having a design capacity of 260 million standard cubic feet per day.

The gases from the three fields when received at the new Gas Process Plant are then combined into one steam and passed through the usual gas processing facilities as described previously under the heading (The Typical Gas Gathering and Processing Plant), which included compression, dehydration, sweetening, expansion through turboexpanders, demethanization, deethanization, depropanization and debutanization.

4. SULPHUR RECOVERY UNITS

Two such units were provided for each LPG train.

Again the process is the same as described under the heading Sulphur Recovery Plant.

5. LPG UNDERGROUND CAVERN STORAGE FACILITY.

A thick layer of salt was discovered near the Kirkuk Gas Processing Plant which presented an ideal opportunity for the creation of salt caverns suitable for the storage of propane and butane produced from the plant.

A salt cavern is created by drilling a well into the salt layer and circulating low salinity water in the hole to dissolve the salt and create a cavity. The resultant brine is forced up from the cavity and sent to a drying pond for evaporation leaving the salt behind. This leaching process is continued until the required size of the cavern is reached. The final cavern usually takes the shape of a pear.

A large diameter casing is installed and cemented to the hole in the ground from the wellhead to the top of the cavern. A second smaller casing is then inserted inside the larger casing and suspended from the wellhead to reach the upper section of the cavern. Finally, a smaller diameter brine pipe is inserted inside the smaller casing and suspended from the wellhead to reach the bottom section of the cavern.

The displacement method is usually the preferred method used in operating the system. Initially, the cavern is full of brine. The product, either propane or butane is pumped between the large and small casings to the top of the cavern to float over the brine and to displace a similar volume of brine to the surface through the suspended brine pipe.

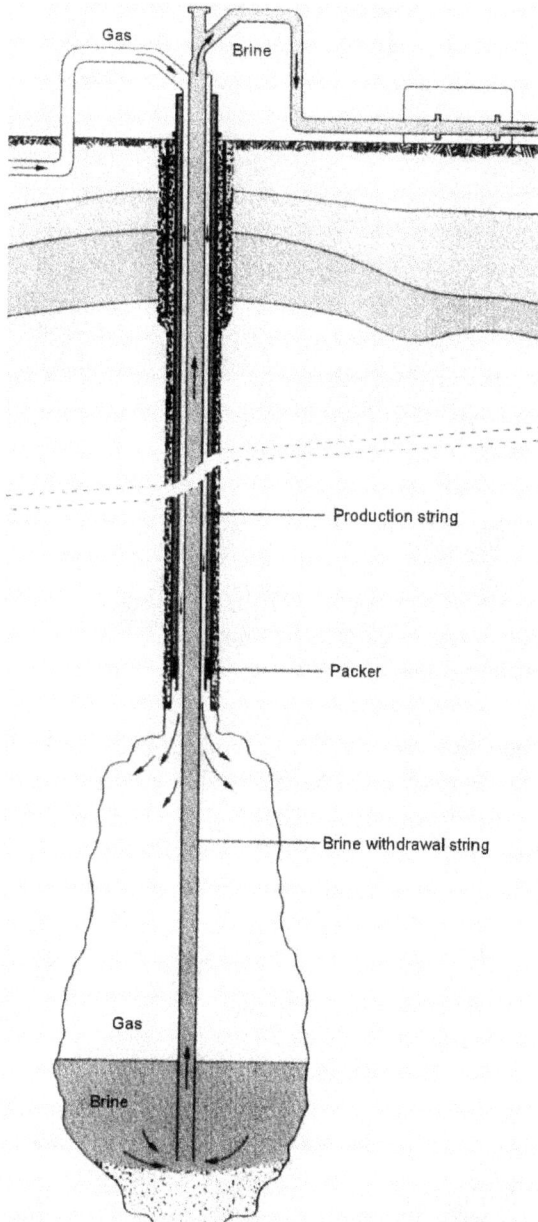

Typical Brine Displacement Salt Cavern.
Similar cavities are used for propane and butane storage at Kirkuk

To extract a product from the cavern the operation is reversed where by brine is injected through the brine pipe into the cavern forcing the product floating above up to the surface through the annulus between the two casings.

The cavern method of storage for crude oil or petroleum products represents one of the most advantageous methods when large volumes are to be stored as well as being both safe and economical.

Originally, five such cavities were created; the volumes of which are approximately (65,000), (61,000), (78,000), (33,000) and (45,000) cubic metres respectively.

A sixth cavity was created at a later date with a volume of around 18,000 cubic metres.

Three of the large cavities are usually used for storing propane with the remaining for butane.

6. SUPPLY OF LPG TO THE OLD KIRKUK BOTTLING PLANT.

An LPG bottling plant had been built earlier on near the old Sulphur plant to provide the local market of Kirkuk and the surrounding region with their requirement of LPG.

Subsequent to the shutdown of the old Sulphur Plant and the completion of the North Gas Project, this plant began to draw its requirement of LPG from the underground storage caverns.

7. LPG PUMPING TO BAGHDAD

Since only a certain proportion of the LPG produced is utilised for the local Kirkuk region, the remaining quantity is pumped to the Taji complex through the existing 8 inch diameter pipeline ex Sulphur Plant.

8. NATURAL GAS PIPELINE DISTRIBUTION SYSTEM

Most of the dry Natural Gas which is produced at the North Gas Complex is sent to the Taji Gas Complex north of Baghdad through the existing 16 inch diameter pipeline ex Sulphur Plant. Other quantities are sent north to Mosul's industrial consumers and further afield to the Badoosh cement factory west of Mosul. While other quantities are sent to the phosphate mines at Okashat west of the river Euphrates with the remaining quantities being supplied to the local industrial consumers in the Kirkuk region.

The other product from the North Gas Complex being condensate (natural gasoline) which is usually blended with other locally produced gasoline for the local market, or otherwise it is either returned back for blending with the export crude oil or injected back into the reservoir.

The South Gas Complex

To utilise the huge quantities of associated gases from the southern oil fields namely Rumaila North, Rumaila South and West Qurnah for the production of natural gas, Natural Gas Liquid, NGL, Liquid Petroleum Gas, LPG and condensates it was decided to construct the South Gas Complex which has a design capacity of 1.55 billion standard cubic feet per day.

The construction work started in 1979 and the project was scheduled for completion in 1983. It was possible for the project to be completed only after a few months delay, in late 1983 in spite of the ongoing Iraq/Iran war.

However the commissioning of the project was postponed due to its proximity to the war zone until 1988. It continued in operation, only to be shutdown during the Gulf War. The following facilities finally returned to continuous operation in 1992.

1. RUMAILA NORTH GAS GATHERING

Rumaila North field has five degassing stations No. 1,2,3,4 and 5. Each degassing station has three stages of gas/oil separation system. The medium pressure gas from the second stage and the low pressure gas from the third stage are compressed to a common pressure equal to that of the first stage gas and then combined with it before being sent to the nearby Rumaila North Gas Processing Plant.

The total quantity of the first stage gas is 440 million standard cubic feet per day; MMSCF/D, while the combined quantity of gas from the second and third stages equal 240MMSCF/D, bringing the combined quantity of gas from this field to a total of 680 MMSCF/D.

2. WEST QURNAH GAS GATHERING

Associated gases are gathered from two of the West Qurnah degassing stations before being compressed, combined and sent through a 40 inch diameter and 50 km long pipeline to the Rumaila North Gas Processing Plant.

The total combined quantity of associated gases from these two degassing stations is 209 million standard cubic feet per day.

3. RUMAILA NORTH GAS PROCESSING PLANT

The incoming gases from the Rumaila North and the West Qurnah fields are combined at the North Rumails Gas Processing Plant. They then have their remaining condensates removed by the slug catchers, Compressed to a higher pressure, dehydrated, sweetened, demethanized and deethanized.

The produced dry natural gas is then fed to the 24 inch diameter Inter –Iraq dry gas pipeline and the 16 inch diameter Strategic dry gas pipeline which runs in parallel with the strategic crude oil pipeline between the Rumaila North Gas processing Plant and K-3 pumping station near Haditha on the river Euphrates.

Meanwile the remaining Natural Gas Liquids of 6,455 ton per day is pumped through a 10 inch diameter and 52 kilometres long pipeline to the Khore al-Zubair Central Gas Processing Plant.

4. RUMAILA SOUTH GAS GATHERING

Rumaila South field has four degassing stations, Gurainat, Shamyah, Central and Janubiah. Each degassing station has three stages of gas/oil separation system similar to that of the Rumaila North field. The gases from these four degassing stations are compressed to a common pressure and combined together before being sent through 48 inch diameter and 35 km long pipeline to the Central Khore al-Zubair Gas Processing Plant.

The total combined quantity of gas from these degassing stations is 700 million standard cubic feet per day.

5. KHORE AL-ZUBAIR CENTRAL GAS PROCESSING PLANT

As we have seen the associated gas from the South Rumaila field and the Natural Gas Liquids from the Rumala North gas processing plant are delivered to Khore al-Zubair Central Gas Processing Plant for their final processing.

This Plant has two trains of Natural Gas Liquid, LNG and three trains of Liquid Petroleum Gas,LPG. The end products from this plant are:-

a. Natural Gas which is fed through two main trunk pipelines:-

The first pipeline of 24 inch diameter and 52 km long feeds four separate branch pipelines to the Hartha power plant, Quarmat WTP, Hamr paper mill and Najibya power plant.

The second pipeline 30 inch diameter and approximately 5.6 km in length, feeds three separate branch pipelines to Khore al-Zubair steel mill, power plant and fertiliser plant.

b. 7,700 tons per day of propane are delivered through a 12 inch diameter pipeline to the refrigerated propane export tanks at Khore al-Zubair tank farm..

c. 5,500 tons per day of butane are delivered through an 8 inch diameter pipeline to the refrigerated butane export tanks at Khore al-Zubair tank farm.

d. 5,400 tons per day of gasoline are delivered through an 8 inch diameter pipeline to the gasoline export tanks at Khore al-Zubair tank farm.

e. Propane, butane and gasoline from this tank farm could also be delivered to other parts of Iraq through the national 14 inch diameter Zubair-Baghdad- Kirkuk products pipeline.

Basra-Baghdad-Kirkuk LPG Pipeline

As we have seen the main centres of LPG production are in Basra and Kirkuk while Baghdad was the main market for the LPG.

As a result it was decided to construct the 14 inch diameter Basra-Baghdad-Kirkuk pipeline to facilitate the revisable pumping and transport of LPG between these three centres. The pipeline also had the additional benefit of supplying the cities and towns along its route with their requirement of LPG.

Iraq-Kuwait Gas Pipeline

It is of interest to record that associated gas from the Rumaila field was exported to Kuwait between 1986 and the Gulf War, through a pipeline 12 inch in diameter and 100 km in length with a capacity of 250 million standard cubic feet per day. The gas was used in Kuwait for power generation and the production of Liquid Petroleum Gas, LPC.

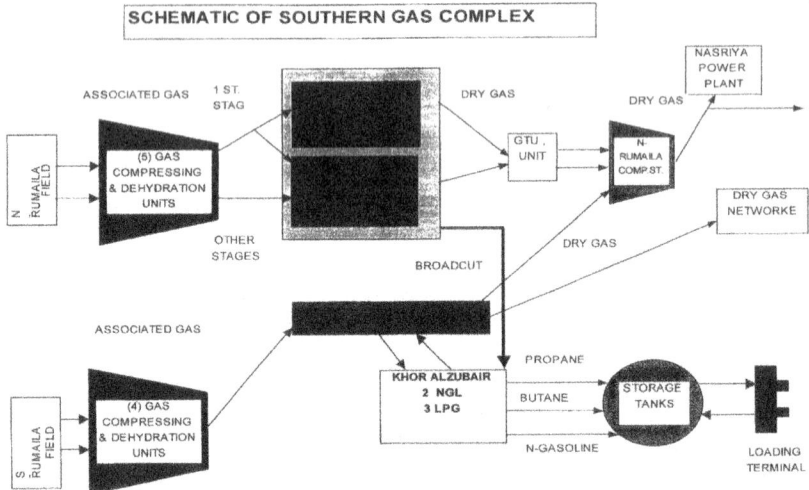

Schematic of Southern Gas Complex

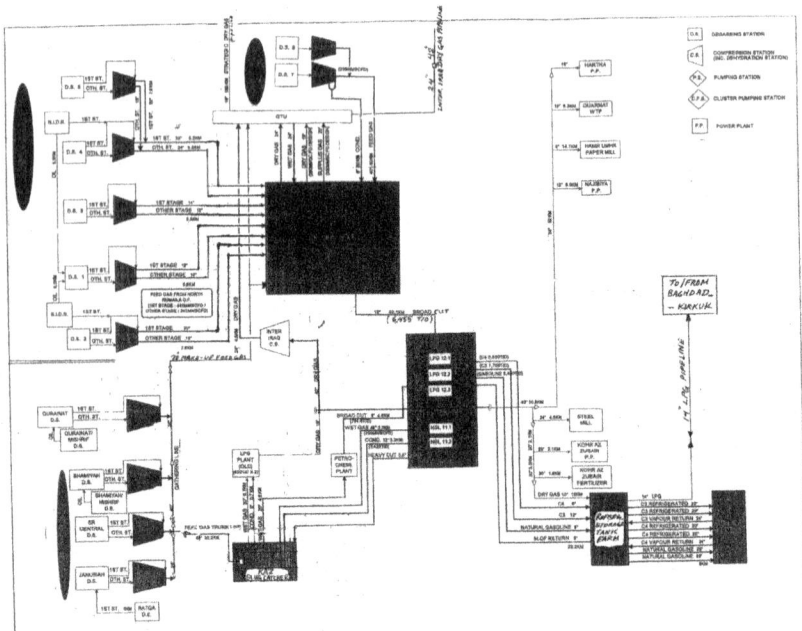

South Gas Project Infrastructure

Fertilizer Plant-Khore al-Zubair

12

IRAQ'S OIL REFINERIES

Crude oil seeping out of underground reservoirs has been collected and used for thousands of years. Petroleum is a complex mixture of hydrocarbons and attempts had been made to extract kerosene from it for lighting since early history. It was distilled in the 9th century AD by the well-known Persian chemist and physician Mohammad Al Razi to produce kerosene in a retort called Alembic (Persian Al Ambiq), which was used in kerosene lamps. It was through the Arabic and Islamic golden civilisation in Spain that the distillation of petroleum became available to Western Europe in the 12th century AD.

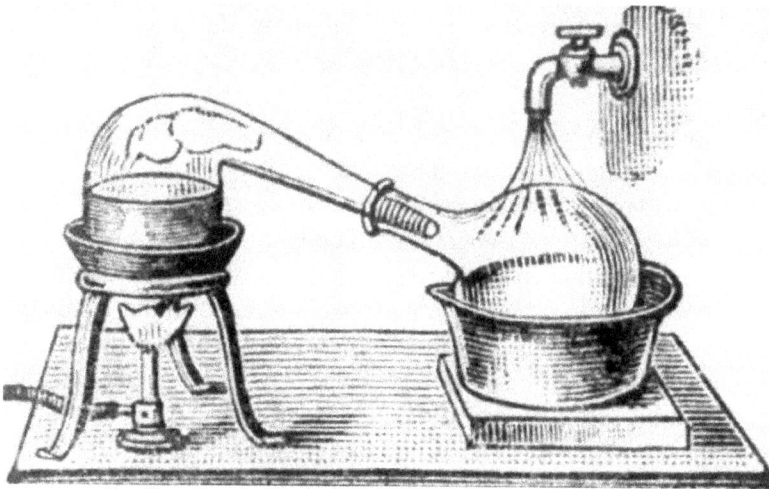

Simple Retort

The process was used on a very limited scale until the early nineteenth century. It was not until the 1840s that serious attempts were made to make use of the distillation process to extract kerosene from crude oil for lighting to replace the popular whale oil which had become less abundant.

The early distillation process was based on the principle of separation by evaporation. The temperature of the crude oil is raised gradually to evaporate the required constituents of the oil before condensing them into liquid again.

449

The original stills for distillation of crude oil were little more than scaled-up version of the traditional retort. They were simple vertical cylindrical steel pots in which the crude oil is heated to the required temperature. The vapour is collected from the top through a metal pipe which is curved over to connect with a condenser consisting of a coil of pipe passing through a tank of running cold water. The distillates are then collected in a tank as a final product. When as much distillates as possible had been collected, the fire was cut off, the residue discarded and the still recharged. These stills had a small capacity of some 20 to 40 gallons of oil.

Later versions of the 1850s and 1860s were made of horizontal steel piping employing the same principle of operation but with a larger capacity of some 100 to 200 gallons of crude oil.

By the 1870s, the same principle, , was being employed on a much larger scale with stills being made from sheets of boiler plate in the form of a horizontal cylinder with a capacity of several hundred barrels. The still was supported on a brick structure and heated from underneath by flue gases from a furnace at the one end.

In 1883, this system was developed further by adapting it to operate on oil supplied in a continuous stream, rather than batch by batch. The new system comprised a battery of horizontal cylindrical stills, each separately heated and provided with its own condenser system. The cylinders are connected in series and were heated so that each successive cylinder was higher in temperature than the previous one. The connections were arranged so that oil could pass in succession along the line of stills, from the coolest to the hottest cylinder, and by locating each cylinder slightly lower than the previous one this flow was achieved by gravity. Thus at the coolest still, the most volatile fraction was evaporated off, condensed and collected, and the residue from this still flowed to the next hotter cylinder, where a distillate of higher specific gravity was collected, and so on, to the last still, from which the residual such as fuel oil was withdrawn. The arrangement of this system is shown in the diagram below. This system continued in operation until the early twentieth century and was actually used in the Ababan refinery which came on stream in 1912.

Later modern refineries were based on the principle of fractionation. The crude oil is pumped through coils of pipe inside a furnace where it is heated to a predetermined temperature and vaporised, the vapour then passing into a tall fractionation column where, as they ascend, they pass through a succession of perforated trays or platforms and are brought into intimate contact with condensed liquid trickling downwards from higher up the column. By tapping off liquid from appropriate trays up the column, closely cut fractions, of gasoline, kerosene, gas oil etc, can then be collected. Modern refineries these days can have enormous capacity of hundreds of thousands of barrels of crude oil per day.

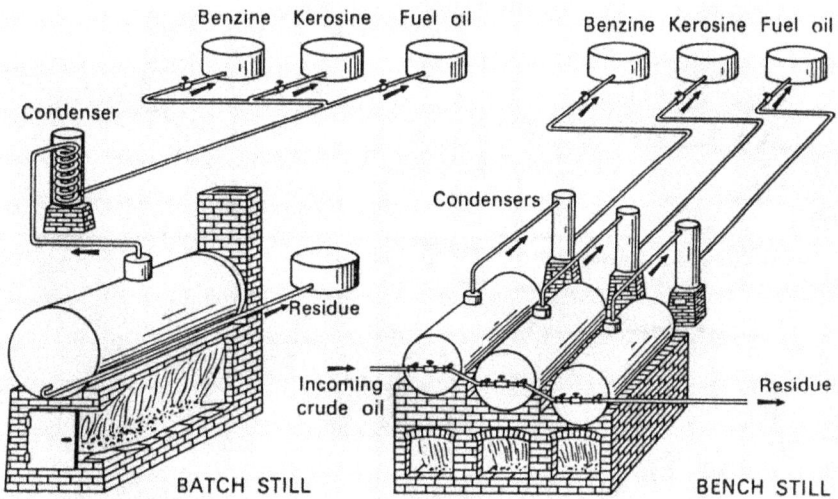

Batch and bench still c. 1912

Source: After Kendall Beaton, *Enterprise in Oil. A History of Shell in the United States* (New York, 1957), p. 86.

Early bench stills, Abadan 1913

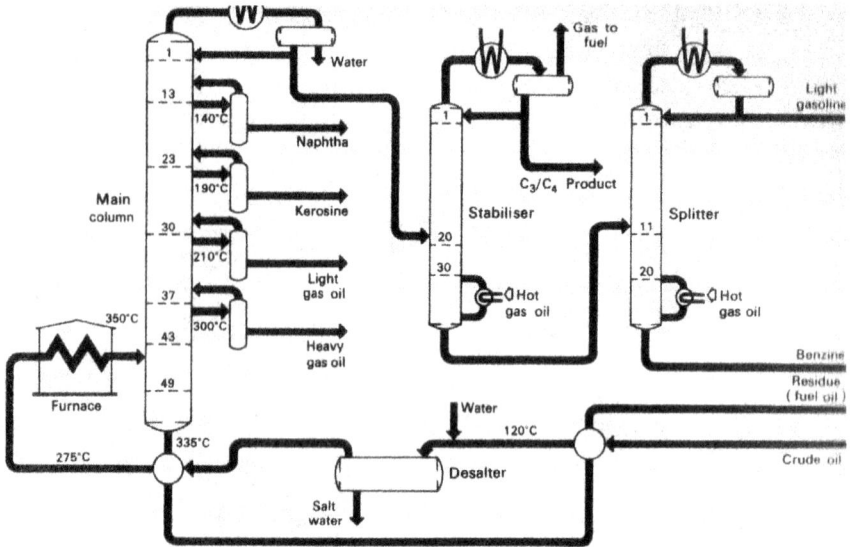

Crude oil distillation

Source: *Our Industry Petroleum* (British Petroleum Company Ltd, 1977), p. 231

Iraq's oil refinery industry did not start until after the country's independence and the discovery of oil in the Naftkhanah oilfield in 1923 which facilitated the construction of its first refinery, Al-Wand, in the Khaniqin region in 1927. This refinery was only able to satisfy part of the country's requirement of petroleum products and it was not until 1955 when the Daura refinery was commissioned when Iraq became self sufficient in petroleum products. Many more much larger capacity refineries were subsequently commissioned as described below.

Qaiyarah Refinery

Heavy oil with asphalt has been seeping to the surface of the ground in the Qaiyarah region from time immemorial and was known to have been used by the Sumerians, in the south of Iraq over five thousand years ago.

The Qaiyarah oil was first produced on a fairly small scale by the Germans in 1908 and then by the British during the First World War. The oil is very heavy with an API, (American Petroleum Institute) gravity ranging from 11-19 degrees, very viscous, highly sulphurous and with an asphaltene content of some 60% by weight.

The early production from this field had been intermittent depending on demand at a rate of some 2,000 barrels per day which was delivered to a small local and simple refinery specifically designed for the production of asphalt.

A more modern refinery was constructed and commissioned in 1956. It had a capacity of some 4,000 barrels of oil per day and an asphalt production rate of 60,000 tons per year. This refinery was shutdown in 1958 for a period of five years as the Daura refinery increased its production of asphalt. However it returned to operation again in 1963 with a large proportion of its asphalt being exported in 33 gallon capacity drums. Instances of such contracts was the one signed in February 1968 with Turkey for the export of Naphtha and fuel oil and another one with Sri Lanka in 1969 for the export of 40,000 tons of asphalt.

However due to the greater demand for asphalt during the late 1970s, a new degassing station was constructed in the 1980s and the production rate from Qaiyarah and the other three fields in the region namely Jawan, Najmah and Qasab was increased to 14,000 barrels per day.

Al-Wand Refinery

The Anglo-Persian Oil Company, which was drilling in the Khaniqin region near the Persian borders, struck oil in May 1923 and the well caught fire and burnt for a week before being brought under control. This oilfield was named Naftkhanah and though it proved to be small, it extended inside Persia and the field there was called Nafti-Shah.

Negotiations followed between the Iraqi Government and the Anglo-Persian Oil Company over the manner of exploiting the Naftkhanah field and an agreement was reached to construct a small refinery near the town of Khaniqin. The refinery was called Al-Wand, and came on stream in February 1927, taking its crude oil feed from the Naftkhanah field.

The Anglo-Persian Oil Company had in anticipation established the Khaniqin Oil Company (KOC) in November 1925 to take over the ownership and operation of the Naftkhanah field and Al-Wand refinery. The KOC then established a subsidiary company by the name of the Rafidain Oil Company which became the main distributor of its petroleum products from Al-Wand refinery in Northern Iraq. It also became the main importer and distributor of additional petroleum products requirement throughout the rest of the country.

It was estimated that by 1932 Al-Wand refinery was refining slightly less than 2,000 barrels per day. This was producing some 22,700,000 gallons of petroleum products per year. The refined products were approximately 55% fuel oil, 17% Kerosene, 12% Benzene, 5% semi-refined, 8% others and 3% losses.

The 17% kerosene, which is equivalent to some 3.9 million gallons per year, was mainly used for lighting and some cooking and was satisfying the needs of nearly 70% (2.55 million people) of Iraq's population, which was estimated at that time at about 3.5 million. This meant that the consumption of kerosene at that time was approximately 1.58 gallons per capita per year, a far cry from the astronomical consumption of the present days.

An agreement was signed in 1951 between the Iraqi government and the Khaniqin Oil Company by which the government purchased Al-Wand refinery and the Rafidain Oil Company's distribution network. However a ten year service contract was signed with the KOC for the operation of the refinery and the products distribution network. The agreement also extended the oil concession of the KOC on the condition that KOC would raise the production capacity from the Naftkhana field and the other small promising structures in that region namely Chia Sarkh, Pika and Buqcha to two million tons per year within a period of seven years.

KOC was unable to abide by the terms of the new concession in producing the two million tons of oil per year and as a result the Naftkhanah field was taken over by the government in December 1958.

Soon after, on the first of July 1959, it was decided to terminate the operation and marketing service contract with KOC as well and as a result the whole oil operations in the Naftkhanah field and Al-Wand refinery were taken over by the Iraqi Administration for Refineries.

It is of interest to record that after the commissioning of the Daura refinery in July 1955, its production of Benzene was enough to satisfy Iraq's requirement and subsequently the quantities of Benzene produced from the Al-Wand refinery became surplus and as a result were injected back in the Naftkhanah field. It is estimated that about one million barrels of such surplus Benzene was injected during the period mid 1955 to the end of 1960.

The capacity of Al-Wand refinery was increased over the decades to reach 12,000 barrels of crude oil per day in the late 1970s. Unfortunately it was bombed just before the start of Iraq-Iran war in July 1980 only to be heavily bombed again at the beginning of the war in September, which rendered it damaged beyond repair and as a result it was abandoned. Since then the refinery had been cannibalised for spare parts.

Haditha Refinery

Two simple refineries (topping Plants) were constructed during the 1930s by the Iraq Petroleum Company, IPC, one in Kirkuk at the main Process Plant and the other at K-3 pump station near the town of Haditha, west of the River Euphrates. They were both of small capacity and designed to supply the IPC's large fleet of vehicles with fuel as well as the hundreds of diesel engines used in the production, processing and pumping of its vast oil operations.

The K-3 refinery which was constructed in 1938 became redundant after the replacement of the diesel pump sets at the IPC's Mediterranean pipeline pump stations by gas turbine driven pump sets and was subsequently handed over to the Iraqi Organisation for Refineries in 1965.

The capacity of this refinery was increased at a later date to 16,000 barrels per day and its products were then utilised to satisfy the needs of the small towns and villages in the region.

Kirkuk Refinery

The old IPC refinery at the Process Plant which was constructed in the 1930s continued to supply, albeit, low quality fuel for the company's large fleet of vehicles and diesel engines used in the production, processing and pumping of its vast oil operations.

With time the refinery had become obsolete and very costly to maintain and as a result it was decided to replace it in the mid 1970s by a modern 20,000 barrels per day capacity refinery.

However, due to the great expansion of the city of Kirkuk and the other towns and villages in that region, the capacity of this refinery was expanded later on to 30,000 barrels per day.

Al-Moftiya Refinery

Al-Wand refinery as we have seen was barely capable of producing enough petroleum products to satisfy the needs of northern Iraq while the south of Iraq was supplied by importing products mainly from Abadan refinery which was owned by the same company that owns Al-Wand refinery i.e. the Anglo Persian Oil Company.

As a result of the increase in demand for petroleum products in Iraq in general after the end of the Second World War, and in view of the availability of new crude oil in southern Iraq from the newly discovered and developed Zubair oil field, it was decided to construct a new refinery in the Basra region by the name of Al-Moftiya.

A pipeline of some 31 kilometres in length and six inch in diameter was constructed between the Zubair oil field and the Moftiya refinery to supply it with the necessary crude oil of 4,000 barrels per day.

The refinery itself was simple and had two units each having a capacity of 2,000 barrels of oil per day. The refinery was completed in 1953 and was able to satisfy a large percentage of southern Iraq's needs of basic petroleum products until mid 1955 when it was made redundant as a result of the commissioning of the Daura refinery. The refinery was subsequently cannibalised for spare parts.

Al-Daura Refinery

As we have seen, Al-Wand refinery which was purchased by the Iraqi government in 1951 from Khaniqin Oil Company was able to satisfy part of the country's increasing consumption of petroleum products. The remaining part was being imported mainly from the Iranian Abadan refinery. This arrangement was considered as unsatisfactory for the following reasons:-

1. Iraq had plenty of crude oil which could easily be refined to satisfy its entire internal requirement of petroleum products.

2. The pricing policy for such vital commodity will be within the control of the Iraqi government and not subject to the international market forces.

3. The import of a large proportion of the country's petroleum products requirement was costing the treasury a lot of hard currency which could be utilised for the construction of vital projects including an oil refinery.

4. It had been considered for a long time as very unwise and risky to keep the country dependent for its vital petroleum products on foreign imports which may be cut or become unavailable for any reason.

    This point of view was greatly strengthened by the oil embargo which was imposed on the export of crude oil and petroleum products from Iran consequent to the nationalisation of Iran's oil industry by Mossadiq in 1951 which deprived Iraq of its cheaper imports of products from Abadan refinery..

As a result, it was decided in 1952 to establish the Iraqi Administration for Refineries to supervise the operations of the Naftkhanah oil field and Al-Wand refinery which were being operated under contract by KOC.

Soon after, a decision was made to construct a new refinery at Daura south of Baghdad. The construction work was started in March 1953 and the refinery was completed and commissioned in June 1955. It was subsequently inaugurated by the late young King Faisal the Second on 28th November 1955.

A new pipeline 215 kilometres in length and 12 inch in diameter was also constructed between the Iraq Petroleum Company pump station of K-2 near the town of Baiji and Daura to supply the new refinery with its feed of crude oil.

The refinery initially had one distillation unit with a capacity of 24,000 barrels of crude oil per day. This unit was expanded soon after in 1956 to 31,000 barrels per day.

A second distillation unit with a capacity of 24,000 barrels per day was added in 1959, which brought the total capacity of the refinery to 55,000 barrels per day

However the capacity of the first unit was increased yet again in mid 1967 to 51,000 barrels per day bringing the total capacity of the refinery to 75,000 barrels per day.

No lubricating oils were produced from the new Daura refinery and as a result of the increasing demand for such oils; a lubrication oils unit with a capacity of 24,000 tons per year was added to the refinery and subsequently opened on first October 1957

A second Lube oils unit with a capacity of 36,000 tons per year was added and was officially opened on 23rd June 1968. This brought the total Lube Oils capacity to 60,000 tons per year which exceeded the needs of the local market and as a result some of the surplus lube oils were exported to Jordan in 1969.

صورة عامة لوحدات الزيوت الثقيلة فى مصفى السـدورة

Daura Refinery

Courtesy Mishal Hammodat

However increasing local market demand in the 1970s necessitated the construction of a third Lube Oils unit with a capacity of 50,000 tons per year. This unit was officially opened on 7th July 1978 bringing the total Lube Oils production capacity to 110,000 tons per year.

A new pipeline 138 kilometres in length and 12 inch in diameter was constructed and commissioned in 1963 between the Naftkhanah oil field and Daura refinery. The pipeline was utilised to supply the Daura refinery with crude oil from the Naftkhanah field which is in excess of the requirement of the Al- Wand refinery as well as the delivery of any surplus quantities of fuel oil from the Al-Wand refinery to Daura.

The capacity of the refinery was expanded further to reach 82,000 barrels per day by 1983. This was increased yet again in 1996 to almost 130,000 barrels per day. However due to a lack of spare parts its actual capacity was limited to 110,000 barrels per day

Basra Refinery

The consumption of petroleum products in the country increased greatly in the late 1960s and early 1970s and as a result it was decided to construct the Basra refinery which was completed in 1974. It had an initial capacity of 70,000 barrels of oil per day. The demand continued to increase dramatically and as a result it was decided to double the capacity of this refinery soon after to 140,000 barrels per day. This expansion was completed in 1978.

It was also decided in 1982 to expand the refinery by adding Lube oil facilities with a capacity of 100,000 tons per year.

Salahuddin Refinery

The demand for the petroleum products in central and northern Iraq was just as dramatic and it was decided to construct the Salahuddin refinery near the town of Baiji on the western bank of the River Tigris. The location is about half way between Baghdad and Mosul and not too far from many of the towns in that region. It is also in the vicinity of the main Mediterranean export pipelines which would conveniently feed it with its crude oil requirements.

This refinery which had an initial capacity of 70,000 barrels of oil per day was completed in the mid 1970s only to be expanded soon after to double its capacity, to 140,000 barrels per day.

Al-Shimal (North) Refinery

This refinery which had a capacity of 70,000 barrels per day was constructed next door to Salahuddin refinery in the late 1970s, only to be expanded soon after to more than double its capacity, 155,000 barrels per day. This second stage expansion was completed during the Iraq-Iran war and was officially opened at the end of March 1983.

The huge Lube oil complex which was added to Salahuddin and Al-Shimal refineries from 1986 onwards has a capacity of some 250,000 tons per year.

A large proportion of the petrol and gasoil from the Salahuddin and Al-Shimal refineries were exported during the Iraq/Iran war by road tankers to Turkey and Jordan. There were surplus quantities of fuel oil which could not be sold and were subsequently returned back to Kirkuk to be injected into the reservoir of the Kirkuk field.

Samawa Refinery

This, 20,000 barrels per day refinery was constructed and commissioned in the early 1980s to satisfy the needs of basic petroleum products of the town of Samawa and the region around it.

Nassiriyah Refinery

This, 30,000 barrels per day refinery was constructed and commissioned in the early 1980s to satisfy the needs of the basic petroleum products of the city of Nassiriyah and the region around it. A reversible pipeline, 298 kilometres in length and 8 inch in diameter was constructed in 1979 between this refinery and the Petroleum Products Depot at the city of Kut on the River Tigris which afforded the necessary flexibility in marketing.

Seniyah Refinery

This, 30,000 barrels per day refinery was constructed to satisfy the needs of the basic petroleum products of the town of Seniyah on the upper reaches of the river Euphrates and the region around it.

Kisik Refinery

This, 10,000 barrels per day refinery was constructed to satisfy the needs of the basic petroleum products of the town of Kisik and the towns and villages around it in the Jezeera region west of the city of Mosul.

Iraq's Refining Capacity

It is estimated that the refining capacities of the country by the end of the twentieth century were as follows:-

	Refinery	Capacity/barrels of oil per day
1	Qaiyara	14,000
2	Wand	Abandoned and cannibalised
3	Haditha	16,000
4	Kirkuk	30,000
5	Moftiya	Abandoned and cannibalised
6	Daura	110,000
7	Basrah	140,000
8	Salahuddin	140,000
9	Shimal	155,000
10	Samawa	20,000
11	Nassiriya	30,000
12	Seniya	30,000
13	Kisik	10,000
	Total	**695,000**

Proposed New Refineries- 2011

It has been reported very recently that two contracts have been awarded for the construction of the following two refineries:

1. KARBALA REFINERY

The design capacity of this refinery is 140,000 barrels per day.

The contract was awarded to a consortium of the Italian company Saipem and an Iraqi company.

2. MOSUL REFINERY

The design capacity of this refinery is 150,000 barrels per day.

The contract was awarded to the Egyptian company Qalaa.

The crude oil for this refinery is to be supplied from the not far away Qaiyara and Najmah oilfields south of Mosul.

Petroleum Product Pipelines

The transportation of Petroleum Refined Products was originally made by road, railway and river tankers. However, as the quantities of these products increased with time it became more economical to transport them by pipelines.

As a result numerous pipelines were constructed over the years with some of the major ones being listed hereunder.

NAFTKHANAH FIELD/DAURA REFINERY PIPELINE

A pipeline, 220 kilometres in length and 12 inch in diameter was constructed and commissioned in 1963 between the Naftkhanah oil field/Al-Wand refinery and Daura refinery. The pipeline was utilised to supply the Daura refinery with crude oil from the Naftkhana field which is in excess of the requirement of the Al-Wand refinery. It was also utilised for the delivery by batching of any surplus quantities of fuel oil from the Al wand refinery to Daura.

DAURA REFINERY/BASRA REFINERY PIPELINE

This pipeline of 545 kilometres in length and 10 inch diameter was constructed between the Daura and Basra refineries. It was designed to transport four types of petroleum products by batching between these refineries as well as feeding some of the cities along its route with their requirement of such products especially the main depot at the city of Kut . The pipeline was officially opened at the end of March 1977.

KUT DEPOT/NASIRIYA REFINERY PIPELINE

This reversible pipeline of 298 kilometres in length and 8 inch in diameter was constructed in 1979 between the Petroleum Products Depot at the city of Kut on the River Tigris and the Nasiriya refinery on the River Euphrates. It is designed to transport three types of petroleum products at the same time by batching in either direction depending on the actual local and seasonal requirements.

SALAHUDDIN-SHIMAL REFINERIES COMPLEX (BAIJI)/HAMAM AL-ALEEL, KIRKUK, MASHAHDA AND AL-QAIM DEPOTS

Four pipelines were constructed from these two refineries at Baiji to supply petroleum products to different regions.

The first pipeline is 153 kilometres in length and 16 inch in diameter to supply the depot at Hammam al-Aleel south of Mosul.

The second is 139 kilometres in length and 12 inch in diameter to supply the depot at Kirkuk.

The third is 177 kilometres in length and 8 inch in diameter to supply the depot at Mashahda near Baghdad.

The fourth is 387 kilometers in length and 16 inch in diameter to supply the depot at Al-Qaim near the Syrian borders.

OTHER PRODUCT PIPELINES

The above pipelines are just a few of the tens of other products pipelines traversing across the length and width of the country.

A summary of all such pipelines is show in the following table.

Petroleum Product Pipelines

	Between	Length (Km)	Diameter (Inches)
1	Baiji - Hammam Alil	153	16
2	Baiji – Kirkuk	139	12
3	Baiji – Mashahdah	177	22
4	Baiji – Mashahda	177	8
5	Baiji – T1	387	16
6	Basrah refinery - Hartha power station		
7	Daura – Baghdad airport	45	8
8	Daura – Rusafa	8	10
9	Daura Refinery - Baghdad power Plant	8	6
10	Daura Refinery - Basra Refinery	545	10
11	Daura Refinery - Cement factory	5	6
12	Daura Refinery - Latifiya Depot		
13	Hammam Alil – Filfel	104	32
14	Karkh – Habania	250	12 / 16
15	Khore al-Zubair – Shuaibah	72	8/10
16	Khore al-Zubair – Shuaibah	75	8/10
17	Mashahdah – Khan Bani Saad Depot	177	12
18	Mashahdah – Rusafa	83	12
19	Naftkhana Field - Daura Refinery	220	12
20	Nasiryah – Daura		10/14
21	Nasiryah – Kut	298	8
22	Nassiriya Refinery - Nassiriya Power plant		
23	North Gas – Salahul Din Refinery	137	8
24	Rusafa – Dialah	40	8
25	Shuaibah – Muftiah	33	10
26	Shuaibah – Muftiah	33	6
27	Shuaibah – Muftiah	33	8
28	Shuaibah – Nasiryah	259	14
29	Taji Plant - Daura Refinery		
30	Wand Refinery - Khaniqin Depot	8	4

13

IRAQ'S OIL PRODUCTION DURING THE TWENTIETH CENTURY

Year	Daily Average 1,000 Barrels	Total Annual 1,000 Barrels	Comments
1923-33	14.8	5,411	
1934	21.1	7,689	
1935	75.1	27,408	
1936	83.3	30,406	
1937	87.2	31,836	
1938	89.4	32,643	
1939	84.4	30,791	
1940	66.4	24,225	Drop was mainly due to the three months shutdown period of the Tripoli 12 inch pipeline in the early 1940s as a result of the dangers to the commercial shipping lanes in the Mediterranean as well as the five weeks total shutdown in spring 1940 during the events that took place during premiership of Rashid Ali Qailani.
1941	34.7	12,650	Drop is due to shipping restrictions during the War.
1942	54.0	19,726	Ditto
1943	68.1	24,848	Ditto
1944	84.8	30,943	
1945	96.2	35,112	
1946	97.7	35,665	
1947	98.2	35,834	

Year	Daily Average 1,000 Barrels	Total Annual 1,000 Barrels	Comments
1948	71.5	26,115	Drop due to the partial shutdown of the 12 inch to Haifa.
1949	84.8	30,957	
1950	136.2	49,726	Rise due to the commissioning of the 16 inch pipeline to Tripoli.
1951	178.4	65,122	
1952	386.6	141,100	Sudden rise due to the commissioning of the 30/32 inch pipeline to Banias.
1953	576.1	210,268	
1954	625.8	228,432	Rise due to the commissioning of the Zubair and Rumala fields.
1955	688.2	251,206	
1956	636.5	232,307	
1957	447.9	163,498	Drop was due to the destruction of the pumping stations in Syria during the Suez crisis.
1958	729.0	266,102	Rise due to the looping of sections of the 30/32 inch pipeline to Tripoli.
1959	852.9	311,311	Ditto
1960	971.5	354,592	Ditto
1961	1,010.0	368,650	Rise was due to the commissioning of the 30/32 inch pipeline to Tripoli.
1962	1,010.0	368,650	
1963	1,160.0	423,400	
1964	1,260.0	459,900	Risewas due to the expansion of the Zubair and Rumaila fields.
1965	1,320.0	481,800	
1966	1,390.0	507,350	
1967	1,230.0	448,950	Drop was due to the 1967 Arab-Israeli war.
1968	1,500.0	547,500	Rise was due to raising the discharge pressures at the main pump stations of the two 30/32 inch pipelines.

Year	Daily Average 1,000 Barrels	Total Annual 1,000 Barrels	Comments
1969	1,520.0	554,800	Ditto
1970	1,550.0	565,750	Ditto
1971	1,690.0	616,850	Ditto
1972	1,470.0	536,550	Drop was due to the nationalisation of the IPC in June 1972.
1973	2,020.0	737,300	Rise was due to the settlement agreement between the Iraqi government and the IPC.
1974	1,970.0	719,050	Drop was due to the oil embargo after the 1973 Arab-Israeli war.
1975	2,260.0	824,900	Rise was due to the expansion of the BPC production and export facilities to 1.6 million barrels per day.
1976	2,420.0	883,300	Ditto and the commissioning of the strategic pipeline.
1977	2,350.0	857,750	The commissioning of the first Iraq/Turkey pipeline.
1978	2,560.0	934,400	
1979	3,480.0	1,270,200	This was highest ever production rate attained by Iraq as a result of expansion of the capacity of the northern fields to 1.4 million barrels per day, the development of new fields by INOC and the bringing into operation of the Strategic and the Iraq/Turkey pipelines.
1980	2,510.0	916,150	Drop was due to the beginning of the Iraq/Iran war in September 1980.
1981	1,000.0	365,000	Drop was due to the damage and shutdown of the southern fields and the destruction of the two deep water terminals in the Gulf as well as the partial shutdown and reduction in throughput of the northern fields.
1982	1,010.0	368,650	The closure of the whole pipeline system going through Syria in April 1982.
1983	1,010.0	368,650	

Year	Daily Average 1,000 Barrels	Total Annual 1,000 Barrels	Comments
1984	1,210.0	441,650	
1985	1,430.0	521,950	
1986	1,690.0	616,850	Rise was due to the commissioning of the first phase of Iraq trans-Saudi pipeline to Yanbu on the Red Sea.
1987	2,080.0	759,200	Rise due to the commissioning of the second Iraq/Turkey pipeline.
1988	2,690.0	981,850	
1989	2,900.0	1,058,500	
1990	2,040.0	744,600	Drop was due to the first Gulf War and the beginning of the sanctions.
1991	310.0	113,150	No crude oil was exported due to the Sanctions. Production was mainly for the supply of the Iraqi refineries.
1992	430.0	156,950	Ditto
1993	510.0	186,150	Ditto
1994	550.0	200,750	Ditto
1995	560.0	204,400	Ditto
1996	580.0	211,700	Ditto
1997	1,160.0	423,400	Rise was due to the start of the United Nations Oil for Food Programme
1998	2,150.0	784,750	Ditto
1999	2,510.0	916,150	
2000	2,570.0	938,050	
2001	2,390.0	872,350	
2002	2,020.0	737,300	
2003	1,310.0	478,150	Drop was due to the invasion of Iraq.
2004	2,010.0	733,650	Production was limited by the maximum available capacity of the production and export of dilapidated facilities after years of wars and sanctions which had left them in need of spares and proper maintenance.

Year	Daily Average 1,000 Barrels	Total Annual 1,000 Barrels	Comments
2005	1,880.0	686,200	
2006	2,000.0	730,000	
2007	2,090.0	762,850	
2008	2,360.0	861,400	
Grand Total		**31,963,373**	

Iraq's Crude oil Production and Export

We have shown in the table above, Iraq's daily rate of production of crude oils and the annual total quantity of oils produced. So from which fields have these crude oils been produced and where have they been delivered to?

It will be near impossible to find out the countries and the international refineries that have been supplied with such crude oils over the past decades.

Hence, instead we shall take 1965 as an example to show the production of each field, the deliveries to the Iraqi, Syrian and Lebanese refineries and the quantities of crude oils exported from the different terminals as shown in the following table.

Iraq's Crude Oil Production and Export - 1945

Field	Production	Refinery	Deliveries	Terminal	Export
	Long Tons		Long Tons		Long Tons
Kirkuk	41.00				
Bai Hassan	2.30				
Jambur	0.60				
IPC Total	**43.90**				
Ain Zalah	1.00				
Butmah	0.30				
MPC Total	**1.30**				
Rumaila	14.50				
Zubair	3.50				
BPC Total	**18.00**				
Iraq's Total	**63.20**				
		Daura	2.05		
		Muftiyah	0.18		
		Homs	1.00		
		Tripoli	0.74		
		Total	**3.97**		
				Tripoli	15.00
				Banias	26.20
				Khore al-Amayah	17.60
				Fao	0.20
				Awaiting shipment	0.23
				Total	**59.23**

14

HOUSING AND SOCIAL AMENITIES

The City of Kirkuk

It is believed that the present city of Kirkuk stands on the site of an ancient city by the name of Arraphkha which dates back to 5,000 BC. The city attained great prominence during the tenth and eleventh century BC under the Assyrian Empire when it came to be known by the name of (Karkha Beit Slookh), which means the (wall protected or immune town). According to the reliable al-Munjid Arabic Dictionary, it flourished greatly after that under the Sassanid Empire 226 to 651 AD which fell to the Islamic armies.

Though the exact origin of the name Kirkuk seems to be in some doubt, it is believed by most of the reliable sources that the name Kirkuk is a modification from its old Assyrian name (Karkha Beit Slookh).

Kirkuk is famous for its Qal'ah or citadel which was built by the famous Assyrian king Ashurnasirlal II between 884 and 858 BC as a military stronghold. However, during the following centuries the citadel was exposed to numerous attacks and suffered damage and fell in disrepair. It was restored and strengthened by King Sluks who built the enormous walls with their 72 towers around it between 319 and 311 BC. It was in 1555 AD when Kirkuk finally came under the rule of the Ottoman Empire.

The Qal'ah today is the focal point of the modern city of Kirkuk, which had expanded around it beyond recognition since the discovery of oil in 1927. It is located on the eastern bank of Khassah Chai River between the two old bridges.

Khassah Chai is a huge dry wadi during the dry season of the year and only runs during the rainy season from November to April. Even during the rainy season it could be reduced to a trickle when the rain stops for a long duration. On the other hand it could swell and roar full like a great river after heavy rain falls and flash floods from the numerous tributary wadis feeding it. It is useful to explain that Khassah Chai, after leaving the Kirkuk region, is known by the name of the Adhaim River.

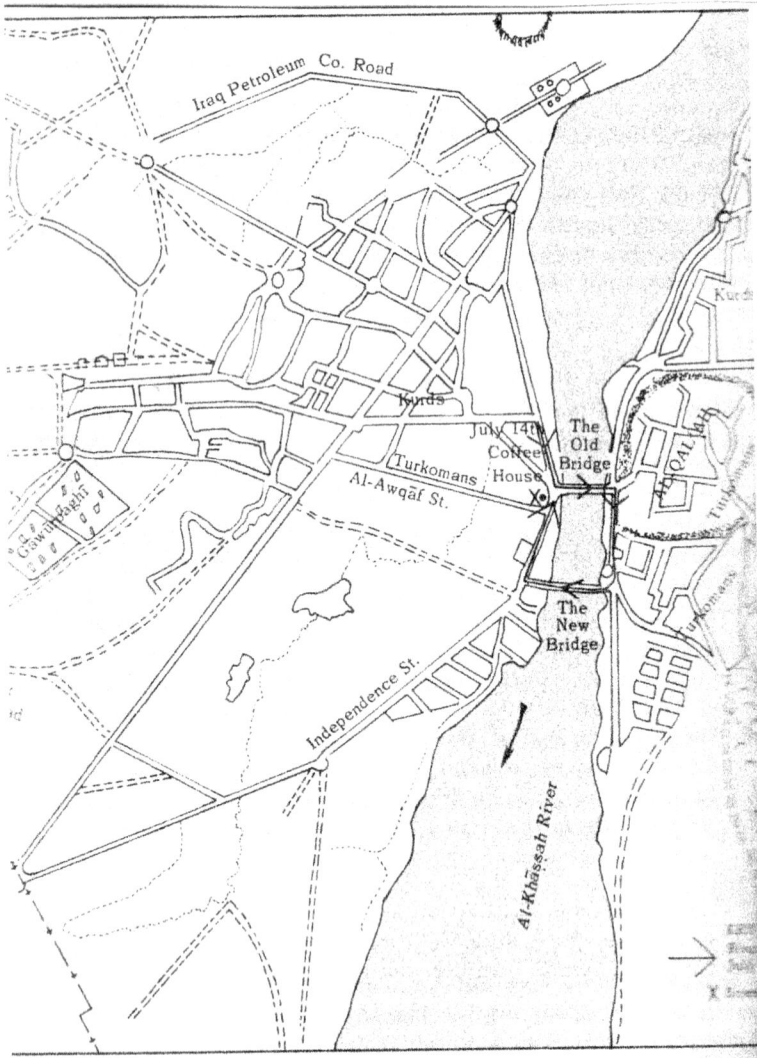

City of Kirkuk

The Qal'ah sits on a mound the top of which is almost 20 metres higher than the surrounding region and has an area of about 25 hectares (approximately 62 acres). The defensive great wall around it is approximate 18 metres high which makes the top of the wall stands some 38 metres above the surrounding plane.

The Qal'ah is divided into three main districts: al- Maidan which is located in the north , al-Qal'ah which is located in the centre and al- Hammam is located in the south and includes the group of mosques and other places of worship.

According to the Director of Antiquities of the Kirkuk province, Ayad Tariq:-

> "The Qal'ah includes many shrines and prominent locations, such as, the Shrine of the Prophet Daniel, Prophet Haneen, and Prophet Uzair. It also includes the Red Church, which is one of the most prominent features of the ancient Qal'ah that is distinguished by the mosaic engraving s on its old walls. It also includes seven mosques amongst which are: the Great mosque, mosque Fuduli, mosque Arian, and the Hassan Backees mosque.
>
> The Qalah is characterised by its unique type of architectures as most of the structures are built with white stones and plaster and its roads are paved with special brickwork called "Farshi".
>
> The Qalah's market became famous from ancient times until present days for what is called (al- Qaisaria), which contains a group of shops and distinguished by its four gates as a metaphor of the four seasons of the year." .

It is of interest also to record that Kirkuk was described in the dictionary of Famous Names, "Qamoos al-Aa'lam", published in Istanbul in 1896, as follows:-

> "Kirkuk is located within the Vilayet of Mosul. It is situated amidst a range of parallel hills next to an extended valley called Adhaim. It is the administrative centre for the Shaharzour Sanjak and had a population of 30,000 inhabitants.
>
> It has a Qal'ah, 36 mosques, 7 schools, 15 Tak'yas, 12 Khans, 1281 shops, 8 public baths, and 3 churches."

Kirkuk and Crude Oil

As we have seen, the name Kirkuk has been associated with Crude Oil and the Eternal Fires for thousands of years. It was therefore not surprising that, after its discovery in 1927, Kirkuk oilfield proved to be one of the giant fields of the world.

Crude oil in the Middle East as well as in many other regions of the world is usually discovered in remote locations far away from inhabited areas. The development of such oilfields requires the skills of geologists, drillers, engineers, administrators, technicians, artisans as well as a large labour force that may not be readily available in the locality and as a result need to be recruited from other far away native towns and cities as well as other countries.

The Qal'ah - Kirkuk

The Old Bridge on the Khassah Chai River with the Qal'ah in the Background-1932

Courtesy of IPC Society Newsletters

Hence it was necessary during the pre-air-travel era to establish residential compounds, if not a small town to accommodate the hundreds if not thousands of such employees in bachelor quarters as well as in married accommodation.

The size of such compounds, villages and towns depended on the size of the operations of the company concerned which could result in sizable towns such as Dhahran in Saudi Arabia.

Though the Kirkuk oilfield is located quite close to the city of Kirkuk and the nearby towns and villages, most of the labour force required by the Iraq Petroleum Company for its vast oil operations was not readily available in the region. Certain skilled labour and artisan were recruited from other cities and towns such as Baghdad, Mosul and Habaniyah. However most of the professional personnel and highly specialised drillers, engineers, technicians etc. had to be recruited from other countries especially the United Kingdom and the United States of America.

The Development of The IPC Housing and Social Amenities

Some of the early recruits had to be settled in temporary accommodation for short durations until permanent accommodation could be provided for them.

The city of Kirkuk during the late 1920s and 1930s could only cater for the accommodation of a small proportion of the large influx of Iraqi and expatriate employees and as a result it was necessary for the IPC to embark on an ambitious programme for the construction of offices and housing estates.

The land between the city of Kirkuk and the centre of oil operations at the Baba Industrial Area which included the Process Plant, some of the degassing stations, workshops, stores, etc was conveniently selected for the IPC's offices and housing requirement.

The area on the north-western boundaries of the city was given the ancient name Arrapha, and was subsequently acquired for the company's headquarters, engineering main offices, finance offices, central administration etc. A large plot of it was also reserved for what came to be known as Arrapha Staff Residential Area and a much larger plot was reserved for the Employee Housing Estate and shops.

Two other staff residential areas by the name Baba East and Baba West were also included in the building programme. Further offices and accommodation quarters were also needed at the Lesser Zab River region, K-1, K-2, K-3 and T-1 pump stations as well as Ain Zalah.

All this was not enough to cater for the large number of staff and employees and hence it was decided in 1953 to adopt the Home Ownership Scheme which resulted in the construction of thousands more homes for the Iraqi staff and employees as will be described later on.

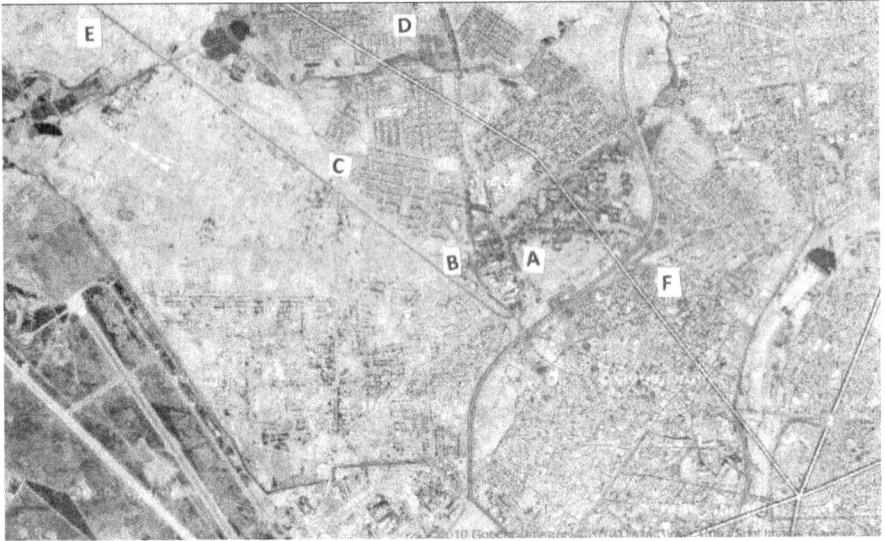

IPC Offices & Housing Estates-Arrapha

Courtesy of Google Earth

The areas marked on the map are as follow:-

A. Arrapha staff Residential Area.

B. IPC Headquarters and Main Offices.

C. Employees Housing Estate and shops.

D. 2,000 Houses Estate.

E. Road to Baba Industrial and Residential Areas.

F. Almas Quarter, mainly IPC Home Ownership Scheme Houses.

ARRAPHA STAFF RESIDENTIAL AREA

The houses in this compound were to cater for accommodation for the senior IPC personnel working in the nearby offices including the General Manager, the divisional managers, some of the heads of departments and other senior staff.

The construction works were started during the 1930s and by end of the decade many such houses were in occupation. The construction of further houses was completed after the Second World War and the early 1950s when the final number of houses reached 42. These early houses had very thick walls and high ceilings to provide insulation and facilitate ventilation against the scorching sun of summer before they were air conditioned in the 1950s.

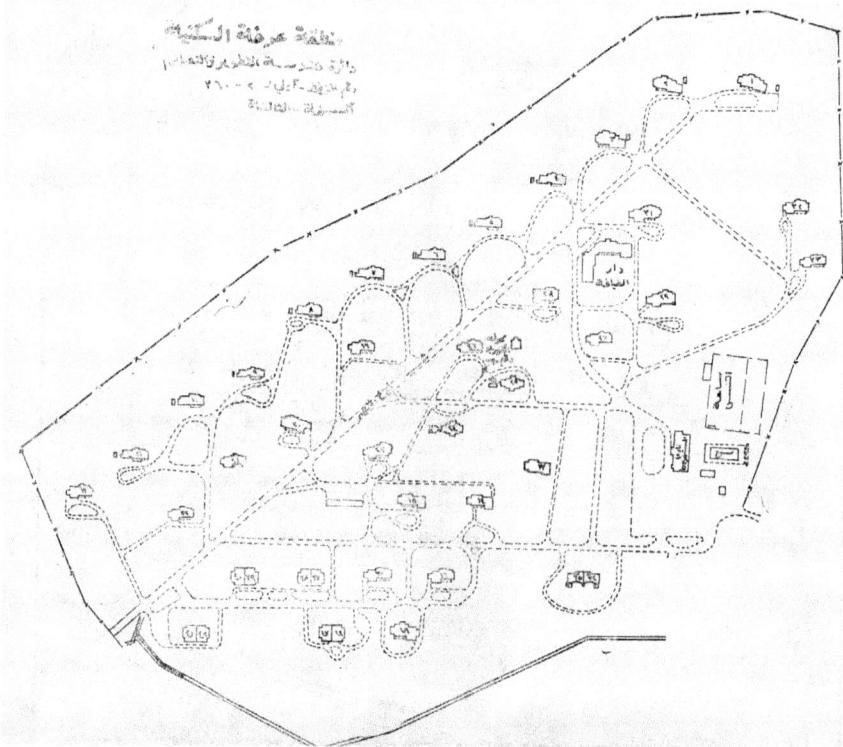

Arrapha Staff Residential Area

Courtesy of IPC

The main company elegant guest house was also built in this area which had been frequented by many of the IPC's chairmen, directors and top management visitors and later on after nationalisation was visited by President Saddam Hussain, Ministers of Oil and other senior Ministry of Oil staff.

The Compound was also famous for "The Feathers", the local bar which used to host very lively gatherings and was famous for its darts competitions.

A tennis court and a play ground with small swimming and paddling pools was also provided for the local residents since the main IPC club was located far away in the Baba Residential Areas.

The author and his family lived in the Arrapha Residential Area for 20 years from 1964 to 1984 during which they resided in houses No. 34, 18, 17 and finally 15 and enjoyed and still cherish the memories of the happy atmosphere of the close knit community of the compound who lived as one big family.

IPC HEADQUARTERS AND MAIN OFFICES

The IPC Headquarters were located at the centre of the Arrapha area and included the offices of the General Manager, Personnel Manager, Finance Manager, Services and administration Manager and some of the departments such as those of Staff , Personnel Development, Costs and Budget, Internal Audit, Industrial relations etc.

The IPC Headquarters with Kirkuk City in the Background – Mid 1940s

Courtesy of IPC

The manager engineering and most of the heads of the engineering departments were accommodated in their own separate office building within a short walking distance from the Headquarters. They included those of the Mechanical, Electrical, Development, Projects and Civil Engineering Departments.

The design and drawing office as well as the quantity survey section of the Development Engineering Department were also accommodated in this building. It is also where the author spent most of his working years with the IPC and later on with the Iraqi Company for Oil Operations/North Petroleum Organisation after nationalisation, progressing over the years from a design engineer to head of that department and head of the Projects Department. He spent twenty happy years in the Engineering office block working closely with other dear friends and colleagues in the same building. He still cherishes the memories of being surrounded and helped by a great team of capable engineers and draughtsmen. The Survey and Printing Sections which were part of the Development Engineering Department were accommodated in nearby separate buildings.

Other offices in the Arrapha area included those of the departments of General Accounts, Training Centre, Lands, Legal and Home Ownership Scheme and other minor sections.

IPC Engineering Offices- Arrapha-Kirkuk

Courtesy of IPC

ARRAPHA EMPLOYEES HOUSING ESTATE AND SHOPS

This housing estate was developed over the years to accommodate the ever increasing number of employees and their families. The estate was completed in the mid 1950s and had some 550 houses and local shops which also catered for the needs of the residents from the nearby Staff Residential Area.

A modern club was also constructed adjacent to the Arrapha Staff Residential Area for the company employees. It was equipped with a social hall, a restaurant and a gymnasium. It also had a huge sports ground for athletics and football.

IPC Sports Day 1947- Employees Club – Arrapha

Courtesy of IPC

BABA INDUSTRIAL AREA

This is the centre of the IPC operations and includes the following facilities:-

1. Baba degassing station.

2. Main Process Plant.

3. Fields Management Offices which included the Departments of Drilling, Petroleum Engineering, Geology and the modern geological, chemical and petroleum engineering laboratories.

4. Main mechanical, electrical and civil engineering workshops.

5. Offices of the Departments of Telecommunications and Instruments and their workshops.

6. Fields Power Station.

7. Transport Department and workshops.

8. Employment Department offices.

9. Fire and Safety department.

10. Mainline Section.

11. Baba East and West Staff Residential Areas.

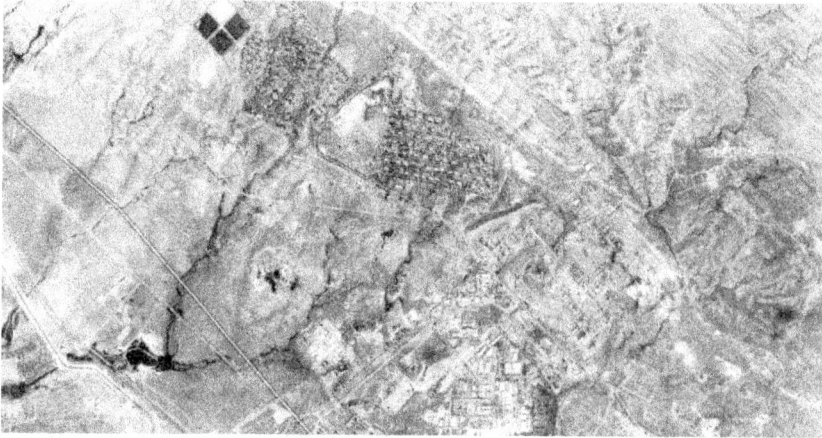

Top-Baba East & West Staff Residential Areas

Bottom – Process Plant & Baba Industrial Area

Courtesy of Google Earth

BABA EAST RESIDENTIAL AREA

The early houses of this area were built during the 1930s. The construction work was resumed after the Second World War and the whole area was completed in the 1950s.

The area included seven parallel roads with a total of 64 houses. These houses were similar in design and construction to those of Arrapha Staff Residential with their very thick walls and high ceilings to provide insulation and facilitate ventilation.

A school, a small church and a shop were also constructed in this area.

These houses were centrally air conditioned later on in the 1950s as part of the construction project of the Baba West Staff Residential Area.

Baba East Staff Residential Area

Courtesy of IPC

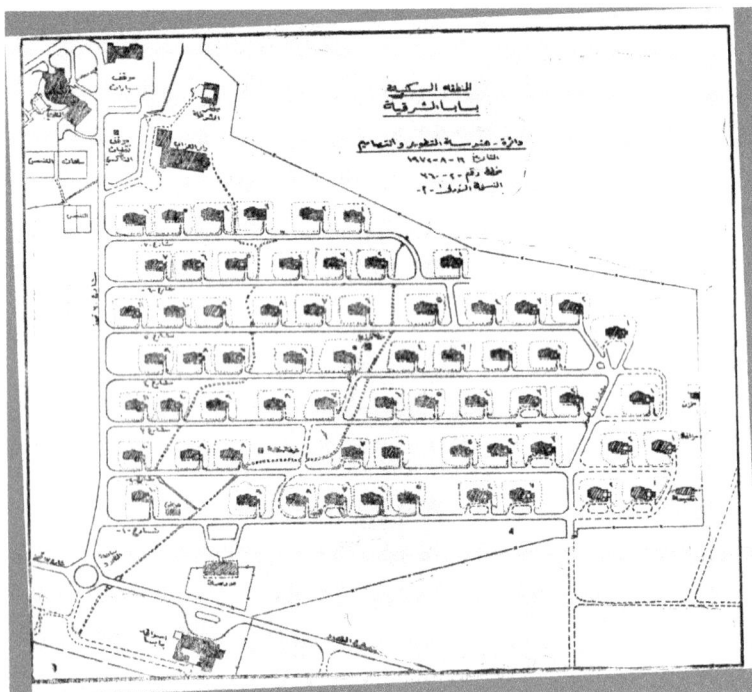

Baba East Staff Residential Area

Top left - Baba Club and Cinema / Bottom Left- School and Spinney's Shop

Courtesy of IPC

BABA WEST RESIDENTIAL AREA

The planned vast expansion of the company's production facilities and the construction of the two 16 inch diameter pipelines to Haifa and Tripoli which were followed immediately by the construction of the 30/32 inch diameter pipeline to Banias brought with it a big construction programme for additional housing accommodation for the increasing number of staff.

This resulted in the construction of the Baba West Staff Residential Area which was built as an extension to the old Baba East area.

The new Estate consisted of seventy modern looking houses with smaller rooms and lower ceilings since they were air conditioned.

It also included a large guest house by the name of Karemiyah House which provided accommodation for the bachelor staff as well as visitors.

The central area between Baba East and West residential areas was utilised for the construction of a fantastic Staff Club. The main circular hall had its walls decorated with thrilling paintings from the famous Arabian one thousand and one nights. The hall was the centre of social activities the year-round including the celebration of the Islamic Eids, Christmas parties and the New-Year's fancy dress parties. Other frequent social activities such as tombola, quiz nights and the occasional Casino night were also held there.

The club's restaurant was excellent with its European and Iraqi menus including the famous Kuba-Mosul and the occasional Kozi Ala Timman, the famous stuffed grilled whole lamb complete with its head and huge fat tail.

The equally famous Chat Noire bar was another attraction for cosy small parties to celebrate birthdays, wedding anniversaries and the like.

The club library was stocked with large number of books which were available for borrowing and which covered many subjects of interest.

The library room was also used during one night of the week for the ever popular game of Bridge with the usual occasional tournaments.

The sports facilities were numerous including tennis, squash, and volley ball and basket ball courts, keep fit classes hall, snooker room, football ground and the inevitable brilliant and popular adults' and children's swimming pools with their stunning surrounding lawns and gardens which were perfect for relaxing and sun bathing.

المنطقة السكنية
بابا الغربية
دائرة هندسة التطوير والتصاميم

Baba West Staff Residential Area

Bottom – Karimiyah House

Courtesy of IPC

The modern cinema was another attraction which showed films on Monday and Thursday nights and a children film on Friday afternoons.

It is of interest to record that a central air conditioning system was installed during the construction of the Baba West Staff Residential area in the mid 1950s which also catered for the Baba East Staff Residential Area as well as the club, cinema etc.

IPC GOLF CLUB

No self respecting oil company could exist without a golf course, at least in the Middle East. Hence an 18 holes beautiful golf course was laid amongst the undulating hills behind the Process Plant very close to the Baba Staff Residential Areas. The tee boxes, fairways and the greens were kept in immaculate condition. The course looked at its best in spring when the whole area around it becomes an endless beautiful meadow full of all sorts of wild flowers of breathtaking colours. The fresh cool breeze and the gentle sun in the mornings and the late afternoons make it a perfect place to forget work and its problems and to enjoy the heavenly atmosphere and the exhilarating walk.

At weekends, after finishing an enjoyable game of golf in the morning, the players were welcomed in the cosy small clubhouse to enjoy a glass of beer, a soft drink or the inevitable cup of tea.

Lunch was served, every Friday, either inside the clubhouse or in the garden which nearly always included that delicious curry dish sprinkled over with sultanas, almond, crushed coconut and fried onions. Golfers are frequently accompanied by their families with children enjoying themselves in the area around the clubhouse.

Competitions were held quite regularly at weekends in winter and spring and usually attracted a crowd of non-playing members and spectators. The atmosphere always resembled a crowd of one big family enjoying a big weekend party since most of these people worked in close association and their families lived in the same residential areas as neighbours.

The scorching heat of summer did not seem to deter the enthusiastic golfers from enjoying a game very early in the morning or the late afternoon.

Finally the region around the golf club seems to have been inhabited by the Sumerians or Babylonians thousands of years ago since rumours had it that a few small cylindrical clay tablets with cuneiform writing had been found on the golf course by some of the enthusiastic amateur archaeologist golfers.

THE IRAQ OPEN - 1971
hosted by the Kirkuk Golf Club.
The prizes were presented by the Mohafidh of Kirkuk,
Sd Ghanim Abdul Jalil.
The winner of the shield was a visitor from Baghdad, name ??

Left to right, DICK PIRIE,   MIKE HARFORD,   ??   THE MOHAFIDH,
ALBERT ISMAIL,   MUNTHER OMAR,   ADNAN TABACHALI.

On Nationalisation in 1972, the Government of Iraq
appointed Ghanim Abdul Jalil
as General Manager Kirkuk, in succession to Allan Gillan.

It is to be noted that the Mohafidh (Governor), Ghanim Abdul Jalil appearing in the Photograph, was one of the top Baath Party members accused, of plotting to overthrow President Saddam Hussain, in July 1979, found guilty and executed as detailed in Chapter (5).

K-1- AREA

This area is an extension of the Baba Industrial Area and includes the following:-

1.   K-1 Tank Farm.

2. K-1 Pump Station.

3. Production and Plant Survey Departments

4. Materials Department with its vast coverer and open air stores.

5. Commissariat Department offices and stores.

6. A few residential houses which were converted to offices for the above mentioned departments after the completion of Baba West Residential Area.

7. K-1 Hospital.

K-1 Hospital

The famous K-1 hospital was constructed in the early days of the IPC operations in Iraq and was opened in 1937 with 44 beds.

It was expanded and improved over the years to reach its final capacity of 140 beds.

K-1 Hospital - Kirkuk
Courtesy of IPC

There was the most modern apparatus of that time in the Operating Theatre, Medical Pathology, and Radiology Departments and in the Dental Centre.

It was staffed with highly qualified surgeons, physicians, an anaesthetist, a dental surgeon, a matron and a number of competent nurses.

The hospital must have seen the birth of hundreds of children of the large number of expatriate staff from countless nationalities. By now, these "children" must be scattered all over the world with the place of birth in their passports showing Kirkuk (i.e. K-1 hospital). Scores of them are known to the author and still talk lovingly about their happy childhood in Kirkuk.

NUMBER 8 CAMP - LESSER ZAB RIVER AREA

One of the main centres of the IPC operations is in the Lesser Zab River region. It includes the following major facilities:-

1. Malhawali, Saralu and Sarbashakh degassing stations.

2. Avanah crude oil pump station.

3. Bai Hassan North, Bai Hassan South and later on Dawood degassing stations.

4. The Water Injection Plant.

5. The IPC domestic water pump station.

6. Kirkuk City water pumping station which was operated and maintained by the IPC.

Number 8 Camp Overlooking the Lesser Zab River - 1947

Courtesy of IPC

The distance between the city of Kirkuk and the Lesser Zab River is some 50 km which made it necessary to provide catering facilities and a limited number of accommodations for the numerous staff and employees operating and maintaining these facilities.

As a result a lovely camp of a few houses and a mess were constructed on top of one of the beautiful hills overlooking the river.

BRICK FIELD

The massive building programme required millions of bricks which were not available from the local markets and as a result, the IPC constructed its own brick production plant. The production continued during the 1950s and early 1960s until the completion of the building programme when it was handed over to the local authorities of Kirkuk city.

PIPELINE PUMP STATIONS, K-2, K-3 AND T-1

Each of these pump stations as well as those built in Syria resembles a small township.

Apart from the industrial facilities of Pump houses, oil tanks, a tangle of pipes, workshops, stores etc., each of these stations has offices, residential areas and a landing strip suitable for light aircrafts for rapid transportation between Kirkuk and other company locations in Iraq, Syria and Lebanon.

K-3 station is the biggest of them all, its staff residential area has 38 houses and that of the employees has scores of houses.

There was also the necessary staff mess with its 16 rooms which accommodates some of the bachelor staff as well as providing accommodation for the frequent staff on duty from Kirkuk and other locations as well as the occasional visitors.

The station also had the usual clubhouses with social halls, restaurants etc as well as the necessary cinema.

The sporting facilities are numerous including tennis courts, volley and basket ball courts, snooker tables, football ground and the inevitable brilliant and popular swimming pools.

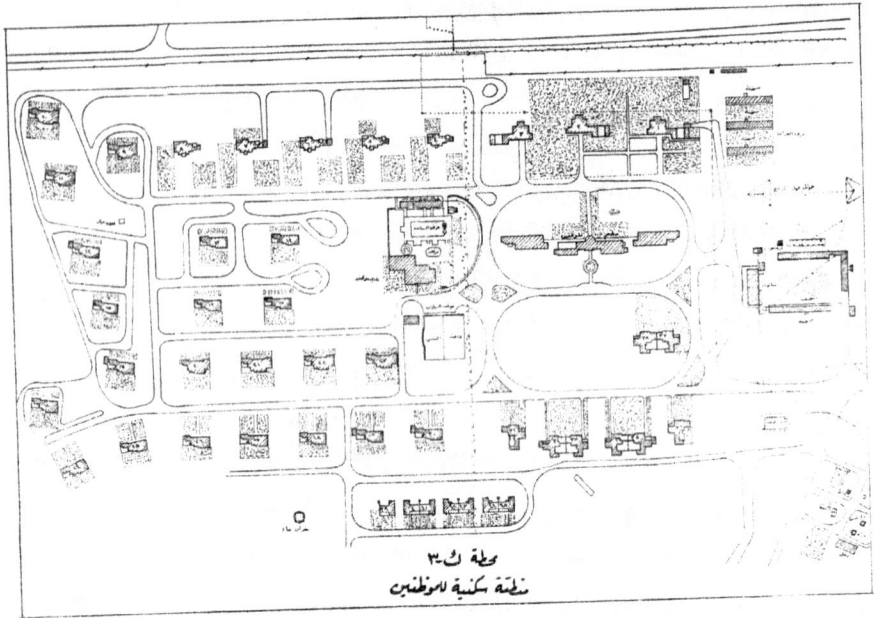

K-3 Pumping Station Staff Residential Area

Courtesy of IPC

HOME OWNERSHIP SCHEME

As it has already been mentioned, the planned vast expansion of the company's production facilities and the construction of the two 16 inch diameter pipelines to Haifa and Tripoli which were followed immediately by the construction and completion of the 30/32 inch diameter pipeline to Banias in 1952 resulted in an unprecedented increase in the number of employees. The Arrapha employee estate became grossly inadequate and the city of Kirkuk had no houses available for rental to satisfy the great demand.

On the other hand the IPC did not want to invest in a massive housing programme and continue to expand the existing Employees Estate in Arrapha which was at that time not yet integrated within the city of Kirkuk. Instead it was thought better to build houses within the boundaries of the Municipality of Kirkuk which would prevent further segregation and help to integrate the employees with the natural life in Kirkuk and allow them to make greater contributions towards the development and prosperity of the city.

Hence the IPC came up with the clever idea of the Home Ownership Scheme for its Iraqi staff and employees, which proved to be beneficial to all the concerned parties, the IPC itself, the employees and the city of Kirkuk.

The scheme is based on the following principles:-

1. The IPC would purchase large plots of land at competitive prices.

2. The land would be divided into hundreds of suitable plots for building houses.

3. The IPC would prepare the necessary services of roads, electric power distribution network , water supply mains, drainage systems etc.

4. The applicant would pay 10% of the estimated cost of his house.

5. The IPC would give the prospective interested applicant a loan for the remaining 90% of the estimated cost of the house equivalent to up to 30 monthly salaries to be repaid in monthly instalments over 25 years. Loans of up to 3,000 Iraqi Dinars would be interest-free and anything above that bear interest, part of which was paid by the company.

6. The company prepared a booklet containing scores of assorted different plans of two, three and four bedroom houses based on the expected allowable loans.

7. Employees who were interested in joining the Scheme would sign the standard contract with the company, chose the district and the type of house they wished to be built and leave the rest for the company to deal with until the house was ready to be handed over to them.

8. The Company would invite approved contractors to tender for each house and sign the relevant contract.

9. Construction of the house would be supervised by the company's own engineers and foremen at no cost to the employee.

10. The Company would waive the whole of the outstanding loan in the case of the death of the employee.

11. The IPC would insure all the houses at no cost to the applicants during the loan term.

The main districts that were developed by the IPC in Kirkuk were Almas, Gower Baghi and Baghdad road. Other smaller areas and individual plots of land were also built in many other districts.

When the author first joined the IPC in Kirkuk in 1961, he was posted to the Home Ownership Scheme Department to work as a site engineer. He worked mainly in the Gower Baghi district which had scores of houses under construction at that time.

It is ironic to highlight that this was the very location where the IPC workers used to assemble during the strike in July 1946 and where the infamous massacre took place as detailed in Chapter 3.

The Gower Baghi Estate consisted mainly of two and three bedroom houses, which varied in cost between 1,200 and 2,500 Iraqi Dinars, bearing in mind that the monthly salary of the semi-skilled labour was between 40 and 50 Dinar while that of the skilled workers, the technical and clerical employees was between 50 and 80 Dinars (One Dinar was to equal 3.3 US Dollar at the official rate of exchange).

The scheme was started in Kirkuk in 1951 and after its success was assured, it was adopted in Basra in 1953 and extended later on to Baghdad, Mosul and the Pipeline Pumping Stations.

The terms of the Home Ownership Scheme were very generous and hence attractive to those who wished to own their own homes and soon after there was a long waiting list from the hundreds of eager applicants.

Modern Home ownership Scheme House-Kirkuk

Courtesy of IPC

By the end of 1965 the number of houses built and those under construction was 2,693 and 111 respectively as shown in the table below.

	Built in 1965	Total Built	Bought in 1965	Total Bought	Total Owned	Being Built
I P C	146	1,537	68	260	1,797	47
B P C	35	595	1	14	609	37
M P C	3	51	0	23	74	11
Baghdad	15	145	12	68	213	16
Total	199	2,328	81	365	2,693	111

2,000 HOUSES ESTATE

The expansion of the oil production and export capacity from one million to 1.2 million and then to 1.4 million barrels per day which took place after the nationalisation of the IPC in 1972, resulted in a similar big expansion in manpower.

This created an acute shortage of accommodation and as a result it was decided to expand the old Arrapha Employee Estate towards Baba Industrial Area, by utilising the adjacent available land along the existing Arrapha-Baba road.

A huge housing project was put in hand in the late 1970s for the construction of 2,000 houses. The project was delayed by shortage of construction materials and was finally completed in the latter years of the 1980s.

AIN ZALAH CAMP

The headquarter of the Mosul Petroleum Company is located at the beautiful resort type camp north-west of Mosul on the picturesque hills of Ain Zalah not too far from the eastern bank of River Tigris.

Its staff residential area consisted of 42 elegant bungalow type dwellings with beautiful gardens, smart lawns, shrubs and flowers. A large guesthouse was also provided for the accommodation of the bachelor staff and frequent visitors from Kirkuk and other locations.

The camp had no houses for the technical and clerical employees. These had their families living in Mosul and normally visited them at weekends. Hence they were accommodated in scores of bachelor quarters.

The unskilled labourers are usually recruited from the surrounding villages of Ain Zalah and either went home at the end of each day or were accommodated in bachelor quarters.

The camp has a cinema and the usual sporting facilities including two sparkling swimming pools, one for the staff and the other for the employees, tennis courts etc, and the inevitable golf course.

The camp also had a landing strip suitable for light aircrafts for rapid transportation between Kirkuk and other company locations.

Due to its higher elevation, the camp's weather is normally kinder, with its temperature being a few degrees lower than that of the city of Kirkuk, which made it attractive for the staff and their families to work and live there, at least for short durations.

BARJISSYAH RESIDENTIAL AREA

The Basra Petroleum Company had the majority of its staff and employees residing in Basra, Zubair and other nearby towns, hence it had only one residential area, Barjissyah, which provided limited married and bachelor accommodation.

Barjissyah also had the usual other amenities found in the other IPC residential areas.

ADDENDUM 1

IRAQ PETROLEUM COMPANY

STAFF LIST MAY 1972

The number of people who had worked in the oil and gas industry in Iraq during the twentieth century must have been over one hundred thousand.

Those of them who had held responsible jobs must number thousands. During the 1930s, 194os and 1950s most of them were expatriates, mainly British, with a limited number of Iraqis but also included others from many different nationalities.

In this book the author would like to give tribute to all those people who have participated in developing and running of this vast industry, but alas to name them all would be an impossible task, and the author would like to apologise for not being able to list all their names.

It is however fortunate that a list of the staff of the Iraq Petroleum Company for May 1972 has come to hand.

This list is significant since it shows the IPC's organisation during the last month before its nationalisation, which was continued to be adopted by its successor the Iraqi Company for Oil Operations, ICOO after nationalisation.

It is also important since it shows the names of the management and the staff who were running the IPC in Kirkuk, and the Pipeline pump stations, before nationalisation and those same people, less the limited number of expatriates, who continued to run the Company after nationalisation and who thus, played a pivotal role in making it a success story.

All the people whose names appear in this Staff List were known to the author. The vast majority were close colleagues and scores of them were and are still his dear friends. Hence it is my pleasure to salute them and their families and hope that the list would be one way of bringing back some nice memories as well as reviving friendship between those who have lost contact over the long years.

With my best wishes to them and their families wherever they may be now.

In the meantime, I beg to be forgiven for being unable to secure similar lists for the equally important oil and gas organisations such as the Ministry of Oil, INOC, BPC, Refineries, Petroleum Products Distribution and many others, but would like to sent to all those who worked for them my sincere and best wishes as well and hope it would be possible to obtain similar lists for them in the future.

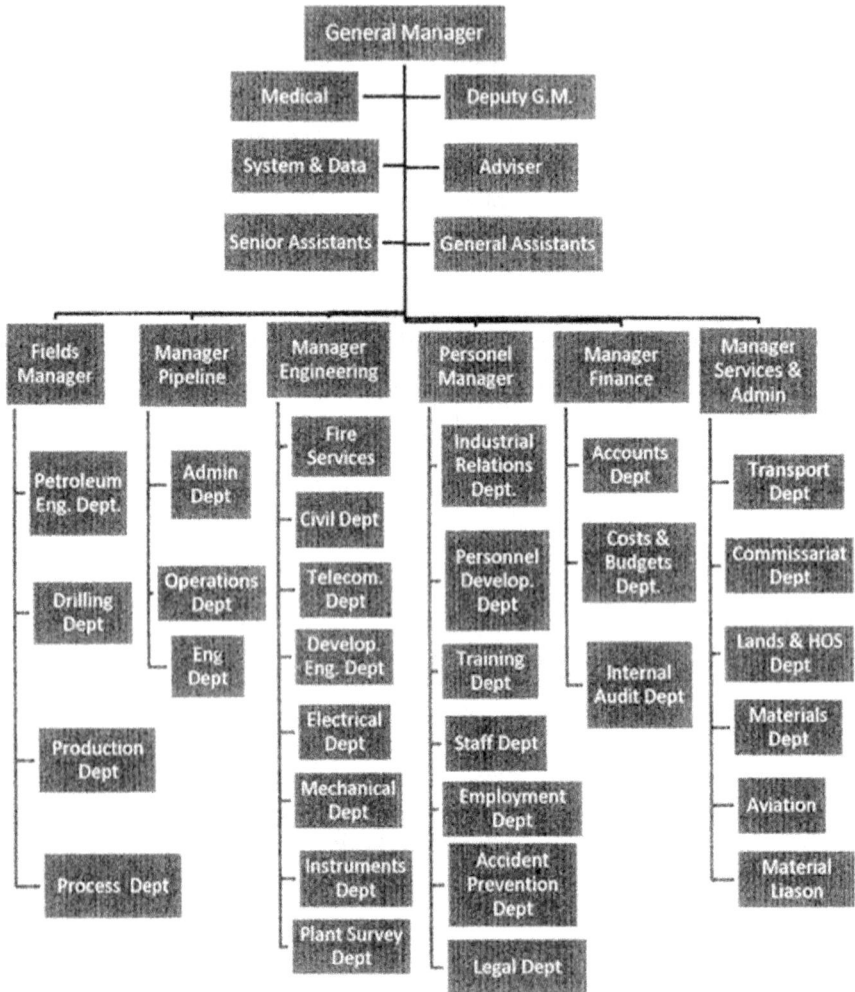

Iraq Petroleum Company - Kirkuk Fields & Pipeline - Organisation Chart-May 1972

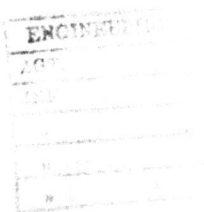

IRAQ PETROLEUM COMPANY, LIMITED
KIRKUK FIELDS & PIPELINE

STAFF LIST AS AT 1ST MAY, 1972

GENERAL MANAGEMENT

General Manager	A. J. A.	Gillan	Kirkuk (L)
Acting General Manager	P. E.	Lane	Kirkuk
Secretary	Clara (Miss)	Basil	Kirkuk
M.B.O. Adviser	Hussam-Eddin Shakir Al-	Dhahi	Kirkuk
Senior Asst. (Management Services)	Samir	Noori	Kirkuk
Asst. (Management Services)	Hazim Abdulla Al-	Sultan	Kirkuk
Senior Assistant	Ghazi Sabir	Ali	Krk.(Sec.to L/O.)
Senior Asst. (Relations)	Ismail Ibrahim Al-	Rawi	Kirkuk
General Asst. (Police Liaison)	Lutfi	Iskander	Kirkuk
General Asst. (Government Relations)	Subhi Mohammed Al-	Algawi	Kirkuk

SYSTEMS & DATA SERVICES

Systems Analyst	Rashid Elias	Haddad	Kirkuk
Systems Analyst	Adnan Younis Al-	Safi	Kirkuk
Supervisor, Computor Operations	Abdul Hak Saeed	Dabdoub	Kirkuk
Maintenance Programmer	Razzak Iskander	Bashoori	Kirkuk
Asst. Programmer	Quraish Muhideen Yousif	Amin	Kirkuk

FIELDS MANAGEMENT

Fields Manager	Abdul Amir	Taki	Krk.(Sec.to L/O.)
Acting Fields Manager	J.	Osborne	Kirkuk

PETROLEUM ENGINEERING

Head of Petroleum Engineering	Faleh Mustafa Al-	Kobaisi	Kirkuk
Reservoir Engineering Adviser	D. M.	Morris	Kirkuk
Technical Assistant	Abdul Muhsin	Ali	Bgd.(Sec.to Petr.Inst.)
General Assistant	Youash Kamber	Iskander	Kirkuk
Senior Petroleum Specialist (Oprs.)	Anwar Al-Sayyid	Ezzadeen	Kirkuk
Senior Petroleum Engineer (Planning)	Tariq Abdul Qadir Al-	Irhayim	Kirkuk
Actg. Area Production Geologist	Ja'far Ahmed Al-	Sakini	Kirkuk
Production Geologist	Shirzad Badi	Nazhat	Kirkuk
Asst. Geologist	Said Hmoud Al-	Dhiab	Kirkuk
Asst. Geologist	Kadir Ridha Al-	Jaff	Krk.(Sec.from Minoil)
Reservoir Engineer	Ghazi Mehdi	Haider	Krk.(Course Baghdad)
Petroleum Specialist	Saib Abdul Aziz Al-	Mutawalli	Krk.(Course Lebanon)
Petroleum Specialist	Sabih	Fatoohi	Kirkuk
Area Petroleum Specialist	Ali Kamil Al-	Rawi	Kirkuk
Petroleum Specialist	Ahmed Shaheen	Sharief	Kirkuk
Petroleum Engineer	Ahmed Thanoon Hussain Al-	Khazraji	Kirkuk
Asst. Petroleum Specialist	Ali Rashid	Mahmoud	Kirkuk
Asst. Petroleum Engineer	Hussain Mahmoud Al-	Mehaidi	Kirkuk
Asst. Petroleum Engineer	Mowaffaq Adeeb Abdul Salam Al-	Samadi	Kirkuk
Asst. Petroleum Engineer (Trainee)	Basil Mohammed	Ismail	Kirkuk

DRILLING

Drilling Superintendent	Fuad	Toma	Kirkuk
Senior Toolpusher	A. J.	Endacott	Kirkuk
Technical Assistant	Ismail Khalil	Ibrahim	Kirkuk
Toolpusher	Mohammed Abid Abood	Bouza	Kirkuk
Toolpusher	Agob Awanes	Bablanian	Kirkuk
Drilling Engineer	Mahmoud Hamid	Ahmed	Kirkuk
Drilling Geologist	Adnan Ismail Al-	Sammarraie	Kirkuk
Driller	Shakir Mohammed Ali Al-	Jammas	Kirkuk
Driller	Yousl	Shamoun	Kirkuk
Driller	Sarkis	Ibrahim	Kirkuk
Driller	Jassim Mohammed Al-	Dhuhban	Krk.(Sec.to BSH.)
Driller	Salahaddin Mohammed	Amin	Kirkuk
Asst. Equipment Supervisor	Belshasar Benjamin	Kalasho	Kirkuk
Driller (Trainee)	Fadheel Elias	Mardilly	Krk.(Sec.to BSH.)
Driller (Trainee)	Ramadhan Abdulla	Swaid	Kirkuk
Driller (Trainee)	Fuad Mahmoud Khidher	Izza	Kirkuk

PRODUCTION

Head of Production	Khalid Ali Khalid Al-	Hijazi	Kirkuk
Senior Production Supervisor (North)	Jawdat Aziz	Searty	Kirkuk
Senior Production Engineer (South)	Hameed Ahmed Al-	Joudi	Krk.(Sec.to Pet.Eng.)
Area Production Supervisor	Imad Hadi El-	Hashimi	Kirkuk
Area Production Supervisor	Adil Mohammed Saleh	Ibrahim	Kirkuk
Area Production Engineer	Abdul Jabbar Khudhayyir	Neseyif	Kirkuk
Area Production Supvr.(Maintenance)	Nishan Sahag Abraham	Sossikian	Kirkuk
Production Supervisor	Abdul Rahman	Mohammed	Kirkuk
Production Engineer	Mohammed Saeed Hassan	Yousif	Kirkuk
Production Engineer	Jafar Safar Shon Ali Al-	Rubai'e	Krk.(Sec.to AZH.)
Production Supervisor	Subhi Abdul Majid	Faris	Kirkuk
Asst. Production Supervisor	Fouad Youaw Al-	Bazi	Kirkuk
Oil Accounting Supervisor	Akram Afram Gewargis	Jezrawi	Kirkuk
Asst. Production Eng. (Maintenance)	Safa Yousif Yacoub	Ashkuri	Kirkuk
Asst. Production Engineer	Adil Ahmed Jawad Al-	Cherchefchi	Krk.
Asst. Production Engineer (Trainee)	Moh'd. Mahmoud Aboush Al-	Sultan	Kirkuk (Course Lebanon)

PROCESS

Head of Process	Abdul Karim Mohammed	Mahmoud	Kirkuk
Acting Senior Operator	Agob Kevork	Boyrazian	Kirkuk
General Assistant	Tahsin Yousif	Abdul-Ahad	Kirkuk
Shift Control Operator	Isaac	Khamis	Kirkuk
Shift Control Operator	Nusraddin Ali Mardan	Nouri	Kirkuk
Shift Control Operator	Khorshid Bahjat Al-	Naqib	Kirkuk
Shift Control Operator	Ahmed Sayed	Tahir	Kirkuk
Shift Control Operator	Mohammed Zaki	Sulaiman	Kirkuk (L)
Shift Control Operator	Fahmi	Habib	Kirkuk
Operator	Nadhim	Shukur	Kirkuk
Operator	Ismail Faraj	Rashid	Krk.(Course Lebanon)
Operator	Abdul Wahid Ahmed	Koozachi	Kirkuk (L)
Operator	Hassan	Hussain	Kirkuk
Operator	Younan Youkhana Al-	Bazi	Kirkuk
Operator	Yousif Saeed	Mahmoud	Kirkuk
Operator	Najib Abdul Qadir	Khidher	Kirkuk
Operator	Nuraddin	Salim	Kirkuk
Operator	Serop Sultan	Sarkissian	Kirkuk
Operator	Qadir Karim	Mohammed	Kirkuk
Operator	Anwar Abdulla	Ridha	Kirkuk
Asst. Operator	Tariq Mahmoud	Kirkchi	Kirkuk
Asst. Operator	Shlimon	Hanna	Kirkuk
Asst. Operator	Adnan Abdul Majid	Younis	Kirkuk (Course UK.)
Asst. Operator	Kamil Ali	Tikrity	Kirkuk
Asst. Operator	Saqi Khidher	Ismail	Kirkuk
Asst. Operator	Auda Fad'ous Moh'd. Al-	Joboori	Kirkuk

P I P E L I N E

Manager Pipeline	Majid Hussain Al-	Hamdani	K-3
Technical Assistant	Waleed Ab. Jalil Jawad Al-	Has'san	K-3

PIPELINE ADMINISTRATION

Actg. Administration Superintendent	Sabah Shakir Al-	Hilal	K-3
Station Administrator	Khaldoon Ahmed	Abdulla	K-3
General Assistant (Trainee)	Rafa' Ahmed Ali Al-	Hashimi	K-3
Station Administrator	Abdul Razzak Muhsin Al-	Nasrawi	T-1

PIPELINE OPERATION & MAINTENANCE

Senior Pipeline Engineer	Jamil Paulus	Hanna	K-3

K-1 Station

Station Engineer	Hikmat Jamil	Khaddour	Kirkuk
Asst. Maintenance Engineer	Mouayed Najib	Rehani	Kirkuk

K-2 Area

Station Supervisor	Abdul Razzak Hussain Al-	Battawi	Kirkuk

K-3 Station

Station Engineer	Abdul Sattar Al-	Jomard	K-3
Actg. Station Operating Supervisor	Abdul Karim Hamood Al-	Rawi	K-3
Station Maintenance Supervisor	Khosrop Sahag	Garabedian	K-3
Maintenance Engineer	Sharief	Ahmed	K-3
Maintenance Engineer	Qays Moh'd. Amin Al-	Doory	K-3
Maintenance Engineer	Nabil Salih Ab. Wahab Al-	Shaibani	K-3
Shift Supervisor	Saleh Qassim Al-	Jaberi	K-3
Shift Supervisor	Chaloob Bani	Mohammed	K-3
Shift Supervisor	Youash Arkhayam	Shamshoun	K-3
Shift Engineer (Trainee)	Talib Ahmed Mohammed Al-	Hadithi	K-3
Shift Engineer (Trainee)	Sa'ad Mahmoud Abdul Karim Al-	Rahim	K-3
Shift Engineer (Trainee)	Hamadallah Hussain	Adwan	K-3

T-1 Station

Station Supervisor	J.	Forsyth	T-1
Station Operating Supervisor	Eydin Hussain Hassan	Awchi	T-1
Station Maintenance Engineer	Tariq Ahmed	Zaki	T-1
Maintenance Supervisor	Petros	Maqsud	T-1
Maintenance Engineer	Nathir Jirjis Ahmed	Omar	T-1
Shift Supervisor	George	Shamoon	T-1
Shift Supervisor	Shamoun	Daoud	T-1
Shift Supervisor	Hadi	Shukur	T-1
Shift Supervisor	Khalil Daoud	Hamid	T-1
Shift Supervisor	Petros Gorgis	Abdul-Ahad	T-1

K-3 Gas Oil Plant

Operator i/c Gas Oil Plant	Khorshid Namiq	Khorshid	K-3

PIPELINE ENGINEERING SERVICES

Senior Services Engineer	Hamid Sadiq Al-	Munshi	K-3
Mechanical Services Supervisor	Turkey Saeed Al-	Abdul Baki	K-3
Electrical Supervisor	Gewargis	Khoshaba	K-3
Electrical Supervisor	Mohammed	Remadhan	K-3
Asst. Electrical Supervisor	Yousif Jajjo	Yousif	K-3
Asst. Electrical Engineer	Maqboul Mahmoud Al-	Chalabi	K-3
Civil Engineer	Sargon Younathan	Hermiz	K-3
Asst. Civil Engineer	Adai Hardan Hasanballa Al-	Hadithi	K-3

<u>E N G I N E E R I N G</u>

Manager Engineering	A. B.	Tavendale	Kirkuk
General Assistant	Leonard Oscar	Fosberry	Kirkuk
Projects Engineer	R.	Bickerdike	Krk.
Mechanical Maint. Superv. (Projects)	J. J. P.	Keal	Kirkuk
Asst. Mechanical Eng. (Trainee)	Thanoon Younis Moh'd. Al-	Dabbagh	Krk.(Sec.to Transport)
Technical Assistant	Abdul Aziz Munim Jabbar Al-	Ghanimi	Kirkuk

<u>FIRE SERVICES</u>

Firemaster	Ibrahim	Samin	Kirkuk
Asst. Firemaster	Mufeed Abdul	Majid	Kirkuk

<u>CIVIL ENGINEERING</u>

Head of Civil Engineering	Ali Mohammed Hassan Al-	Khayatt	Kirkuk

H.Q.S. Construction

Building Supervisor	Hussain	Juma	Kirkuk
Building Engineer	Issam Fouad	Sarsam	Kirkuk
Asst. Civil Engineer	Abdul Basit	Mustafa	Kirkuk
Asst. Building Supervisor	Abdul Qadir Mahmoud Al-	Jeboori	Kirkuk

Works Section

Building Supervisor	Mudhaffar	Ezzat	Kirkuk
Asst. Building Supvr.(Process Plant)	Youash Lazar	Khana	Kirkuk
Asst. Building Supervisor	Hanna	Daniel	Kirkuk (L)
Asst. Civil Engineer (Trainee)	Akram Ismail Moh'd. Al-	Amin	Kirkuk

Building Section

Civil Engineer	Akram Bashir	Rassam	Kirkuk
Asst. Building Supervisor	Albert Mardiros	Alexander	Kirkuk
Asst. Civil Engineer	Ali Hussain	Mohammed	Kirkuk

Road Section

Civil Engineer	Bakir	Jabbar	Kirkuk
Asst. Building Supervisor	Warda	Odisho	Kirkuk

<u>TELECOMMUNICATIONS ENGINEERING</u>

Head of Telecommunications	Ali	Mustafa	Kirkuk
Asst. Electrical Engineer (Trainee)	Khalil Ibrahim	Ahmed	Kirkuk
Asst. Telecommuns. Engineer (Trainee)	Wajdi Fawzi Moh'd. Al-	Khateeb	Kirkuk

Radio & Transmission Section

Telecommunications Engineer	Mohammed Fuad Mulla	Karim	Kirkuk (L)
Asst. Telecommunications Engineer	Falah Kadhim Jassim Al-	Khawaja	Kirkuk
Asst. Telecommunications Supervisor	Noeh Qoryakos Al-	Jajjoka	Kirkuk

Exchanges & Subscribers Section

Telecommunications Supervisor	Edward	Habib	Kirkuk
Asst. Telecommunications Supervisor	Nuraddin Ali	Hassan	Kirkuk

Operations

Telecommunications Supervisor	Salman Saleh Al-	Adhami	Kirkuk

Workshops

Telecommunications Supervisor	Saleeba Yousif Marcus	Qassab	Kirkuk

Pipeline Section

Telecommunications Engineer	Yousif Jawad	Muhiddin	K-3
Asst. Telecommunications Supervisor	Hassan Moh'd. Amin Al-	Salihi	K-3

- 5 -

DEVELOPMENT ENGINEERING

Development Engineering Superintendent	Ghanim Abid Khalil	Anaz	Kirkuk
Materials Control & Drawing Office Records Supervisor	Dinha Gorgis	Dikho	Kirkuk

Drawing Office

Senior Designer Engineer	M. J. L.	Rogers	Kirkuk
Designer Engineer	E. H.	Anderson	Kirkuk
Designer Engineering	Baba Shimshoon	Jacob	Kirkuk
Designer Engineering	Hanna Nasir	Khoury	Kirkuk
Designer Engineering	Ali Mohammed	Ali	Krk.(Sec.to Projects Eng.)
Designer Engineering	Abdul Munim Abdul Aziz	Ghazal	Kirkuk
Asst. Mechanical Engineer	Sargon Karim	Jabri	Kirkuk

Q.S. & E. Section

Senior Quantity Surveyor	Saib Bahjat	Majid	Krk.(Course Bgd.)
Actg. Senior Quantity Surveyor	Johnson John	Paulus	Kirkuk

Survey Section

Surveyor	Nafie Aboudi Al-	Siliq	Kirkuk

ELECTRICAL ENGINEERING

Head of Electrical Engineering	Faik Mohammed	Abdul Aziz	Krk.
Senior Electrical Engineer (P/L.& Ser.)	Munthir Hassan	Omar	Kirkuk
Electrical Supervisor	Hashim	Qassim	Kirkuk
Asst. Electrical Engineer	Muhammed Hamdi Ab. Latif Al-	Shaikhly	Kirkuk

Fields

Senior Electrical Engineer (Fields)	Abdul Amir Yousif Al-	Azzawi	Kirkuk
Senior Electrical Engineer	P. J.	Beresford	Kirkuk
Electrical Engineer No. 1 Area	Hashim Ali Khalid Al-	Hijazi	Kirkuk
Electrical Supervisor No. 2 Area	Hanna	Habib	Kirkuk
Electrical Supervisor No. 3 Area	Zain-Abdin Moh'd. Al-	Bayati	Kirkuk
Electrical Supervisor No. 4 Area	Mohammed Amin	Siddiq	Kirkuk
Electrical Supervisor No. 5 Area	Samson	George	Kirkuk (L)
Distribution Engineer	Ahmed Rawshan	Ahmed Shukri	Krk.
Testing & Switchgear Supervisor	Awikan	George	Kirkuk
Protection & Substations Supervisor	Abdul Qadir	Mohammed	Kirkuk

Fields Power Station

Power Station Superintendent	Mohammed Abdulla	Shali	Krk.(Course Bgd.)
Electrical Engineer	Zaki	Habib	Kirkuk
Mechanical Engineer	Adnan	Bashir	Kirkuk
Electrical Engineer	Nohad Ismail Khalil Al-	Tuwaijiry	Kirkuk
Shift Supervisor	Sarkis Younan	Georgis	Kirkuk
Shift Supervisor	Jawad Kadhim Al-	Rubai'e	Kirkuk
Shift Supervisor	Mohammed Ismail	Najjar	Kirkuk
Shift Supervisor	Sulaiman	Ahmed	Kirkuk
Shift Supervisor	As'ad Ali	Abdulla	Kirkuk
Asst. Shift Engineer	Moh'd. Bakir Abbas Al-	Tabatabaie	Krk. (L)

MECHANICAL ENGINEERING

Head of Mechanical Engineering	Shakir Abdul Razzak	Anani	Kirkuk
Asst. Mechanical Engineer	Rahif Abdul Rahman	Qattan	Krk.(Sec.to Dev. Eng.)
Asst. Mechanical Engineer	Mohammed Ali Abbas Al-	Haidari	Kirkuk

FIELDS

Senior Mechanical Engineer	Anis Ibrahim Al-	Jassar	Kirkuk

Zab Area

Mechanical Engineer	Subhi Abdul Majid Al-	Ani	Kirkuk
Mechanical Engineer	Fakhri Farid Shiltagh Al-	Sharief	Kirkuk
Asst. Mechanical Engineer	Muhanned Mahmoud Al-	Durrah	Kirkuk

Process & Production Maintenance

Maintenance Superintendent	Khalid Jamil	Mahmoud	Kirkuk
Maintenance Supervisor	Mirco	Sulaiman	Kirkuk
Asst. Mechanical Engineer	Sabah Yousif Daoud Al-	Ayoubi	Kirkuk
Asst. Mechanical Engineer	Hassan Salman Al-	Amiri	Kirkuk
Asst. Mechanical Engineer	Manaa Abdulla	Michbas	Kirkuk

Turbine Maintenance

Maintenance Superintendent	Abdul Karim Yousif Abdul	Rahman	Kirkuk
Mechanical Engineer	Abdul Illah Moh'd. Amin Al-	Khattat	Kirkuk
Mechanical Engineer	Tariq Abdul Razzak Al-	Salihi	Kirkuk
Asst. Mechanical Engineer	Ibrahim Injad Jandal Al-	Jumaili	Krk.(Course UK.)
Asst. Mechanical Engineer	Mawloud Ab. Hakim Mahmoud Al-	Mamizdeni	Kirkuk
Asst. Mechanical Engineer	Hamid Abdul Razzak Al-	Sa'adi	Kirkuk

SERVICES

Actg. Senior Mechanical Engineer	J. H.	Appelbe	Kirkuk

Air Conditioning & Refrigeration

Air Condtg. & Refrigeration Supdt.	Warkes Ohanes	Chubukjian	Kirkuk
Mechanical Engineer	Thamir Muhsin Al-	Khozaie	Kirkuk
Asst. Mechanical Engineer	Zaki Hassan Hadi Al-	Hadi	Kirkuk

Mechanical Workshops

Workshops Superintendent	Salahaddin Mohammed	Sa'adallah	Kirkuk
Mechanical Supervisor	Jassim Moh'd. Saleh Al-	Obaydi	Kirkuk
Mechanical Supervisor	Nafie Ibrahim	Haddad	Kirkuk
Mechanical Supervisor	Hassan Ali	Khidher	Kirkuk
Asst. Mechanical Supervisor	Tahir Shaban	Ramadhan	Kirkuk

Fields Services

Fields Services Engineer (Kirkuk)	Yacoub Yousif	Yessi	Kirkuk
Mechanical Engineer (Services)	Hisham Al-Sayid Fakhri	Jerjis	Kirkuk
Maintenance Supervisor	Dadisho	David	Kirkuk
Fixed Plant Supervisor	Salim Hassan Taha Al-	Ani	Kirkuk
Rig Maintenance Supervisor	Ali	Abdulla	Kirkuk

MAINLINE MAINTENANCE

Mainline Superintendent	Ali Attiyah Al-	Doory	Kirkuk
Mainline Supervisor	Ezbar Anizan Al-	Sagri	K-3
Asst. Mainline Supervisor	Sarkis Jean	Gazian	Kirkuk
Asst. Mechanical Engineer	Adeeb Mohammed Al-	Fakhry	Kirkuk

CONTROL INSTRUMENT SERVICES

Head of Control Instrument Services	Sabah Moh'd. Ali	Jumah	Kirkuk
Senior Instrument Engineer (Fields)	Qais Karim Al-	Dabbagh	Kirkuk
Area Instrument Supervisor (P/Line)	Ali	Sharief	K-3
Area Instrument Engineer	Akram Fathulla	Hannoudi	K-3
Instrument Supervisor	Barkev	Stephan	Kirkuk
Instrument Supervisor	Hussain Ali Al-	Janabi	Kirkuk
Instrument Supervisor	Hussamaddin Marouf	Ismail	Kirkuk
Instrument Engineer	Ghazi Faidhulla Al-	Talabani	Kirkuk
Instrument Engineer	Hussam Mahdi Ja'far Al-	Khunmali	Kirkuk
Asst. Instrument Engineer	Iqdam Rashid	Derzi	K-3
Asst. Instrument Engineer	Adil Moh'd. Mustafa Al-	Qazzaz	Kirkuk
Asst. Instrument Engineer	Nadhim Ibrahim Abdulla Al-	Nafousi	Kirkuk
Asst. Instrument Engineer	Hamid Majid Mohammed Al-	Khateeb	Kirkuk
Asst. Instrument Engineer	Salah Aziz	Karim	Kirkuk
Asst. Instrument Supvr. (Trainee)	Hayas Kaka Al-	Kakiya	Kirkuk
Asst. Instrument Supvr. (Trainee)	Rajab Telfah	Hawija	Kirkuk

PLANT SURVEY

Plant Inspection Superintendent	Sabah Siddiq Al-	Damluji	Krk.(Course UK.)
Plant Inspector	Sadeq Abed Al-	Yacoub	Kirkuk
Plant Inspector	Anis	Samarchi	Krk.(Sec.from Elect.)
Plant Inspector	Ghazi Towfiq Al-	Saoudi	Kirkuk
Inspection Services Supervisor	Jalal Shamoon	Botani	Kirkuk
Corrosion Supervisor	Awni Mohammed	Younis	Kirkuk
Asst. Plant Inspector	Zuhair Rashid	Amin	Kirkuk
Asst. Plant Inspector	Mowaffaq Moh'd. Nassem	Towfiq	Kirkuk

PERSONNEL

Personnel Manager	Sa'adi	Nazhat	Kirkuk
Senior Assistant	Hanna Abdul Aziz	Hindi	Kirkuk

INDUSTRIAL RELATIONS

Actg. Head of Industrial Relations	Sabah Mahmoud Al-	Jadooa	Kirkuk
Personnel Assistant	Salman Fadhil	Hamdi	Kirkuk
Personnel Assistant	Sabri Al-Din Aziz	Mustafa	Kirkuk
Personnel Assistant	Abdul Hassan Munhil	Khafaji	Kirkuk

PERSONNEL DEVELOPMENT

Head of Personnel Development	Daoud Ibrahim Al-	Jeboori	Kirkuk
Personnel Assistant	Fredrick Michael	Farnon	Kirkuk
Personnel Assistant	Petros	Garabet	Kirkuk
Personnel Assistant	Tariq Rashid	Abdulla	Krk.(Att.to I.R.)

TRAINING

Training Superintendent	Mahdi Hassan	Zuwailif	Kirkuk
Personnel Assistant	Maurice	Porter	Kirkuk
Training Supervisor (Emp. Develop.)	Matti Fathulla	Hayali	Kirkuk
Training Supervisor (Commerce)	Khoshaba	Camber	Kirkuk
Training Supervisor (Language)	Salah-Al-Din Ali	Irfan	Kirkuk
Training Supervisor	Safa Mustafa	Shibeeb	Kirkuk
Training Supervisor	Michael	Naoum	Kirkuk
Training Engineer	Ali Moh'd. Khedher Al-	Shatri	Kirkuk
Workshop Supervisor	Subhi Omar	Kirdar	Kirkuk
Asst. Training Supervisor	Fadhil Shehab Ahmed Al-	Ani	Kirkuk
Asst. Training Engineer	Tariq Naji Al-	Shamsi	Kirkuk

S T A F F

Staff Superintendent	Jerjis Raouf	Nannis	Kirkuk
Personnel Assistant	Zia Aprim	Younan	Kirkuk
Personnel Assistant	Normess Ohanes	Bablanian	Kirkuk
Personnel Assistant	Majid Ali	Kadhim	Kirkuk

Junior School

| Schoolteacher | S. A. (Miss) | Nightingale | Kirkuk |

EMPLOYMENT

Employment Superintendent	James Paul	Malik	Kirkuk
Personnel Assistant	Abdul Wahid	Fahmi	Krk.(Att.to Legal)
Personnel Assistant	Karim Mohammed	Ismail	Kirkuk
Personnel Assistant	Tariq Taha Al-	Rekhaisa	K-3
Personnel Assistant	Sa'doon Ibrahim	Hilmi	Kirkuk
Personnel Assistant	Fakhraddin Taha Al-	Dabbagh	Kirkuk

ACCIDENT PREVENTION

Head of Accident Prevention	Ezzat	Taha	Krk.(Course UK.)
Actg. Head of Accident Prevention & Senior Instrument Eng. (P/Line).	Tahir Abdul Ghani Al-	Khudri	Kirkuk
Accident Prevention Supervisor	Ali Majid Al-	Bayati	Kirkuk
Accident Prevention Supervisor	Saddiq Majid	Abdulla	Kirkuk
Personnel Assistant	Nadhim Mahmoud Moh'd. Al-	Zubaidi	Kirkuk

LEGAL

| Legal Superintendent | Adnan Raouf Al- | Naqib | Kirkuk |
| Legal Assistant | Shakir Ameen | Mukhlus | Kirkuk |

SERVICES AND ADMINISTRATION

Manager Services & Administration	Mahidh Al-	Jadir	Kirkuk
Administrative Assistant	Amin Abdul Ghani Al-	Karaghouli	Kirkuk
General Assistant	Emmanuel Shmouel	Youkhana	Kirkuk
General Assistant (Translation)	Ja'far Moh'd. Jawad Mehdi	Shahrabanli	Kirkuk
General Assistant	Bulus Sulaiman	Abdulla	Kirkuk

MATERIALS LIAISON

| Materials Liaison Engineer | Falih Abdul Karim Sd. | Hatem | Kirkuk |
| Materials Liaison Assistant | Hamid Mahmoud Al- | Fattah | Kirkuk |

AVIATION AND MOVEMENTS

Aviation Superintendent	Shamsiddin	Abdullah	Kirkuk
Movements Assistant	Roland	Noori	Kirkuk
Aircraft Maintenance Supervisor	Hussain Ahmed	Azzawi	Kirkuk

COMMISSARIAT

Commissariat Superintendent	Albert	Ismail	Kirkuk
Commissariat Supervisor	Odisho Warda	Enwiya	Kirkuk
Commissariat Supervisor	Michael	Odisho	Kirkuk
Commissariat Supervisor	Bahjat Turkey	Khaddour	Kirkuk
Asst. Commissariat Supervisor	Mahmoud Mohammed Jamil	Tahir	Kirkuk
Fields Club Supervisor	Farid Yacoub	Questo	Kirkuk

LANDS, AND H.O.S.

Lands & H.O.S. Superintendent	Anwar	Marouf	Kirkuk
Lands Supervisor	Ghanim Majid	Sha'ya	Kirkuk
Asst. Lands Supervisor	Daniel	Youkhana	Kirkuk
H.O.S. Assistant	Bahjat Hanna	Misho	Kirkuk
Asst. Lands Engineer (Surveyor)	Noel Fattohi	Rammo	Kirkuk

MATERIALS

Head of Materials	Noel Jean	Maghak	Kirkuk
Senior Materials Assistant	Mowaffaq Moh'd. Ibrahim Al-	Assad	Kirkuk
Senior Materials Assistant (Ops.)	Megerditch Espeare	Bagheshian	Kirkuk
Senior Materials Assistant (Planning and Procedure)	Hisham Ahmed Al-	Rawi	Kirkuk
Purchasing Assistant	Mohammed Saleh	Qassab	Kirkuk
Materials Assistant	Sabri Yessagh Handal Al-	Mashyahi	Kirkuk
Materials Assistant	Anwar Abdul Qadir	Wajdi	Kirkuk
Materials Assistant	Nimrod Israil	Ibrahim	K-3
Materials Assistant	Fakhir Amin	Kirdar	Kirkuk

TRANSPORT

Head of Transport	Faleh Hussain Al-	Hamdani	Kirkuk
Senior Workshops Supervisor	James	Abdul-Noor	Kirkuk
Workshop Supervisor	Nureddin	Majid	Kirkuk
Workshop Supervisor	Kamal	Bakri	Kirkuk
Workshop Supervisor	Elia Michael	Samber	Kirkuk
Workshop Engineer	Dhafir Rashid Salman	Selbi	Kirkuk
Asst. Workshop Engineer	Talal Abdulla Hassoon Al-	Najin	Kirkuk
Asst. Workshop Engineer (Trainee)	Akram Omer	Mohammed	Kirkuk
Senior Traffic Supervisor	Salim Abdulla	Diab	Kirkuk
Traffic Supervisor	Samuel	Sada	Kirkuk
Asst. Traffic Supervisor (Trainee)	Khalil Ali	Hamid	Kirkuk
Transport Supervisor (P/Line)	Hazim Abdul Wahab Al-	Saky	K-3

FINANCE

Manager Finance	C.	Hopwood	Kirkuk

GENERAL ACCOUNTS

Head of General Accounts	Abbas Abdullah	Abdul-Karim	Kirkuk
Cashier	Hanna Matti	Sabbagh	Kirkuk
Accountant (General Ledgers)	Azzam Badi	Bakir	Kirkuk
Actg. Accountant (Staff & Pay)	Yousif Daoud	Mumar	Kirkuk
Accountant(Pay)	Jamil	Karim	Kirkuk
Asst. Accountant (Pay)	Adouniya Elia	Enwiya	Kirkuk
Accountant (Administration)	Namir Mahmood	Khawaja	Krk.(Course UK.)
Asst. Accountant	Raghib Ali Abdul Hamid Al-	Alusi	Kirkuk

INTERNAL AUDIT

Senior Internal Auditor (Iraq)	M. J.	McVeigh	Krk.(Sec.from Bgd.)
Accountant	Anwar Tahir	Saleh	Krk.(Course UK.)
Accountant	Tariq Towfiq	Ibrahim	Kirkuk
Accountant	Aziz Salman	Abid	Kirkuk
Asst. Accountant	Ibrahim Ali Shuaib Al-	Jebouri	Krk.(Course UK.)

COSTS & BUDGETS

Head of Costs and Budgets	A. J.	Winckworth	Kirkuk
Cost Accountant	Saeed Stepho	Jajjoka	Kirkuk
Accountant (Budgets)	Lewis Mansour	Nissan	Kirkuk
Accountant	Jamil Fathulla	Anayi	Krk.(Sec.from Gen.Accts.
Accountant	Muyassar Adeeb Abdul Salam Al-Semadi		Kirkuk
Accountant (Trainee)	Hikmat Kadhim Sadiq Al-	Bahrani	Krk.(Sec.from Minoil)

M E D I C A L

Senior Medical Officer	I. S.	Holle	Kirkuk
Senior Pharmacist	Zaki Hanna	Semhery	Kirkuk
General Assistant	William Eshaya	Khammo	Kirkuk
Medical Officer Public Health	Elia Daoud	Sulaiman	Kirkuk
Medical Officer Ophthalmology	Sami Qassim Al-	Duri	Kirkuk
Fields Medical Officer	Nafeh	Habboosh	Kirkuk
Medical Officer	Michael Rahoumi	Saour	Kirkuk
Medical Officer	Mudhaffar	Emmanuel	Krk.(Course K.)
Medical Officer	Abdul Razzak Ibrahim Al-	Mashhadani	Kirkuk
Medical Officer	Faik Naji Al-	Kifaishi	Kirkuk
Medical Officer	Samir Abdul Rahim Al-	Sayegh	Kirkuk
Dental Officer	Subhi	Hassan	Kirkuk
Pipeline Medical Officer	Bayan Abdul Latif Al-	Tai	K-3
Medical Officer	Rafiq Tahir	Chalabi	K-3
Medical Officer	Tariq Abbass	AbdulWahab	K-3
Dental Officer	Aziz Ghafour Zainal	Imam Oglu	K-3
Pharmacist	Amjad Jibrail Hanna	Mekha	K-3
Nursing Sister	Zarouhi (Miss)	Shirinian	K-3
Medical Officer	Ali Hussain Hamoudi Al-	Hamdani	T-1
Surgeon Specialist	A. A.	Belton	Kirkuk
Physician	Idris Daoud	Sulaiman	Kirkuk
Anaesthetist	Abdul Amir	Abdul Karim	Kirkuk
Medical Officer/Surgical Assistant	Othman Omar	Shangonul	Kirkuk
Senior Pharmacist	Baithon	Habib	Kirkuk
Pharmacist	Naoum George	Naoum	Kirkuk
Pathological Lab. Technician	Khalid Amin	Haidari	Kirkuk
Pathological Lab. Technician	Badri	Ab. Majid	Kirkuk
Radiographer	Jalil Mohammed	Amin	Kirkuk
Radiographer	Ramzi Shukur	Qadir	Kirkuk
Senior Nursing Sister	N. (Miss)	Connell	Kirkuk
Nursing Sister	J. H. (Miss)	Ross	Kirkuk
Nursing Sister	Esther Brimon Tatto (Miss)	Abraham	Kirkuk
Nursing Sister	C. A. (Miss)	Robson	Kirkuk
Ward Charge	Hanna Jibrail Hanna	Hachie	Kirkuk .

CONTRACTORS

IRAQI AIRWAYS

Faik Towfiq Al-	Saoudi	Kirkuk
Mohammed Reyad Al-	Janabi	Kirkuk
Zaki Noor	Zaki	Kirkuk
Basil Ibrahim Al-	Ali	Kirkuk
Basil Salim	Kalian	Kirkuk
Anwar Makki	Mahmoud	Kirkuk

UNITED HELICOPTERS LTD.

D. L.	Wolff	(Sec.to BPC.)
F.	Shields	(Sec.to BPC.)

LLOYDS REGISTER OF SHIPPING (NON) MARINE DEPARTMENT

P. S.	Tindall	Kirkuk

SCHLUMBERGER

P. A.	King	Kirkuk

WHINNEY MURRAY

P. F.	Lecoutre	Kirkuk
Eshaya Hormiz	Isaac	Kirkuk

I.B.M.

P. E.	Veritsis	Kirkuk

- 12 -

		Kirkuk	K-3	T-1	Total	Grand Total
Own Strength	(F) (N)	20 324	- 42	1 11	21 377	
		344	42	12	398	398
Attached From						
Contractors	(F) (N)	6 7	- -	- -	6 7	
IPC. Ltd., Baghdad	(F)	1	-	-	1	
Minoil & Minerals	(N)	2	-	-	2	
		16	-	-	16	
Grand Total		360	42	12		414

ZAY/RMI.

Kirkuk - Staff Department

29th April, 1972.

<u>RECONCILIATION STATEMENT STAFF LIST - 1ST MAY, 1972</u>

<u>GENERAL MANAGEMENT</u>

Page   1.   <u>Delete</u>:   Hosan Arif, on transfer to B.P.C. Basrah with
                          effect from 8th April, 1972.

<u>ENGINEERING DIVISION</u>

Page   5.   <u>Add</u>:   P. J. Beresford, on transfer from B.P.C. Basrah
                        with effect from 15th April, 1972.

<u>MEDICAL DIVISION</u>

Page   10.   <u>Delete</u>:   Dr. Ihsan Mahfoudh, on expiry of secondment from
                           B.P.Co., Ltd., Basrah with effect from
                           18th April, 1972.

REFERENCES

1. The Iraq Petroleum Company and Its Associated Companies' Handbook, first Edition 1948, compiled in the Companies' Head Office, 214 Oxford Street, London, W1.

2. Other different IPC publications.

3. Scores of Newsletters published by the IPC Society limited, Brettenham House, 1 Lancaster Place, London WC2E 7EE.

4. The Political History of the Oil Concessions in Iraq, between 1925-1952, a Ph. D. thesis by Nori Abdul Hamid Khalil, first published in 1980 with the assistance of Baghdad University, (Arabic language).

5. Iraq's Oil Negotiations between 1952- 1968, by Abdullah Ismail, ISBN 1-870326-202, first published in 1989 by Laam Ltd, P.O.Box 249A, Surbiton, Surrey, KT6 5AX, UK (Arabic language).

6. Iraq-International Relations and National Development, by Edith and E.F Penrose, ISBN 0-89158-804-3, first published in 1978 by Ernest Benn Limited, 25 New Street Square, Fleet Street, London EC4A 3JA.

7. The History of the British Petroleum Company, Volume 1, The developing Years 1901-1932, by R.W. Ferrier, first published in 1982 by the Press Syndicate of the University of Cambridge, the Pitt Building, Trumpington Street, Cambridge CB2 1RP.

8. The Engineering Data Book, tenth edition 1987, by the Gas Processors Suppliers Association, Tulsa, Oklahoma 74145, USA.

9. The James A. Baker III Institute for Public Policy, Rice University-March 2007.

10. Case Study on Iraq's Oil Industry by Amy Myers Jaffe, James A. Baker III Institute for Public Policy.

11. Cross Borders Oil and Gas Pipelines, Problems and Prospect, June 2003, a joint UNDP/World Bank-Energy sector Management Assistance Programme.

12. The development of the Gas Industry in Iraq by Mishal Hammodat, first published in 1982 by Al Adeeb Press, Baghdad, (Arabic language).

13. Mishal Hammodat, Memoirs and Work for the Development of Iraq's Oil Sector, first published in 2010 by Al- Okhowa Press-Mosul, Iraq, (Arabic language).

14. The Old Social classes and the Revolutionary Movements of Iraq, by Hanna Batatu, first published in 1978 by New Jersey: Princeton University press.

15. The Modern History of Iraq, by Phebe Marr, first published in 1985 in the UK by Longman Group Ltd, Longman House, Burnt Mill, Harlow, Essex CM20 2JE, England.

16. The Seven Sisters, by Anthony Sampson, first published in 1975 by Hodder and Stoughton Limited, St. Paul's House, Warwick Lane, London EC4P 4AH.

17. The Economics of the Middle Eastern Oil, by Charles Issawi and Mohammed Yeganeh, first Published in 1962 by Faber and Faber Ltd. 24 Russell Square, London W.C.1.

18. The Growth of Firms, Middle East Oil and Other Essays, by Edith Penrose, first published in 1971 by Frank Cass and Company, 67 Great Russell Street, London WC1B 3BT.

19. National Gas Museum-History of gas, UK.

20. Fuel on the Fire/Oil and Politics in Occupied Iraq, by Greg Muttitt, first published in 2010 by The Bodley Head, London.

www.ingramcontent.com/pod-product-compliance
Lightning Source LLC
Chambersburg PA
CBHW061229220326
41599CB00028B/5378